USING LATIN

Annabel Horn, Wesleyan College

John Flagg Gummere, William Penn Charter School

Margaret M. Forbes, University of Minnesota

SCOTT, FORESMAN AND COMPANY
Chicago   Atlanta   Dallas   Palo Alto   Fair Lawn, N. J.

BOOK ONE

The meeting place of the Roman Senate, called the Curia, was built, destroyed, and rebuilt many times. The first building was burned in 52 B.C. This brick building, ornamented with stucco and marble, was the last. Its original bronze doors were removed for use in the Church of St. John Lateran in Rome. The cover design of the Using Latin series is derived from the ornamentation of those doors.

CONTENTS

How Much Latin Do You Know?   **8**   Introduction to Word Mastery
1. Word Mastery   **8**   Words Ending in -a

INTRODUCTION   **9**

A. A Roman Villa   **10**   Nominative and Accusative Singular; Subject; Direct Object; Predicate Noun/Adjective
B. An American House   **13**   Ablative with Preposition
C. Roman Aqueducts   **21**   Plural Nouns; Verb Endings -t, -nt
D. American Aqueducts   **24**   Ablative/Accusative with Prepositions
E. Roman Roads   **26**   Apposition; Position of Adjectives
F. American Highways   **28**   Review of Case/Verb Endings/Case Uses
2. Word Mastery   **30**   Words Ending in -ia, -tia/-cia, -ula

UNIT I   **31**

I. Roman Provinces   **32**   Genitive Case; Possession
II. Africa   **34**   Tense; Forms of *sum*; Person, Number
III. Britain   **38**   Dative Case; Indirect Object
IV. Sicily   **43**   Dative with Adjectives; Masculine Nouns in -a

UNIT II   **47**

V. Pirates and Hidden Treasure   **48**   Questions and Answers
VI. Latona and the Frogs   **51**   Declension I: Summary of Cases and Case Uses
VII. The Ant and the Grasshopper   **54**   Conjugations I, II: Infinitives, Present Stem/Tense

UNIT III   **63**

3. Word Mastery   **64**   Verbs
VIII. The Moon and Stars   **64**   Indicative, Imperative; Vocative Case
IX. Anna and the Bear   **68**   Clauses, Conjunctions
4. Word Mastery   **71**   Verbs: Variations in Spelling
X. The Great Bear   **72**   Summary: Adverbs, Conjunctions, Prepositions
XI. Cassiopeia and Andromeda   **75**   Forms of *possum*; Complementary Infinitive

UNIT IV   **81**

XII. Gods and Goddesses of Rome   **82**   Declension II Nouns in -us, -er/-r; Vocative in -e
XIII. Diana, Goddess of the Moon   **88**   Gender; Nouns in -um; Declension I-II Adjectives
5. Word Mastery   **92**   Declension II Nouns and Adjectives
XIV. Daphne and Apollo   **93**   Agreement of Adjectives and Nouns in Gender
XV. Apollo and Mercury   **97**   Conjugations I, II: Future Tense
XVI. Kingdom of the Dead   **102**   Ablative Without Preposition

UNIT V 107

XVII. Vulcan **108** Perfect Tense: Conjugation, Endings
XVIII. Minerva and Medusa **112** Principal Parts of Verb; Perfect Stem
XIX. The Best Gift **114**
XX. The Gift of Fire **117** Variations of Perfect Stem
6. Word Mastery **123** Compound Verbs with Simple Prefixes

OPTIONAL UNIT A 127

1. The Pleiades **127**
2. Orion, the Hunter **128**

UNIT VI 129

XXI. Shepherd of Admetus **130** Conjugations III, IV: Present Tense; Infinitives
XXII. Messengers of the Gods **134** Conjugations III, IV: Future Tense
XXIII. School of the Centaurs **137** Conjugations I, II, III, IV: Imperfect Tense
XXIV. Vesta, Keeper of the Flame **141** Differences Between Perfect/Imperfect
XXV. The First Physician **146** Summary of Present System of Verbs

UNIT VII 151

XXVI. The Magic Shield **152** Superlative of Adjectives
XXVII. The Golden Touch **154** Irregular Superlative Forms
XXVIII. Too Much Wind **156** *Nunc/Jam;* Imperatives of Conjugations III, IV; Negative Commands
XXIX. The Golden Bough **160** Irregular Imperatives: *dīc, dūc, fac, fer*
7. Word Mastery **166** Word Families: Nouns, Adjectives, Verbs

OPTIONAL UNIT B 167

3. Closing of the Gates **167**
4. Janus, a God with Two Faces **168**

UNIT VIII 169

XXX. Hercules and the Lion **170** Conjugations III, IV: Perfect Tense
XXXI. People for a King **173** Perfect Tense: Summary and Review
XXXII. King and Woodpecker **176** Summary: Present, Imperfect, Future, Perfect

UNIT IX 183

XXXIII. Perseus and the Gorgon **184** Demonstrative *is, ea, id:* Pronoun/Adjective
XXXIV. The Land of Forgetfulness **188** Reflexive Adjective *suus, -a, -um; suus/ejus*
8. Word Mastery **191** Compound Verbs with Assimilation/Internal Change
XXXV. Arachne **192** Demonstratives *hic* and *ille*
XXXVI. Echo and Narcissus **196** Intensive *ipse, ipsa, ipsum*
XXXVII. New Race on Earth **199** Declension and Use of *īdem, eadem, idem*

4

UNIT X 207

XXXVIII. A Man Who Was
Not Afraid **208** Relative Pronoun: Declension, Use; with *cum*
XXXIX. Androcles and
the Lion **214** Reflexive Pronoun in Third Person
XL. Manlius and the Geese
Save Rome **217** Personal Pronouns *ego/tū*; Reflexives; with *cum*
XLI. Deceiving the Enemy **220** Interrogative Pronoun
XLII. Vesuvius **223** Interrogative Adjective

OPTIONAL UNIT C 230

5. A Trick of War **230**

UNIT XI 231

XLIII. Small Beginning of
a Great War **232** Declension III Nouns: Case Endings (M./F.)
XLIV. A Pyrrhic Victory **236** Declension III Neuter Nouns: Case Endings
XLV. A Roman Statesman **239** Declension III Nouns Ending in *-tor/-or;* Nouns
ending in *-is/-ēs;* Genitive Plural in *-ium*
9. Word Mastery **241** Latin Nouns Ending in *-or/-tor* Formed from Verbs
10. Word Mastery **243** Latin Diminutives
11. Word Mastery **246** Nouns Designating Family Relationships

UNIT XII 247

XLVI. The Twelve Tables **248** Nouns Ending in *-tās/-tūdō*
XLVII. The Tiber **250** Nouns Ending in *-iō/-ō/-en*
12. Word Mastery **253** Nouns in *-tās, -tūdō/-iō* Formed from Adjectives/Verbs
XLVIII. A Letter from the
Front **254**

OPTIONAL UNIT D 260

6. The Tarpeian Rock **260**

UNIT XIII 261

XLIX. A Man Who Panicked **262** Declension III Adjectives
L. A Tall Tale **265** Comparison of Adjectives; Comparatives Declined
LI. Expensive Books **268** Irregular Comparison of Adjectives
LII. Romans Capture Veii **274** Comparison of Adjectives Ending in *-lis/-er*
LIII. A Life for a Friend **276** Regular and Irregular Comparison of Adverbs
13. Word Mastery **280** Latin and English Suffixes: Adjectives/Nouns

UNIT XIV 281

LIV. A Stolen Bride **282** Latin Numbers; Ablative of Time
LV. Four Impossible Tasks **285** *Mille* and *Milia*
LVI. Pandora's Box **288** Present Active Participles
LVII. A Lost Wife **292** Accusative of Extent of Space/Time
14. Word Mastery **296** More Latin and English Suffixes: Adjectives/Nouns

5

UNIT XV 297

LVIII. The Golden Ram **298** Active/Passive Voice; Present System in Passive Voice
LIX. A Man with One Shoe **301** Ablative of Agent
LX. A Cruel Plot **304** Perfect Participles; Fourth Principal Part
LXI. The Golden Fleece **310** Past Perfect/Future Perfect Active
LXII. Jason's Return **314** Perfect System in Passive Voice

OPTIONAL UNIT E 319

7. A Reckless Driver **320**
8. The First Aviator **321**
9. Theseus Meets the
Minotaur **322**

THE TROJAN WAR 323

UNIT XVI 325

LXIII. Gift for the Fairest **326** Present Infinitives Active/Passive
LXIV. Paris Gets His Reward **329** Indirect Statement with Present Infinitive
LXV. Ulysses' Trick **332** Perfect Infinitive; Tense in Indirect Statement
LXVI. Beggar or Spy? **335** Conjugation of *eō* and Compounds
LXVII. The Wooden Horse **337** Future Active Participles/Infinitives
15. Word Mastery **342** English Word Families from Latin Verbs

UNIT XVII 343

LXVIII. In Search of a
Promised Land **344** Ablative Absolute
LXIX. No Permanent Home **347** Free Translation of Ablative Absolute
LXX. A Fateful Storm **350**
LXXI. By Bees and Fire
Foretold **352** Ablative With/Without Preposition
LXXII. A Royal Dilemma **356**
16. Word Mastery **360** Borrowed Words; Place Names; Zodiac; Proper Names

OPTIONAL UNIT F 361

10. The Old Man of the Sea **361**
11. The White Stag **361**

UNIT XVIII 363

LXXIII. Aeneas Seeks Aid **364** *Volō/Nōlō*
LXXIV. The War Is On **367** Declension IV Nouns
LXXV. A Broken Treaty **370** Declension V Nouns
LXXVI. Renewed Conflict **373**
LXXVII. Jupiter Ends the War **374**

IPHIGENIA 376

OPTIONAL UNIT G 377

12. A False Letter **378**
13. Unexpected Guests **379** Mood; Present Subjunctive
14. Achilles Discovers the
Plot **382**
15. Sacrifice of Iphigenia **383**
16. A Fateful Meeting **383**

**OPTIONAL REVIEW
UNIT H** 385

17. Return of Ulysses **386**
18. Reunion of Father and
Son **387**
19. Recognition of Ulysses **388**
20. Rescue of Penelope **389**
21. Revelation to Ulysses **390** Exercises for General Review

ROMAN LIFE

Roman Houses **16**
Furnishings and Decoration
of Roman Houses **18**
Roman Food and Meals **56**
Religion of the Romans **86**
Roman Dress **124**
Education of Roman Children **144**
Archaeology **164**
Roman Baths **180**
The Roman Empire **204**
Streets, Roads, and
Water Supply **212**
Roman Trade **228**
Roman Industries **244**
Roman Theaters and Plays **258**
Circuses and Racing **272**
Gladiators and Amphitheaters **308**

LEARNING AIDS

Map of the Roman Empire **206**
Exercises for General Review **391**
Useful Latin **394**
Latin for Fun **396**
Pronunciation of Latin **398**
General Vocabulary **399**
Summary of Grammar **426**
Index of Grammar **442**
Grammatical Terms **445**

7

| junior | plus | major | maximum | interior | superior |
| senior | minus | minor | minimum | exterior | inferior |

What student is not familiar with these words? Yet, all are Latin words taken over into English without change.

animal	basis	genius	militia	radius	spectator
area	census	impetus	neuter	rumor	stimulus
auditorium	favor	index	omen	senator	vacuum

Who needs a dictionary to tell him the meaning of these words? Look them up in either a Latin or an English dictionary. You will find them in both, spelled the same and with the same (or almost the same) meanings.

Caution: Some words have the same spelling in English as in Latin, but their meanings are different. For example, what is the meaning of each of these words as used in English?

alumna (foster daughter) **arēna** (sand) **pūpa** (little girl, doll)
campus (field) **lacūna** (pool) **sinister** (on the left)

At intervals throughout this book are word studies that have been worked out to help you increase not only your Latin vocabulary, but also your English vocabulary. These studies are called "Word Mastery."

WORD MASTERY 1

When a Latin word is taken over into English, its spelling sometimes changes a little, although its original meaning often remains the same.

The final letter **-a** may disappear as in **mūsica**/music, **longa**/long. What do the following words become in English?

fōrma **jūsta** **poēta** **splendida** **urna** **valida**

In other English words the final **-a** of the Latin word is replaced by -e as in **pictūra**/picture, **antīqua**/antique. Apply this principle to these Latin words.

| agricultūra | figūra | irāta | oliva | prima | sōla |
| fāma | fortūna | lyra | pirāta | rosa | statua |

INTRODUCTION TO L A T I N

Rome, located on the Tiber River in Italy, was the home of the Romans, whose language was Latin. The influence of the Romans and their language spread over most of Europe and the Near East. Many modern languages, including English, reflect this influence.

9

A

Vīlla est vīlla Rōmāna.° Vīlla nōn est parva. Vīlla est magna. Vīlla est antīqua. Vīlla est alta et longa. Magna vīlla parvam lacūnam° habet. Lacūna nōn est longa. Lacūna nōn est alta.

°**Rō mā′na*** Roman • **la cū′na** pool

Noun		Verbs	
*vil′la	villa, house	**est**	is
Adjectives		**ha′bet**	has
al′ta	high, tall, deep	Adverb	
*an ti′qua	old	***nōn**	not
*lon′ga	long	Conjunction	
mag′na	large, great	**et**	and
par′va	small		

PRONUNCIATION OF LATIN WORDS The first word in the story (**vīlla**) is a Latin noun brought over into English with the same spelling and meaning, but with a different pronunciation.

Latin	English
vīl′la (weel′la)	vil′la (vĭl′ə)

The marking of long vowels in Latin gives a key to pronunciation. Most consonants stand for approximately the same sounds in Latin as in English.

Vowels			Consonants	
Long	Short		Latin	English
ā (father)	a (aha)		c	like **k** (**c**ook)
ē (they)	e (met)		g	as in **g**ood
ī (meet)	i (pin)		qu	like **kw** (**qu**ick)
ō (lone)	o (obey)		s	as in **s**ay
ū (cool)	u (full)		v	like **w** (**w**all)

°Latin words with the symbol (°) do not appear in the unit vocabulary. They are listed separately from the regular lesson vocabulary in the order of their first occurrence.

*Words with (*) contain clues to their meaning through related English words.

The House of Meleager in Pompeii, like many Roman houses, had a garden court, including a pool.

USE YOUR EYES Which of the Latin adjectives used in this story would best describe the villa in this picture? What can you say, in Latin, about this pool?

THE POSITION OF THE LATIN VERB[1] is usually at the end of a sentence.[1] However, **est** and other forms of the verb meaning "to be" are generally found immediately after the subject.[1]

Villa lacūnam habet. The villa has a pool.
Villa est magna. The villa is large.

[1]All grammatical terms used in this book are listed alphabetically and defined on pages 445-446.

CASES OF A LATIN NOUN A Latin noun has different forms which signal meanings by showing how the noun is used in the sentence. These forms are called cases.

In "A Roman Villa" two cases are used, nominative and accusative. In this story the nominative ends in **-a** and the accusative in **-am.**

Villa lacūnam habet. The villa has a pool.[1]

THE SUBJECT of the sentence is in nominative case.

Villa lacūnam habet. The villa has a pool.

THE DIRECT OBJECT of the verb is in accusative case.

Villa lacūnam habet. The villa has a pool.

A PREDICATE NOUN is linked to the subject by **est** or by another form of the verb meaning "to be." It is in the same case as the subject.

Villa est villa Rōmāna. The villa is a Roman villa.

A PREDICATE ADJECTIVE is linked to the subject by **est** or by another form of the verb meaning "to be." It is in the same case as the subject.

Villa est magna. The villa is large.

LOOK AND THINK The same Latin word **(alta)** means both "tall" and "deep." What is the meaning of **alta villa?** Of **alta lacūna?**

LATIN LIVES TODAY Find in "A Roman Villa" Latin words related to key words in these sentences. Explain each statement.

1 The plane reached an altitude of ten thousand feet.
2 His mother likes antique furniture.
3 Your sister has an alto voice.
4 Father could not read fine print without a magnifier.

[1]Since Latin has no such words, "the," "a," or "an" is supplied as needed in translating a Latin noun.

American houses are often built around a central garden court, as were Roman houses.

B

AN AMERICAN HOUSE

In pictūrā casam Americānam° vidēmus.° Casa nōn est antīqua; casa est nova. Casa nōn est alta, sed casa est lāta. Casa est in viā longā. Casa lacūnam habet. In lacūnā est aqua. Aqua nōn est alta.

°**A me ri cā'na*** American • **vi dē'mus** we see

Nouns	
a'qua	water
ca'sa	house, cottage
*pic tū'ra	picture
vi'a	street, road, highway, way
Adjectives	
lā'ta	wide, broad
no'va	new, modern
Conjunction	
sed	but
Preposition	
*in	(with abl.) in, on

THE ABLATIVE CASE in Latin, when used with **in,** answers the question, "Where?" In this story the ablative case ends in long **a** (**-ā**).

In pictūrā casam vidēmus. In the picture we see a house.

A PREPOSITIONAL PHRASE is made up of a preposition and its object—usually a noun. In this story nouns which follow the preposition **in** are in the ablative case, and the phrase expresses place where.

An adjective used with a noun in such a phrase is in the same case as the noun.

In lacūnā est aqua. In the pool there is water.[1]

Casa est in viā longā. The house is on a long street.

DIVIDING A LATIN WORD into syllables often makes it easier to pronounce. A Latin word has as many syllables as it has vowels or diphthongs.

(A diphthong is two vowels pronounced together, as **ae** in **Caesar**—pronounced kī'sär in Latin; sē'zər in English.)

| pic tū ra | la cū na | vi a | est |

A consonant between two vowels is pronounced with the vowel which follows it.

| Rō mā na | an ti qua[2] | no va | ca sa |

Two consonants between two vowels are usually divided.

| al ta | vil la | lon ga | mag na |

A SYLLABLE IS LONG if it contains a long vowel or a diphthong, or if it ends in a consonant; otherwise, it is short.

| vīl la | Cae sar | la cū na | mag na |

[1] In translating **est** or **sunt** it is sometimes necessary to supply the expletive "there" ("there is" or "there are"). Latin has no such expletive.

[2] The combination **qu** in Latin, though pronounced as two consonants (kw), is treated as a single consonant (**a′qua**) in syllabication.

THE ACCENT in words of two syllables always falls on the first syllable.

al'ta   ca'sam   vi'a   a'qua   lā'tam

In words of more than two syllables the accent falls on the next to the last syllable, if that syllable is long.

A me ri cā'na   an ti'qua   la cū'na   cis ter'na

When the next to the last syllable is short, the one immediately preceding it is stressed.

Ī ta'li a   A me'ri ca   ta'bu la   ha'bi tat

PRACTICE IN PRONUNCIATION Divide the words below into syllables and mark the accented syllable of each; then pronounce the word.

arēna	fōrma	fortūna	movent	periculōsa[1]
quoque	rēgīna	alumna	memoria	agenda
mīrābile	tuba	poēta	dictātor	fēmina

LATIN LIVES TODAY If the eighteenth-century adventurer Casanova had wanted to change his name from Italian to English, would his name have been Highville, Longway, or Newhouse?

.On a map, which lines show longitude? Which show latitude? In "An American House" find two Latin words related to the English words "longitude" and "latitude."

SING IT IN LATIN

America (Latin version by Professor George D. Kellogg)

Tē canō, Patria	My country, 'tis of thee,
Candida, libera,	Sweet land of liberty,
Tē referet.	Of thee I sing.
Portus et exulum	Land where my fathers died,
Et tumulus senum;	Land of the pilgrims' pride,
Libera montium	From every mountain side
Vōx resonet.	Let freedom ring.

[1]In a very long word the stress is still on the next to the last syllable, if that syllable is long: **lā ti tū'dō, me mo ran'dum.**

15

ROMAN HOUSES

Roman houses varied with their period in history, with their location, and with the means of their occupants. Originally the house was a single large room called the "atrium," which had an opening (compluvium) in the roof for light and air, and a basin (impluvium) below to catch rain water. In time, rooms were added around the sides, and one at the rear became the owner's office or study (tablinum). The front entrance, which originally opened off the street, later led into a hallway from a vestibule.

Still later, in houses of the well-to-do, an open court (peristylium) lay beyond the tablinum. Shrubs, flowers, and sometimes a fountain with a decorative pool made this outdoor living room attractive. Small rooms around both peristyle and atrium were used for many purposes—bedrooms, dining rooms, servants' quarters, and perhaps a library. Two facing wings off the atrium were devoted to the display of busts and wax masks of ancestors. To save on plumbing, kitchens and bathrooms were near each other, usually at the rear of the peristyle. Elaborate houses sometimes had a second story, but atrium and peristyle remained open to the sky to provide light and air, since windows were not so common as they are today.

Buildings were heated by portable charcoal braziers of metal or, especially in colder northern provinces, by circulating warm air under floors and through walls.

Ordinary city dwellers lived in no such luxury. Large apartment buildings called "insulae" provided small quarters for the majority. In both houses and apartment buildings, rooms facing on the street were rented as shops.

Above left: Compluvium and impluvium in the atrium of the House of the Silver Wedding in Pompeii were larger than usual; therefore, pillars were required to support the roof. Above right: Peristyle of the Pompeian House of the Vettii with restored planting in bloom and ornamental statuary in place.

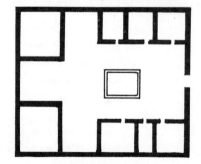

Right: Floor plan of a simple Roman house showing entrance at right leading into the atrium with its impluvium, small enclosed rooms, and alcoves or wings (alae) at each side. The tablinum at the rear is flanked by rooms not open to the atrium.

Left: Elaborate mosaic fountain which ornamented the garden of a Pompeian house known as the House of the Great Fountain.

Above: Remains of atrium and tablinum of the House of the Faun, so called from the graceful dancing figure on a pedestal in the impluvium.

Above left: Scale model of the ruins of a Roman apartment building discovered near the Capitoline Hill. With at least five stories, this insula was typical, since its first-floor rooms facing on the street were arranged for use as shops.

Right: Section of a street in Herculaneum, partly restored, with doors obviously of modern construction.

Below left: View through part of ruined atrium of the House of Pansa in Pompeii looking toward the peristyle, where sixteen pillars formed a colonnade around a pool. A "Cave canem" mosaic adorned the floor of the entrance to this house.

Right: Massive ruins which give an impression of the lavish villas of wealthy Romans at Baiae, a seaside resort.

FURNISHINGS AND DECORATION OF ROMAN HOUSES

Because their furniture was scanty, Roman houses might seem bare to us. There were chairs and stools, couches which served also as beds, and a variety of tables, cabinets, and chests. Although not much wooden furniture has survived, it is known from paintings to have existed. Tables were of bronze and marble as well as wood.

Dining-room furniture consisted of three couches for reclining at a small table. Couches and chairs were enhanced by colorful cushions, pads, and draperies. Dishes and utensils, finely designed, were of pottery, bronze, glass, and silver.

To us a Roman house would seem dark, because during the day the only light came from the compluvium and from open doors, and at night oil lamps of pottery or bronze gave a flickering light from their small wicks. Often several lamps were hung on one standard for more light. Candles were uncommon.

Rooms were made more cheerful by wall decorations, usually frescoes painted on fresh plaster. The commonest subjects of these frescoes, whose colors and designs have remained remarkably intact, were scenes from daily life and from mythology. Cupids were often shown engaged in various commonplace activities.

Floors were of mosaic in simple geometric patterns or elaborate pictorial designs. Some of the finer mosaics that have survived were wall decorations, but most were floors. Exceptionally delicate mosaic pictures made of thousands of tiny glass or stone tesserae were generally covered to avoid wear. Vestibules sometimes had the figure of a watchdog in mosaic, with the inscription "Cave canem" (Beware the dog).

Above left: Ornament from a Roman couch in the form of a mule's head of bronze inlaid with silver.

Left: Example of a "Cave canem" mosaic, common on entrance floors.

Above: Part of a mosaic, probably the most famous of antiquity, illustrating the Battle of Issus. This portion shows the Persian King Darius fleeing from the triumphant Alexander the Great, whose likeness is on a badly defaced portion not included here.

Upper left: Part of a fresco in which Ulysses and his men approach the cave of the witch Circe. Lower left: Painting of armed goddesses. Above right: Fresco showing a street with an elaborate villa.

Above left: Glass bottle partially encased in silver with design of a mask.
Center: Hanging lamp with six holes for wicks.

Above: Dining room richly decorated in mosaic, with recess for a table and three built-in couches.

Left: Famous garden fresco from the villa of a royal lady, Livia, wife of Augustus and mother of Tiberius.

19

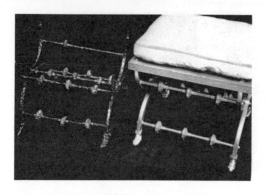

Roman furniture and utensils 2000 years old. Top left and right: Folding chair with cushion restored and a wooden cabinet.

Center: Silver spoons, fork (for serving and cooking only), and jugs for wine or oil beside a room containing a baby's bed (in case).

Bottom left: Though badly defaced, the wall decorations of this room are typical. The burned wooden divan and table (in case) remain where they were found.

Bottom right: Bathtub in the garden of a house.

C

Prīmō Rōma° antīqua bonam aquam nōn habet.[1] In puteīs° aqua est contāmināta.° In cisternīs° aqua est bona, sed cisternae nōn sunt magnae.

Prope Rōmam est aqua incontāmināta.° Rōmānī° aquam bonam in urbem° per magnās Aquās° dūcunt. In urbe,° 5 prīma Aqua est sub terrā. Rōma magnās cloācās° habet. Magnae cloācae sunt sub terrā.

°**Rō'ma*** Rome • **in pu'te īs** in wells • **con tā mi nā'ta*** contaminated, impure • **cis ter'na*** cistern, reservoir • **in-con tā mi nā'ta*** uncontaminated, pure • **Rō mā'nī*** (nom. pl.) the Romans • **in ur'bem** • into the city • **A'qua*** aqueduct, conduit • **in ur'be** in the city • **clo ā'ca** sewer

	Noun	
	ter'ra	land, earth, ground
Adjectives		
	bo'na	good
	*pri'ma	first
Verbs		
	dū'cunt	bring, lead, carry
	sunt	are
Adverb		
	*pri'mō	at first
Prepositions		
	per	(with acc.) through
	pro'pe	(with acc.) near
	sub	(with abl.) under

NOMINATIVE PLURAL ending of nouns and adjectives whose nominative singular ends in **-a** is **-ae** (pronounced "i" as in "like").

Cisterna nōn est magna. The cistern is not large.
Cisternae nōn sunt magnae. The cisterns are not large.

[1]Translate **nōn habet** "does not have." English requires the use of "do" or "does" with the verb of a negative sentence.

Portions of the Claudian Aqueduct, begun in A.D. 38 by Emperor Caligula, can still be seen on the plains near Rome. Many sections of its channel were under ground.

ACCUSATIVE PLURAL ending of nouns and adjectives whose accusative singular ends in **-am** is **-ās.**

> **Rōma magnam cloācam habet.** Rome has a large sewer.
> **Rōma magnās cloācās habet.** Rome has large sewers.

Many other nouns and adjectives with accusative singular in **-m** have the accusative plural in **-s.**

> **Majōrem vidēmus urbem.** We see a larger city.
> **Majōrēs vidēmus urbēs.** We see larger cities.

ABLATIVE PLURAL ending of nouns and adjectives whose ablative singular ends in **-ā** is **-īs.**

> **In cisternā aqua est bona.** In the cistern the water is good.
> **In cisternīs aqua est bona.** In the cisterns the water is good.

ACCUSATIVE WITH PREPOSITIONS Some prepositions are followed by nouns in the accusative case. Two such prepositions (**prope** and **per**) are used in this story.

> **per magnās Aquās** through great aqueducts
> **prope Rōmam** near Rome

CASE ENDINGS

	Singular	Plural		Singular	Plural
Nom.	-a	-ae	Nom.	ca'sa	ca'sae
Acc.	-am	-ās	Acc.	ca'sam	ca'sās
Abl.	-ā	-īs	Abl.	ca'sā	ca'sīs

VERB ENDINGS A verb with a singular subject ends in -**t**; a verb with a plural subject ends in -**nt**.

Rōma Aquās habet. Rome has aqueducts.
Casae aquam habent. The houses have water.

An English verb sometimes changes according to whether the subject is singular or plural.

Singular:	he calls	he gives	he carries
Plural:	they call	they give	they carry

USE YOUR EYES What is the meaning of **Aqua?** Of **aqua?** Explain the syllable division and accent of the words in the vocabulary; then pronounce each word.

LATIN LIVES TODAY With the help of one Latin word in "Roman Aqueducts" tell what each of these phrases means. Use an English dictionary if necessary.

primary colors	prime number
primary election	prime meridian
primary school	primitive art
prime minister	primitive man

WHAT'S IN A NAME? The word "America" comes from **Americus,** the Latinized first name of an explorer. Since many of the discoverers of parts of North and South America spoke Italian, Spanish, or French—languages derived from Latin—we have numerous place names which are either Latinized forms of persons' names or really of Latin origin.[1] Such are Argentina (**argentum,** silver), Carolina (**Carolus,** Charles), Florida (**flōrēs,** flowers), Montana (**montēs,** mountains).

[1] Some place names ending in -**a** are from Indian words; e.g., Iowa, Minnesota, Oklahoma.

Part of New York City's water supply is carried by the Croton Aqueduct on the Hudson River. Its arches resemble those of a Roman aqueduct.

D

AMERICAN AQUEDUCTS

Urbēs° Americānae aquam habent bonam. Interdum cōpia nōn est magna. Itaque magnae Aquae in urbēs aquam dūcunt. Aquae sunt altae et longae. Aquae aquam in casās et vīllās dūcunt.

Interdum in America° Aquae aquam sub terram dūcunt. 5 America quoque magnās sub terrā cloācās habet.

°**ur′bēs** (nom., acc. pl.) cities • **A me′ri ca*** America

Noun		Conjunction	
cō′pi a	supply, abundance	**i′ta que**	and so; therefore
Verb		Prepositions	
ha′bent	have	**in**	(with acc.) into
Adverbs		**sub**	(with acc.) under
in ter′dum	sometimes		
quo′que	also		

PREPOSITIONS WITH ABLATIVE OR AC-CUSATIVE

A few Latin prepositions are sometimes followed by the ablative and sometimes by the accusative. When the noun in such a prepositional phrase is in the ablative case, the phrase expresses place where.

Aqua est in lacūnā. Water is in the pool.

Magnae Aquae sunt sub terrā. Large conduits are under ground.

With the accusative, **in** means "into" and the prepositional phrase implies motion (place into which).

Aquae aquam in casās dūcunt. Conduits bring water into houses.

Aquae aquam in urbem dūcunt. Conduits bring water into the city.

Likewise, when **sub** is followed by the accusative, the phrase implies motion (place to which).

Aquae aquam sub terram dūcunt. Conduits carry water under ground.

PRACTICE IN PHRASES

(I) Change the phrases below to show place into or to which instead of place where.

1 **in magnā villā**
2 **in viā longā**
3 **sub casīs parvīs**

4 **in lacūnīs altīs**
5 **in casīs parvīs**
6 **sub magnā villā**

(II) Change the phrases below from singular to plural.

1 **per viam lātam**
2 **per aquam altam**
3 **sub casā parvā**

4 **prope casam magnam**
5 **in altā cisternā**
6 **sub casam parvam**

USE YOUR EYES

Find two clues that tell whether **Urbēs** (first word in story) is singular or plural and whether it is nominative or accusative. How is **urbēs** used in line 2 of "American Aqueducts"?

LATIN LIVES TODAY

In meaning, the English noun "copy" is only a distant relative of **cōpia**. Two derivatives more closely related in meaning are "copious" and "cornucopia." What do these words mean? Consult a dictionary if necessary.

E

Viae Rōmānae sunt antīquae. Initiō° Rōma viās strātās°
nōn habuit.° Appius Claudius° prīmam viam strātam fēcit.°
"Viam¹ Appiam"° Rōmānī viam¹ nōminant. Via Appia ab
urbe Rōmā ad urbem Capuam° dūcit. Posteā viae Rōmānae
ad prōvinciās Rōmānās dūcunt.

°**in i'ti ō** in the beginning • **strā'ta** paved • **nōn ha'bu it**
did not have • **Ap'pi us Clau'di us*** name of a famous Roman
fē'cit made • **Vi'a Ap'pi a*** Appian Way • **Ca'pu a***
Capua (name of Italian city)

Noun	
*prō vin'ci a	province
Verbs	
dū'cit	leads
nō'mi nant	name, call
Adverb	
²**post'e ā**	later, afterward
Prepositions	
³**ā, ab**	(with abl.) from, away from
ad	(with acc.) to, toward

APPOSITION A noun set beside another noun to explain
its meaning is called an appositive and is said to be in apposition with the noun it explains.

Via ab urbe Rōmā ad urbem Capuam dūcit. A highway leads
from the city Rome to the city Capua.

An appositive is in the same case as the noun it explains.
In translating a noun and its appositive we often use "of."

A highway leads from the city (of) Rome to the city (of) Capua.

¹In Latin as in English, some verbs have two direct objects. Here, **viam** is the first
object of **nōminant** and **Viam Appiam** is the second: "The Romans call the highway the
Appian Way."

²The adverb **posteā** is made up of two words, **post** and **eā**. This accounts for the
unusual division of syllables.

³Before a vowel or "h," **ab** is used; before most consonants, **ā** is used.

TWO ADJECTIVES, when they modify the same noun, are sometimes connected by **et,** or one may precede the noun and the other follow.

magnae et longae viae   great (and) long roads

magnae viae longae   great, long roads

magnae longae viae   great, long roads

Roman roads were so well constructed that sections are still in use, not only in the vicinity of Rome, but elsewhere—from Britain to North Africa and the Near East.

A LATIN ADJECTIVE often follows its noun, but an adjective denoting size or number commonly precedes its noun.

terra pulchra   beautiful land   **magna terra**   large country

LOOK AND THINK Who built the first paved road? What was it called? How far did it go?

LATIN LIVES TODAY Below are common English words in everyday use. How can they help you with the meaning of some of the Latin words in "Roman Roads"? To which Latin word is each one related?

initial	nominate	urban	viaduct
initiation	nomination	suburban	provincial

F

AMERICAN HIGHWAYS

America quoque multās habet viās. Multae viae Americānae sunt longae et lātae. Multae viae Americānae ab alterā° ōrā ad alteram° ōram dūcunt. Fāma viārum Americānārum est magna.

Urbēs Americānae viās habent strātās. Viae strātae sunt lātae.

°**ab al'terā . . . ad al'teram**   from one . . . to the other

Nouns		Adjective	
*****fā'ma**	fame	**mul'tae**	many (plural)
ō'ra	coast, shore		

LOOK AND THINK In which paragraph of "American Highways" is "streets" a suitable translation for **viās** and **viae?** In which paragraph is "highways" more appropriate?

Are the forms **viārum Americānārum** (line 3) unfamiliar? Translate **Fāma . . . est magna;** then ask yourself: "The fame OF WHAT is great?" The answer is **viārum Americānārum.**

Will complex American highways like this endure two thousand years of traffic?

THINGS TO REMEMBER

Case Endings

	Singular	Plural
Nominative:	**-a**	**-ae**
Accusative:	**-am**	**-ās**
Ablative:	**-ā**	**-īs**

Case Uses

Nominative: subject or predicate noun

Accusative: direct object; with prepositions: **in** and **sub** (motion implied); **ad, per, prope**

Ablative: with prepositions: **in, sub, ā/ab**

Any case: noun in apposition (same case as noun it explains)

Verb Endings

-t singular subject   **-nt** plural subject

29

SCRAMBLED SENTENCES Unscramble the words to make sentences and translate. Watch word endings. They make the meaning clear, regardless of word order.

1 aquam Aquae in dūcunt incontāminātam urbēs multae.
2 Rōmāna lacūnam vīlla habet magnam.
3 magnā in est aqua lacūnā.

WORDS TO REMEMBER

Nouns	Adjectives	Verbs	Conjunctions
aqua	alta	dūcit, dūcunt	et
casa	*antīqua	est, sunt	itaque
cōpia	bona	habet, habent	sed
*fāma	lāta	nōminant	Prepositions
ōra	*longa	Adverbs	ā, ab
*pictūra	magna	interdum	ad
*prōvincia	multae	*nōn	*in
terra	nova	posteā	per
via	parva	*prīmō	prope
*vīlla	*prīma	quoque	sub

WORD MASTERY 2

Latin nouns ending in **-ia** have sometimes become English words ending in -y as in **familia**/family, **glōria**/glory. If you change **-ia** to -y in the following words what English words appear?

harmonia   industria   injūria   lūxuria   memoria

The ending **-tia/-cia** often becomes -ce in corresponding English nouns; for example, **pestilentia**/pestilence, **jūstitia**/justice. Apply this principle to these Latin words.

absentia   dīligentia   prōvincia   sapientia   scientia

Latin nouns in **-ula** sometimes become English words without undergoing any change or with final **-a** replaced by -e. Occasionally the **-u-** of the Latin ending disappears, so that the derivative ends in -le; for example, **fābula**/fable. For each word below give the corresponding Latin word.

capsule   clavicle   epistle   formula   table

Romans called the world "orbis terrarum" (the circle of lands), because the Empire centered around the Mediterranean Sea. This view of the Mediterranean, which the Romans called "Mare Nostrum" (Our Sea), is from the site of ancient Soluntum, on the north coast of Sicily.

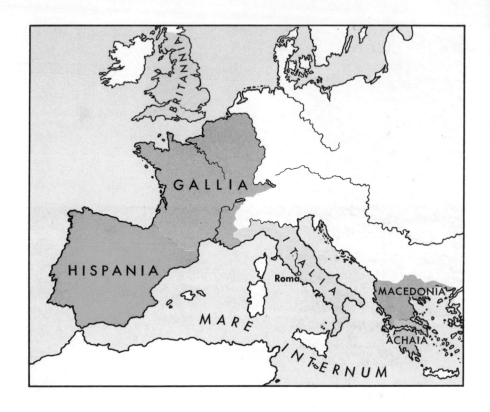

I

ROMAN PROVINCES

In tabulā° Rōmam et prōvinciās Rōmae vidētis.° Rōma multās et magnās prōvinciās habet. Inter nōtās prōvinciās Rōmānās sunt Britannia,[1] Gallia, Hispānia, Achāia, Macedonia. Lingua prōvinciārum Rōmānārum est lingua Latīna.°

Britannia est parva prōvincia; Hispānia et Gallia sunt 5 magnae prōvinciae. Achāia nōn est īnsula; est paenīnsula. Estne Hispānia paenīnsula? Figūra Ītaliae est figūra caligae.°

°**ta′bu la, -ae** map • **vi dē′tis** (pl.) you see • **La ti′na***
(adj.) Latin • **ca′li ga, -ae** boot, shoe

---

[1]Names of persons and places and their English equivalents are given in the General Vocabulary at the back of this book.

In multīs prōvinciīs sunt silvae; silvae sunt magnae et obscūrae. In silvīs obscūrīs sunt bēstiae mīrae. 10

In magnīs prōvinciīs sunt Aquae longae. Aquae aquam ad urbēs dūcunt. Per prōvinciās dūcunt viae. Viae prōvinciārum sunt lātae et longae.

Nouns	
[1]*bēs′ti a, -ae	wild beast
*fi gū′ra, -ae	shape, figure
īn′su la, -ae	island
[2]lin′gua, -ae	tongue, language
*pae nīn′su la, -ae	peninsula
sil′va, -ae	forest, wood
Adjectives	
mi′ra	wonderful, strange
nō′ta	famous, noted
[3]*ob scū′ra	dark, dim
Preposition	
in′ter	(with acc.) between, among
Interrogative	
-ne	(attached to word; indicates question)

THE GENITIVE CASE in Latin shows possession. Nouns with nominative singular in **-a** have the genitive singular in **-ae** and the genitive plural in **-ārum**.

Silvae īnsulae sunt magnae. The forests of the island are large or The island's forests are large.

Bēstiae silvārum sunt magnae. The wild beasts of the forests are large or The forests' wild beasts are large.

Genitive singular **-ae** and nominative plural **-ae** are easily distinguished.

1 The genitive usually follows the noun on which it depends.
2 When the subject is nominative plural the verb ends in **-nt.**

[1]Beginning with this vocabulary, the genitive singular ending of each noun is indicated along with the nominative.

[2]Pronounced **ling′gwa.** Between **n** and a vowel, **gu** represents the sound of **gw,** as in English (lan**gu**age).

[3]When three or more consonants occur between two vowels, the syllable division is usually made after the first consonant.

In writing, most English nouns show possession by adding an apostrophe and -s ('s). When the noun already ends in -s or an "s" sound, as in most plurals, the apostrophe alone shows possession. English nouns which show possession are said to be in the possessive case.

girl's, girls'   man's, men's   princess', princesses'

Possession is often shown in English by "of" and the noun in place of the possessive case.

the dresses of the girls   the homes of the people

LOOK AND THINK In the last two paragraphs of "Roman Provinces" the verb **sunt** is used five times. When is it better translated just "are" (without the expletive) and when "there are"? (See footnote 1 on page 14.)

USE YOUR EYES **Paenīnsula** is a combination of **paene** (almost) and **insula** (island). What is a peninsula? What does the Italian peninsula look like on a map?

SCRAMBLED SENTENCES Unscramble the words to make sentences, and translate. Watch word endings. They make the meaning clear, regardless of word order.

1 **longās habent prōvinciae Aquās Rōmānae.**
2 **bona in aqua est Aquīs.**
3 **obscūrīs bēstiae silvīs in magnae insulārum sunt.**

II

AFRICA

Anna Cornēliae salūtem dīcit[1]; sī valēs, bene est; valeō.[2]
Prīmō erāmus in Siciliā; nunc sumus in Āfricā; mox erimus in Ītaliā. Nunc in Āfricā cum amitā meā sum.

[1]This phrase is equivalent to the salutation "Dear Cornelia" in a personal letter an American girl might write; literally, "Anna says a greeting to Cornelia."

[2]**Sī valēs, bene est; valeō** was an expression so often used by the Romans in letter writing that it was usually abbreviated: **s.v.b.e.v.** It means "If you're well, that's good; I am well," and may be compared with a similar expression still used by some letter writers.

Āfrica est magna prōvincia Rōmae; est terra mīra. Ōra
maritima Āfricae est pulchra et aqua maritima est quiēta. ₅
Multae vīllae Rōmānae in ōrā sunt. Vīllae sunt albae et
pulchrae, sed casae parvae nōn sunt pulchrae.

Āfrica est ārida.° Nōn procul ab ōrā maritimā est terra
arēnōsa.° In viīs angustīs vidēmus bēstiās mīrās—ele-
phantōs° et camēlōs.° ₁₀

Es nunc in Britanniā; mox eris in Galliā. Nārrā° mihi° dē
Britanniā. Estne Britannia terra frīgida°? Suntne viae lātae
in Britanniā? Dūcuntne Aquae aquam in urbēs? Suntne
silvae obscūrae? In ōrā Āfricae silvās nōn vidēmus.

Amita mea mē° vocat. Valē.[1] ₁₅

°**ā′ri da*** dry, arid • **a rē nō sa** sandy • **e le phan′tōs***
(acc. pl.) elephants • **ca mē′lōs*** (acc. pl.) camels • **nār′rā**
(a command) tell • **mi′hi** (to) me • **fri′gi da*** cold, frigid
mē* me

Noun	
a′mi ta, -ae	aunt
Adjectives	
al′ba	white
an gus′ta	narrow
***ma ri′ti ma**	of the sea; (with **ōra**) seacoast
me′a	my, mine
[2]**pul′chra**	beautiful
***qui ē′ta**	quiet
Verbs	
vi dē′mus	we see
vo′cat	calls, is calling
Adverbs	
mox	soon
nunc	now
pro′cul	far, far away
Prepositions	
cum	(with abl.) with
dē	(with abl.) about, concerning

[1]**Valē,** the Roman expression meaning literally "Farewell," is equivalent to our "Goodby" (God be with you).

[2]In syllabication, **ch** is treated as a single letter. Its sound is that of "c" in "can."

35

TENSE Time as it is shown by verbs is called tense. Verbs indicate tense by different forms.

TENSE FORMS OF THE VERB sum which show present, past, and future time are these.

Present		Imperfect (Past)		Future	
Singular		Singular		Singular	
1 **sum**	I am	**e'ram**	I was	**e'rō**	I shall be
2 **es**	you are	**e'rās**	you were	**e'ris**	you will be
3 **est**	he is	**e'rat**	he was	**e'rit**	he will be
Plural		Plural		Plural	
1 **su'mus**	we are	**erā'mus**	we were	**e'rimus**	we shall be
2 **es'tis**	you are	**erā'tis**	you were	**e'ritis**	you will be
3 **sunt**	they are	**e'rant**	they were	**e'runt**	they will be

PERSON AND NUMBER OF A VERB are shown by verb endings.

		Singular		Plural	
1	First person:	**-m (ō)**	I	**-mus**	we
2	Second person:	**-s**	you	**-tis**	you
3	Third person:	**-t**	he (she, it)	**-nt**	they

Roman mosaic from North Africa, showing musicians in a boat.

AGREEMENT OF VERB AND SUBJECT

The person and number of a Latin verb are always the same as the person and number of its subject. A noun subject is in third person.

Singular

1 **Sum in Āfricā.** I am in Africa.
2 **Es amita mea.** You are my aunt.
3 **Via est angusta.** The street is narrow.

Plural

1 **Sumus in Āfricā.** We are in Africa.
2 **Estis pulchrae.** You are beautiful.
3 **Silvae sunt obscūrae.** The forests are dark.

OMISSION OF THE SUBJECT
When a Latin verb is first or second person, its subject is usually omitted. The subject of a verb in third person may also be omitted, if it is clear what or who the subject is. In translating a verb with subject omitted, a pronoun subject is supplied.

Sum in Āfricā; est pulchra. I am in Africa; it is beautiful.
Casae sunt parvae, sed sunt pulchrae. The houses are small, but they are beautiful.

PRACTICE IN VERB FORMS
The verbs in these sentences all show present time.

1 **Bēstiae sunt in silvā.**
2 **Sum in Galliā.**
3 **Es in casā.**
4 **Sumus in Galliā.**
5 **Estis in Āfricā.**
6 **Anna est in vīllā.**

Change the verbs so that each sentence will show (a) past time and (b) future time. Keep the same person and number. Translate.

I For each verb in the lettered list, choose all appropriate subjects and/or direct objects from the numbered list of nouns. Translate each noun and verb combination.

1 amita
2 bēstiās
3 casam
4 īnsulīs
5 linguārum
6 pictūrae
7 silva
8 viae

a) dūcunt
b) est
c) habent
d) sunt
e) vocat
f) nōminant
g) dūcit
h) habet

LOOK AND THINK Besides the forms of **sum,** these verb forms appear in stories I and II of this unit.

vidētis (I, 1)   **valēs** (II, 1)   **vidēmus** (II, 9)

dīcit (II, 1)   **valeō** (II, 1)   **Dūcunt** (II, 13)

What are the person and number of each of these verb forms? What are the clues? What pronoun is used in translating each form?

USE YOUR EYES In the story, "Africa," **bēstiās** (line 9), **elephantōs** and **camēlōs** (lines 9-10), and **urbēs** (line 13) are all accusative plural. In what way are their endings alike? How do they differ?

LATIN LIVES TODAY For each sentence choose the word which makes the statement true. Explain your choice.

1 An albino is sometimes/never black.
2 To a shipowner maritime law is important/unimportant.
3 Miss America usually has great/no pulchritude.
4 Land is arid when it is flooded/dry.

III

BRITAIN

Cornēlia Annae salūtem dīcit: s.v.b.e.v.

Amita mea in vīllā nostrā in Britanniā habitat. Britannia est magna īnsula. Circum īnsulam est alta et frīgida aqua, sed inter Galliam et Britanniam aquae nōn sunt frīgidae.

Vīlla nostra est prope ōram maritimam. Nōn procul ā ⁵ vīllā nostrā sunt thermae.° In thermīs sunt et aqua tepida° et aqua frīgida. Prope vīllam nostram est via lāta, sed via nōn est longa. Nōn sunt multae vīllae in viā nostrā.

In Britanniā Rōmānā sunt scholae Rōmānae et vīllae

°ther'mae, -ārum the baths • te'pi da* lukewarm, tepid

Rōmānae et ārae Rōmānae. Sed in Britanniā Celticā° sunt 10
silvae. Silvae sunt obscūrae et perīculōsae. In silvīs obscūrīs
sunt bēstiae mīrae. Per silvās viae Rōmānae nōn pertinent.°
Incolae silvārum in parvīs casīs habitant. Prope casās nōn
sunt ārae, sed procul in silvīs sunt ārae mīrae.

Briganta est ancilla° amitae meae. Briganta in silvīs 15
obscūrīs habitat. Briganta mihi et amitae meae multās dē
Britanniā Celticā fābulās nārrat. Amitae et mihi sēmitam°
obscūram silvae mōnstrat, sed casās nōn vidēmus Celticās.
Interdum Briganta amitae meae herbās novās dat.

Mox erimus in Galliā. Erisne in Āfricā? Eritne amita tua 20
in Ītaliā? Erō beāta in Galliā. Valē.

°**Cel′ti ca*** (adj.) Celtic • **per′ti nent** extend • **an cil′la,
-ae** maid • **sē′mi ta, -ae** path

Nouns	
ā′ra, -ae	altar
***fā′bu la, -ae**	story, fable
***her′ba, -ae**	herb, plant
in′co la, -ae	inhabitant, resident
***scho′la, -ae**	school
Adjectives	
be ā′ta	happy
nos′tra	our
pe ri cu lō′sa	dangerous
tu′a	your, yours (of one person)
Verbs	
dat	gives
ha′bi tat	lives, dwells
mōn′strat	shows, points out
nār′rat	tells
Conjunctions	
et . . . et	both . . . and
Preposition	
***cir′cum**	(with acc.) around

I N D I R E C T   O B J E C T A word denoting the person to
whom something is given, said, told, or shown is an indirect
object.

Ancilla Annae pictūram dat. The maid gives a picture to Anna.

Anna amitae pictūram mōnstrat. Anna shows the picture to her aunt.

Anna ancillīs fābulam nārrat. Anna tells a story to the maids.

In English "to" is often omitted with the indirect object.

The maid gives Anna a picture.

Anna shows her aunt the picture.

Anna tells the maids a story.

D A T I V E   C A S E   A Latin noun used as an indirect object is in the dative case. Nouns with nominative singular in **-a** have the dative singular in **-ae** and the dative plural in **-īs**.

ancillae   **ancillīs**

Dative singular **-ae** is easily distinguished from genitive singular **-ae** and nominative plural **-ae**.

1 The dative usually precedes the direct object.
2 The dative is found with verbs meaning "give," "say," "tell," or "show."
3 The genitive usually follows the noun on which it depends.
4 When the subject is nominative plural the verb ends in **-nt.**
5 The sentence makes sense in translation if the proper distinction is made.

Dative plural **-īs** and ablative plural **-īs** are easily distinguished.

1 The dative is found with verbs meaning "give," "say," "tell," or "show."
2 The ablative is often found after a preposition.

A roof tile from Roman London bears the imprint of a hob-nailed boot that had stepped on it before it had dried. The sole of a similar boot is at the right.

Remains of a fort along Hadrian's Wall, built across Northern Britain to defend Roman territory from the barbarians

LOOK AND THINK Which form in the list below can be ablative only? Which can be either ablative or dative? Which can be nominative, genitive, or dative? Which, genitive only? Accusative only? Nominative only? Which can be singular only? Which, plural only?

silvīs   casae   viā   casārum   Rōmam   amita

I Change singular verbs to plural and plural verbs to singular. Translate both forms, supplying appropriate pronoun subjects for each.

1 dat	4 mōnstrātis	7 eram	10 nārrāmus
2 dūcunt	5 eris	8 vidēs	11 vocant
3 vocās	6 habitat	9 sum	12 habet

II Supply missing case endings to complete each sentence.
1 Cornēlia amit- (sing.) pictūram dat.
2 Amita Cornēli- fābulam nārrat.
3 Fābul- amit- sunt bon-.
4 Amit- incol- (pl.) casās mōnstrat.
5 Incol- in cas- (pl.) amit- nostrae habitant.

Unscramble the words to make sentences, and translate. Watch word endings. They make the meaning clear, regardless of word order.

1 ārae in sunt silvīs multae magnīs.
2 prōpe sunt nōn ārae viās.
3 mihi pictūrās mea casārum mōnstrat amīta; sed pictūrās mihi dat nōn.

LATIN LIVES TODAY Select the word which completes each sentence correctly. Explain your selection.

beatific	**habitable**	**scholastic**
fabulous	**perilous**	**tepid**

1 Because they are found only in stories, talking animals are —.
2 A place where people can live is —.
3 Falling stones made the journey —.
4 The water was neither hot nor cold, but —.
5 Since he was studious, his chief interests were —.

Ancient theater at beautiful Taormina in Sicily, with Mt. Aetna in the background

IV

Sicilia est magna īnsula inter Ītaliam et Āfricam. Antīquitus Sicilia erat paenīnsula Ītaliae; nunc Sicilia est īnsula.
Inter Siciliam et Ītaliam aquae sunt angustae. Inter Siciliam
et Āfricam aquae sunt altae et lātae.

Antīquitus Sicilia erat terra opīma.° Incolae erant agri- 5
colae et nautae. Vīllae agricolārum erant in terrā opīmā;
casae nautārum erant in ōrā maritimā.

Incolae Siciliae dīcēbant, "Sunt multae ārae deārum in
Siciliā. Deae sunt terrae nostrae benignae; incolīs īnsulae
sunt amīcae. Itaque in Siciliā multās vidētis ārās deārum." 10

In īnsulīs Siciliae propinquīs erant pīrātae. Interdum
pīrātae incolās necābant et casās īnsulae vāstābant.

Aetna est in Siciliā. Incolae Siciliae flammās Aetnae vidēbant. Aetnam timēbant, sed dīcēbant, "Deae nostrae erunt
benignae; incolās Siciliae servābunt.°" 15

°**o pī′ma** fertile, rich • **ser vā′bunt** will save

Nouns	
a gri′co la, -ae	M., farmer
de′a, -ae	F., goddess
***flam′ma, -ae**	F., flame
nau′ta, -ae	M., sailor
***pī rā′ta, -ae**	M., pirate
Adjectives	
a mī′ca	friendly
***be nig′na**	kind
pro pin′qua	near
Verbs	
[1]**dī cē′bant**	used to say; said
ne cā′bant	used to kill; killed
ti mē′bant	used to fear; feared
vās tā′bant	used to destroy; destroyed
Adverb	
***an tī′qui tus**	in ancient times

[1]With **-ba-** or **-bā-** inserted before the person ending, the time changes from present
to past in all Latin verbs (except **sum** and compound verbs containing **sum**).

DATIVE WITH ADJECTIVES With adjectives meaning "kind," "friendly," "near," and some others the dative is often translated by an English phrase with "to."

Sicilia est Italiae propinqua. Sicily is near (to) Italy.
Deae nautīs sunt benignae. Goddesses are kind to sailors.
Dea Siciliae est amīca. The goddess is friendly to Sicily.

This dative commonly precedes its adjective.

MASCULINE NOUNS ENDING IN -a Most nouns with nominative singular ending in -a are feminine, but a few referring to males are masculine: **agricola,** farmer; **nauta,** sailor; **pīrāta,** pirate. **Incola,** inhabitant, naturally may be either masculine or feminine.

Adjectives with the nominative singular ending in -a are always feminine and are never used with masculine nouns.

LOOK AND THINK What do **necābant** and **vāstābant** in line 12 of "Sicily" have in common? How do **erant** (11) and **erunt** (14) differ in meaning?

USE YOUR EYES In the last paragraph of "Sicily" find three verbs with the same time signal as **necābant** and **vāstābant** (12).

I Complete the prepositional phrases by adding appropriate case endings. When two different cases may be used with the same preposition, give both. Translate.

1	ab īnsul-	(sing.)	6 circum ār-	(pl.)
2	sub terr-	(sing.)	7 inter bēsti-	(pl.)
3	ad vīll-	(sing.)	8 cum naut-	(pl.)
4	dē pīrāt-	(sing.)	9 in silv-	(pl.)
5	prope lacūn-	(sing.)	10 per vi-	(pl.)

II Select the correct word or phrase to complete each sentence.
1 Flammae vīllīs/vīllās propinquae sunt.
2 Deae nauta/nautae benignae sunt.
3 Amita mea incolīs/ad incolās amīca est.
4 Via meae casae propinqua ad ōram/ōrae dūcit.
5 Bēstiae silvae incolam/incolae īnsulae amīcae sunt.

PRACTICE   Change all verbs in present time to past time and all verbs in past time to present time. (See footnote on page 43.) Translate each verb in both tenses.

erat	mōnstrābāmus	nārrant	vidēbātis
habēbant	mōnstrābat	nōminātis	vidēmus
habēbās	mōnstrās	timēbāmus	vidēs
habet	nārrābās	timent	vocābātis
habētis	nārrāmus	vāstābant	vocat

LATIN LIVES TODAY   Explain these phrases. Which words in the lesson vocabulary contain clues to the meaning?

flammable materials   amicable relations

nautical clothes   benign manner

REVIEW OF UNIT I

LESSONS I-IV

Nouns	Adjectives	Verbs	Adverbs
agricola, -ae	alba	dat	*antīquitus
amita, -ae	amīca	dīcēbant	mox
āra, -ae	angusta	habitat	nunc
*bēstia, -ae	beāta	mōnstrat	procul
dea, -ae	*benigna	nārrat	
*fābula, -ae	*marītima	necābant	Conjunctions
*figūra, -ae	mea	timēbant	et . . . et
*flamma, -ae	mīra	vāstābant	
*herba, -ae	nostra	vidēbant	Prepositions
incola, -ae	nōta	vidēmus	*circum
īnsula, -ae	*obscūra	vocat	cum
lingua, -ae	perīculōsa		dē
nauta, -ae	propinqua		inter
*paenīnsula, -ae	pulchra		
*pīrāta, -ae	*quiēta		Interrogative
*schola, -ae	tua		-ne
silva, -ae			

I From each group select the singular and plural nouns in the case specified.

1 (Dative)   nautae, amitīs, deārum, vīllās, viam
2 (Nominative) linguae, schola, aquam, fābulās, āra
3 (Accusative) bēstiae, cisternīs, cōpiam, fāma, ōrās
4 (Genitive)   silvārum, agricolās, casam, terrā, prōvinciae
5 (Ablative)   īnsulam, pīrātae, pictūrā, flammīs, incola

II From the forms in parentheses select the appropriate object or objects for each preposition, and translate all phrases.

1 cum   (pīrātae, cōpiam, amitīs)
2 dē   (scholā, fābulīs, casam)
3 circum (silvārum, paenīnsulam, lacūnīs)
4 inter   (nautae, deārum, agricolās)
5 in   (aquam, herbīs, āra)
6 per   (linguae, viā, aquam)
7 prope   (flammīs, bēstiae, vīllās)
8 ā (ab) (terrā, ōrīs, prōvinciae)
9 ad   (pictūra, īnsulam, deās)

III Explain how the verbs of each pair differ, and translate.

1 dīcit/dīcēbant   6 vidēs/vidētis
2 mōnstrās/mōnstrātis   7 erant/erunt
3 estis/eritis   8 habent/habēbant
4 nārrāmus/nārrābāmus   9 timeō/timēmus
5 sum/eram   10 habitat/habitābat

IV Select from the underlined words examples of the uses listed at the right; state whether singular or plural, and translate the sentences.

1 Casa silvae propinqua erat.   subject
2 Aqua lacūnae est alta.   predicate adjective
3 Agricolae fābulam nārrāmus.   possessive
4 Amitam meam ad scholam dūcunt.   indirect object
5 Ārae in silvā erunt.   dative with adjective
6 Timēsne incolās īnsulārum?   direct object
7 Nautīs benignae sumus.   accusative with preposi-
8 Per prōvinciam via dūcit.   tion
9 Cum pīrātīs prope ōram erimus.   ablative with preposition

46

UNIT II

The sails are furled on this boat pictured in mosaic, and oars are plainly visible. Roman ships had square-rigged sails, hung from a spar which crossed the mast at right angles. This fine mosaic was found in North Africa in 1954.

Ancient pirates of the Mediterranean probably knew this coast of Sicily. Caesar, captured in his youth by pirates, later got revenge in his campaign against them.

V

PIRATES AND HIDDEN TREASURE

Galba et Silvānus in ōrā maritimā Siciliae ambulant. Galba est nauta; Silvānus est agricola.

Silvānus. Hodiē° aquae sunt quiētae. Ōram amō maritimam cum undae sunt quiētae.

Galba. Ita; hodiē undae et ōra sunt quiētae, sed mox ōra ₅ erit perīculōsa. Pīrātae sunt in īnsulīs propinquīs. Mox pīrātae erunt in īnsulā tuā.

Silvānus. Nōn timeō pīrātās. Vīlla mea nōn est ōrae propinqua. Nōnne vidēs vīllam meam prope altam Aetnam?

Galba. Aetna est longinqua, sed videō vīllam prope altam ₁₀ Aetnam. Nōnne timēs flammās Aetnae?

Silvānus. Minimē. Interdum flammae sunt clārae, sed flammae nōn sunt perīculōsae. Cūr flammās timēs?

°ho′di ē   today

Galba. Nōn timeō flammās; sed pīrātās timeō. Pīrātae casās et ārās vāstant. Pīrātae incolās necant. Ōlim noctū° ambulō 15 in ōrā. Stellae et lūna sunt clārae. Nōn procul videō pīrātās in ōrā! Pīrātae magnam arcam° portant. Arca est longa et alta. In arcā videō gemmās et pecūniam.°

Silvānus. Ubi sunt gemmae et pecūnia? Habēsne arcam gemmārum et pecūniae? 20

Galba. Minimē. Pīrātae terram posteā effodiunt°; cēlant arcam in terrā. Pīrātae mē nōn vident. Timeō pīrātās!

°**noc'tū** at night • **ar'ca, -ae** F., box, chest • **pe cū'ni a, -ae** F., money • **ef fo'di unt** dig up

Nouns	
*gem'ma, -ae	F., gem, jewel
*lū'na, -ae	F., moon
*stel'la, -ae	F., star
un'da, -ae	F., wave
Adjectives	
*clā'ra	bright, clear
loн gin'qua	distant, far away
Verbs	
*am'bu lō	walk, am walking
a'mō	like, love
*cē'lō	hide, conceal
*por'tō	carry
Adverbs	
cūr	why
i'ta	yes; thus, in this way
mi'ni mē	no; not at all
ō'lim	once
u'bi	where
Conjunction	
cum	when

Q U E S T I O N S Ubi (where), cūr (why), and other interrogative words introduce questions.

Ubi est casa tua? Where is your house?
Cūr pīrātās timēs? Why do you fear pirates?

The syllable **-ne** attached to a verb is a sign of a question.

Vidēsne flammās? Do you see the flames?
Estne casa in ōrā? Is the house on the shore?

Nōnne asks a question which expects the answer "Yes."

Nōnne vidēs flammās? Don't you see the flames?
Nōnne est casa in ōrā? Isn't the house on the shore?

A N S W E R S   T O   Q U E S T I O N S   are generally made in the form of a statement in Latin. Sometimes in place of a sentence **minimē** is used for "No" and **ita** for "Yes."

U S E   Y O U R   E Y E S   What does the ending **-ō** of a verb tell about the subject? The ending **-s? -t? -nt? -m?**

P R A C T I C E   I N   V E R B   F O R M S   Pronounce these words and translate each so as to show person and number.

> erunt, erās, es, sunt, eritis, erātis, erō, estis, erimus,
> sum, erat, erit, est, erāmus, eris, eram, sumus, erant

(A) Select the verbs that show present time and arrange them in order according to person and number.

(B) Select the verbs that show past time and future time and arrange each group according to person and number.

I Answer in complete Latin sentences the following questions about "Pirates and Hidden Treasure."

1 Ubi Galba et Silvānus ambulant?
2 Estne Silvānus nauta?
3 Nōnne Galba nauta est?
4 Cūr agricola pīrātās nōn timet?
5 Ubi vīlla agricolae est?
6 Estne Aetna parva?
7 Timetne Galba flammās?
8 Estne Aetna prope ōram maritimam?
9 Cūr Galba pīrātās timet?
10 Ubi pīrātae cēlant arcam?

L A T I N   L I V E S   T O D A Y   Combine each noun under A with an appropriate adjective under B.

A (Nouns)		B (Adjectives)	
patient	month	portable	stellar
loss	motion	lunar	pecuniary
rôle	typewriter	undulant	ambulatory

VI

Incolae Graeciae antīquae saepe deās vidēbant. Deās in viīs nōn vidēbant, sed deae saepe in silvīs ambulābant. Deae multās ārās in silvīs Graeciae habēbant.

Dea Lātōna erat incolīs multīs Graeciae cāra quod erat dea benigna. In Graeciā erant multae ārae Lātōnae. Aliārum° quoque deārum ārae erant pulchrae.

Dea Lātōna in silvīs Graeciae saepe ambulābat. Ōlim Lātōna cum parvīs līberīs° per magnam silvam ambulābat.

Ut° fābula est, Diāna, parva fīlia Lātōnae, aquam in lacūnā propinquā videt. Subitō Diāna lacūnam mōnstrat et aquam ōrat. Prope lacūnam sunt agricolae.

Lātōna agricolās vocat et dīcit, "Mea fīlia aquam ōrat."

Aqua est bona, sed agricolae deae dīcunt, "Aqua lacūnae nōn est bona." Itaque Diānae, parvae fīliae Lātōnae, aquam nōn dant.

Lātōna īrāta subitō clāmat, "Nunc estis agricolae; nunc in casīs habitātis. Nōn jam in casīs habitābitis,° quod fīliae meae bonam aquam lacūnae nōn datis. Nunc in lacūnā est bona aqua! Nōn jam aqua erit bona, quod in lacūnā habitābitis. Eritis rānae.°"

°a′li a   other   •   li′be rīs   (dat., abl. pl.) children   •   ut   as
ha bi tā′bi tis   (pl.) you will live   •   rā′na, -ae   F., frog

Nouns		Adverbs	
[1]fi′li a, -ae	F., daughter	nōn [2]jam	no longer
*la cū′na, -ae	F., pond, pool	sae′pe	often
Adjectives		su′bi tō	suddenly
cā′ra	dear	Conjunction	
*ī rā′ta	angry	quod	because
Verbs			
clā′mō	shout, cry		
ō′rō	ask for		

[1]filia and dea have the ending -ābus instead of -īs in the dative and ablative plural.

[2]Pronounced "yäm." Jam is sometimes spelled iam, Latin i being a consonant (with sound of "y") as well as a vowel. In this book, J is used to represent consonant i.

51

This painting of Latona punishing the boorish farmers who refused to let her have water for her thirsty children is in the Fitzwilliam Museum at Cambridge University. It is attributed to the German painter Adam Elsheimer (1578-1610).

DECLENSION A list of the cases and numbers of a noun, adjective, or pronoun given in order is called a declension. When you give all the forms of such a word you decline it.

DECLENSION OF silva

Singular

Nom.	**sil′va**	forest	Subject; Pred. Noun
Gen.	**sil′vae**	forest's, of a forest	Possessive
Dat.	**sil′vae**	to or for a forest	Ind. Obj.; with Adj.
Acc.	**sil′vam**	forest	Dir. Obj.; with Prep.
Abl.	**sil′vā**	in, from, with a forest	With Prep.; without Prep.

Plural

Nom.	**sil′vae**	forests	Subject; Pred. Noun
Gen.	**silvā′rum**	forests', of forests	Possessive
Dat.	**sil′vīs**	to or for forests	Ind. Obj.; with Adj.
Acc.	**sil′vās**	forests	Dir. Obj.; with Prep.
Abl.	**sil′vīs**	in, from, with forests	With Prep.; without Prep.

FIRST DECLENSION Nouns with nominative singular ending in -**a** and genitive singular in -**ae** belong to the first declension. All first-declension nouns have the same case endings as **silva**. Latin has five regular noun declensions.

The part of a noun to which the endings are added is called the base. The base is found by dropping the genitive singular ending. Thus, the base of **silva** (from genitive singular **silvae**) is **silv-**. The vocabularies throughout this book give the nominative and genitive singular of each noun.

USES OF LATIN CASES

	Singular	Plural
Nom.	**Nauta casam habet.**	**Sumus nautae.**
Gen.	**Casa nautae est parva.**	**Casa nautārum est parva.**
Dat.	**Galba nautae arcam dat.**	**Nautīs benignae estis.**
Acc.	**Galba nautam videt.**	**Galba prope nautās habitat.**
Abl.	**Galba cum nautā ambulat.**	**Galba cum nautīs ambulat.**

I Translate the parts of the sentences that are underlined, using words in the list and applying appropriate endings.

1 They walk with the pirates.   agricola
2 He walks around the island.   amita
3 There are forests near the city.   aqua
4 The farmer is walking from the villa.   āra
5 The house of my aunt is not far away.   īnsula
6 He gives the herbs to the farmer.   nauta
7 A long road leads to the provinces.   pīrāta
8 The flames of the altars are bright.   prōvincia
9 She was kind to the sailors.   silva
10 The water is not deep.   vīlla

II From each statement below form a question, using an interrogative word or syllable in the list. Translate each question and the statement which answers it.

cūr -ne nōnne ubi

1 Deae saepe in silvīs Graeciae ambulābant.
2 In Graeciā erant multae ārae Lātōnae.
3 Lātōna multīs incolīs cāra erat, quod dea benigna erat.
4 Diāna parva fīlia Lātōnae erat.

53

Unscramble the words to make sentences, and translate. Watch word endings. They make the meaning of a Latin sentence clear, regardless of word order.

1 aquam lacūnae habent bonam nōn parvae multae.
2 saepe lacūnae est aqua quiēta.
3 saepe in bēstiās silvā vidēbat Diāna.
4 necābant vāstābant et urbēs Graeciae incolās interdum pīrātae.

VII

THE ANT AND THE GRASSHOPPER

In parvā casā prope magnam silvam formīca° impigra habitābat. Aestāte formīca labōrābat et cibum° in casam portābat. Laeta erat, sed nōn cantābat.°

Prope casam formīcae impigrae cicāda° pigra habitābat. Formīca impigra pigram cicādam monēbat, sed cicāda nōn 5 labōrābat; semper cantābat. Hieme formīca cibum habēbat; cicāda cibum nōn habēbat.

Ōlim, ut fābula est, cicāda misera parvam casam formīcae videt. Ad casam volat; jānuam pulsat.° Formīca domī° est, sed jānuam nōn aperit.° Per fenestram formīca cicādam 10 spectat.

Misera cicāda jānuam iterum pulsat et clāmat, "Tū[1] cibum habēs; ego[1] cibum nōn habeō; cibum ōrō."

Per fenestram formīca clāmat, "Tū pigra es! Aestāte ego labōrō; aestāte tū nōn labōrās. Formīcae sunt impigrae; 15 nōs[1] labōrāmus aestāte; hieme cibum nōs habēmus. Cicādae

°**for mi′ca, -ae** F., ant • **ci′bum** (acc. sing.) food • **can′tō, -āre** sing • **ci cā′da, -ae** F., cicada, grasshopper • **pul′sō, -āre** beat, knock (on) • **do′mī** at home • **nōn a′pe rit** does not open

[1]Latin verbs with first- or second-person endings usually do not have the pronoun subject expressed. Here the pronouns **tū, ego, nōs, vōs** are used for emphasis. How can you tell which is which? There are clues to help you translate them correctly as "I," "you," or "we."

A sense of humor is reflected in this mosaic designed for a dining room floor. Fish, shrimp, chicken, nuts, berries, and vegetables are among the identifiable scraps.

aestāte nōn labōrant; hieme vōs cibum nōn habētis. Vōs pigrae estis! Cūr nōn labōrātis?"

Cicāda misera ā casā formīcae volat. Nōn jam cantat.

Nouns		Verbs	
fe nes'tra, -ae	F., window	***la bō'rō, -āre**	work
jā'nu a, -ae	F., door	***spec'tō, -āre**	watch, see,
aes tā'te	in summer		look, look at
hi'e me	in winter	**vo'lō, -āre**	fly
Adjectives		**mo'ne ō, -ēre**	warn
[1]**im'pi gra**	industrious	Adverbs	
[1]**pi'gra**	lazy	**i'te rum**	again
lae'ta	happy	**sem'per**	always
***mi'se ra**	unhappy, poor		

[1]An exception to the rule that two consonants between two vowels are divided. If the first is a stop consonant (**g** or **c, b** or **p, d** or **t**) and the second is **l** or **r**, both are pronounced with the vowel that follows.

ROMAN FOOD AND MEALS

In the early days, Romans ate dinner (cena) at noon. Other meals were breakfast (jentaculum) and supper (vesperna). Later, dinner was the evening meal, and lunch (prandium) was eaten at noon, especially in the cities. Bread, olive oil, and wine were basic foods of the Romans, who also ate many of the same meats, poultry, seafoods, vegetables, and fruits that we eat. Exceptions were tomatoes, potatoes, and corn. Sugar, coffee, tea, and chocolate also were unknown to the Romans, and butter was not used by them as food. Eggs were popular as an appetizer, while dessert was regularly fruit. "From egg to apples" accordingly came to mean "from beginning to end" or, as we say, "from soup to nuts."

Above: Butcher's shop on an ancient relief, in which spareribs, part of a ham, and a side of bacon are recognizable. Pork was the favorite meat of the Romans; beef was regarded by them as a luxury food.

Below: Wine jug and bowl decorated with a bird and flowers are examples of handsome Roman tableware.

Left: Decorative mosaics show a partridge, ducks, guinea fowl, and various seafoods. The Romans ate all kinds of fish and fowl, but oysters and fresh fish were especially prized. The wealthy raised fish in private fishponds for their own table use. Wild fowl were raised on large estates, as well as domestic fowl, which were cultivated both as meat and for eggs.

Above: This Roman bowl, made by fusing rods of varicolored glass, is similar to our millefiori (Italian for "a thousand flowers"). Right: Bowl of red Arretine pottery, a common type of everyday ware used all over the Roman world.

Above: Olive orchards like this produced oil for the Romans. Below: Open-air dining room with sloping couches where Romans reclined on cushions as they ate a leisurely late-afternoon cena. Right: Wall painting of a loaf of bread, figs, and a small bird. Romans enjoyed eating songbirds, as their descendants still do.

THE INFINITIVE ENDING of most Latin verbs is
-re. In English, such verb forms as "to carry" and "to warn"
are called infinitives.

portāre	**monēre**
to carry	to warn

THE PRESENT STEM of most verbs can be found by
dropping the -re of the infinitive.

Verb	Infinitive	Present Stem
portō	**portāre**	**portā-**
moneō	**monēre**	**monē-**

PRESENT TENSE shows that an act is taking place or that
a condition exists in present time. Verbs in the present tense
are made up of the present stem plus person endings.

A CONJUGATION is the arrangement in regular order
of the forms of a verb. There are four main conjugations of
Latin verbs.

Verbs with infinitive **-āre** are of the First Conjugation.
Verbs with infinitive **-ēre** are of the Second Conjugation.

CONJUGATIONS I AND II IN PRESENT TENSE

	I			II	
	Singular			Singular	
1	**por'tō**	I carry		**mo'neō**	I warn
2	**por'tās**	you carry		**mo'nēs**	you warn
3	**por'tat**	he carries		**mo'net**	he warns
	Plural			Plural	
1	**portā'mus**	we carry		**monē'mus**	we warn
2	**portā'tis**	you carry		**monē'tis**	you warn
3	**por'tant**	they carry		**mo'nent**	they warn

First-conjugation verbs are conjugated like **portō**. Second-
conjugation verbs are conjugated like **moneō**.

Notice that before **-ō** the stem vowel **-ā-** disappears, while
-ē- remains, but is shortened. Both **-ā-** and **-ē-** become short
before **-nt** and final **-t**.

For translating Latin verbs in the present tense, a phrase like "I am carrying," "you are carrying"; "I am warning," "you are warning," etc. is often preferable to "I carry," "you carry," etc.

PAST TIME may be shown by the sign **-ba-/-bā-** in all verbs (except **sum** and its compounds). This sign, which appears between the stem and the person ending, indicates an action or condition that was continuous, repeated, or customary in past time.

Singular			Plural		
I **portābam**	**portābās**	**portābat**	**portābāmus**	**portābātis**	**portābant**
II **monēbam**	**monēbās**	**monēbat**	**monēbāmus**	**monēbātis**	**monēbant**

Verbs with the sign **-bā-** are in imperfect tense and may be translated "I used to carry," "I carried," "I was carrying," etc.; "I used to warn," "I warned," "I was warning," etc.

REVIEW OF VERBS IN -āre (FIRST CONJUGATION)

ambulō, -āre	walk
amō, -āre	like, love
cēlō, -āre	hide, conceal
clāmō, -āre	shout, cry
[1]**dō, -ăre**	give
habitō, -āre	live, dwell
labōrō, -āre	work
mōnstrō, -āre	show, point out
nārrō, -āre	tell, relate
necō, -āre	kill
nōminō, -āre	name, call
ōrō, -āre	ask for
portō, -āre	carry
spectō, -āre	watch, see
vāstō, -āre	destroy, lay waste
vocō, -āre	call, summon
volō, -āre	fly

[1]**dō, dăre** differs from other first-conjugation verbs in that it has short **a** in the infinitive and in the first and second persons plural: **dō, dās, dat; damus, datis, dant.**

REVIEW OF VERBS IN -ēre
(SECOND CONJUGATION)

habeō, -ēre	have, hold
moneō, -ēre	warn
timeō, -ēre	fear, be afraid of
valeō, -ēre	be well, be strong
videō, -ēre	see

I Identify each of the verb forms below as present tense, past tense, stem, or infinitive. Translate.

1	cēlāre	5	nārrātis	9	amant
2	habēbat	6	erāmus	10	dās
3	timent	7	sumus	11	timēbant
4	vidē-	8	dare	12	habēre

SCRAMBLED SENTENCES Rearrange the words to make sentences, and translate.

1 **prope cicāda casam pigra formīcae habitat parvam.**
2 **pigra es aestāte; sed aestāte et sum impigra hieme.**
3 **quiētae aquae hodiē nōnne sunt?**
4 **cāra Graeciae Lātōna est incolīs dea.**
5 **timent Diānam agricolae nōn Lātōnae filiam parvam.**

MENU FOR A ROMAN BANQUET

Antecēna (Appetizers)

Ostreae (Oysters) **Asparagus** (Asparagus) **Ōva** (Eggs)

Caepae (Onions) **Lactūca** (Lettuce) **Mulsum** (Honeyed Wine) [1]

Cēna (Main Course)

Assum vitulīnum (Roast veal) **Carōtae** (Carrots)

Perna (Ham) **Bētae** (Beets)

Gallīnae (Chickens) **Brassicae** (Cabbages)

Piscēs (Fish) **Pānis et mel** (Bread and honey)

Fabae (Beans) **Vīnum** (Wine—diluted) [1]

Secunda Mēnsa (Dessert)

Ūvae (Grapes) **Māla** (Apples) **Vīnum** (Wine) [1]

Pira (Pears) **Castaneae** (Chestnuts)

[1]Fruit juice or soft drinks may be used in place of wine.

Ēsuriō. I'm hungry.   **Sitiō.** I'm thirsty.   **Lac bibō.** I drink milk.

Dā mihi salem/piper, quaesō. Please pass the salt/pepper.

Grātiās tibi/vōbīs agō. Thanks!—I thank you (sing./pl.).

REVIEW OF UNIT II

LESSONS V—VII

Nouns	Adjectives	Verbs	Adverbs	Conjunctions
fenestra, -ae	cāra	*ambulō, -āre	cūr	cum
filia, -ae	*clāra	amō, -āre	ita	quod
*gemma, -ae	impigra	*cēlō, -āre	iterum	
jānua, -ae	*īrāta	clāmō, -āre	minimē	
*lacūna, -ae	laeta	*labōrō, -āre	nōn jam	
*lūna, -ae	longinqua	ōrō, -āre	ōlim	
*stella, -ae	*misera	*portō, -āre	saepe	
unda, -ae	pigra	*spectō, -āre	semper	
aestāte		volō, -āre	subitō	
hieme		moneō, -ēre	ubi	

I Keeping in mind the stories of this unit, combine each numbered expression with one or more lettered phrases to make complete sentences. Add **et** or **sed,** if necessary.

1 Formīca impigra   a) aquam ōrat   f) lacūnam mōnstrat
2 Cicāda pigra   b) aestāte cantat   g) hieme cibum habet
3 Pīrātae   c) casās vāstant   h) incolās necant
4 Diāna parva   d) subitō clāmat   i) aestāte labōrat
5 Dea īrāta   e) cibum ōrat   j) "Eritis rānae."

II Translate each numbered verb form and select its infinitive from the lettered list.

1 timeō   7 dant   a) ambulāre   g) ōrāre
2 spectātis   8 portatne   b) clāmāre   h) portāre
3 ambulō   9 habētis   c) dare   i) spectāre
4 habitat   10 labōrat   d) habēre   j) timēre
5 volant   11 clāmāmus   e) habitāre   k) vidēre
6 ōrās   12 vidēmus   f) labōrāre   l) volāre

61

III Translate the underlined English words by selecting appropriate Latin words from the lettered list and supplying proper endings.

1 The moon magna et clāra est.
2 Jānuae of the school altae sunt.
3 Āra the cottage propinqua est.
4 Pīrāta a jewel cēlat.
5 Cūr monētis agricolās dē the beast?
6 Nostrae daughters in silvā ambulant.
7 In vīllā longinquā the sailors' amita habitat.
8 The farmers fābulam nārrō.
9 Timēsne the waves?
10 E the windows spectāmus.

a) lūna
b) schola
c) arca
d) lacūna
e) gemma
f) casa
g) bēstia
h) jānua
i) fīlia
j) nauta
k) agricola
l) unda
m) fenestra
n) stella

USE YOUR EYES When you have applied the correct endings to the appropriate nouns in III, what do you observe about the order in which the forms occur?

IV Choose suitable nouns as objects of each preposition. If a preposition occurs with either of two cases, give all possible phrases. Translate each completed phrase. Which forms cannot be objects of prepositions?

1 ā
2 ab
3 ad
4 circum
5 cum
6 dē
7 in
8 per
9 prope
10 sub

a) amitīs
b) casā
c) stellā
d) īnsulā
e) scholam
f) undās
g) nautārum
h) terra

V Add each word in lettered list to one of the numbered groups, making sure it is like other words in the group. Explain your decision.

1 mox, saepe, procul, posteā
2 dūcit, vocātis, habent, monēs
3 cum, in, prope, circum
4 tua, alba, prīma, quiēta
5 ōra, cōpia, lingua, fīlia
6 sed, et, itaque, cum

a) ab
b) antīquitus
c) valeō
d) inter
e) quod
f) ita
g) fāma
h) multae
i) clāmāre
j) propinqua
k) āra
l) monētis
m) per
n) semper

UNIT III

Urania, the Muse of astronomy, sits beside a globe of the heavens. Mythological figures representing the constellations appear on the celestial globe. This painting by Eustache Leseuer (1616-1655) is in the Louvre.

Dropping the final **-ō** of a Latin verb will often reveal an English verb.

errō	**expectō**	**laudō**	**moveō**	**prōvideō**	**vexō**
err	expect	laud	move	provide	vex

Some English verbs replace the final **-ō** with -e.

adōrō	**accūsō**	**dēclārō**	**excitō**	**invītō**	**salūtō**
adore	accuse	declare	excite	invite	salute

You may find other English verbs by substituting -ate for the final **-ō** of the Latin verb.

agitō	**alternō**	**dōnō**	**nāvigō**	**penetrō**
agitate	alternate	donate	navigate	penetrate

When a repeated consonant precedes final **-ō** in a Latin verb, you may find the corresponding English verb by dropping not only the **-ō** but also one of the consonants.

admittō	**excellō**	**expellō**	**occurrō**	**permittō**
admit	excel	expel	occur	permit

What English verbs come from these Latin verbs?

cōnsūmō	**comparō**	**contendō**	**dēscrībō**	**labōrō**
commūnicō	**compellō**	**creō**	**explōrō**	**nārrō**

VIII

THE MOON AND THE STARS

Duae° puellae, Anna et Tullia, prope fenestram stant. Clāra, amita Annae, in camerā° sedet.

Tullia. Nōn videō lūnam. Nūbēs° lūnam cēlant.

Clāra. Noctū in Ītaliā lūna et stellae sunt pulchrae. Sed interdum sunt nūbēs in caelō.° 5

°**du'ae***	(nom.) F., two	•	**in ca'me rā**	in (the) room, bedroom
nū'bēs	(nom., acc. pl.) F., clouds	•	**in cae'lō**	in the sky

64

Anna. Mox lūna erit clāra.

Tullia. Spectāte! Nūllae nūbēs sunt in caelō!

Anna. Vidēte! Nunc lūna et stellae sunt clārae.

Tullia. Lūnam clāram et stellās amō clārās! Nārrā nōbīs,°
Clāra, dē lūnā. 10

Clāra. Lūna in caelō est dea pulchra. Dea lūnae est Diāna. Diāna sagittās habet; radiī° lūnae sunt sagittae Diānae. Sagittae Diānae sunt clārae.

Tullia. Cūr interdiū lūnam nōn vidēmus?

Clāra. Noctū Diāna in caelō habitat, sed interdiū in terrā 15 ambulat. Diāna, dea lūnae, silvārum quoque est dea. Diāna silvās obscūrās et bēstiās silvārum amat.

Anna. Nārrā nōbīs dē stellīs. Ambulantne stellae quoque in terrā, amita?

Clāra. Minimē. Stellae semper manent in caelō. 20

Tullia. Diāna sagittās habet. Habentne stellae sagittās?

Clāra. Minimē. Stellae nōn sunt deae; sunt gemmae Diānae.

Anna et Tullia (ad fenestram). Tuae gemmae sunt clārae, dea lūnae! Spectāte nōs,° stellae clārae! Spectā nōs, Diāna pulchra! 25

°ra′di ī (nom. pl.) rays • nō′bīs (dat. pl.) us, to us • nōs (acc. pl.) us

Nouns	
pu el′la, -ae	F., girl
sa git′ta, -ae	F., arrow
Adjective	
*nūl′la	no, none
Verbs	
stō, -āre	stand, stand still
ma′ne ō, -ēre	stay, remain
se′de ō, -ēre	sit
Adverbs	
in ter′di ū	by day, in the daytime
*noc′tū	by night, at night
Preposition	
+ad	at, near

+Latin words which have occurred in earlier vocabularies and appear again with a new meaning or function bear the symbol (+).

This painting of Diana and her maidens in medieval dress by Dutch artist Jan Vermeer de Delft (about 1653) hangs in the Mauritshuis at The Hague.

T H E   I N D I C A T I V E   A verb which states a fact or asks a question is in the indicative.

> **Spectō stellās.** I am watching the stars.
> **Cūr stellās spectās?** Why are you watching the stars?

T H E   I M P E R A T I V E   A verb which expresses a command is in the imperative.

> **Nārrā nōbīs dē lūnā.** Tell us about the moon.
> **Spectāte nōs!** Look at us!
> **Monē puellās!** Warn the girls!
> **Vidēte stellās!** See the stars!

The singular imperative of most Latin verbs is like the present stem. The plural is made up of the present stem and **-te.**

	I	II
Infinitive:	**nārrāre**	**monēre**
Present Stem:	**nārrā-**	**monē-**
Singular Imperative:	**nārrā**	**monē**
Plural Imperative:	**nārrāte**	**monēte**

THE VOCATIVE CASE of a noun is used in Latin in addressing a person or persons. In most Latin nouns the vocative has the same form as the nominative.

> **Noctū, Anna, stellās vidēmus.** At night, Anna, we see stars.
> **Spectāte, puellae, stellās in caelō!** Girls, watch the stars in the sky!
> **Cūr lūnam spectās, Anna?** Why are you looking at the moon, Anna?

In Latin the vocative is usually not the first word in a sentence.

SCRAMBLED SENTENCES Rearrange the words to make sentences, and translate.

1 **spectāte.in puellae stellās caelō; et lūnam vidētisne stellās?**
2 **habet Diāna quod dea sagittās lūnae est.**

I Complete each statement by choosing the correct word or items from the list.

1 — is verb stem and singular imperative.
2 —, —, and — are infinitives.
3 — is plural imperative.
4 — and — are person endings.
5 — is a past tense.

a) amāte
b) cēlābam
c) dare
d) eris
e) est
f) habēre
g) manē
h) ō
i) servābunt
j) tis
k) volāre

II From each group of verbs select the singular and plural imperatives.

1 videō, vidēte, vidēre, vidē, videt
2 monent, monēs, monē, moneō, monēte
3 habitā, habitāre, habitās, habitāte, habitat
4 nārrāre, nārrant, nārrāte, nārrā, nārrō
5 habēmus, habet, habē, habēte, habēs

III Use a verb from the list to complete each sentence.

1 ___ , Anna, puellīs fābulam.
2 Cūr puella in silvā ___ ?
3 Pīrātae gemmās in arcā ___ .
4 Noctū agricolae clārās stellās ___ .
5 Diāna, ___ nōs!

a) ambulat   f) nārrā
b) cēlābant   g) nārrat
c) erunt   h) servā
d) habitāmus   i) servāte
e) monēre   j) vident

LATIN LIVES TODAY   What is wrong here? Explain.

1 A permanent wave that does not last
2 A sedentary job for which a man must stand up to do his work
3 A stationary platform that is moved from place to place
4 A nocturnal animal that is active in the daytime

IX

ANNA AND THE BEAR

Anna est fīlia Galbae. Galba est agricola; prope magnam silvam habitat. In silvā dēnsā sunt multae ursae. Galba fīliam dē ursīs saepe monet.

"Silva est perīculōsa, quod ursae sunt in silvā," dīcit. "Ambulā semper in sēmitā lātā."   5

Ōlim autem Anna sōla in magnā et obscūrā silvā ambulat. Caelum,° nōn sēmitam, spectat. Mox ā viā errat. Subitō magnam ursam videt. Ursa stat; Annam expectat. Ursa Annam spectat; Anna ursam spectat.

Anna territa clāmāre temptat, sed nōn clāmat. Viam nōn 10 videt, sed celeriter ambulat per dēnsam silvam. Ursa quoque celeriter ambulat. Anna lentē ambulat; ursa quoque lentē ambulat. Dēnique ursa prope sēmitam stat et pede° Annae viam mōnstrat.

Nunc laeta Anna casam videt; pater° et māter° prō casā 15 stant. Anna dē ursā nārrat.

Galba dīcit, "Ursa benigna est Callistō. Ōlim Callistō erat

°**cae′lum** (acc. sing.) sky • **pe′de** (abl. sing.) with (her) paw
pa′ter (nom. sing.) father • **mā′ter** (nom. sing.) mother

fēmina pulchra; nunc est ursa pulchra. Saepe agricolae ursam necāre temptant, sed ursam nōn necant."

Nouns	
*fē'mi na, -ae	F., woman
sē'mi ta, -ae	F., path
ur'sa, -ae	F., bear
Adjectives	
*dēn'sa	thick, dense
*sō'la	alone, only
*ter'ri ta	frightened
Verbs	
di'cit	says
*er'rō, -āre	wander, stray, err
*ex pec'tō, -āre	wait for
[1]*temp'tō, -āre	try, attempt
Adverbs	
au'tem	however, but
ce le'ri ter	quickly, fast
dē'ni que	finally, at last
len'tē	slowly
Preposition	
prō	(with abl.) in front of, before

A CLAUSE regularly contains a subject and a predicate. Clauses are of two kinds, independent and dependent.

An independent clause expresses a complete thought and can stand alone as a sentence.

Silva est perīculōsa. The forest is dangerous.

A dependent clause is related to the main (independent) clause and functions only as part of a sentence.

Silva est perīculōsa, quod ursae sunt in silvā. The forest is dangerous because there are bears in the forest.

The dependent clause **quod ursae sunt in silvā** serves as an adverb, adding the idea of cause.

---

[1]An exception to the rule that calls for division of syllables after the first consonant when three or more consonants occur between two vowels.

69

Roman children may have encountered bears while walking or playing in wooded areas like the one in the Sabine Hills near Rome pictured here.

A CONJUNCTION joins words, phrases, or clauses.

> **Galba et filia prope silvam habitant.** Galba and his daughter live near a forest.

The conjunction **et** connects the words **Galba** and **filia**.

> **Rānae in aquā et in terrā habitant.** Frogs live in water and on land.

Here **et** connects the phrases **in aquā** and **in terrā**.

> **Incolae Aetnam timent, sed Siciliam amant quod est terra pulchra.** The inhabitants are afraid of Etna, but they love Sicily because it is a beautiful land.

The conjunctions **sed** and **quod** join the three clauses of the sentence.

I Choose the most suitable clause or phrase to complete each sentence. Translate the completed sentences.

1 Incolae gemmās cēlābant quod
- ōram maritimam amābant.
- pīrātās in ōrā maritimā vidēbant.
- puellae bēstiās timēbant.

2 Līberī in viā ambulant
- quod flammae clārae sunt.
- quod casae magnae sunt.
- sed in silvā nōn ambulant.

3 Rōma magnam cōpiam aquae habet quod
- lacūna propinqua est.
- multās Aquās habet.
- lacūna pulchra est.

4 Antīquitus nautae in īnsulā habitābant, ubi nōn jam
- bēstiās timent.
- aqua quiēta est.
- incolae habitant.

5 Anna labōrāre nōn amat quod
- in vīllā habitat.
- pigra est.
- laeta est.

SCRAMBLED SENTENCES Unscramble the words to make sentences, and translate. Watch word endings.

1 amitae mōnstrābant līberī villae pictūram.
2 agricola puellās dē ursā monēbat.
3 habitant in rānae tepidā saepe aquā.
4 pecūnia cāra est nautae.
5 sed formīca cicāda est pigra cūr impigra?

WORD MASTERY 4

A Latin verb occasionally undergoes changes more extensive than those made in the ending before it reaches its actual form in modern English. These changes may involve internal variations of spelling, the addition of a prefix, or both.

ambulō	cantō	cēlō	habitō	maneō
amble	chant	conceal	inhabit	remain

What Latin verbs are suggested by these English verbs?

demonstrate	exclaim	export	invoke	produce
devastate	expect	inspect	nominate	salute

MOTTO: **Labōrāre est ōrāre.** To work is to pray. (Benedictine Monks)

The most familiar constellations in the sky are Ursa Major (the Greater Bear) and Ursa Minor (the Lesser Bear), more commonly called "the big dipper" and "the little dipper." Bears were associated with certain deities not only by the Greeks and Romans but also by other peoples both earlier and later. This bronze statuette shows a Gallic goddess with a bear, indicating that the animal was sacred to her.

X

THE GREAT BEAR

Galba fīliae fābulam nārrat; Annae dē Magnā Ursā nārrat.

Callistō, fēmina pulchra et superba, ōlim in terrā Arcadiā habitābat. Interdum in silvīs cum amīcīs fēminīs Arcadiae ambulābat.

Jūnō est dea pulchra. Jūnō in caelō habitat, sed saepe in 5 terrā ambulat. Jūnō est invidiōsa et pulchrās nōn amat fēminās.

Hodiē Callistō et duae fēminae in silvā Arcadiae ambulant. Callistō superba dīcit, "Pulchra sum, et incolae Arcadiae mē laudant. Jūnō quoque est pulchra, sed incolae deam nōn 10 laudant, quod Jūnō est invidiōsa."

Jūnō, quae° ex caelō° fēminās spectat, dīcit, "Nunc,

°**quae** F., who • **ex cae′lō** from the sky

Callistō, es fēmina pulchra, sed nōn semper eris pulchra. 15
Nōn semper eris fēmina; eris ursa."

Itaque in silvīs incolae magnam ursam interdum vident.
Ursa est Callistō. Saepe agricolae ursam necāre temptant.

Juppiter autem, rēx° deōrum,° ursam servāre dēsīderat.
Itaque in caelō stellam novam pōnit. Callistō est stella clāra 20
et nova in caelō. Incolae multārum terrārum clāram spectant
stellam; inter stellās Magnam Ursam vident. Ursa Magna est
Callistō.

Anna autem dīcit, "Callistō nōn est in caelō. Callistō est
ursa; ursa in terrā est. Hodiē Callistō mihi° viam mōnstrāvit." 25

Māter dīcit, "Ita, Anna, Callistō est ursa, sed in terrā nōn
jam habitat. Interdum Callistō in silvīs interdiū ambulat, sed
noctū Callistō est stella. Noctū Magnam Ursam in caelō
vidēmus."

°**rēx de ō'rum** king of the gods • **mi'hi** (dat.) to me, me

Adjectives	
in vi di ō'sa	jealous, envious
su per'ba	proud, haughty
Verbs	
pō'nit	places, puts
dē si'de rō, -āre	desire, want
*****lau'dō, -āre**	praise, speak well of
ser'vō, -āre	save, keep
Adverb	
ho'di ē	today
Preposition	
[1]**ē, ex**	(with abl.) from, out of

SCRAMBLED SENTENCES Unscramble the words to
make sentences, and translate. Watch word endings. They
make the meaning clear, regardless of word order.

1 **habet pulchra arēnōsam insula ōram.**
2 **est multās habet nōn īrāta quod dea ārās.**
3 **Latīna prōvinciae erat prīmō lingua.**
4 **terram timēbat fēmina mīram.**

---

[1]Before a vowel or **h**, **ex** is used; **ē** and **ex** both appear before consonants.

REVIEW OF ADVERBS, CONJUNCTIONS, PREPOSITIONS

Which of these words are adverbs? Which are conjunctions? Which are prepositions? Which word is sometimes a conjunction and sometimes a preposition?

ā, ab	ē, ex	minimē	procul
ad	hodiē	mox	prope
antīquitus	in	noctū	quod
autem	inter	nōn	quoque
celeriter	interdiū	nunc	saepe
circum	interdum	ōlim	sed
cum	ita	per	semper
cūr	itaque	posteā	sub
dē	iterum	prīmō	subitō
dēnique	lentē	prō	ubi

1 Combine a preposition with each of these nouns to form sensible phrases; translate.

casā silvīs terrā casam silvam agricolīs lūnā casās

2 Combine an adverb with each of these verb forms to show time or frequency of action; translate.

ambulant vidēmus nārrat portās eritis erant

3 Which conjunction introduces a reason or cause?
4 Which adverbs may introduce questions?
5 Which adverbs may answer questions by "Yes" and "No"?

I Choose from the list a word or phrase to translate each underlined English word or phrase. Translate the completed sentences.

1 <u>At night</u> autem in silvā ambulāre nōn amō.
2 <u>In ancient times</u> deae <u>often</u> in terrā habitābant.
3 <u>Afterwards</u> Callistō erat ursa.
4 <u>No longer</u> beātae estis.
5 <u>And so</u> fēminam nōn laudat.
6 Casa <u>near</u> ōram maritimam est.
7 Puellae <u>also</u> flammās vidēbant.

a) antīquitus h) nōn jam
b) autem i) nunc
c) et . . . et j) posteā
d) itaque k) prope
e) iterum l) quoque
f) jam m) saepe
g) noctū n) subitō

"Motion picture" of Andromeda's rescue painted by Italian Piero di Cosimo

XI

CASSIOPEIA AND ANDROMEDA

Cassiopēa, rēgīna terrae antīquae, erat superba quod erat pulchra. Andromeda autem, fīlia rēgīnae pulchra, nōn erat superba.

Ōlim rēgīna et fīlia in ōrā maritimā stābant. Rēgīna aquam quiētam spectābat.

"In aquā, fīlia mea, nymphae pulchrae habitant," dīcit mater, "sed nymphae sunt invidiōsae quod tam pulchra sum."

"Spectā!" Andromeda clāmat. "Vidē! Nunc aqua nōn est quiēta."

Subitō vident Neptūnum, rēgem° aquārum. "Fēmina superba nymphīs meīs nōn grāta est," dīcit Neptūnus. "Nymphae sunt īrātae, et nymphae meae sunt mihi cārae. Sacrificium° postulō; fīliam tuam Andromedam postulō. Mox multa¹ aqua erit in terrā tuā, et in aquā mōnstrum° erit.

°**rē′gem** (acc. sing.) king • **sa cri fi′ci um*** (acc. sing.) sacrifice • **mōn′strum*** (nom., acc. sing.) monster

¹In the singular this adjective means "much."

75

Incolae terrae tuam fīliam servāre nōn poterunt. Tū es 15
rēgīna, sed fīliam tuam servāre nōn poteris."

Cassiopēa autem dīcit, "Ego° meam fīliam servāre possum.
Nymphīs tuīs meās dabō° gemmās."

Neptūnus rēgīnae superbae dīcit, "Nymphīs meīs gemmae
tuae nōn sunt grātae." 20

Incolae Andromedam ad ōram maritimam dūcunt, ubi
mōnstrum puellam necāre poterit. Sed Perseus ex caelō
mōnstrum et puellam miseram videt. Celeriter dē caelō volat
et statim mōnstrum necat.

Andromeda erat lībera. Cassiopēa erat laeta, quod fīlia 25
lībera erat. Posteā rēgīna et fīlia et līberātor° erant stellae.
Noctū in caelō Cassiopēam et Andromedam et Perseum
vidēre possumus.

°**e′go** (nom. sing.) I • **da′bō** I shall give • **li be rā′tor***
(nom. sing.) rescuer, liberator

Nouns	
*nym′pha, -ae	F., nymph
*rē gi′na, -ae	F., queen
Adjectives	
grā′ta	pleasing
*li′be ra	free
Verbs	
pos′sum, pos′se	be able, can
pos′tu lō, -āre	demand
Adverbs	
sta′tim	at once, immediately
tam	so, to such a degree
Preposition	
⁺dē	(with abl.) down from

T H E   V E R B **possum** is a combination of **pot-** (base of **potis**, able)
and the verb **sum**. For ease of pronunciation, **pos-** is used
instead of **pot-** in combining with the **s** sound, as in **possunt**. Similarity of forms of **sum** and **possum** can easily be seen
from the parallel arrangement of their conjugations on page 77.

⁺Latin words which have occurred in earlier vocabularies and appear again with a new
meaning or function bear the symbol (⁺).

Singular			Plural		
Present			Present		
1 **pos′sum**	**sum**		**pos′sumus**	**su′mus**	
2 **po′tes**	**es**		**potes′tis**	**es′tis**	
3 **po′test**	**est**		**pos′sunt**	**sunt**	
Past			Past		
1 **po′teram**	**e′ram**		**poterā′mus**	**erā′mus**	
2 **po′terās**	**e′rās**		**poterā′tis**	**erā′tis**	
3 **po′terat**	**e′rat**		**po′terant**	**e′rant**	
Future			Future		
1 **po′terō**	**e′rō**		**pote′rimus**	**e′rimus**	
2 **po′teris**	**e′ris**		**pote′ritis**	**e′ritis**	
3 **po′terit**	**e′rit**		**po′terunt**	**e′runt**	

The infinitive of **possum** is **posse**; the infinitive of **sum** is **esse**.

TO TRANSLATE THE FORMS OF possum, the word "able" may be added to the translation of the corresponding forms of **sum**.

possum I am able   **poteram** I was able   **poterō** I shall (I'll) be able

Often "can" and "could" are used in translating forms of **possum**. In English "can" refers to the future as well as to the present, while "could" is used for the past tense.

possum I can   **poteram** I could   **poterō** I can

A COMPLEMENTARY INFINITIVE is required to complete the meaning of the verb **possum**, just as it is in English with "I am able," "you are able," etc. With "can" and "could" a complementary infinitive is also required, but the word "to" is not used with the infinitive after these verbs.

Perseus Andromedam servāre potest. Perseus is able to save Andromeda, or Perseus can save Andromeda.

Perseus Andromedam servāre poterat. Perseus was able to save Andromeda, or Perseus could save Andromeda.

Perseus Andromedam servāre poterit. Perseus will be able to save Andromeda, or Perseus can save Andromeda.

I Translate those parts of the sentences which are underlined. What is the person, number, and tense of each verb?

1 <u>You will be</u> happy in school.   (Sing.)
2 <u>Will you be able to see</u> Aetna at night?   (Pl.)
3 Sometimes Anna <u>is able to remain</u> at the villa.
4 Why <u>can't they walk</u> to the seashore?
5 We <u>couldn't live</u> in the cottage, but <u>we can</u> always <u>stay</u> at the villa.
6 I <u>can walk</u> through the forest.
7 Soon <u>we shall be</u> happy.
8 The sailors <u>were able to work</u>.

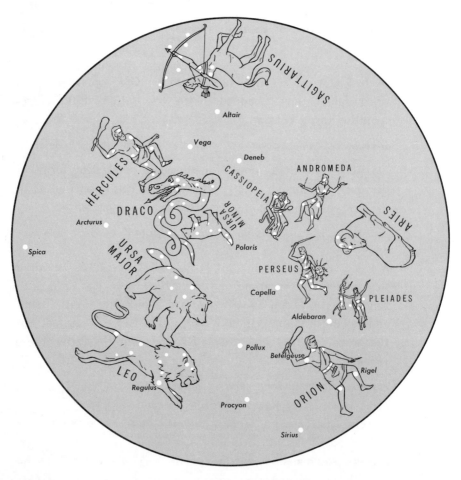

The Romans imagined they saw a host of mythological figures in the constellations. These figures were the subjects of many myths and stories told by the Romans.

REVIEW OF UNIT III

LESSONS VIII—XI

Nouns	Adjectives	Verbs	Adverbs
*fēmina, -ae	*dēnsa	dēsīderō, -āre	autem
*nympha, -ae	grāta	*errō, -āre	celeriter
puella, -ae	invidiōsa	*expectō, -āre	dēnique
*rēgina, -ae	*libera	*laudō, -āre	hodiē
sagitta, -ae	nūlla	postulō, -āre	interdiū
sēmita, -ae	*sōla	stō, -āre	lentē
ursa, -ae	superba	servō, -āre	*noctū
	*territa	*temptō, -āre	statim
		maneō, -ēre	tam
		sedeō, -ēre	
		dīcit	Prepositions
		pōnit	ē, ex
		possum, posse	prō

I With the underlined words or phrases as clues, select the character described by each sentence.

1 <u>Lūna</u> est dea pulchra.   Andromeda
2 Ōlim <u>ursa benigna</u> fēmina pulchra erat.   Callistō
3 <u>Dea invidiōsa</u> fēminās pulchrās nōn amat.   Cassiopēa
4 <u>Rēgina</u> erat superba quod pulchra erat.   Diāna
5 <u>Fīlia rēginae pulchra</u>, nōn superba erat.   Jūnō
6 <u>Rēx aquārum</u> sacrificium postulat.   Juppiter
    Neptūnus

II Choose six verbs in the present tense and arrange in sequence of 1st, 2nd, 3rd person, singular and plural. Repeat for past (imperfect), and future tenses. Explain all other forms and translate.

1 poteris	9 errās	17 dare
2 erāmus	10 eritis	18 erit
3 esse	11 servābant	19 possumus
4 dō	12 stāte	20 habitant
5 timēbat	13 posse	21 potest
6 erās	14 poterimus	22 postulā
7 manēte	15 poteram	23 poterātis
8 erō	16 estis	24 erunt

III Translate, then point out examples of grammatical points listed below.

1 In silvīs noctū nōn errāmus, quod ursās timēmus.
2 Cūr fīliās agricolae semper laudābās?
3 Puellae, Anna et Clāra, stellās spectant.
4 Clāra dīcit, "Spectā, Anna, sagittās Diānae."
5 Mox lūnam vidēre poteris.
6 Rēgīna clāmat, "Servāte, fīliae, nymphās territās."

a) adverb of time
b) apposition
c) complementary infinitive
d) conjunction
e) dependent clause
f) future tense

g) imperative
h) interrogative adverb
i) past tense
j) prepositional phrase
k) present tense
l) vocative

IV Select from the list on the right Latin words to replace the underlined English expressions; then translate the completed sentences.

1 Pīrātae per viās at night ambulābant.
2 Fēminae prope lacūnam now sedent.
3 Vīllam amitae nostrae vidēre soon poteritis.
4 In ancient times ārae multae in īnsulā erant.
5 Incolae nautās afterwards timēbant.
6 Nōnne rēgīnam amīcam today expectātis?
7 Stellās in the daytime vidēre nōn possumus.
8 Agricolae bēstiās sometimes necābant.
9 Errāsne, parva puella, often ā scholā ad ōram?
10 At last rēgīnae grātae eritis.

antīquitus
dēnique
hodiē
interdiū
interdum
mox
noctū
nunc
posteā
saepe

LATIN LIVES TODAY Use each of these words in a sentence. All of them are related to **sōla,** an adjective introduced in this unit.

sole	soliloquy	solitary	solo
solely	solitaire	solitude	soloist

Select one or more of the following Latin adjectives and (using a dictionary) find as many English words as possible that are related to the Latin word/words.

dēnsa **grāta** **lībera** **nūlla**

UNIT IV

The Greeks located the home of the gods on the summit of Mount Olympus, where Jupiter and Juno ruled over the other gods.

This bronze statuette of Jupiter is only about three inches high, but it conveys a feeling of the majesty attributed by the Romans to the deity they worshiped as king of the gods.

XII

GODS AND GODDESSES OF ROME

Prīmō Rōmānī deōs deāsque agrōrum et silvārum et aquārum adōrābant. Dī et deae Rōmānōrum ārās prope vīcōs et in silvīs habēbant. Ārās quoque in viīs vīcōrum et in ōrā maritimā habēbant.

Posteā multōs deōs Rōmānī adōrābant. Juppiter, rēx° deōrum, erat amīcus incolārum terrae. Juppiter Rōmānōs saepe juvābat. Habitābat in rēgiā pulchrā; ā rēgiā incolās terrae spectāre amābat.

°rēx* (nom. sing.) king

Jūnō erat rēgīna deōrum. Rēgīna erat superba, sed erat fēminīs terrae cāra. In magnīs oppidīs° et parvīs vīcīs Jūnō 10 ārās habēbat, sed in silvīs ārās nōn habēbat.

Deus bellī° erat Mārs; hastam et gladium portābat. Mārs agricultūrae quoque deus erat. Multās ārās in oppidīs et in agrīs Ītaliae habēbat.

Minerva, dea bellī, sapientiae quoque dea erat. Ārae 15 Minervae erant in oppidīs, nōn in silvīs.

Diāna erat dea benigna; Rōmānīs cāra erat. Diāna silvās et bēstiās silvārum amābat. Ārae Diānae erant in silvīs.

Rōmānī deum Neptūnum, rēgem° fluviōrum, adōrābant. Neptūnus multās ārās in ōrā maritimā habēbat. Rōmānī in 20 Ōceanō nōn saepe nāvigābant, quod tempestātēs° timēbant.

Vesta erat Rōmānīs cāra; multās ārās in parvīs casīs et in magnīs vīllīs habēbat. In ārīs Vestae flammae semper ārdē-bant.° Vesta erat dea focī.

°**op'pi dīs**   (abl. pl.) towns   •   **bel'lī**   (gen. sing.) of war
rē'gem   (acc. sing.) king   •   **tem pes tā'tēs***   (nom., acc. pl.)
storms, tempests   •   **ār dē'bant**   used to burn

	Nouns	
has'ta, -ae	F., spear
***rē'gi a, -ae**	F., palace, royal residence
sa pi en'ti a, -ae	F., wisdom
a'ger, a'grī	M., field
***a mi'cus, -ī**	M., friend
de'us, -ī	M., god; nom. pl., **dī** or **deī**
flu'vi us, -ī	M., stream, river
fo'cus, -ī	M., hearth, fireplace
gla'di us, -ī	M., sword
vi'cus, -ī	M., village
	Verb	
ju'vō, -āre	help, aid
	Conjunction	
-que	(attached to word) and

SECOND-DECLENSION NOUNS all have geni-tive singular ending in **-ī**, but in the nominative some end in **-us**, others in **-um,** and a few in **-er**.

SECOND-DECLENSION NOUNS IN -us are declined like **amīcus**, friend.

DECLENSION OF amīcus

Singular

Case	
Nom.	ami'cus
Gen.	ami'cī
Dat.	ami'cō
Acc.	ami'cum
Abl.	ami'cō

Plural

Case	
Nom.	ami'cī
Gen.	amicō'rum
Dat.	ami'cīs
Acc.	ami'cōs
Abl.	ami'cīs

CASE USES OF amīcus

Singular

Amicus casam habet.

Casa **amici** est parva.

Amicō casam dant.

Nauta **amicum** habet.

Cum **amicō** ambulō.

Plural

Amici casam habent.

Casa **amicōrum** est parva.

Amicis casam dant.

Nauta **amicōs** habet.

Cum **amicis** ambulō.

SECOND-DECLENSION NOUNS IN -er AND -r are like **amīcus** except in the nominative singular.

Case								
Nom.	**magister**	teacher	**liber**	book	**ager**	field	**vir**	man
Gen.	**magistrī**		**librī**		**agrī**		**virī**	

Most -er nouns drop the -e- of the nominative singular in other cases. A few -er nouns keep the -e- in all cases: **puer, puerī,** boy; **vesper, vesperī,** evening.

This difference in spelling also appears in corresponding English derivatives: magistrate, library, agriculture; puerile, vespers.

THE VOCATIVE CASE of Latin nouns is usually the same as the nominative. Most Declension II nouns in -us, however, end in -e in vocative singular. In the plural, the vocative is always the same as the nominative.

Case	Singular	Plural	Singular	Plural	Singular	Singular
Nom.	amīcus	amīcī	puer	puerī	Anna	Mārcus
Voc.	amīce	amīcī	puer	puerī	Anna	Mārce

Deus has no special vocative form; in the plural, both **dī** and **deī** are used for vocative as well as for nominative.

I Translate these phrases into Latin.

1 From the shore
2 To the forest
3 With a friend
4 Concerning the village

5 In the stream
6 In front of the fireplace
7 Near the altars
8 Through the fields

II Each group contains a word which does not belong with the others. Find it and identify the group to which it belongs.

1 amīcus, vīcum, nautae, cum, deus
2 possum, nūllum, sōlī, dēnsus, pigrum
3 semper, statim, dēnique, inter, iterum
4 circum, tam, sub, ad, prope
5 et, sed, agrō,- que, quod
6 dō, altō, habeō, amō, nārrō

III Change singular nouns to plural and plural nouns to singular wherever possible, and make other changes as needed.

1 Dea laetam nympham laudābat.
2 Nauta fābulās dē Neptūnō nārrābat.
3 Cum incolīs vīcī manēre poteram.
4 Territae puellae clāmāre nōn poterant.

SCRAMBLED SENTENCES Unscramble the words to make sentences, and translate. Watch word endings. They make the meaning of a Latin sentence clear, regardless of word order.

1 **terrās Perseus per errābat multās.**
2 **laudat filiam Jūnō rēgīnae.**

LATIN LIVES TODAY Complete each sentence with a word related in meaning to the word underlined and to a Latin word in the lesson vocabulary.

1 A gladiator fought with a —.
2 A focal point in a home is often the —.
3 The fluent speech flowed on like a —.
4 A — encourages amicable relations.
5 Agrarian laws pertain to —.
6 A deified emperor was thought of as a —.
7 Due to violent — our voyage was tempestuous.

85

RELIGION OF THE ROMANS

Few aspects of Roman life changed as greatly with time as religious beliefs and observances. The earliest Romans believed in and offered sacrifices to spirits or powers everywhere in nature, although they did not ascribe human form to them.

As Rome grew and contact with other peoples increased, the Romans began to adopt other beliefs—especially of the Greeks—in gods who were much like men, but larger, more powerful, and immortal. Some ancient gods, particularly the lares and penates and Vesta, were worshiped at household shrines. Priests and priestesses led worship of many other gods—and Vesta, too, in temples as a State religion.

Janus was one of the gods peculiar to Roman religion. He was the patron of doors and beginnings, and was associated with war and peace. Jupiter, whose Greek counterpart was Zeus, was regarded as king and father of the gods. His wife was Juno (Greek Hera), queen of the gods. The Romans also worshiped Minerva (Athena) and Neptune (Poseidon), Diana and Apollo, Venus and Mars, Ceres and Proserpina, and many others. There were also lesser gods and demigods, such as Hercules, Aesculapius, and the twin gods Castor and Pollux.

Foreign gods, such as Mithras and Magna Mater (Cybele) from the East and Isis from Egypt, exercised a strong influence on Roman religion. Secret oriental cults called "mysteries" had many adherents. Rome also sheltered numerous Jews who retained their own religion; and finally Christianity, which began its advance during the Empire, supplanted the worship of pagan gods.

Above: Temple at Agrigentum in Sicily, though built by a colony of Greeks, is similar to many Roman temples.

Top left: A lar—a Roman household deity—with a priest beside him. Covering the head with a fold of the toga while offering a sacrifice was a reverent gesture.

Below: Statue of Mars and head of Juno, called the Ludovisi Mars and Juno from the name of an Italian family which once owned them.

86

Above: Relief showing Minerva, Jupiter, and Juno, with Hercules, Bacchus, Ceres, and Mercury behind them. The head of Apollo is the famous Apollo Belvedere. Right: Statuette representing the Roman goddess Fortuna, with cornucopia in hand, who is identified with the Egyptian Isis and here wears her typical headdress.

Above: Behind the ruins of the temple of Julius Caesar in the Forum stands the temple of Antoninus and Faustina.

Above: Family shrine where the household gods (lares and penates) were worshiped in the House of the Menander in Pompeii. Incense was burned and a little wine poured out daily at the altar. On special occasions a pig might be sacrificed there, too.

Left: Temple at Paestum, once believed to be sacred to Ceres, now called the Athena (Minerva) temple.

This fresco of Diana, who was goddess of the hunt as well as goddess of the moon, shows her in the rôle of huntress. This wall painting ornamented a house in Stabiae, near Pompeii.

XIII

DIANA, GODDESS OF THE MOON

Ōlim in Ītaliā prope dēnsam silvam habitābat agricola. In silvā erat templum Diānae antīquum. Agricola deōs agrōrum et silvārum adōrābat. Deam Diānam quoque amābat, quod Diāna erat dea silvārum.

Nauta, amīcus agricolae, hieme in vīcō propinquō habitābat. Aestāte nauta procul ab Ītaliā nāvigābat et multās terrās spectābat. Nauta Neptūnum adōrābat, quod Neptūnus erat deus maritimus. Templa Neptūnī erant ōrae maritimae propinqua.

Agricola fābulās Diānae amīcō nārrābat, sed nauta semper 10
dīcēbat, "In templō antīquō, amīce, dea nōn habitat. Sunt
nūllae flammae in ārā; sunt nūlla dōna prō ārā."

Nunc, ut fābula est, nauta noctū in silvā obscūrā ambulat.
Lūnam in caelō vidēre nōn potest. Subitō autem prope templum Diānae flammās videt clārās. Per jānuam apertam 15
nauta deam pulchram vidēre potest. Dea cum multīs puellīs
prope āram stat.

Nauta audit verba deae. "Habeō multa templa in multīs
terrīs," Diāna puellīs dīcit, "sed in hāc° terrā incolae ārās
nōn servant meās; mihi dōna nōn dant. In terrā ubi incolae 20
āram deae nōn servant manēre nōn possum. Date mihi
lucernās, puellae; eritis stellae in caelō. Ego lūna in caelō
erō."

Puellae lucernās deae dant. Subitō templum est obscūrum;
nūllae flammae sunt in ārā. Sed lūna est clāra; stellae sunt 25
clārae. Celeriter ex silvā nauta properat.

Posteā nauta lūnam et stellās in caelō saepe spectābat. In
templō Diānae autem āra erat semper obscūra. Iterum
atque iterum nauta amīcīs dē templō antīquō et dē deā
puellīsque nārrābat. 30

"Dea cum multīs puellīs erat in templō," dīcēbat. "Nunc
Diāna est lūna; puellae sunt stellae in caelō. Noctū lūnam
et stellās vidēre possumus; Diānam et puellās in caelō
vidēmus."

°**in hāc ter′rā**   in this country

Nouns	
lu cer′na, -ae	F., lantern, lamp
cae′lum, -ī	N., sky, heaven
***dō′num, -ī**	N., gift, offering
***ver′bum, -ī**	N., word
Adjective	
a per′tus, -a, -um	open
Verbs	
au′dit	hears, listens to
pro′pe rō, -āre	hasten, hurry
Conjunction	
at′que	and, and also

GENDER Latin nouns have what we call gender. In language, gender is the grouping of nouns into classes, such as masculine, feminine, and neuter. Words for males are naturally masculine; for females, feminine: **deus** (M.); **dea** (F.).

Words for things may be either masculine or feminine, or they may be neuter (neither): **vīcus**, village (M.); **silva**, forest (F.); **templum**, temple (N.). There are some clues to the gender of Latin words for things.

1 Most nouns with nominative singular ending in **-us** are masculine.
2 All nouns with nominative singular ending in **-a** are feminine (except a few which refer to males).
3 All nouns with nominative singular ending in **-um** are neuter.

Obviously, English nouns have no such artificial gender, and natural gender is indicated by the meaning of the word: man, woman; boy, girl; waiter, waitress; god, goddess. (In English the names of things are naturally neuter.)

THE ''NEUTER LAW'' All neuter nouns of all Latin declensions have the same form for both nominative and accusative. In the neuter plural these cases always end in **-a.**

SECOND-DECLENSION NOUNS IN -um are declined like **templum,** temple.

DECLENSION OF templum

CASE USES OF templum

	Singular		Singular
Nom.	**tem'plum**		**Templum est magnum.**
Gen.	**tem'plī**		**Jānua templī est aperta.**
Dat.	**tem'plō**		**Aqua templō propinqua est.**
Acc.	**tem'plum**		**Nauta templum videt.**
Abl.	**tem'plō**		**In templō flammās videt.**
	Plural		Plural
Nom.	**tem'pla**		**Templa sunt magna.**
Gen.	**templō'rum**		**Jānuae templōrum sunt apertae.**
Dat.	**tem'plīs**		**Aqua templīs propinqua est.**
Acc.	**tem'pla**		**Nauta templa videt.**
Abl.	**tem'plīs**		**In templīs flammās videt.**

ADJECTIVES OF DECLENSION I-II Many adjectives have the same endings as the noun **amīcus** for the masculine and as the noun **templum** for the neuter. Such adjectives as **bona** and **magna** have second-declension as well as first-declension endings: **bonus** (M.), **bona** (F.), **bonum** (N.).

A few adjectives, such as **pulchra,** have second-declension endings like those of the noun **ager** for the masculine: **pulcher** (M.), **pulchra** (F.), **pulchrum** (N.).

Like some **-er** nouns, a few second-declension adjectives with masculine in **-er** keep the **-e-** in all forms: **miser** (M.), **misera** (F.), **miserum** (N.).

I Select the neuter nouns and arrange them in regular declension order. A word may be used more than once.

agricolae	amīcus	dōnōrum	templō	lucerna
caelīs	dōna	vīcum	verbī	templum

II Choose the verb or noun which completes each sentence sensibly, and translate.

1 Ambulā/Ambulant/Ambulātisne/Ambulāte, nautae miserī, ad templum.
2 Stāre/Stāte/Stō/Stās prope casam, incolae!
3 Mihi nārrā/nārrat/nārrō/nārrāte, puellae, fābulam Diānae.
4 Vidēsne, amīcum/amīce/amīcōs/amīcī, templa deārum?

SCRAMBLED SENTENCES Unscramble the words to make sentences, and translate. Watch word endings. They make the meaning of a Latin sentence clear, regardless of word order.

1 **per ambulābant lātōs multī nautae agrōs.**
2 **multa postulābat Juppiter dōna.**
3 **portant deae templum incolae vīcōrum dōna ad.**
4 **in erant antīqua dēnsā templa silvā deōrum.**
5 **estne templum altus prope fluvius?**

LATIN LIVES TODAY Explain these phrases, using words in the lesson vocabulary as clues.

celestial bliss	celestial equator	verbal message
celestial blue	verbal agreement	verbal picture

Some English nouns are identical with Latin nouns ending in **-us/-um**.

alumnus   circus   focus   medium   mōmentum   stadium

Many other English nouns (and adjectives also) come from Declension II nouns and adjectives, undergoing changes similar to those that apply to Declension I words.

Final **-us/-um** may disappear; for example, **patrōnus**/patron, **ōrnāmentum**/ornament, **timidus**/timid. Drop final **-us/-um** from the following words and watch English words appear.

frīgidus   tepidus   angelus   signum   factum
magicus   Ōceanus   documentum   tacitus   testāmentum

In other English words -e replaces final **-us/-um**; for example, **captīvus**/captive, **fātum**/fate, **dēnsus**/dense. Substitute -e for final **-us/-um** in the following words.

fugitīvus   modus   vōtum   templum   mūlus
dīvīnus   sānus   plānum   marīnus   globus

Sometimes Latin words in **-ius/-ium** have become English words in -y, while others have -e replacing **-ium**; for example, **sacrificium**/sacrifice, **testimōnium**/testimony.

contrārius   mātrimōnium   officium   exilium   suffrāgium

A few English words in -ce come from Latin words in **-tium**.

servitium   silentium   sōlstitium   spatium   vitium

English adjectives in -ous often come from Latin adjectives in **-ōsus**. Change **-ōsus** to -ous in these adjectives.

cōpiōsus   cūriōsus   fābulōsus   glōriōsus   invidiōsus

A few English words in -er come from Latin nouns in **-rum**.

membrum   mōnstrum   scēptrum   sepulchrum   spectrum

LOOK   AND   THINK Beginning with Unit IV, words covered by principles explained under "Word Mastery" will be omitted from lesson vocabularies. Try to make an intelligent guess before consulting the General Vocabulary.

XIV

DAPHNE AND APOLLO

Apollo's pursuit of Daphne was painted by a rather obscure Italian artist, Andrea Appiani (1754-1817). Apollo as the hunter carries his quiver of arrows on his hip. Daphne's arms are shown turning into leafy branches and her feet into the roots of a tree. This picture is in the Art Museum of Brera in Milan, Italy.

In silvīs Thessaliae habitat nympha Daphnē. Daphnē multīs° grāta est, quod est pulchra. Multī° nympham in mātrimōnium dūcere° dēsīderant. Daphnē autem mātrimōnium semper recūsat.

"Lībera esse dēsīderō," dīcit. "In silvīs sōla errāre amō; 5 mātrimōnium recūsō."

In silvā propinquā autem parvus deus Cupīdō habitat. Per dēnsam silvam errāre amat quoque Cupīdō.

Ōlim Cupīdō in silvā ambulat; in pharetrā° et sagittās aureās et sagittās plumbeās portat. Deus Phoebus Apollō 10 puerum videt parvum.

Apollō jocōsē° dīcit, "Multās sagittās in tuā pharetrā portās, sed tuae sagittae bēstias necāre nōn possunt. Pharetram habēs magnam, sed in pharetrā sunt parvae sagittae aureae et plumbeae."
15

Celeriter Cupīdō sagittam mittit° auream. Sagitta vulnerat Phoebum. Mox Phoebus Apollō pulchram nympham Daphnēn videt; statim deus nympham in mātrimōnium dūcere dēsīderat.

"Tē° amō, Daphnē," dīcit Phoebus. "Sagitta aurea parvī 20 deī mē vulnerāvit.° Sum deus medicīnae, sed nūlla medicīna mē juvāre potest. Tū° sōla mē juvāre poteris. Tē amō; tē in mātrimōnium dūcere dēsīderō."

Daphnē territa per silvam properat. Apollō quoque properat.
25

Dēnique Daphnē properāre nōn jam potest; territa nympha ōrat, "Servāte mē, dī benignī. Mūtāte fōrmam meam! Tum Apollinī grāta nōn erō."

Statim dī benignī fōrmam nymphae mūtant. Nōn jam comam, sed folia habet Daphnē. Nōn jam bracchia, sed 30 rāmōs habet. Daphnē est pulchra laurus.

Apollō laurum pulchram spectat et dīcit, "Nōn jam es nympha, sed tē amō, Daphnē. Mea laurus es, et corōna laurea erit semper signum victōriae."

°**mul'tīs** (dat. pl.) to many (men) • **mul'tī** (nom. pl.) many (men)
in mā tri mō'ni um dū'ce re   to marry; to lead into marriage
pha're tra, -ae F̣., quiver (for arrows) • **jo cō'sē** jokingly
mit'tit sends; shoots (an arrow) • **tē** (acc. sing.) you
vul ne rā'vit has wounded • **tū** (nom. sing.) you

Nouns	
co'ma, -ae	F., hair
*****co rō'na, -ae**	F., crown
*****lau'rus, -ī**	F., laurel tree
pu'er, -ī	M., boy
rā'mus, -ī	M., branch (of tree)
brac'chi um, -ī	N., arm
*****fo'li um, -ī**	N., leaf
Adjectives	
au're us, -a, -um	gold, golden; of gold
*****lau're us, -a, -um**	laurel; of laurel
plum'be us, -a, -um	lead, leaden
Verbs	
mū'tō, -āre	change
re cū'sō, -āre	refuse
vul'ne rō, -āre	wound
Adverb	
tum	then

AGREEMENT OF ADJECTIVES AND NOUNS IN GENDER

An adjective agrees with its noun in gender, as well as in case and number.

bonus amīcus (M.)   **casa alba** (F.)   **magnum templum** (N.)
good friend   white house   large temple

amīcus miser (genitive, **amīci miseri**) M., an unhappy friend
magnus ager (genitive, **magni agri**) M., a large field
puer piger (genitive, **puerī pigrī**) M., a lazy boy

POSITION OF ADJECTIVES

Since in Latin an adjective does not always stand next to its noun, a knowledge of gender and the principle of agreement is useful in linking words together.

Subitō templum est obscūrum. Suddenly the temple is dark.
Incolae ārās nōn servant meās. The inhabitants do not keep my altars.

Most adjectives follow nouns they modify; but **bonus, malus, magnus, parvus, multus, tōtus** usually precede their nouns.

ADJECTIVES WITH NOUNS OF DIFFERENT DECLENSION

An adjective always agrees in gender with the noun it modifies, but a noun and its modifying adjective may belong to different declensions.

Most first-declension nouns are feminine; the few that are masculine (**agricola, nauta, pīrāta, poēta,** and sometimes **incola**) are modified only by masculine adjectives.

Most second-declension nouns in **-us** are masculine, but names of islands, towns, and trees are usually feminine: **Rhodus** (Rhodes), **Corinthus** (Corinth), **laurus** (laurel tree). Adjectives modifying such nouns are also feminine.

Thus, a modifying adjective often reveals the gender of its noun: **bonus nauta** (M.), **laurus pulchra** (F.).

I Choose the group of case endings of nouns appropriate for each use. A group may be used more than once.

Case Endings	Use
1 -a, -us, -er, -ae, -ī	direct object
2 -um, -ās, -am, -ōs, -a	indirect object
3 -ae, -ārum, -ī, -ōrum	possession
4 -ae, -ō, -īs	object of preposition
5 -ā, -ō, -īs	subject
6 -a, -ae, -e, -ī	vocative

II Complete the phrases by using as many of the listed endings as possible.

1 cum puer- īrāt-
2 inter dōn- grāt-
3 in fluvi- angust-
4 ō, fēmin- superb-!
5 dē naut- benign-
6 ad templ- magn-
7 prope ōr- maritim-
8 per agr- bon-

-a, -ā, -ae, -am, ās, -e, -ī, -īs, -ō, -ōs, -um, -us

III Translate each sentence into Latin. Tell the case and use of every noun in the sentence.
1 I have a good friend.
2 The kind sailor is pleasing to the queen.
3 The happy farmer walks through the fields.
4 I cannot remain in the temple.
5 The door of the house is open.

Mercury is truly the winged god, with wings on his caduceus, his helmet, and his sandals. This famous bronze by Giovanni da Bologna is in the Uffizi Gallery.

XV

APOLLO AND MERCURY

Phoebus Apollō est deus sōlis.° Deus incolīs terrae grātus est, quod radiī sōlis sunt Phoebī sagittae. Sagittae deī incolās et agrōs ā perīculō morbī dēfendunt.

Apollō est deus jūstus; populō bonās lēgēs° dat. Pācem° amat, sed arma nōn vītat. Phoebō cāra est lyra, quod est 5 deus mūsicae. Graecī fābulam nōtam dē lyrā prīmā nārrant.

°sō′lis (gen. sing.) of the sun • lē′gēs (acc. pl.) laws
pā′cem (acc. sing.) peace

Ōlim, ut fābula est, Apollō parvum deum Mercurium ex caelō spectat. Mercurius est īnfāns.°

Hodiē inter saxa silvae parvus deus testūdinem° subitō videt. Testūdinem celeriter necat; testam° autem servat. 10 Chordās trāns testam Mercurius pōnit; tum ē testā mūsicam ēvocat grātam. Apollō mūsicam chordārum audit, et ad terram statim volat; parvum deum laudat.

"Lyra tua est bona; mūsica tuae lyrae mihi° grāta est," dīcit Apollō. "Dabisne mihi lyram?" 15

Parvus Mercurius invītus Phoebō lyram dat. Gaudium Phoebī est magnum. "Semper lyram portābō," dīcit Apollō, "quod sum deus mūsicae."

Deinde Apollō laetus Mercuriō dīcit, "Tibi° cādūceum magicum dabō. Semper cādūceum habēbis; cādūceus magicus 20 tē juvābit. Trāns terram et aquās Ōceanī volāre poteris."

°in'fāns*[1] (nom. sing.) infant, child • tes tū'di nem (acc. sing.) tortoise • tes'ta, -ae F., shell • mi'hi (dat.) to me, me ti'bi (dat. sing.) you, to you

Nouns	
*cā dū'ce us, -ī	M., wand, staff
mor'bus, -ī	M., disease, illness
*po'pu lus, -ī	M., people
ra'di us, -ī	M., ray
*ar'ma, -ōrum	N. pl., arms, weapons
gau'di um, -ī	N., joy
pe ri'cu lum, -ī	N., danger, peril
sax'um, -ī	N., rock, stone
Adjective	
in vī'tus, -a, -um	reluctant, unwilling
Verbs	
*ē' vo cō, -āre	evoke, call forth
vī'tō, -āre	avoid, shun
Adverb	
de in'de	then, next; in the second place
Preposition	
*trāns	(with acc.) across

[1] A vowel before **ns** or **nf** in Latin is always long.

98

This Roman bowl, made of silver and adorned with sprigs of laurel sacred to Apollo, may have commemorated an ancient victory.

THE STEM OF THE FUTURE TENSE of most verbs is the present stem.

Verb	Infinitive	Present Stem
portō	**portāre**	**portā-**
moneō	**monēre**	**monē-**

THE FUTURE TENSE SIGN OF CONJUGATIONS I AND II is -bi- (-b-, -bu-) added to the present stem and followed by person endings.

portā+b+ō   portā+bi+s (+t, +mus, +tis)   portā+bu+nt

monē+b+ō   monē+bi+s (+t, +mus, +tis)   monē+bu+nt

CONJUGATIONS I AND II IN FUTURE TENSE

	I		II	
	Singular		Singular	
1	**portā′bō**	I shall carry	**monē′bō**	I shall warn
2	**portā′bis**	you will carry	**monē′bis**	you will warn
3	**portā′bit**	he will carry	**monē′bit**	he will warn
	Plural		Plural	
1	**portā′bimus**	we shall carry	**monē′bimus**	we shall warn
2	**portā′bitis**	you will carry	**monē′bitis**	you will warn
3	**portā′bunt**	they will carry	**monē′bunt**	they will warn

I In the list of verbs below change all present tenses to future. Give person and number of each verb already in future tense.

1 dēsīderābitis	4 videō	7 valēs
2 clāmant	5 poterunt	8 habet
3 sedent	6 monēbit	9 manētis

II Give verb forms indicated.

1 First person plural, present tense of **postulō**
2 Third person singular, future tense of **moneō**
3 Second person singular, future tense of **clāmō**
4 First person plural, future tense of **habeō**

III Translate the phrases into Latin.

1 He was not able	3 They will remain
2 I see	4 You (pl.) will be

IV Translate.

1 Mox nautae per perīculōsās aquās nāvigābunt.
2 Bēstiās aut sagittīs aut hastīs necāre poterimus.
3 Ītalia magnam habēbit fāmam.

SCRAMBLED SENTENCES Unscramble the words to make sentences, and translate.

1 **nōn puer ad poterat rēgiam properāre.**
2 **gladiōsque portābunt hastās deī.**
3 **manēbunt in incolae quod vīcō multī territī sunt.**

USEFUL LATIN The caduceus (Mercury's magic staff) has become the symbol of the medical profession. Many physicians use Latin abbreviations in writing their prescriptions.

aq. (aqua) water
dil. (dīlue) dilute
h.s. (hōrā somni) at bedtime (hour of sleep)
M. (miscē) mix
q.s. (quantum sufficit) enough (as much as is sufficient)
R/ (recipe) take

ut dict. (ut dictum) as directed
t.i.d. (ter in diē) three times a day
gtt. (guttae) drops
cap. (capiat) let him take
o.d. (oculus dexter) right eye
o.s. (oculus sinister) left eye
S (signā) indicate

100

THE PLANETS, with one exception, were named after mythological characters. How many of these characters can you identify? (Consult an English dictionary, if necessary.) "Minerva" has been suggested to replace the one non-Roman name. Which planet would be renamed?

Earth	Mars	Neptune	Saturn	Venus
Jupiter	Mercury	Pluto	Uranus	

COMPARISON OF NOUN ENDINGS

	I (F., M.)	II (M., F.)	II (N.)	OTHER (M., F.)[1]
	Singular	Singular	Singular	Singular
Nom.	-a	-us, -er (M.)	-um	(Varied)
Gen.	-ae	-ī	-ī	-is
Dat.	-ae	-ō	-ō	
Acc.	-am	-um	-um	-em
Abl.	-ā	-ō	-ō	-e
	Plural	Plural	Plural	Plural
Nom.	-ae	-ī	-a	-ēs
Gen.	-ārum	-ōrum	-ōrum	
Dat.	-īs	-īs	-īs	
Acc.	-ās	-ōs	-a	-ēs
Abl.	-īs	-īs	-īs	

COMPARISON OF ADJECTIVE ENDINGS

	I (F.)	II (M.)	II (N.)
	Singular	Singular	Singular
Nom.	-a	-us, -er	-um
Gen.	-ae	-ī	-ī
Dat.	-ae	-ō	-ō
Acc.	-am	-um	-um
Abl.	-ā	-ō	-ō
	Plural	Plural	Plural
Nom.	-ae	-ī	-a
Gen.	-ārum	-ōrum	-ōrum
Dat.	-īs	-īs	-īs
Acc.	-ās	-ōs	-a
Abl.	-īs	-īs	-īs

[1]Only case endings which have been used up to this point are given here.

XVI

THE KINGDOM OF THE DEAD

Initiō dī in summō Olympō° habitābant; Tītānī in terrā habitābant. Tītānī invidiōsī autem longīs bellīs pugnābant et Olympum occupāre temptābant. Dēnique post multōs annōs dī Olympī Tītānōs superāvērunt.°

Post victōriam Juppiter in conciliō deōrum et deārum 5 dīxit,° "Nōn jam Tītānī terram habēbunt; sub terrā in Tartarō obscūrō semper habitābunt. Ego et terram et caelum habēbō."

Neptūnō Juppiter dīxit, "Tibi, Neptūne, rēgnum aquārum dabō; tū eris rēx fluviōrum et Ōceanī."

Deinde rēx deōrum dīxit, "Tū, Plūtō, eris rēx Orcī 10 obscūrī; tū rēgnum mortuōrum[1] habēbis."

Itaque Plūtō est rēx regiōnis° subterrāneae; in magnā rēgiā habitat, sed rēgia nōn est pulchra. Canis trīceps,° Cerberus, prope jānuam rēgiae semper vigilat.

Circum rēgiam sunt silvae dēnsae; in silvīs umbrae mīrae 15 errant. Rēgnum subterrāneum semper obscūrum est.

Circum Orcum est fluvius Styx, frīgidus et obscūrus. Deus Mercurius mortuōs[1] ad rīpās fluviī dūcit; parvā nāviculā nauta Charōn mortuōs trāns fluvium frīgidum portat.

Charōn mortuōs sine pecūniā portāre recūsat. Itaque 20 mortuus[1] quī° pecūniam nōn habet prope rīpam fluviī per centum° annōs errat. Dēnique post centum annōs Charōn miserās umbrās trāns fluvium portābit sine pecūniā.

°**in sum'mō O lym'pō** on top of Olympus • **su pe rā vē'runt** defeated, overcame • **dīx'it**[2] said • **re gi ō'nis*** (gen. sing.) region, district • **ca'nis trī'ceps** (nom. sing.) three-headed dog • **quī** M. (nom. sing., pl.) who • **cen'tum*** (indeclinable) a hundred

The decoration on this ancient Greek vase in the Louvre shows Charon landing his boat on the shore in Hades, as he serves as ferryman of the Styx.

[1]In Latin, as in English, some adjectives are used alone and stand for both noun and adjective. In this story, **mortuōrum** (of the dead), **mortuōs** (the dead), and **mortuus** (a dead man) are all adjectives used as nouns.

[2]The letter **x** between two vowels is pronounced with the first vowel.

nā vi'cu la, -ae	F., little boat
pe cū'ni a, -ae	F., money
rī'pa, -ae	F., bank (of a river)
um'bra, -ae	F., shade, ghost
***an'nus, -ī**	M., year
bel'lum, -ī	N., war
***con ci'li um, -ī**	N., council, assembly
***in i'ti um, -ī**	N., beginning
***rēg'num, -ī**	N., kingdom

Adjective

***mor'tu us, -a, -um**	dead

Verbs

***oc'cu pō, -āre**	seize, occupy
pug'nō, -āre	fight
vi'gi lō, -āre	stand watch, be on guard

Prepositions

post	(with acc.) after, behind
si'ne	(with abl.) without

A B L A T I V E   W I T H O U T   A   P R E P O S I T I O N   in Latin requires an English connective in translation. Such prepositions as "with," "by," "at," "in," or "from" and phrases like "by means of" or "because of" may be tried for sense.

Parvā nāviculā Charōn mortuōs trāns fluvium portat. By means of a small boat Charon carries the dead across the river.

Sagittā Cupīdō vulnerat Phoebum. With an arrow Cupid wounds Phoebus.

Initiō dī in summō Olympō habitābant. In the beginning the gods lived on top of Olympus.

I Tell to which classification listed at the right each verb form belongs, and translate.

1 vītābunt	6 ēvocāre	11 manē	16 sumus		Infinitive
2 mōnstrā	7 recūsātis	12 monētis	17 erunt		Present
3 manēte	8 erāmus	13 esse	18 dās		Imperfect
4 monēbis	9 poteris	14 necābis	19 vulnerāte		Future
5 amābat	10 dare	15 videt	20 posse		Imperative

II The following sentences are taken from the stories of this unit. Answer the questions regarding the sentences.

1 **Vesta erat Rōmānīs cāra; multās ārās in parvīs casīs et in magnīs villīs habēbat.**

What is the case of **Rōmānīs?** How can you tell?

What is the meaning of **in** used with **casīs** and **villīs?**

Does **habēbat** denote present time, future time, or continuous action in past time?

2 **Agricola fābulās Diānae amīcō nārrābat, sed nauta semper dīcēbat, "In templō antīquō, amīce, dea nōn habitat."**

What is the gender of **agricola?** Why?

Explain the use of **amīcō** and of **Diānae.**

What is the best translation of **dīcēbat?**

What is the case of **amīce?**

3 **"Servāte mē, dī benignī. Mūtāte fōrmam meam! Tum Apollinī grāta nōn erō."**

Explain the forms ending in **-te.**

What other form could be used as well as **dī?**

Why is **Apollinī** in the dative case?

4 **"Dabisne mihi lyram?"**

If the expected answer were "yes," how would the question change?

What does the ending **-bis** signify?

5 **Initiō dī in summō Olympō habitābant; Tītānī in terrā habitābant.**

What does the ending **-bant** signify?

LATIN LIVES TODAY Explain each statement by relating each key word to a word in the lesson vocabulary.

1 Pecuniary property may mean money in the bank.
2 Riparian property is on the bank of a river.
3 An umbrella gives a little shade.
4 Umbrage is suspicion of being put in the shade.
5 An annual is a yearbook; also a flower blooming each year.
6 An annuity provides a yearly income.
7 Initiation begins membership in an organization.
8 Initials are the letters that begin one's name.
9 A vigilant person is watchful and on guard.
10 A mortician works with dead people in a mortuary.

REVIEW OF UNIT IV

LESSONS XII — XVI

Nouns	Nouns (cont.)	Adjectives	Adverbs
coma, -ae	morbus, -ī	apertus, -a, -um	deinde
*corōna, -ae	*populus, -ī	aureus, -a, -um	tum
hasta, -ae	puer, puerī	invītus, -a, -um	
lucerna, -ae	radius, -ī	*laureus, -a, -um	Conjunctions
nāvicula, -ae	rāmus, -ī	*mortuus, -a, -um	atque
pecūnia, -ae	vīcus, -ī	plumbeus, -a, -um	-que
*rēgia, -ae	*arma, -ōrum		
rīpa, -ae	bellum, -ī	Verbs	Prepositions
sapientia, -ae	bracchium, -ī	*ēvocō, -āre	post
umbra, -ae	caelum, -ī	juvō, -āre	sine
ager, agrī	*concilium, -ī	mūtō, -āre	trāns
*amīcus, -ī	*dōnum, -ī	*occupō, -āre	
*annus, -ī	*folium, -ī	properō, -āre	
*cādūceus, -ī	gaudium, -ī	pugnō, -āre	
deus, -ī	*initium, -ī	recūsō, -āre	
fluvius, -ī	perīculum, -ī	vigilō, -āre	
focus, -ī	rēgnum, -ī	vītō, -āre	
gladius, -ī	saxum, -ī	vulnerō, -āre	
*laurus, -ī	*verbum, -ī	audit	

I Give the gender of each noun in the list; then complete the statement which justifies your answer.

1 Most nouns with a nominative singular ending in **-a** are ____ gender.
2 Most nouns with a nominative singular ending in **-us** are ____ gender.
3 All Declension II nouns with a nominative singular ending in **-um** are ____ gender.
4 Declension II nouns that are names of islands, towns, and trees are ____ gender.

a) amīcus
b) Corinthus
c) fīlia
d) gaudium
e) laurus
f) lyra
g) rāmus
h) Rōma

II In each sentence change singular nouns to plural and plural nouns to singular. Make other changes as needed. Translate.

1 Bonī incolae vīcōrum bellum vītābunt.
2 Puer amīcīs fābulās nārrābit.
3 Saxum agrō amīcī meī propinquum est.

105

III From the list below select (a) pairs of opposite meaning, (b) words referring to people, (c) kinds of buildings, and (d) geographical terms. Translate any remaining words.

1 aestāte	11 hieme	21 rāmus
2 ager	12 incola	22 rēgia
3 amita	13 īnsula	23 schola
4 beāta	14 interdiū	24 sedeō
5 casa	15 lucerna	25 silva
6 coma	16 misera	26 stō
7 dēnique	17 noctū	27 templum
8 fīlia	18 nunc	28 tum
9 fluvius	19 prīmō	29 ursa
10 gladius	20 puer	30 vīlla

IV Some of the following statements are only partially true. By adding to them make all statements completely true. Then check items for agreement with instructions.

1 Declension I endings used for one case only are **-a, -ārum, -ās.**
2 Declension II endings used for more than one case are **-ī, -īs.**
3 In Declension I nouns, **-ae** is used in genitive singular and nominative plural.
4 Masculine nouns of Declension II end in **-ī** in nominative and vocative plural.
5 In Declension II masculine nouns, only the endings **-um** and **-ōrum** appear in one case each.
6 In all nouns of Declensions I and II, dative and ablative plurals end in **-īs.**
7 Neuter nouns of Declension II have **-um** in nominative and accusative singular, and **-a** in nominative plural.
8 Masculine nouns of Declension I are **agricola, nauta,** and **poēta.**
9 **Laurus** is a feminine noun, but belongs to Declension II.

V Change all verbs in the present and past tenses to corresponding person and number of the future. Identify any other forms. Translate.

1 cēlāte	6 juvātis	11 postulāre
2 eram	7 laudant	12 recūsās
3 erāmus	8 manētis	13 sedēs
4 errō	9 nārrat	14 timēbant
5 habēmus	10 possum	15 vītāmus

Old Greek artists who made the designs for vases had a sense of humor, as this grinning caricature of Medusa, complete with snaky hair and wings, shows. The vase is in the Louvre.

Vulcan works on Achilles' shield, while a workman completes the helmet.

XVII

VULCAN

Vulcānus est deus perītus. Magnā cum cūrā rēgiās splendidās deōrum deārumque in Olympō aedificāvit. Rēgiae erant aureae; jānuae rēgiārum erant aureae. Ā fenestrīs apertīs rēgiārum dī Olympī terrās et aquās orbis° terrārum vidēre poterant.

In summō Olympō erat magna rēgia Jovis.° In rēgiā Vulcānus splendidum ātrium aedificāvit; hūc Juppiter concilium convocābat. In ātriō erant magnae urnae; urnae gemmīs erant adōrnātae.

In Olympō Vulcānus fulmina° Jovis, galeās aureās, scūta

°**or′bis terrā′rum**   of the world (of the circle of lands)   •   **Jo′vis**
(gen.) of Jupiter   •   **ful′mina**   (acc. pl.) thunderbolts

splendida, hastās validās faciēbat.° Aliīs quoque deīs arma Vulcānus dabat. Juppiter īrātus Vulcānum vocāvit.

"Bene labōrāvistī, Vulcāne, sed inimīcōs meōs jūvistī!" dīxit rēx deōrum. "Quod inimīcīs meīs arma dedistī, tē dē Olympō jactābō." 15

Mox Vulcānus miser ad terram cadēbat.° Post multās hōrās in īnsulam Siciliam pervēnit.° In Siciliā est Aetna alta. Aetna flammās perpetuās ēmittit.°

Vulcānus flammās Aetnae spectāvit et dīxit, "In Aetnā meam incūdem° habēbō. Dōna pulchra atque arma bellī 20 facere° poterō; erō amīcus incolārum terrae."

Incolae Ītaliae flammās Aetnae saepe vidēre possunt, quod Sicilia Ītaliae propinqua est.

"Hodiē flammae Aetnae sunt clārae," dīcunt. "Vulcānus incūde° labōrat. Vulcānus est amīcus noster." 25

°faciē'bat used to make • **cadē'bat** was falling • **pervē'- ·nit** came (to) • **ēmit'tit*** sends forth • **incū'dem** (acc. sing.); **incū'de** (abl. sing.) anvil • **fa'cere** to make

[1]**cū'ra, -ae**	F., care
[2]**ga'lea, -ae**	F., helmet
hō'ra, -ae	F., hour
*ā'trium, -ī	N., hall, main room, atrium
scū'tum, -ī	N., shield
*adōrnā'tus, -a, -um	decorated, adorned
inimī'cus, -a, -um	unfriendly; M. (as noun), enemy
perī'tus, -a, -um	skilled, experienced
*va'lidus, -a, -um	strong, powerful; well
aedi'ficō, -āre, -ā'vī	build, construct
*con'vocō, -āre, -ā'vī	summon, call together
jac'tō, -āre, -ā'vī	hurl, throw, cast
be'ne	well; (with **labōrō**), work hard
hūc	here; to this place

[1]Beginning with the vocabulary of this lesson, the labels "Nouns," "Adjectives," "Verbs," etc. are omitted, although words are still grouped according to parts of speech.

[2]Hereafter, except for accented syllables, the syllabication of words is not indicated in lesson vocabularies.

PERFECT TENSE in Latin tells something that happened in the past. It usually indicates a single past act, not continuous nor repeated action.

Juppiter Vulcānum vocāvit. Jupiter summoned Vulcan.

PERSON ENDINGS OF THE PERFECT are the same for all Latin verbs but different from the endings regularly seen in other tenses.

	Singular				Plural	
	Regular	Perfect			Regular	Perfect
1	-ō (-m)	-ī		1	-mus	-imus
2	-s	-istī		2	-tis	-istis
3	-t	-it		3	-nt	-ērunt

CONJUGATION OF VERBS IN PERFECT TENSE

	I			II	
	Singular			Singular	
1	portā'vī	I carried		mo'nuī	I warned
2	portāvis'tī	you carried		monuis'tī	you warned
3	portā'vit	he carried		mo'nuit	he warned
	Plural			Plural	
1	portā'vimus	we carried		monu'imus	we warned
2	portāvis'tis	you carried		monuis'tis	you warned
3	portāvē'runt	they carried		monuē'runt	they warned

In perfect tense, **sum** and **possum** have the same endings as other verbs.

| **sum:** | fuī | fuistī | fuit | fuimus | fuistis | fuērunt |
| **possum:** | potuī | potuistī | potuit | potuimus | potuistis | potuērunt |

TRANSLATION OF VERBS IN PERFECT TENSE   When a Latin perfect indicates a single past act, as it usually does, the verb should be translated as a simple past tense in English. Occasionally a Latin perfect may be translated with "have" or "has" or with "did." For questions in English, such "helping verbs" are necessary: "Did I carry ... ?" or "Have I carried ... ?"

(portō)	**portāvī**	I carried, I have carried, I did carry
(moneō)	**monuī**	I warned, I have warned, I did warn
(sum)	**fuī**	I was, I have been
(possum)	**potuī**	I could (was able), I have been able

LOOK AND THINK In paragraph four of "Vulcan" three verbs have the same ending. The first **(labōrāvistī)** gives a clue to the person, number, and tense of the others: **jūvistī (juvō)** and **dedistī (dō)**.

I Which of these endings are used only for the perfect?

1 -ērunt   4 -imus   7 -t
2 -ō   5 -tis   8 -istis
3 -istī   6 -it   9 -ī

II Complete each verb with a different ending from I; translate.

1 recūsāv-   3 habitāv-   5 mūtāv-
2 timu-   4 potu-   6 habu-

III Change any verb in present to perfect, in perfect to present; in future to present.

1 pugnāvistis   5 laudābunt   9 stābō
2 monet   6 clāmant   10 monēmus
3 temptat   7 habuit   11 habitābimus
4 potuimus   8 juvābit   12 fuī

LATIN LIVES TODAY in English words derived from the name of the Roman fire-god. The name of this ancient god had two acceptable spellings **(Vulcānus/Volcānus)**. Therefore, some derivatives also have two spellings, while others are based on only one of the Latin spellings.

Vulcānus		**Volcānus**
vulcanian	vulcanism/volcanism	volcanic
vulcanite	vulcanology/volcanology	volcanicity
vulcanize	vulcanologist/volcanoligist	volcano

Each year on August 23 the Romans held a festival in honor of Vulcan—the **Volcānālia**. At a place near the Tiber River that was sacred to Vulcan **(area Volcānī)** heads of families bought small fish and threw them into a fire.

XVIII

Ōlim Medūsa, puella pulchra, in terrā obscūrā habitābat
ubi neque sōl° neque lūna appārēbat. Terra obscūra puellae
grāta nōn erat. Medūsa igitur Minervam adōrāvit.

"Dea sapientiae, audī mē," puella misera ōrāvit. "Juvā
mē! Terra obscūra, ubi habitō, mihi grāta nōn est. Pulchra 5
sum; pulchram comam atque faciem° pulchram habeō. Nēmō°
autem in terrā obscūrā mē vidēre potest. Dēsīderō in terrā
clārā habitāre."

Dea autem Medūsam juvāre recūsāvit. Tum puella īrāta
Minervae dīxit, "Invidiōsa es quod tam pulchra sum! Popu- 10
lum mē vidēre nōn dēsīderās!"

Tum dea īrāta pulchram comam puellae mūtāvit.

"Tū fuistī superba propter comam pulchram atque faciem
pulchram. Ego comam tuam in serpentēs° mūtāvī," dea

°**sōl** (nom. sing.) sun • **fa'ciem*** (acc. sing.) face • **nē'mō**
(nom. sing.) no one • **serpen'tēs*** (nom., acc. pl.) serpents

This head of Medusa forms the central medallion of a vestibule's mosaic floor.

112

dīxit īrāta. "Nōn jam tua coma erit pulchra. Tua faciēs° 15
erit pulchra, sed nēmō tē spectāre poterit. In saxa tua
faciēs virōs mūtābit."

°fa′ciēs* (nom. sing.) face

vir, vi′rī	M., man
***appā′reō, -ēre, -uī**	appear
au′dī	(imperative sing.) hear! listen!
i′gitur	therefore
ne′que . . . ne′que	neither . . . nor; **neque** (alone) nor, and not
prop′ter	(with acc.) because of

PRINCIPAL PARTS OF A VERB Certain forms
of a Latin verb are called principal parts because they are key
words on which all forms of a conjugation are based. Most
Latin verbs have four principal parts. Three of these have
already appeared in this book.

(First Person Singular)		(First Person Singular)
Present	Infinitive	Perfect
I **portō**	**portāre**	**portāvī**
II **moneō**	**monēre**	**monuī**
sum	**esse**	**fuī**
possum	**posse**	**potuī**

THE STEM OF THE PERFECT TENSE can
be found by dropping **-ī** from the third principal part, just as
the stem of the present tense is found by dropping **-re** from
the infinitive (second principal part).

Present Stem	Perfect Stem
I **portā-**	**portāv-**
II **monē-**	**monu-**

I Translate each Latin verb. Give infinitive and first person
singular present tense.

1 habēbitis	4 habitās	7 fuī
2 portāvērunt	5 appārēmus	8 dabitis
3 stābō	6 mūtat	9 monuistī

113

II Supply the other two principal parts of the verbs listed.

1 spectō   3 habēre   5 cēlāvī

2 sum   4 posse   6 jactō

III Complete each sentence with one or more of the underlined verbs or verb phrases therein and translate.

1 Pīrātae arma vidēmus/cēlāre possunt/esse poterant.

2 Date/Habuistī/Potuimus, nautae, incolīs cibum.

3 Virī vīcī fuī/fuērunt/poterō aegrī.

4 Hodiē in casā erō/posse/manēre nōn potes.

5 Fuit/Fuistīne/Stātis in ōrā maritimā cum puerīs?

6 Cūr bēstiam amāre/timuistī/timēs, mea puella?

XIX

THE BEST GIFT

Neptūnus, rēx fluviōrum, rēgiam sub aquīs Ōceanī habēbat.

Minerva erat dea Rōmāna bellī et sapientiae. Graecī deam bellī et sapientiae "Athēnam" appellābant.

Ōlim Neptūnus et Minerva oppidum novum vīdērunt. 5 Oppidum erat prope ōram maritimam.

Neptūnus rogāvit, "Habetne oppidum nōmen°?"

Incolae oppidī respondērunt, "Minimē. Oppidum est novum; nōmen nōn habet."

Deinde Neptūnus dīxit, "Oppidō nōmen dabō." 10

Athēna (Minerva) quoque oppidō nōmen dare dēsīderāvit.

Dēnique Juppiter, rēx deōrum, dīxit, "Neptūnus dōnum

°**nō′men***   (nom., acc. sing.) name

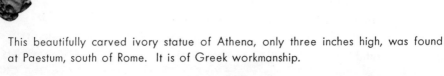

This beautifully carved ivory statue of Athena, only three inches high, was found at Paestum, south of Rome. It is of Greek workmanship.

114

creābit; oppidō novō dōnum dabit. Athēna quoque dōnum creābit et dabit. Creātor dōnī optimī oppidum appellābit."

Sine morā Neptūnus prīmum dōnum creāvit; dōnum 15 Neptūnī erat equus.

"Equus optimum dōnum est," dīxit Neptūnus, "quod equus incolās oppidī juvābit. Equum creāvī; oppidō equum dabō."

"Dōnum meum optimum erit," Athēna dīxit. "Arborem° 20 novam creāvī; olīvam dabō. Olīva bācās habet, et bācae oleum dant."

Incolae oppidī dōna spectāvērunt et clāmāvērunt, "Equus bonus est, sed olīva est dōnum optimum. Equus est signum bellī; olīva est signum pācis.°" 25

Tum Juppiter dēclārāvit, "Olīva est dōnum optimum. Dā, Athēna, nōmen oppidō!"

Itaque hodiē nōmen oppidī nōtī Graeciae est Athēnae, quod antīquitus Athēna creāvit olīvam.

°ar′borem* (acc. sing.) tree • pā′cis (gen. sing.) of peace

bā′ca, -ae	F., berry, small fruit
mo′ra, -ae	F., delay
e′quus, -ī	M., horse
*o′leum, -ī	N., oil
op′pidum, -ī	N., town
*op′timus, -a, -um	best; very good
appel′lō, -āre, -ā′vī	name
ro′gō, -āre, -ā′vī	ask

I In each group point out one form that does not belong with the others. Explain your decision, and identify the group to which it does belong.

1 monēbant, adōrābant, habitant, erat, habēbat
2 mūtābit, eris, adōrāvit, poterit, spectābit
3 dare, mūtāvistī, potuimus, fuistī, laudāvistis
4 es, monēbit, dēsīderō, possumus, adōrō
5 fuērunt, dā, respondēte, portā, juvāte
6 amāvērunt, nārrāre, esse, posse, appārēre

115

II Translate.

1 I shall sail.
2 They wandered.
3 You (pl.) are remaining.
4 They are changing.
5 I was unable to praise.
6 Hurry! (pl.)

7 They worshiped.
8 You (sing.) will see.
9 We have asked.
10 They will fight.
11 He has tried.
12 It will be.

III For each of the verb forms below supply the matching form in present and future. Translate. Give three principal parts of each.

1 vocāvērunt
2 habuit
3 mūtāvit
4 creāvī
5 adōrāvērunt

6 servāvistī
7 timuī
8 rogāvimus
9 potuistis
10 spectāvī

The Acropolis with its ancient temples still looms over modern Athens.

Modern representation of Prometheus in a mural at the New York Public Library

XX

THE GIFT OF FIRE

Initiō Promētheus, Tītānus amīcus, incolās terrae creāvit.
Incolae autem erant miserī. Aut in cavernīs obscūrīs aut
in casīs frīgidīs habitāvērunt.

Neque deōs neque templa incolae habuērunt. Nūlla arma
praeter clāvās, magna saxa, et hastās ligneās habuērunt. 5
Promētheus incolās terrae amāvit.

"Ignis° incolās terrae miserōs juvābit," dīxit Promētheus. "Ignis erit dōnum bonum. Ignem° ad terram portābō dē Olympō."

Juppiter autem Promētheō ignem dare recūsāvit. "Ignis in Olympō manēbit," dīxit rēx deōrum. ₁₀

Promētheus nōn respondit, sed cōnsilium bonum cēpit. Noctū volāvit sēcrētō in ātrium deōrum. Celeriter Promētheus taedam flammeam cēpit et ignem in baculō° cēlāvit. Deinde dē Olympō ad terram volāvit. ₁₅

Promētheus, ubi in terram pervēnit, incolās convocāvit. "Bonum dōnum in meō baculō habeō—ignem," dīxit. "Ignis autem dōnum perīculōsum est. Flammae magnam injūriam facere° possunt. Semper cūrāte ignem! Ita flammae injūriam facere nōn poterunt." ₂₀

Mox erant multae flammae clārae in terrā; cavernae et casae neque frīgidae neque obscūrae erant; propter dōnum Promētheī incolae terrae in clārīs et calidīs casīs hodiē habitant.

°**ig′nis** (nom. sing.); **ig′nem** (acc. sing.) fire • **ba′culum, -ī** N., cane, hollow stick • **fa′cere** to do

clā′va, -ae	F., club, stick
tae′da, -ae	F., torch
*****cōnsi′lium, -ī**	N., plan
ca′lidus, -a, -um	warm
*****flam′meus, -a, -um**	flaming, fiery
lig′neus, -a, -um	wooden, made of wood
cū′rō, -āre, -ā′vī	tend, care for
cē′pit	seized, took; (with **cōnsilium**), formed a plan
*****sēcrē′tō**	secretly, stealthily
+**u′bi**	when (with verb in perf. tense)
aut . . . aut	either . . . or
prae′ter	(with acc.) except

VARIATIONS OF THE PERFECT STEM occur in all conjugations. Many Latin verbs have perfect stems ending in **-v-**: **portāv-** (**portō**), **creāv-** (**creō**), **audīv-** (**audiō**). Some have **-u-** at the end of the perfect stem: **monu-** (**moneō**).

Many have **-s-**, which sometimes combines with a preceding consonant: **māns- (maneō), dīx-** from **dīcs- (dīcō).**

A few have no added letter at the end, but have an extra syllable (called reduplication) at the beginning of the verb: **ded- (dō), stet- (stō).**

Others have no addition at beginning or end. Some of these show the perfect tense by lengthening the vowel of the verb stem: **jūv- (juvō), vīd- (videō).**

Some verb stems remain unchanged in the perfect: **respond- (respondeō).**

The following is a summary, in perfect tense, of verbs that have already appeared in other tenses.

Most verbs of Conjugation I have **-v-** at the end of the perfect stem, like **portāvī** (perfect stem **portāv-**).

			Exceptions
appellāvī	**nāvigāvī**	**pugnāvī**	
dēclārāvī	**occupāvī**	**rogāvī**	**dedī (dō)**
expectāvī	**postulāvī**	**temptāvī**	**jūvī (juvō)**
mūtāvī	**properāvī**	**vulnerāvī**	**stetī (stō)**

With the exception of **dō, juvō,** and **stō,** all Conjugation I verbs that have occurred so far in this book have the perfect stem ending in **-v-**. See review of Conjugation I verbs on page 59. Give the perfect stem of each.

What is the perfect stem of each of these Conjugation I verbs?

adōrō	**convocō**	**dēsīderō**	**jactō**	**servō**
aedificō	**creō**	**errō**	**laudō**	**vigilō**
amō	**cūrō**	**ēvocō**	**recūsō**	**vītō**

Perfect stems of Conjugation II verbs are varied.

appāruī (appāreō)	**respondī (respondeō)**	**mānsī (maneō)**
habuī (habeō)	**sēdī (sedeō)**	
timuī (timeō)	**vīdī (videō)**	

A few verbs of other conjugations have appeared in the stories. Their perfect stems are also varied.

fuī (sum)	**dīxī (dīcō)**	**fēcī (faciō)**
potuī (possum)	**dūxī (dūcō)**	**dēfendī (dēfendō)**
posuī (pōnō)	**cēpī (capiō)**	**audīvī (audiō)**

119

I In "The Gift of Fire" find an example of each of the following.

1 Present infinitive (Conjugation I)
2 Third person singular, perfect tense (Conjugation I)
3 Neuter singular noun; neuter plural noun (Declension II)
4 Indirect object
5 Third person singular, future tense (Conjugations I and II)
6 Plural imperative (Conjugation I)
7 Third person plural, imperfect tense (**sum**)
8 Direct object
9 Masculine noun (Declension I)
10 Third person plural, future tense (**possum**)

II Select from the numbered list the corresponding perfect tense for each verb in the unnumbered list.

stāmus	dēlēbō	valēs	dīcit	juvō
poterunt	sedēmus	habēbit	monēs	vidētis

1 habitāvī   6 mānsistī   11 jūvī
2 dēlēvī   7 dīxit   12 dedit
3 valuistī   8 stetimus   13 sēdimus
4 potuērunt   9 volāvistis   14 vīdistis
5 habuit   10 monuistī   15 volāvērunt

III With one or more words from the lettered list, replace any item in each group which has no relation to the other items. Justify your decision.

1 aqua, coma, unda, Ōceanus   a) ager   k) jānua
2 arma, caverna, gladius, sagitta   b) āra   l) lacūna
3 urna, terra, īnsula, ōra   c) camēlus   m) populus
4 īnfāns, puella, līberī, perīculum   d) cōpia   n) puer
5 fābula, incola, fēmina, amita   e) elephantus o) rēgia
6 bēstia, ursa, canis, taeda   f) equus   p) rīpa
7 laurus, rāmus, injūria, folium   g) fīlia   q) sacrificium
8 schola, bracchium, casa, vīlla   h) fluvius   r) scūtum
9 morbus, deus, dea, templum   i) hasta   s) silva
10 ātrium, lingua, fenestra, focus   j) ignis   t) vir

USEFUL LATIN These verbs became English nouns.

Affidavit (he has stated on oath) = a sworn statement
Deficit (there is lacking) = a shortage
Placebo (I'll please) = medicine given to please a patient

REVIEW OF UNIT V

LESSONS XVII — XX

Nouns	Adjectives	Verbs (cont.)
bāca, -ae	*adōrnātus, -a, -um	audi
clāva, -ae	calidus, -a, -um	cēpit
cūra, -ae	*flammeus, -a, -um	
galea, -ae	inimīcus, -a, -um	Adverbs
hōra, -ae	ligneus, -a, -um	bene
mora, -ae	*optimus, -a, -um	hūc
taeda, -ae	perītus, -a, -um	igitur
equus, -ī	*validus, -a, -um	*sēcrētō
vir, -ī		+ubi
*ātrium, -ī	Verbs	
*cōnsilium, -ī	aedificō, -āre	Conjunctions
*oleum, -ī	appellō, -āre	aut . . . aut
oppidum, -ī	*convocō, -āre	neque . . . neque
scūtum, -ī	cūrō, -āre	
	jactō, -āre	Prepositions
	rogō, -āre	praeter
	*appāreō, -ēre	propter

I From the numbered list select terms which suggest the mythological characters in the lettered list as mentioned in stories of this unit. Any term may be used more than once.

1 Aetna	13 Ōceanus	a) Vulcan
2 Athēna	14 olīva	
3 coma	15 Olympus	b) Medusa
4 dōnum	16 perītus	
5 equus	17 pulchra	c) Minerva
6 fluviī	18 rēgia	
7 focus	19 sapientia	d) Jupiter
8 fulmina	20 saxum	
9 ignis	21 serpentēs	e) Neptune
10 īrātus	22 Sicilia	
11 laurus	23 taeda	f) Prometheus
12 miser	24 Tītānus	

121

II Find three principal parts of as many verbs as possible. Identify the remaining forms.

1 dabō	6 possum	11 esse	16 poterō	21 potuī
2 audī	7 sedeō	12 mānsī	17 dō	22 postulāvī
3 jūvī	8 dare	13 juvāre	18 sum	23 juvō
4 maneō	9 jactāvī	14 fuī	19 habēbit	24 dedistī
5 stāre	10 manēre	15 monuī	20 dedī	25 posse

III Complete each sentence by replacing the blank with a suitable verb from the list. Use each verb only once.

1 Hodiē malī erāmus; nōn semper _____ bonī
 possumus.
2 Puerī ad ōram ambulāre nōn _____ ; in
 scholā fuērunt.
3 Lacūnam nautīs mōnstrō quod aquam _____ .
4 Virōs dē perīculō saepe _____ .
5 Nōnne, virī, noctū in fluviō _____ ?
6 _____ diū in parvō vīcō?
7 Multōs pīrātās in ōrā maritimā _____ .
8 Nauta altus et validus galeās _____ .

esse
habuitne
mānsistīne
monēbimus
nāvigāvistis
portāvit
poteram
potuērunt
rogāvērunt
vīdimus

IV Add each person ending to all possible verb elements in the group it follows. Translate the completed forms.

Verb Elements | Person Endings
1 respond-, māns-, potu-, creāv- | -ērunt
2 vīd-, fu-, da-, timē- | -ī
3 eru-, stet-, monu-, sēd- | -istī
4 sedē-, errā-, mūtā-, erā- | -tis
5 fēc-, pertinē-, habitāv-, dīx- | -it
6 clāma-, nārrābi-, eri-, potera- | -t
7 mūtābi-, mone-, juva-, aedifica- | -nt
8 appāre-, poter-, jūv-, dab- | -ō
9 cūrā-, potera-, monē-, errābā- | -te

TRADE NAMES often come from Latin words. Here are a few. Look for others in newspaper and magazine advertisements.

Aquascutum raincoat

Bon Ami (French from **bonus**
amīcus) scouring powder

Atlas cement

Corona typewriter

Magnavox record player

122

In the foregoing units you have become acquainted with the meanings and uses as prepositions of **ā/ab, ad, circum, cum,**[1] **dē, ē/ex, in, inter, per, post, prō, sub,** and **trāns.** These words are also used as adverbial prefixes to form compounds, in which their meanings sometimes differ from the originals. Other such prefixes are **prae** (before), which becomes English pre-, and **ob** (toward), as in **objectum** (object).

ad+**ōrō** =**adōrō**	speak to, address, beseech, adore
ē +**vocō**=**ēvocō**	call from, call out, evoke
in +**dūcō**=**indūcō**	lead or draw on, induce

In addition to these adverbial prefixes certain other particles are used in forming compound verbs.

re-	(again, against, back)+**vocō** =**revocō**	call back
dis/dī-	(apart, away) +**putō** =**disputō**	discuss, argue

Some compound verbs can easily be translated.

removeō	**prōdūcō**	**convocō**	**praeparō**
remove	produce	convoke	prepare

An apparent English derivative, however, is not always a suitable translation. Frequently specialized meanings develop, and only the context can provide the correct answer.

invideō envy   **oppugnō** attack, besiege   **expectō** wait for

No English verb is derived directly from either **invideō** or **oppugnō.** **Invideō** means "look upon with envy or hatred." Originally it meant "look upon with evil eye." A related adjective is **invidiōsus**/invidious (full of envy, hateful). The meaning of **oppugnō** becomes apparent from a translation of its parts **(ob/pugnō).** Look up "impugn" and "repugnant."

Give a suitable meaning for an English derivative of each of the following Latin compounds.

dēdūcō	**circumnāvigō**	**perambulō**	**prōvocō**	**repugnō**
dēportō	**collabōrō**	**prōvideō**	**importō**	**recreō**

---

[1]The form **cum** is used only as a preposition; in compounds it appears as **co-, col-, com-, con-, cor-:** cogitō (cum/agitō), collabōrō, commūtō, convocō, corrōborō.

ROMAN DRESS

The basic article of clothing worn by all Romans—men, women, and children—was a simple tunic, usually made of wool. Children, workingmen, and slaves frequently wore nothing more. The tunic might hang free or be pulled up by means of a belt to a convenient length. Sometimes there were two tunics, an inner and an outer one.

The badge of citizenship, worn by Roman men, was a plain white toga—a large, semicircular piece of material draped in such a way as to leave the right arm bare. The free end of the toga was thrown over the left shoulder and held in place by its own weight. Although trousers were despised by the Romans, who considered them the mark of barbarian races, they were sometimes used for warmth by soldiers.

The outer garment of women, put on over the tunics, was the stola. Since it was too long for walking, it was belted in loose folds to floor length. A draped one-piece cloak called "palla," simpler than the toga, served as an outdoor wrap.

Most Roman garments were white or the natural color of the wool from which they were made. A colored stripe bordering a man's toga or extending from the hem of his tunic over each shoulder indicated the rank of the wearer. Women's clothes were more likely to be colorful than those of men, especially during the Empire, when various colors were popular. Earlier, shades of purple were the only colors used to relieve the plain white or natural color of clothing materials. In women's clothing, the colored border appeared around the neck and on the lower edge of the stola. True dyes were imported and therefore expensive, so that when certain shades of garnet and violet were worn, they were a mark of great luxury.

Roman shoes were of leather, made on a last, but only the upper classes could afford them. Sandals with straps were more common footwear. The Romans ordinarily went bareheaded, although small hats were sometimes worn by men while traveling or by very old men. Both women and men could pull parts of their outer garments up over their heads for protection when necessary.

Styles of hairdressing changed from time to time more than did clothing styles. Women often had elaborate hair arrangements. Men sometimes were clean-shaven, and at other times beards were popular.

Men seldom used any jewelry except a seal ring worn for practical reasons. Women, especially wealthy ones, adorned themselves with much handsome jewelry, of which many specimens have survived. Romans especially valued beautiful pearls, but they also had jewelry set with nearly every kind of precious stones except diamonds, as well as ornaments made of plain gold.

Left and right: These busts show elaborate hair styles worn by Roman women of various periods. Bust of Emperor Caracalla dates from a time when beards were popular. Earlier, in the days of Caesar and Cicero, beards were scorned as effeminate, and most men were clean-shaven.

124

Above: Box of inlaid ivory containing a woman's jewelry and toilet articles, found in a tomb at Cumae, including gold ring, earrings, ivory hairpins, cosmetics containers, and a metal mirror.

Above: Mirror and hairpins, comb and vial, probably made of alabaster as a container for perfume.

Below and right: Gold necklaces, pins, earrings, bracelet, and rings.

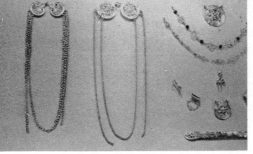

Below: Roman gold rings with and without sets, found in Switzerland. Such valuable objects have often been found where they had been hidden in times of invasion or other danger.

Lower right: Found near ancient military camp in Germany, this shoe of a Roman woman, together with a modern reproduction, is not too different from shoes worn by women today.

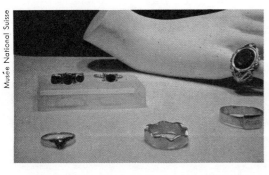

Left: Fresco from Villa of the Mysteries, Pompeii, shows a woman wearing colorful clothing. The scarf worn over the head probably was required at the religious rite the woman was watching.

Below: Vase painting shows women with colored pallae and stolae.

Below left: Empress Agrippina (seated) and the Vestal (standing) both wear the formal stola and palla in white wool.

Upper right: Statue of a camillus, a young man who took part in religious rites. The extra width of the tunic made the sleeves longer. The garment could be shortened by pulling it up over the belt knotted around the waist, thus allowing greater freedom of movement. The sandals were soles held on by an elaborate arrangement of narrow straps of leather.

Lower right: Sculptured panel shows men wearing white woolen togas over unbelted tunics. The third figure from the left shows how folds of the garment were held in place by the end of the toga thrown over the shoulder. As was proper with the toga, all the men wear shoes.

1

THE PLEIADES

Antīquitus septem sorōrēs erant. Pater erat Atlās; māter, Plēionē. Pulchrae puellae erant; erant nymphae deae Diānae.

Ōlim septem sorōrēs in silvā errābant. Subitō erant clāmōrēs. Nymphae vidēbant vēnātōrem, canēs, bēstiās ferās. Ōrīōn erat vēnātor; bēstiās agitābat. 5

Vēnātor sagittās portābat, quod bēstiās ferās necāre amābat. Bēstiae territae fugiēbant.

Territae quoque erant septem puellae; fugere dēsīderābant. Nymphae autem fugere nōn poterant, quod vēnātōrem et canēs timēbant. 10

"Ō Diāna, nōs audī! Servā nōs!" clāmābant puellae.

Ex caelō Diāna septem nymphās spectābat. Canēs et

septem seven • **sorōrēs** (nom.) sisters • **pater** (nom.) father • **māter** (nom.) mother • ***clāmōrēs** (nom.) noises **vēnātōrem** (acc.) hunter • **canēs** (acc.) dogs • **agitābat** was hunting • **fugiēbant** were fleeing • **fugere** flee **nōs** (acc.) us

Delos as it appears from the air

vēnātōrem quoque spectābat. Clāmōrēs audiēbat Diāna; puellās territās audiēbat.

Subitō puellae pulchrae et timidae nōn jam in terrā erant. 15 Septem nymphae erant stellae in caelō.

Hodiē septem stellās noctū spectāre possumus. Stellās appellāmus Plēiades, quod fīliae Plēionēs sunt.

Plēiades, quod in terrā vēnātōrem fugere dēsīderāvērunt, in caelō quoque Ōrīōnem fugere temptant. 20

2

ORION, THE HUNTER

Ōrīōn vēnātor deam Diānam amābat. Apollō autem, frāter Diānae, Ōrīōnem nōn amābat.

"Ōrīōn mē nōn dēlectat," dīxit Apollō. "Bonus nōn est; Diānam in mātrimōnium dūcere nōn poterit."

Ōlim prope ōram maritimam ambulābant Apollō et soror 5 Diāna. Deus et dea arcūs et sagittās portābant. Ōrīōn procul in aquīs natābat.

Subitō Apollō dīxit, "Spectā, Diāna, saxum in aquīs. Longinquum est, sed in saxum sagittam mittere possum. In saxum, quod est longinquum, sagittam mittere nōn potes." 10

"Manē!" respondit Diāna. "Saxum videō. Sagittam in saxum mittere facile possum. Spectā!"

Statim erat clāmor. Nōn erat saxum in aquīs; erat caput Ōrīōnis. Sagitta Diānae Ōrīōnem necāvit. Vēnātor mortuus est, et undae corpus ad ōram maritimam portāvērunt. 15

Nunc Diāna misera lacrimābat. Frāter Apollō autem nōn lacrimābat. Diāna erat tūta, quod vēnātor mortuus erat.

Posteā Juppiter Ōrīōnem et canēs in caelō posuit. Nōn jam Ōrīōn in silvīs vēnātor est; stella in caelō est.

vēnātor (nom.) hunter • **frāter** (nom.) brother • **dēlectat** pleases • **in mātrimōnium dūcere** marry • **soror** (nom.) sister • **arcūs** (acc.) bows • **natābat** was swimming **mittere** (to) shoot, send • **facile** easily • **caput** (nom.) head • **mortuus** dead • **corpus** (acc.) body • **lacrimābat** was crying • **tūta** safe • **posuit** put

128

In this mosaic, Alcestis is being led by Mercury to the underworld. It is part of a series called the Porcareccia Mosaics in the Vatican.

XXI

THE SHEPHERD OF ADMETUS

Ōlim Juppiter īrātus Phoebum Apollinem ad terram mittere in animō habet; fīlium pūnīre cupit.

Phoebō fīliō dīcit, "In Olympō manēre nōn potes. Per annum eris servus in terrā."

Phoebus Apollō ad Thessaliam, rēgnum Admētī, volat; in 5 rēgiam venit. Admētō dīcit, "Servus sum; in agrīs tuīs labōrābō."

Admētus laetus est quod bonum servum dēsīderat. Phoebō rēx dīcit, "Servum dēsīderō; eris pāstor° in agrīs meīs."

Phoebus Apollō est deus sōlis°; itaque per annum agrī 10 Admētī magnam cōpiam frūmentī dant. Incolae Thessaliae sunt laetī.

Interim autem ōrāculum monet rēgem Admētum, "Moritūrus° es!"

Apollō territum Admētum juvāre cupit; auxilium igitur 15 Fātōrum rogat.

"Admētus, bonus rēx Thessaliae, est amīcus meus," dīcit. "Date vītam Admētō aeternam."

Fāta autem respondent, "Vītam Admētō aeternam dare nōn possumus sine auxiliō incolārum Thessaliae. Statim 20 incola vītam prō Admētō dare dēbet."

Populus maestus[1] verba Fātōrum audit. Nūllus autem incola Thessaliae vītam prō Admētō dare cupit.

Dēnique Alcestis, rēgīna Thessaliae, verba Fātōrum audit et magnō cum gaudiō vītam prō Admētō dat. Statim Juppiter 25 Phoebum ad Olympum revocat. Rēx et amīcī rēgīnam mortuam ad sepulchrum° portant. Tum Admētus maestus[1] ad rēgiam revenit.

Interim Herculēs, amīcus Admētī, ad Thessaliam venit. Herculēs dē sacrificiō Alcestis audit; statim ad sepulchrum 30

°**pās′tor** (nom. sing.) shepherd • **sō′lis** (gen. sing.) of the sun
moritū′rus, -a, -um about to die • **sepul′chrum, -ī*** N., grave, sepulchre

---

[1]Translate as an adverb: "sadly." In Latin an adjective is frequently used with adverbial force. Here **maestus** serves as an adverb that answers the question "How?"

properat. Vincere mortem° et rēgīnam servāre in animō habet.

Prope sepulchrum Herculēs cum deō mortis° pugnat et rēgīnam bonam līberat. Juppiter et Alcestī et Admētō dōnum vītae longae dat. ³⁵

°**mor′tem** (acc. sing.); **mor′tis** (gen. sing.) death

*vī′ta, -ae	F., life
a′nimus, -ī	M., mind; **in animō habēre,** intend, have in mind
fī′lius, -ī	M., son
ser′vus, -ī	M., slave, servant
*auxi′lium, -ī	N., help, aid
frūmen′tum, -ī	N., grain
maes′tus, -a, -um	sad
dē′beō, -ēre, -uī	ought (with infinitive)
cu′piō, -ere, -i′vī	desire, wish
mit′tō, -ere, mī′sī	send
vin′cō, -ere, vī′cī	conquer
*pū′niō, -īre, -i′vī	punish
ve′niō, -īre, vē′nī	come
*in′terim	meanwhile
⁺prō	(with abl.) for, for the sake of

CONJUGATIONS III AND IV IN PRESENT TENSE

III	III-iō	IV	Person Endings
Singular	Singular	Singular	Singular
1 di′cō	ca′piō	au′diō	-ō
2 di′cis	ca′pis	au′dīs	-s
3 di′cit	ca′pit	au′dit	-t
Plural	Plural	Plural	Plural
1 di′cimus	ca′pimus	audī′mus	-mus
2 di′citis	ca′pitis	audī′tis	-tis
3 di′cunt	ca′piunt	au′diunt	-nt

Capiō is like **dīcō** in all forms of present tense except first person singular and third person plural, which are like **audiō**.

Mittō and **vincō** (in this lesson) are conjugated like **dīcō**

131

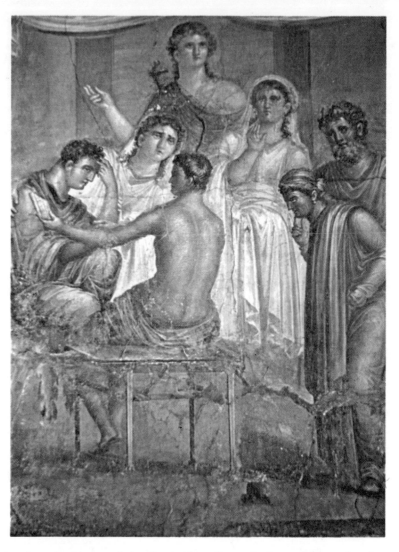

Wall painting from the House of the Tragic Poet, Pompeii, shows Admetus hearing the oracle's prophecy from a messenger. Alcestis, dressed as a bride, tries to comfort her husband, as her parents and a horrified bridesmaid stand by. The figure in the rear, with a quiver of arrows, is either Diana or Apollo.

in the present system, as are also **dēfendō, dūcō,** and **pōnō,** forms of which were introduced earlier.

Cupiō (in this lesson) and **faciō** (earlier) are like **capiō.**

Pūniō, reveniō, and **veniō** (all in this lesson) are like **audiō.**

THIRD AND FOURTH CONJUGATIONS

Verbs of third conjugation have **-ere** in the infinitive: **dīcere** (say), **capere** (take).

Verbs of fourth conjugation have **-īre: audīre** (hear).

I Translate. Point out verbs of Conjugations III and IV.

1 Pīrātae gemmās capere nōn potuērunt.
2 Agricolae equōs habēre dēbent.
3 Athēna incolās Graeciae juvāre amāvit.
4 Servus in Ītaliā habitāre cupit.
5 Rēgīna prōvinciam vincere poterit.
6 Audīsne mūsicam lyrae?

II Translate.

1 They take.
2 He hears.
3 Do you (sing.) punish?
4 He is able to say.
5 You (sing.) want to walk, don't you?
6 You (pl.) come.
7 I can conquer.
8 We say.

III Give the present stem of each verb, using the present infinitive as a clue.

1 līberō
2 nūntiō
3 dēbeō
4 audiō
5 dēleō
6 recūsō
7 veniō
8 videō
9 dīcō
10 capiō
11 spectō
12 respondeō

SCRAMBLED SENTENCES

Unscramble the words, if necessary, to make sentences, and translate.

1 cupit bonus bellum nōn vir.
2 dēfenduntne Rōmam dī?
3 dēbēs servum nōnne pūnīre pigrum?
4 interdiū silvā errāmus in saepe.

USEFUL LATIN EXPRESSIONS

Prō certō habeō I'm sure
Sententiam dīcere to express an opinion
Verba facere to make a speech
Verba dare to be impudent

133

Plate of Italian majolica with Jupiter, Mercury, Iris, and the rainbow pictured in the decorative enamel that coats this kind of pottery

XXII

MESSENGERS OF THE GODS

Antīquitus Juppiter, rēx deōrum, dīxit, "Dīvidam orbem° terrārum in tria° rēgna. Rēx erō caelī terraeque. Jūnō rēgīna mea erit. In Olympō habitābimus, sed incolae terrae nōs° interdum in templīs atque in silvīs vidēbunt."

Deinde Juppiter dīxit, "Neptūnus reget Ōceanum et 5 aquās quae° in Ōceanum fluunt. Scēptrum nōn habēbit; semper tridentem° portābit."

Dēnique Juppiter dīxit, "Plūtō erit rēx mortuōrum; sub terrā in rēgnō Orcī reget."

Saepe rēx deōrum nūntiōs ad Plūtōnem, ad Neptūnum, 10 ad rēgna terrae mittere cupit.

Itaque ōlim Mercurium Juppiter vocāvit et dīxit, "Eris

°**or′bem terrā′rum** the world • **tri′a*** N. (nom., acc. pl.)
three • **nōs** (nom., acc. pl.) we, us • **quae** F. (nom. pl.)
which • **triden′tem*** (acc. sing.) three-pronged spear, trident

nūntius deōrum. Ālās habēbis—ālās in soleīs° et ālās in petasō.° Cādūceus tuus et jānuās et portās semper aperiet."

Itaque Mercurius etiam jānuās sepulchrōrum aperit et 15 mortuōs ad rēgnum Plūtōnis dūcit. Dum Mercurius petasum gerit, mortālēs° nūntium deōrum vidēre nōn possunt.

Jūnō, rēgīna deōrum, nūntiam quoque habet. Īris, dea arcūs pluviī,° jussa° Jūnōnis ad mortālēs portat. In pallā deae multī sunt colōrēs.° Cum Īris per caelum volat, multī 20 colōrēs sub radiīs sōlis lūcent.

°so'lea, -ae* F., sole, sandal • **pe'tasus, -ī** M., hat **mortā'lēs*** (nom., acc. pl.) mortals • **ar'cūs plu'viī** (gen. sing.) of the rainbow • **jus'sa** N., (nom., acc. pl.) orders **colō'rēs*** (nom., acc. pl.) colors

ā'la, -ae	F., wing
nūn'tia, -ae	F., messenger
*pal'la, -ae	F., cloak, palla; tapestry
*por'ta, -ae	F., gate
nūn'tius, -ī	M., messenger; message, news
lū'ceō, -ēre, lūx'ī	shine
*flu'ō, -ere, flūx'ī	flow
ge'rō, -ere, ges'sī	wear, carry, conduct
re'gō, -ere, rēx'ī	direct, rule
ape'riō, -īre, -uī	open
et'iam	also, even
dum	(with pres. tense) while

FUTURE TENSE SIGN OF CONJUGATIONS III AND IV

is -ē-, followed by the person endings. Before final -t and -nt the -e- is short, and in first person singular -a- occurs instead of -e-.

	Singular		Plural	
First Person:	**-am**	I shall ...	**-ēmus**	we shall ...
Second Person:	**-ēs**	you will ...	**-ētis**	you will ...
Third Person:	**-et**	he will ...	**-ent**	they will ...

Verbs of -iō conjugations (III-iō and IV) have -i- before the tense sign: **capiam** (I shall take); **audiēs** (you will hear).

135

CONJUGATIONS III AND IV IN FUTURE TENSE

III	III-iō	IV	Person Endings
Singular	**Singular**	**Singular**	**Singular**
1 **dī′cam**	**ca′piam**	**au′diam**	-m
2 **dī′cēs**	**ca′piēs**	**au′diēs**	-s
3 **dī′cet**	**ca′piet**	**au′diet**	-t
Plural	**Plural**	**Plural**	**Plural**
1 **dīcē′mus**	**capiē′mus**	**audiē′mus**	-mus
2 **dīcē′tis**	**capiē′tis**	**audiē′tis**	-tis
3 **dī′cent**	**ca′pient**	**au′dient**	-nt

I Change all present tenses to future and all future tenses to present. Translate each verb form with a suitable pronoun subject.

1 audīs
2 dēbēs
3 manent
4 nārrābunt
5 capitis
6 habēbō
7 habitābunt
8 poterō
9 erunt
10 dīcent
11 capiam
12 veniunt

II Complete each Latin sentence by translating the underlined English words. Translate the completed sentences.

1 Mox rēx servō auxilium will give.
2 Meus amīcus neque templum neque ōrāculum vidēre wishes.
3 Will Juppiter invidiōsam fēminam punish?
4 Rōmānī mox rēgiam splendidam will build.
5 Pīrātae saepe frūmentum agricolārum seize.
6 You will come ad meam casam, amīcī, won't you?

III From the list select endings for future tense of verbs of Conjugations III-IV. Combine each verb element with a different ending to form a complete "conjugation" in future tense.

Verb Elements	Endings		
audi-	-am	-bis	-ēs
capi-	-āmus	-bitis	-et
dīc-	-ant	-bō	-ētis
ger-	-bam	-bunt	-imus
veni-	-bant	-ēmus	-ō
vinc-	-bās	-ent	-unt

136

XXIII

SCHOOL OF THE CENTAURS

The Italian artist Batoni (1708-1787) painted Chiron, teacher of Achilles.

Magnīs in silvīs Graeciae habitābant Centaurī, quī° capita° virōrum, sed corpora° equōrum habēbant. Centaurus ēgregius erat Chīrōn, quī erat magister magnae scholae.

In scholā Chīrōn dē vēnātiōne,° dē medicīnā, dē mūsicā, dē stellīs caelōque discipulīs multa mōnstrābat. 5

Antīquitus, dum rēgna dēfendunt, multī rēgēs° fīliōs in scholam Centaurōrum mittēbant.

Interdum fīliī per multōs annōs apud Centaurōs manēbant. Inter discipulōs ēgregiōs erant Jāsōn, Achillēs, Herculēs, quī in scholā Centaurōrum arma gerere discēbant. Chīrōn 10 magister bonus erat.

Achillēs hastā gladiōque bene pugnābat; laetus erat quod Chīrōn cōnsilia bellī docēbat.

"Aliquandō," inquit Achillēs, "meō prō populō et meā prō patriā pugnābō. Magna erit mea glōria et populus mē 15 laudābit."

Jāsōn autem bellum nōn amābat; magnum rēgnum cupiē-bat. Jāsōn studiīs medicīnae, mūsicae, stellārum caelīque sē° dedit.

Saepe dīcēbat, "Aliquandō magnum rēgnum habēbō. 20 Nāvigābō multa per perīcula; habēbō magnam glōriam."

Herculēs erat altus et validus; propter magnam vim° aliōs superābat puerōs. In silvīs bēstiās perīculōsās celeriter aut sagittā aut hastā aut clāvā interficere poterat.

Saepe Chīrōn dīcēbat, "Achillēs, Jāsōn, Herculēs magnam 25 glōriam terrā marīque° habēbunt, sed Herculēs sōlus locum inter deōs Olympī habēbit."

Mox Chīrōn, Centaurus ēgregius, quoque locum in caelō habet. Sagittārius est Chīrōn inter stellās.

°**quī** M. (nom. sing., pl.) who • **ca'pita*** (nom., acc. pl.) heads **cor'pora*** (nom., acc. pl.) bodies • **vēnātiō'ne** (abl. sing.) hunt-ing • **rē'gēs** (nom., acc. pl.) kings • **sē** (acc. sing.) himself **vim*** (acc. sing.) force, power, strength • **ter'rā mari'que** on land and sea

---

***pa'tria, -ae**	F., native country
***disci'pulus, -i**	M., pupil, student, disciple
lo'cus, -i	M., place (pl. usually N., **lo'ca**)
magis'ter, -trī	M., master, teacher

¹**a′lius, -a, -ud**	other, another
ēgre′gius, -a, -um	excellent, distinguished
su′perō, -āre, -āvī	defeat, overcome
do′ceō, -ēre, -uī	teach
dis′cō, -ere, di′dicī	learn
interfi′ciō, -ere, -fē′cī	kill
in′quit	says, said (after one or more words of a quotation)
aliquan′dō	at some time
a′pud	(with acc.) at, with

IMPERFECT TENSE in Latin indicates continuous, repeated, or customary action in past time.

Continuous: **Interdum filiī per multōs annōs apud Centaurōs manē-bant.** Sometimes the sons stayed with the Centaurs for many years.

Repeated: **Chīrōn saepe dīcēbat, "Achillēs magnam glōriam habēbit."** Chiron often said, "Achilles will have great glory."

Customary: **Achillēs hastā gladiōque bene pugnābat.** Achilles used to fight well with sword and spear.

TENSE SIGN OF THE IMPERFECT of verbs in all four conjugations is **-bā- (-ba-** before final **-m** or **-t,** and before **-nt).** It is followed by the person endings.

CONJUGATIONS I, II, III, IV IN IMPERFECT TENSE

I	**portā**		**-bam, -bās, -bat**	Singular
II	**monē**	+		
III	**dīcē**		**-bāmus, -bātis, -bant**	Plural
III-**iō**	**capiē**			
IV	**audiē**			

The tense sign **-bā-** is attached directly to the present stem in Conjugations I and II; **portā-bam, monē-bam.**

Verbs of all conjugations except the first have **-ē-** before the tense sign; **-iō** verbs (Conjugations III-**iō** and IV) have **-iē-: monē-bam, dīcē-bam;** but **capiē-bam, audiē-bam.**

---

¹Has two irregular forms in singular (all genders): **alte rius** (gen.), **a liī** (dat.).

TRANSLATION OF IMPERFECT TENSE To translate a Latin verb in the imperfect so as to show continuous, repeated, or customary action, a phrase is often needed.

portābam   I was carrying   or   I used to carry
dīcēbat   he was saying   or   he used to say

Sometimes a simple past tense is all that is needed in an English translation.

Saepe dīcēbat   He often said

Here "often" in the English sentence indicates repeated or customary action.

I Combine a verb element and ending to translate each verb phrase.

	Elements	Endings
1 They will teach	regē-	-mus
2 I kill	pūni-	-et
3 He was ruling	poteri-	-bant
4 Will you (sing.) hear	docē-	-ō
5 They were changing	dīc-	-itis
6 Will we be able	nec-	-bunt
7 You (pl.) say	audi-	-bat
8 He will punish	mūtā-	-ēs

II Change the following verbs to as many other tenses as possible, in corresponding person and number. Translate.

1 capiō	4 audiēmus	7 sum
2 gerunt	5 vincēbās	8 dīcit
3 regēs	6 docēbunt	9 properāmus

III In the sentences below select the verbs in imperfect tense and determine whether they denote continuous, repeated, or customary action. Translate the sentences.

1 Rōmānī saepe magna templa aedificābant.
2 Puerī per silvam ambulant.
3 Semper Apollō lyram portābat.
4 Multī fluviī in Ōceanum fluunt.
5 Graecī deōs Olympī adōrābant.

140

XXIV

VESTA, KEEPER OF THE FLAME

Vestals were chosen by lot from a group of girls, six to ten years old, from freeborn families. Each served thirty years, after which she could leave and marry, but seldom did. The main duty of the six vestals was to tend the sacred fire of Vesta. To let it go out was punishable by being buried alive. Statues like this of the Vestal Claudia lined the garden of the Atrium Vestae.

Initiō dea Vesta in Olympō habitābat, sed maesta erat quod dī deaeque saepe inter sē° disputābant. Vesta pācem° amābat; itaque in terram dēscendere cupiēbat.

Dēnique Vesta dīxit, "Incolae terrae flammās habent, sed ārās nōn habent." 5

Juppiter respondit, "Ad terram tē mittam; eris dea flammārum sacrārum. Incolae multārum terrārum ārās tuās aedificābunt et cūrābunt. Virī flammās ab ārīs tuīs ad terrās novās portābunt. Flammae ab ārīs Vestae semper ascendent."

Tum Vesta ad terram dēscendit. Multōs post annōs in- 10 colae Ītaliae urbem Rōmam aedificāvērunt. Mediā in urbe erat magnum templum deae Vestae. Prīmō flammae sacrae in ārā semper ārdēbant. Posteā autem Rōmānī āram nōn cūrābant; nōn jam flammae ab ārā Vestae ascendēbant.

Dea Vesta īrāta fuit. "Cūr meās flammās nōn custōdītis?" 15 rogāvit. "Flammae semper in magnā ārā ārdēre dēbent. Sī flammās dīligenter custōdiētis, tūta semper erit Rōma; aliter dī Rōmānōs pūnient."

Rōmānī respondērunt, "Puellās dēligēmus, quās° 'Virginēs Vestālēs' nōminābimus. Noctū atque interdiū Virginēs 20 Vestālēs flammās sacrās custōdient; magnam āram cūrābunt. In templō Vestae flammae semper ārdēbunt."

Posteā Rōmānī semper flammās ab ārā Vestae ad aedificium novum portābant. In focō aedificiī novī flammās sacrās pōnēbant; dea focī erat Vesta. 25

°**in'ter sē** with each other (among themselves) • **pā'cem** (acc. sing.) peace • **quās** (acc. pl.) F., whom

***aedifi'cium, -ī**	N., building, edifice
***me'dius, -a, -um**	mid; middle of
***sacer, -cra, -crum**	holy, sacred
tū'tus, -a, -um	safe, secure
***ār'deō, -ēre, ār'sī**	burn, glow
dē'ligō, -ere, -lē'gī	pick, choose
***custō'diō, -īre, -ī'vī**	guard, watch
a'liter	otherwise
***dīligen'ter**	carefully
sī	if

DIFFERENCES IN PAST TENSES (PER-FECT AND IMPERFECT) Perfect and imperfect are both past tenses in Latin. Both describe actions or circumstances in the past.

Imperfect: Continuing, repeated, customary action in the past
Perfect: A single, completed action in the past

Dī deaeque saepe inter sē disputābant. The gods and goddesses often quarreled among themselves.

In this sentence the verb in the imperfect **(disputābant)** tells of a repeated or customary action in the past. Without **saepe** it could also describe a continuing action ("were quarreling").

Incolae Ītaliae urbem Rōmam aedificāvērunt. The inhabitants of Italy built the city of Rome.

In this sentence the verb in the perfect **(aedificāvērunt)** describes a single action completed in the past.

TRANSLATE the following sentences and explain the tense of each verb.

1 **Rōmānī multōs deōs adōrābant.**
2 **Anna viam vidēre temptābat.**
3 **Nūntium nōn audīvī, quod labōrābam.**
4 **Mercurius Phoebō lyram dedit.**
5 **Herculēs in vīcum properāvit.**
6 **Herculēs clāvam portābat.**

I Change imperfects to perfects and perfects to imperfects. Translate.

1 interficiēbat	3 nārrāvit	5 dīcēbāmus	7 mānsistī
2 docuit	4 eram	6 audīvistis	8 potuērunt

II In each sentence translate only the verb or verb phrase.
1 The pupils helped the teacher.
2 The master used to teach many things about the stars.
3 At first Rome was a small village.
4 The messenger of the Gods used to fly from heaven to earth.
5 Mercury flew from Rome to Sicily.

EDUCATION OF ROMAN CHILDREN

Roman mothers took charge of training their daughters as homemakers, although some girls were allowed to attend primary school with the boys. By assisting their fathers at the day's work, boys gained practical knowledge through a sort of apprentice system.

Since Romans married very young, a girl on the eve of her wedding discarded her toys as a symbol of attaining maturity. A boy's elevation to manhood at the age of fourteen to seventeen was marked by a formal ceremony in the presence of relatives and friends. At the family shrine of the lares (household gods) a young man laid aside his bulla—a good luck charm he had worn from infancy—and exchanged his bordered toga praetexta for a pure white toga virilis. He was then escorted to the registry office for enrollment as a Roman citizen, and returned home for a festive dinner with his family and friends.

There was no system of public schools, but individual teachers maintained private elementary schools. The teachers were proverbially strict, and beatings were not uncommon. Children were often taken to school by a slave called a paedagogus. Boys might receive further instruction from scholars at Rome or be sent abroad, especially to Athens or Rhodes, for advanced work.

Writing was done on tablets of wax in a wooden frame, the letters being formed by scratching the wax surface with a stylus which had a flattened end for erasing. A large percentage of Romans could read and write, a fact proved by comments scratched or painted by ordinary people on walls, pillars, and other objects.

Arithmetic was difficult because of the unwieldy Roman numerals. Children learned to count on their fingers, and to use an abacus such as the Chinese still use.

Advanced education included the study of literature, geometry, and music, public speaking, and sports such as wrestling, swimming, discus throwing, and racing.

Right: A Roman boy as he might have appeared during his coming-of-age ceremony. Having put on the toga virilis, he had not yet removed his bulla, which was probably of gold like the one at the left. The boy in the fresco painting is reading a Roman book (volumen), a long sheet of papyrus rolled on two sticks.

Above: Books stored in cabinet, with title tag exposed.

Above left: Pen and styli and (center) wax tablet with cursive writing, and a mosaic of musicians beside a portable case for storing books.

Left: Rag doll from Roman Egypt shown beside a marble relief of teacher and pupil from the museum of the school at Harrow, England.

Below: Painting of Roman pupils with their teacher.

145

Temple of Aesculapius, with huge statue of the god, as envisioned by modern artist Robert Thom. Plaques and symbolic images given by grateful patients adorn the walls.

XXV

THE FIRST PHYSICIAN

Aesculāpius, quamquam fīlius Apollinis erat, in Olympō nōn habitābat; in terrā habitābat.

Aesculāpius puer in silvīs errāre amābat; ibi herbās colligēbat et medicīnam parābat. Aesculāpius vīcīnōs aegrōs medicīnā cūrāre temptābat.

Ex caelō Apollō fīlium saepe spectābat. Scientia puerī deō medicīnae grāta erat.

Apollō dīxit, "Puer magnam herbārum scientiam habet; erit medicus prīmus. Puerum ad scholam Centaurōrum dūcam."

Itaque Apollō Aesculāpium ad scholam dūxit et magistrō dīxit, "Magnam intelligentiam, Chīrōn, et parvam herbārum scientiam habet Aesculāpius. Accipiēsne puerum in scholam?"

Chīrōn fīlium Apollinis libenter accēpit. Per paucōs annōs Aesculāpius in scholā Centaurōrum manēbat.

Dēnique Chīrōn dīxit, "Medicus clārus eris; magnum in Graeciā templum aedificābis. Aegrī ā multīs terrīs ad templum tuum venient." [15]

Itaque Aesculāpius in Graeciam properāvit; ibi templum aedificāvit. Medicus ēgregius multōs aegrōs cūrābat; magister quoque erat medicae scientiae. Multī discipulī ad medicum [20] clārum veniēbant.

Magister Aesculāpius discipulīs saepe dīcēbat, "Bonī medicī herbās salūbrēs° cognōscent; medicīnam parābunt."

Posteā Aesculāpius nōn sōlum aegrōs cūrābat, sed etiam mortuōs ex sepulchrīs revocābat. [25]

Plūtō īrātus ad Olympum properāvit ab Orcō; ibi dīxit, "Aesculāpius nōn sōlum aegrōs cūrat, sed etiam vītam mortuīs dat. Sum rēx mortuōrum. Mox in rēgnō meō incolae nōn jam erunt."

Juppiter respondit, "Aesculāpius deīs magnam injūriam [30] facit. Scientiam sine sapientiā habet. Meīs fulminibus° Aesculāpium interficiam."

°**salū'brēs** (nom., acc. pl.) healthful • **fulmi'nibus** (dat., abl. pl.) thunderbolts

*scien'tia, -ae	F., knowledge, science
*me'dicus, -ī	M., doctor, physician
*vīci'nus, -ī	M., neighbor
ae'ger, -gra, -grum	sick, ill
*me'dicus, -a, -um	medical, healing, of medicine
pau'cī, -ae, -a	(pl.) few
pa'rō, -āre, -ā'vī	prepare, furnish
*acci'piō, -ere, -cē'pī	take, receive, accept
cognōs'cō, -ere, cognō'vī	become acquainted with, recognize
col'ligō, -ere, -lē'gī	bring together, collect
fa'ciō, -ere, fē'cī	do, make
i'bi	there, in that place
liben'ter	with pleasure, gladly
nōn sō'lum ... sed et'iam	not only ... but also
quam'quam	although

THE PRESENT SYSTEM OF VERBS consists of the present, imperfect, and future tenses. Each verb form in these tenses begins with the present stem.

SUMMARY OF THE PRESENT SYSTEM

	I	II	III	III-iō	IV
Present:	cūrat	habet	regit	facit	venit
Imperf.:	cūrābat	habēbat	regēbat	faciēbat	veniēbat
Future:	cūrābit	habēbit	reget	faciet	veniet

A complete table of conjugations may be found in the Summary of Grammar at the back of this book.

I Select the verb form which correctly completes each sentence, and translate.

1 Sōl in cavernam obscūram nōn lūcēbant/lūcēs/lūcēbat.
2 Puellae timidae erant, sed saepe in silvā ambulāvit/ambulō/ambulābant.
3 Mox ārsimus/ārdēbat/ārdēbunt multae flammae clārae in ārīs.
4 Dēnique fēmina pulchra vītam prō servō dat/dedit/dabit.
5 Posteā rēgīna superba et fīlia sunt/fuit/erant stellae in caelō.
6 Veniēsne/Vīdistīne/Vocatne hodiē ursam prope vīcum?

II Translate each sentence first with one Latin verb, then with the other. In translating each version omit all unnecessary Latin words.

1 Paucī pīrātae arcās aureās capiunt/cupiunt.
2 Puerī cum servō in silvā errant/erant.
3 Dēbuistīne apud nōs manēre/nōs monēre?
4 Virī validī galeās gerēbant/hastās gerēbant.
5 Fīliae multa grāta nōbīs dīcent/nōs docent.

SCRAMBLED SENTENCES Unscramble the words to make sentences, and translate.

1 paucī custōdient aedificium dīligenter virī.
2 ad portāvit sacrum nūntius scēptrum Olympum.
3 discipulī grātum erat studium magistrō.

148

REVIEW OF UNIT VI

LESSONS XXI—XXV

Nouns	Adjectives	Verbs (cont.)	Adverbs
āla, -ae	alius, -a, -ud	cognōscō, -ere	aliquandō
nūntia, -ae	ēgregius, -a, -um	colligō, -ere	aliter
*palla, -ae	maestus, -a, -um	cupiō, -ere	*dīligenter
*patria, -ae	*medicus, -a, -um	dēligō, -ere	etiam
*porta, -ae	*medius, -a, -um	discō, -ere	ibi
*scientia, -ae	tūtus, -a, -um	faciō, -ere	*interim
*vīta, -ae	aeger, -gra, -grum	*fluō, -ere	libenter
animus, -ī	*sacer, -cra, -crum	gerō, -ere	
*discipulus, -ī	paucī, -ae, -a	interficiō, -ere	Conjunctions
*filius, -ī		mittō, -ere	dum
locus, -ī	Verbs	regō, -ere	nōn sōlum
magister, -trī	parō, -āre	vincō, -ere	sed etiam
*medicus, -ī	superō, -āre	aperiō, -īre	quamquam
nūntius, -ī	ārdeō, -ēre	*custōdiō, -īre	sī
servus, -ī	dēbeō, -ēre	*pūniō, -īre	
*vicīnus, -ī	doceō, -ēre	veniō, -īre	Preposition
*aedificium, -ī	lūceō, -ēre	inquit	apud
*auxilium, -ī	*accipiō, -ere		
frūmentum, -ī			

I Bearing in mind the stories of this unit, connect each numbered statement with the lettered statement to which it logically belongs.

1 Incolae terrae arcum pluviī saepe in caelō vidēbant.
2 Puerī in scholā arma gerere discēbant.
3 Ālās habēbat—ālās in soleīs et ālās in petasō.
4 In pallā deae multī colōrēs erant.
5 Flammae sacrae semper in magnā ārā ārdēre dēbent.
6 In focō aedificiī novī flammās sacrās pōnēbant.
7 Scientia puerī deō medicīnae grāta erat.
   a) Mercurium Juppiter vocāvit.
   b) Centaurus ēgregius erat Chīrōn.
   c) Aesculāpius fīlius Apollinis erat.
   d) Īris jussa Jūnōnis ad mortālēs portābat.
   e) Vesta in terram dēscendere cupiēbat.

149

II Select from each group the verb form which differs in some respect from the rest, and justify your answer.

1 errāmus, dēbēbās, dīcēbātis, amābant, pūniēbam
2 respondit, jūvistī, accēpērunt, custōdītis, rogāvimus
3 poterō, audiam, mittunt, vidēbunt, veniēmus
4 aperīmus, nūntiāvit, dūcit, manēs, accipiunt
5 stā, vince, date, pugnā, ārdē

III Add all possible endings to each verb element and translate each completed verb. If certain vowels are changed in length, additional combinations are possible.

Elements		Endings	
1 pōnē-	6 cupi-	a) -s	e) -te
2 veni-	7 timēb-	b) -m	f) -nt
3 dīx-	8 nūntiābā-	c) -istī	g) -it
4 cognōsce-	9 pūnia-	d) -ō	
5 accipiēba-	10 habu-		

IV Using underlined words as clues, complete each sentence with the appropriate verb form.

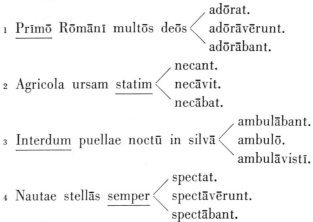

1 Prīmō Rōmānī multōs deōs ⟨ adōrat.
adōrāvērunt.
adōrābant.

2 Agricola ursam statim ⟨ necant.
necāvit.
necābat.

3 Interdum puellae noctū in silvā ⟨ ambulābant.
ambulō.
ambulāvistī.

4 Nautae stellās semper ⟨ spectat.
spectāvērunt.
spectābant.

V Translate each sentence with each of the verb forms, bringing out the difference in tense.

1 Flammae clārae in ārīs deae ārdēbunt/ārdēbant/ārdent.
2 Puer ā virīs novīs fūgit/fugit/fugiet, quod nautās timet.
3 Flammās ab ārā dēsīderābāmus/dēsīderāvimus/dēsīderāmus.
4 Gemmās per nostrōs amīcōs dīvidētis/dīviditis/dīvidēbātis.
5 Jānuam scholae magnō cum gaudiō aperuī/aperiam/aperiēbam.

Though badly damaged, this carved relief from the Ara Pacis (Altar of Peace), erected by Augustus, gives an impression of majesty. It represents Aeneas, first ancestor of the Romans, conducting a sacrifice. One attendant carries cakes and wine, the other drives a pig to be offered to the gods.

XXVI

Per multōs annōs Numa, rēx secundus, Rōmam regēbat.
Numa erat vir bonus.

Ōlim Numa dīxit, "Deus Mārs est amīcus populī Rōmānī.
Aedificābimus magnum templum pulcherrimum."

Templum novum erat deō grātum et Mārs populum saepe 5
juvābat. Ōlim autem erat pestilentia magna in Ītaliā. Numa
dolēbat, quod multī incolae Rōmae aegerrimī erant.

Tum agricola bonus ad rēgiam vēnit; scūtum novum portābat. Numae dīxit, "Hodiē in meō agrō labōrābam. Subitō
clārissimam flammam in caelō vīdī; magnum sonum audīvī; 10
prope mē in agrō scūtum clārissimum vīdī."

Tum agricola Numae scūtum mōnstrāvit. Subitō vōx° dē
caelō clāmāvit, "Sum deus Mārs! Servā scūtum dīligenter;
ita pestilentia nōn erit in terrā tuā!"

Numa statim virōs ēgregiōs convocāvit. Scūtum mōnstrā- 15
vit et dīxit, "Scūtum ex caelō vēnit; scūtum servāre dēbēmus.
Sī scūtum servābimus, scūtum nōs servābit. Ita incolae
aegrī iterum validī erunt; pestilentia in terrā nōn erit."

Virī ēgregiī autem rogāvērunt, "Ubi scūtum erit tūtum?"

"Cēlābimus scūtum," Numa respondit. "Ūndecim° scūta 20
faciēmus. Scūta nova et scūtum magicum in locō tūtō
pōnēmus."

Itaque ūndecim scūta nova virī fēcērunt. Numa scūtum
magicum inter ūndecim scūta nova cēlāvit. Nōn jam erat
pestilentia in Italiā. Scūtum magicum erat tūtissimum. 25

°**vōx** (nom. sing.) voice • **ūn′decim** eleven

so′nus, -ī	M., sound
***secun′dus, -a, -um**	second
do′leō, -ēre, -uī	grieve, suffer

THE SUPERLATIVE OF ADJECTIVES An
adjective describes or qualifies a noun. This description or
quality may vary in degree.

Grave relief of soldier, showing fine Roman shield, as well as his other weapons

REGULAR SUPERLATIVE FORMS

Positive	Superlative
altus, -a, -um tall	**altissimus, -a, -um** tallest, very tall
fidus, -a, -um faithful	**fidissimus, -a, -um** most (very) faithful

The simple form of an adjective is called the positive. Latin indicates the highest degree, called the superlative, by a special ending. An adjective with the positive in **-us** ends in **-issimus** in the superlative, which is declined like any adjective in **-us**.

An adjective with the positive in **-er** ends in **-errimus** in the superlative, which is also declined like any adjective in **-us**.

Positive	Superlative
miser, -era, -erum unhappy, wretched	**miserrimus, -a, -um** very unhappy, unhappiest, most wretched
pulcher, -chra, -chrum handsome, beautiful	**pulcherrimus, -a, -um** handsomest, very beautiful, most beautiful

153

I Translate each sentence three times, using each adjective separately.

1 Magister discipulōs miserrimōs/ēgregiōs/validissimōs statim convocāvit.

2 Virī scūta clārissima/tria/pulcherrima cēlāvērunt.

3 Benignī/Inimīcissimī/Impigerrimī nūntiī erant.

4 Incolae invidiōsī/aegerrimī/īrātī erunt.

5 Rēx scēptrum aureum/novissimum/pulchrum servābat.

II Give the superlative of each adjective in the same number, gender, and case.

1 cārae	3 miserōs	5 sacrum	7 clārārum
2 dēnsō	4 pulchram	6 lātī	8 aeger

III Give the positive of each superlative adjective in the same number, gender, and case.

1 maestissimīs	3 pulcherrimās	5 pigerrimī	7 sacerrima
2 novissimō	4 altissimōrum	6 perītissimus	8 miserrimōs

XXVII

THE GOLDEN TOUCH

Mīdās maximā in rēgiā habitābat, ubi plūrimae arcae, urnae, lucernae, statuae erant. Mīdās erat rēx, sed beātus nōn erat, quod multum aurum cupiēbat.

Ōlim rēx Mīdās amīcum deī jūvit. Itaque deus dīxit, "Tibi,° Mīdās, praemium dabō. Quid° cupis?" 5

Mīdās respondit, "Multī multum aurum habent; aurum quoque amō. Dā mihi contāctum° aureum. Multa[1] mūtābō contāctū° aureō; tum plūrimum aurum erit in rēgiā meā."

Deus dōnum virō laetissimō dedit. Statim Mīdās multa mūtāre temptāvit. Per hortum ambulāvit; rosae fuērunt 10

°**ti′bi** (dat. sing.) to you, you • **quid** (introduces question) what
contāc′tum* (acc. sing.) **contāc′tū** (abl. sing.) touch, contact

---

[1]The neuter plural of an adjective is used alone to refer to things: **multa,** many things.

aureae. Per rēgiam ambulāvit; lucernae, urnae, statuae fuērunt aureae. Mīdās erat vir laetissimus, quod aurum spectāre amāvit.

Vesperī multōs amīcōs convocāvit; amīcīs aurum mōn-strāvit. 15

Deinde cēnam bōnam dēsīderāvit. "Parāte cēnam opti-mam," dīxit.

Mīdās autem, ubi cēnam edere temptāvit, edere nōn potuit. Cibus erat aureus! Aquam bibere temptāvit, sed aqua quoque erat aurea! Mīdās territus contāctum aureum nōn jam dē- 20 sīderābat; cēnam dēsīderābat. Nōn jam multum aurum dēsīderābat; aquam dēsīderābat.

Tum rēx miserrimus deum vocāvit. "Juvā mē! Juvā mē!" clāmāvit.

Deus erat īrātissimus, sed virum miserum servāvit; con- 25 tāctū aureō Mīdam līberāvit.

ar′ca, -ae	F., chest, box
cē′na, -ae	F., dinner
ci′bus, -ī	M., food
***hor′tus, -ī**	M., garden
au′rum, -ī	N., gold
***prae′mium, -ī**	N., reward, premium
***bi′bō, -ere, bi′bī**	drink
***e′dō, -ere, ē′dī**	eat
***ves′perī**	in the evening

These bronze cups made in the shape of a ram's head and lion's head were found at Gordion in modern Turkey in 1957. Archaeological evidence points to the fact that these cups were buried in a royal tomb, possibly that of king Midas' predecessor. They date from the eighth century B.C.

IRREGULAR SUPERLATIVE FORMS OF ADJECTIVES

Some adjectives have an entirely different word for the superlative. These examples of irregular superlatives all end in **-imus,** and have the forms of a **-us** adjective.

Positive		Superlative	
bonus, -a, -um	good	**optimus, -a, -um**	best, very good
magnus, -a, -um	large	**maximus, -a, -um**	largest, very large
malus, -a, -um	bad	**pessimus, -a, -um**	worst, very bad
multus, -a, -um	much, many	**plūrimus, -a, -um**	most, very many
parvus, -a, -um	small, little	**minimus, -a, -um**	smallest, very small

I Translate the English adjectives into Latin.

1 bad
2 best   } **puerōs**
3 good
4 largest   } **dōna**
5 smallest
6 little   } **puellae**
7 smallest
8 very bad
9 very many } **virī**
10 worst

II Translate. Caution: Give special thought to 3, 4, and 6.

1 with the longest spear
2 of a very faithful friend
3 to the largest town
4 the smallest house
5 in a very deep pond
6 on the most sacred altars
7 in the newest buildings
8 of the strongest horses

XXVIII

TOO MUCH WIND

Rēx Aeolus in parvā īnsulā Aeoliā habitābat. Rēgnum erat parvum, sed Aeolus laetus erat. Rēx in patriā ventōrum regēbat. Ventī bonī nautās juvābant, sed ventī malī magnam injūriam faciēbant. Aeolus saepe nautās juvāre temptābat.

Post bellum Trōjānum Ulixēs et sociī ad rēgnum Aeolī 5 nāvigāvērunt. Rēx benignus Graecīs auxilium dedit.

Graecī diū apud Aeolum mānsērunt. Tum Aeolō Ulixēs dīxit, "Audī mē, Aeole! Laetissimī sumus in īnsulā tuā, sed

nunc Pēnelopē, uxor° mea cārissima, mē in rēgnō Ithacā expectat; Tēlemachus quoque, fīlius meus cārissimus, mē 10
expectat. Mitte nōs ad Ithacam sine morā!"

Deinde Aeolus Graecīs nova vēla et rēmōs validōs dedit.
Ulīxī autem magnum saccum ventōrum dedit et dīxit, "Nōlī
aperīre saccum! Omnēs ventī praeter Zephyrum in saccō
sunt. Multī ventī malī sunt, sed Zephyrus ventus benignus 15
est; tē celeriter ad patriam tuam portābit."

Auxiliō Zephyrī Ulīxēs per altās aquās celeriter nāvigāvit.
Post multōs diēs° Graecī laetī ōram Ithacae vīdērunt. Nautae
malī autem, ubi terram vīdērunt, dīxērunt, "Ulīxēs multum
aurum in magnō saccō habet. Ulīxēs sē° somnō dabit. 20
Deinde saccum aperiēmus et aurum capiēmus."

Dum Ulīxēs dormit, nautae saccum aperuērunt. Statim
omnēs° ventī malī ex saccō volāvērunt. Ulīxem ex somnō excitāvit sonus ventōrum. Jam ventī aquās excitābant. Ulīxēs
et nautae ad īnsulam Aeoliam iterum vēnērunt. 25

Jam autem Aeolus Graecōs juvāre recūsāvit. "Audīte
ventōs," inquit. "Ventī īrātissimī sunt. Jūnō quoque est
īrātissima. Discēdite statim ab īnsulā meā! Vōs° nōn juvābō."

°**ux′or** (nom. sing.) wife   •   **diēs** (nom., acc. pl.) days   •   **sē**
(acc. sing.) himself   •   **om′nēs** (nom., acc. pl.) all   •   **vōs**
(nom., acc. pl.) you

rē′mus, -ī	M., oar
***sac′cus, -ī**	M., bag, sack
so′cius, -ī	M., companion, associate, partner
som′nus, -ī	M., sleep
***ven′tus, -ī**	M., wind
vē′lum, -ī	N., sail
ma′lus, -a, -um	bad, evil, wicked; (as noun) N. evil
***ex′citō, -āre, -ā′vī**	awaken, stir up
discē′dō, -ere, -ces′sī	go away, depart
***dor′miō, -īre, -ī′vī**	sleep
di′ū	long (of time only)
jam	now, already

157

Painted frieze by Pellegrino Tibaldi (1527-1597) in ducal palace, Bologna, Italy, shows Ulysses' adventures. Here Neptune stirs up waves, driving ships ashore.

NUNC AND JAM Both **nunc** and **jam** mean "now," but often a distinction in time is shown by their use.

Nunc Pēnelopē mē expectat. Penelope is waiting for me now.
Jam ventī aquās excitābant. Now the winds were stirring up the waters.

Nunc indicates a single point of time: "now"; that is, "at this time."

Jam contrasts a time with a preceding one. (Something is true now that was not true before.) **Jam** means "now"; that is, "already," "by this time."

When used with the future, **jam** may mean "soon."

IMPERATIVES OF CONJUGATIONS III AND IV

	III	III-**iō**	IV
Infinitive:	**mittere**	**capere**	**audīre**
Present Stem:	**mitte-**	**cape-**	**audī-**
Singular Imperative:	**mitte**	**cape**	**audī**
Plural Imperative:	**mittite**	**capite**	**audīte**

As in Conjugations I and II, the singular imperative of most verbs in Conjugations III and IV is the present stem. The plural imperative is the present stem with **-te** added. Notice that in Conjugation III the vowel changes to **-i-** before the ending **-te**.

158

NEGATIVE COMMANDS in Latin are expressed by **nōlī** (singular) or **nōlīte** (plural) and the infinitive of the verb.

Singular: **Nōlī aperīre saccum!** Don't open the sack!

Plural: **Nōlīte aperīre saccum!** Don't open the sack!

When only one person is addressed, the singular is used; when the command is given to more than one, the plural is used.

I Translate and explain the special significance, if any, of the adverbs.

1 Pīrāta aurum in hortō meō jam cēlāvit.
2 Nunc in ōrā maritimā virī dormiunt.
3 Pestilentia in rēgnō nōn jam erat.
4 Diū sociōs puerī in nāviculā expectābant.
5 Rēx contāctum aureum jam habet.
6 Magister līberīs fābulam jam nārrābit.

II Give the superlative of each adjective with the ending required for its use in the sentence. Translate the completed sentences.

1 Aeolus in parv- īnsulā habitābat.
2 Rēgnum nōn erat magn-, sed Aeolus laet- erat.
3 Ventī bon- nautās juvābant.
4 Aeolus Graecīs benign- erat.
5 Post mult- annōs Graecī patriam vīdērunt.
6 Ulīxēs per alt- aquās nāvigāvit.

III Give singular and plural imperatives of each verb.

1 interficiō	5 ascendō
2 custōdiō	6 dēligō
3 labōrō	7 gerō
4 doceō	8 accipiō

SCRAMBLED SENTENCES

1 **pulcherrima saepe accipiēbat rēx praemia.**
2 **prope ambulāre līberī propter nōlīte silvam obscūram bēstiās.**

XXIX

Ōlim in cavernā oppidō Cūmīs propinquā, Sibylla nōta habitābat. Post bellum Trōjānum Aenēās, dux° Trōjānus, plūrimīs cum virīs ad oppidum Cūmās nāvigāvit.

Hīc Aenēās ante jānuam cavernae Sibyllae stetit et clāmā- vit, "Audī mē, Sibylla! Ē rēgnō mortuōrum Anchīsēs, pater 5 meus, mē vocat. Dūc mē ad Orcum."

Sibylla respondit, "Noctū et interdiū jānua Orcī aperta est. Multī in rēgnum mortuōrum dēscendērunt, sed patriam iterum nōn vidēbunt. Tē ad Orcum dūcere nōn possum. Nūllī vīvī ad rēgnum mortuōrum īre° possunt." 10

"Dea Venus māter mea est," Aenēās clāmāvit. "Mē juvā- bit māter mea."

"In silvā propinquā est sacer rāmus aureus," inquit Sibylla. "Prīmum ad mē fer° rāmum aureum! Properā! Deinde tibi portam rēgnī mortuōrum mōnstrābō." 15

Aenēās sine morā in silvam obscūram properāvit. Ibi columbās geminās vīdit; lentē volābant. Columbae deae sacrae Aenēae viam mōnstrābant. Subitō Aenēās per rāmōs aurum splendidum cōnspexit.

"Ecce! Rāmus aureus!" Aenēās laetus[1] rāmum aureum 20 cēpit et ad cavernam Sibyllae portāvit.

Sibylla dīxit, "Dī tē amant. Ecce! Jānua cavernae aperta est. Nunc portābimus rāmum aureum ad Prōserpinam, rēgīnam mortuōrum."

Aenēās et Sibylla in cavernam properāvērunt; per viās 25 perīculōsās et obscūrās ambulāvērunt. Auxiliō rāmī aureī, altissimum atque lātissimum fluvium——etiam ātrum[2] Stygem——trānsīre° potuērunt.

Deinde Sibylla rēgiam Prōserpinae mōnstrāvit, et Aenēās rāmum aureum in jānuā rēgiae posuit. Dōnum erat rēgīnae 30 grātissimum.

°**dux** (nom. sing.) leader • **ī're** to go • **fer** (sing.) bring!
trānsī're to go across, to cross

---

[1]An adjective may sometimes be translated as an adverb, as here: "Aeneas joyfully," etc.
[2]**Āter** (black) and **albus** (white) are found only in the positive.

Dēnique Aenēās cum Sibyllā per Campōs Ēlysiōs ad locum quiētum vēnit, ubi Anchīsēs fīlium expectābat. Hīc Anchīsēs fīliō multa futūra nārrāvit et multa Orcī mōnstrāvit.

colum'ba, -ae	F., dove
***mā'ter**	F., mother
***pa'ter**	M., father
ā'ter, -tra, -trum	black
ge'minus, -a, -um	twin-born, twin
vī'vus, -a, -um	alive, living
cōnspi'ciō, -ere, cōnspex'ī	catch sight of, look at
ec'ce	see! behold!
hīc	here
***prī'mum**	(at) first
***an'te**	(with acc.) in front of, before

IRREGULAR IMPERATIVES

Dūc mē ad Orcum! Lead me to Orcus!
Dīc nōbīs nōmen tuum. Tell us your name.

The imperatives of **dīcō, dūcō, faciō,** and **ferō** differ from those of other verbs in the singular: **dīc, dūc, fac, fer.** The plurals of the first three are regular: **dīcite, dūcite, facite.** The plural of **fer** is **ferte.**

I Give imperative singular of each verb.

1 dīcō   3 dormiō   5 edō   7 juvō
2 dō   4 dūcō   6 faciō   8 moneō

II Complete each sentence by translating each underlined English word or phrase with a suitable word from the list. Translate the completed sentences.

1 To many Mīdās fābulam nārrāvit.   a) aedificāre
2 Magister to the pupils benignissimus erat.   b) dēbēmus
3 Amīcōs juvāre semper we ought.   c) discipulīs
4 Puerī casam parvam to build temptant.   d) monēte
5 Virī jānuās templī dēfendere nōn were able.   e) multīs
6 Warn agricolās dē perīculō.   f) poterant

161

REVIEW OF UNIT VII

LESSONS XXVI—XXIX

Nouns	Nouns (cont.)	Verbs	Adverbs
arca, -ae	aurum, -ī	*excitō, -āre	diū
cēna, -ae	*praemium, -ī	doleō, -ēre	ecce
columba, -ae	vēlum, -ī	*bibō, -ere	hīc
cibus, -ī	*māter	cōnspiciō, -ere	jam
*hortus, -ī	*pater	*edō, -ere	*prīmum
rēmus, -ī	Adjectives	discēdō, -ere	*vesperī
*saccus, -ī	āter, -tra, -trum	*dormiō, -īre	Preposition
socius, -ī	geminus, -a, -um		*ante
somnus, -ī	malus, -a, -um		
sonus, -ī	*secundus, -a, -um		
*ventus, -ī	vīvus, -a, -um		

I By changing, adding, or subtracting only one letter make as many other verb forms as possible from those given, and translate. If necessary, length of vowels may be changed.

1 servābit
2 jacēbant
3 erunt
4 pōnēmus
5 jūvit
6 dūc
7 posuit
8 potuistī
9 mitte
10 dormī
11 regēbat
12 volābitis
13 poteris
14 faciunt
15 videō
16 aperiēmus
17 potes
18 respondet

II Change all singular imperatives to plural, and all plural imperatives to singular.

1 dolē
2 facite
3 stā
4 rege
5 ferte
6 pōnite
7 audī
8 dūc
9 dīcite
10 discēde

III Using the vocative expressions as clues, supply the appropriate form of the verb in parentheses.

1 (**Juvō**) nōs, dī benignī.
2 (**Nārrō**) mihi, Mārce, fābulam dē pīrātīs.
3 (**Mittō**), agricolae, puerōs ad agrōs.
4 (**Ferō**) ad mē, amīce, scūta novissima.
5 (**Audiō**), sociī, ōrāculum deae.
6 (**Dūcō**) fīliōs tuōs ad ōram maritimam, nauta.

162

IV Select from the list an appropriate adjective to replace each English expression, and apply the proper ending.

1. Incolae <u>smallest</u> vīcī erant <u>very ill</u>.
2. Puer <u>most miserable</u> cēnam <u>very good</u> edere cupiēbat.
3. Virī <u>strong</u> cēlāre arcās aurī in locō <u>safest</u> recūsant.
4. Flammās <u>very bright</u> <u>of a great many</u> lucernārum in cavernā <u>dark</u> vīdimus.
5. Fīliae <u>twin</u> rēgīnae dolēbant, quod columba <u>sacred</u> mortua erat.
6. Fer mihi scūta <u>largest</u> et <u>best</u>.
7. Etiam dōna <u>worst</u> erunt deae <u>pleasing</u>.

a) aegerrimus
b) beātissimus
c) bonus
d) clārissimus
e) geminus
f) grātus
g) maximus
h) minimus
i) miserrimus
j) obscūrus
k) optimus
l) pessimus
m) plūrimus
n) sacer
o) tūtissimus
p) validus

V Find as many pairs of words as possible which have contrasting meanings.

1. accipere
2. aestāte
3. albus
4. ante
5. āter
6. audīre
7. bellum
8. bibere
9. cum
10. discipulus
11. edere
12. hieme
13. longinquus
14. magister
15. pācem
16. post
17. posteā
18. propinquus
19. recūsāre
20. schola
21. sedēre
22. servāre
23. sine
24. stāre
25. statim
26. templum
27. vāstāre
28. vidēre

VI Change affirmative commands to negative, and negative commands to affirmative.

1. Dā mihi rāmum aureum.
2. Nōlī facere puerīs injūriam.
3. Nōlīte accipere auxilium deae superbae.
4. Cape taedam ā nūntiō.
5. Dormī in hortō.

VII Supply a vocative of one of the nouns below for each imperative in VI, using each noun once.

magister   fēmina   servus   amīcus   dea

ARCHAEOLOGY

How have we acquired our knowledge of the ancient Romans—who they were and how they lived two thousand years ago? The two most important sources are literature and archaeology, which often verify each other.

Literature frequently provides eye-witness accounts of Roman life, descriptions of people and objects, and reports of events. Archaeology, which is the science of "digging up the past," uncovers the material remains of cities and people, such as buildings (public and private), graves and monuments, tools and utensils, clothing and jewelry, statues and paintings.

An eruption of Vesuvius in A.D. 79 buried Pompeii and Herculaneum, and preserved those cities as a showcase of Roman life. Excavation work is still going on in both cities, and archaeologists have uncovered wall paintings, furniture, charred food, and ancient coins. Enough traces of plantings have been found to restore Roman gardens, as well as the original pipes—in need of little or no repair—with which to water them. There are even replicas of bodies of Romans who died where they had fallen, choked in the rain of ashes or asphyxiated by deadly gases. (Plaster poured into the hollow impressions molds itself to the likeness of the long-dead victims.) Of the two cities, Herculaneum is harder to excavate, because it was engulfed by rivers of mud, now hardened into rock, while Pompeii was buried under layers of hot ashes. More furniture and books, however, survived in Herculaneum.

Not all discovery is by digging. Desert sands and waters of the sea and the rivers also play a part in archaeology. In the deserts of North Africa whole cities have been uncovered by brushing and blowing away drifts of sand. Other cities, left under water by changing shorelines, have been found elsewhere in the Roman world. Dredging of the Thames in London brought to light a wooden boat that had sunk at its mooring in Roman times, and divers have recovered ancient ships together with their cargoes, as an exciting achievement of underwater archaeology.

The Romans' habit of picturing everyday activities on walls and tombstones has told us much about their clothes, tools, furniture, and food.

Left: Blue glass vase with raised decorations in white enamel, called the "Portland Vase."
Above: Archaeologists at work on Ischia, island near Naples.

164

Above: Tomb relief showing bakers at work.

Below left. Temple where Augustus' record *(Res Gestae)* was inscribed.

Above right: Ruins of Sabratha, a Roman city rescued from the sands of Libya.

Right: Roman boat dredged up in the Thames River.

Bottom left: Diver with aqua-lung inspects cargo of a Roman ship sunk centuries ago off the coast of the Riviera. The jars probably held wine.

Bottom right: A ship's figurehead in form of Minerva, from Actium, site of sea battle in which Augustus defeated Antony and Cleopatra.

Nouns and adjectives of Declensions I-II and regular verbs of all four conjugations have now been presented. Many of these have English derivatives which are similar or even identical, and many belong to groups of related Latin words. Such related groups may be described as "word families."

Latin Word Families	English Word Families
liber, -era, -erum (adj.) free	liberal (adj.)
liberātor (noun) one who frees	liberator (noun)
liberō, -āre (verb) set free	liberate (verb)
sacer, -cra, -crum (adj.) sacred	sacred (adj.)
sacrificium (noun) sacrifice	sacrifice (noun)
sacrificō, -āre (verb) sacrifice	sacrifice (verb)

There are other groups of related words which have already been included in unit vocabularies or are soon to appear.

antīquus	**longus**	**prope**	**medicīna**
antiquitus	**longinquus**	**propinquus**	**medicus**
ager	**spectāculum**	**amīcus**	**perīculum**[1]
agricola	**spectō**	**amō**	**perīculōsus**
agricultūra	**expectō**	**inimīcus**	**perītus**

Nouns that have been used in the preceding units are related to certain verbs already introduced.

nōmen	**dux**	**creātor**	**vōx**	**nāvicula**
nōminō	**dūcō**	**creō**	**vocō**	**nāvigō**

To help associate these pairs of related words try forming word families of their English derivatives; for example, navicular, navigate, navy, naval, navigation.

What Latin nouns, adjectives or other verbs do you know that are related to the following verbs?

ōrō   discō   cūrō   nūntiō   fluō   aedificō

[1]Meanings of **perīculum** include not only "danger" but also "trial," "test," and "attempt," implying risk or danger of failure. Hence, **perīculōsus** and **perītus** belong rightly to the same word family, although the former means "dangerous" and the latter, "experienced" or "expert," describing one who has practised or tried something often.

3

CLOSING OF THE GATES

Lūcia et Anna per angustam viam Rōmae properant.

Anna. Ecce! Videō Secundam!

Lūcia. Properā, Secunda! Venī nōbīscum! Mox erunt multī virī, fēminae, līberī in Forō. Portās templī vidēre nōn poterimus. 5

Advena. Cūr properātis? Quō populus currit?

Lūcia. Hodiē Caesar Augustus, noster imperātor, portās templī Jānī claudere poterit.

Advena. Cūr Augustus portās templī Jānī claudet? Nōnne via per portās templī Jānī dūcit? 10

nōbīscum with us • **līberī** children • **quō** whither, where to • **currit** run • **imperātor** (nom.) emperor • **claudere** to close • **claudet** will close

The Roman Forum, where the temple of Janus once stood.

Secunda. Ita; viae autem aliae sunt. Jam est pāx Rōmāna. Posthāc Rōma nūlla bella geret. Erit pāx aeterna. Bellō Jānus mīlitēs Rōmānōs juvat; pāce in templō manet.

Anna. Frāter meus est mīles, sed frāter meus bellō nōn pugnābit. In prōvinciīs vigilābit; pācem servābit. 15

Secunda. Ecce! Videō Virginēs Vestālēs! Ecce! Videō Augustum, nostrum imperātōrem! Nunc portās claudit.

Lūcia. Jam Jānus in templō manēbit. Jam vērō erit pāx!

---

pāx (nom.) peace • **posthāc** after this • **bella...
geret** will wage wars • **aeterna*** eternal • **mīlitēs**
(acc.) soldiers • **bellō...pāce** in war...in peace • **frāter**
(nom.) brother • **mīles** (nom.) soldier • **pācem** (acc.)
peace • **imperātōrem** (acc.) emperor • **claudit** closes
vērō indeed, really

4

JANUS—A GOD WITH TWO FACES

Antīquae statuae deī Jānī duās faciēs habent—altera faciēs porrō, altera faciēs retrō spectat. Jānuae et portae quoque duās faciēs habent—altera faciēs intus, altera faciēs extrā spectat. Nōnne deus quoque jānuārum et portārum duās faciēs habēre dēbet? 5

Prīma diēs mēnsis est Jānō sacra. Prīmus mēnsis annī est Jānuārius. Nōnne Jānus deus initiōrum est?

Deus pācis bellīque quoque est Jānus. Dum bellum Rōmānī gerunt, portae templī Jānī sunt apertae. Deus abest; Rōmānōs mīlitēs juvat. Dum pācem Rōmānī servant, portae 10 templī sunt clausae; deus in templō manet.

---

duās faciēs (acc.) two faces • **altera faciēs...altera faciēs**
(nom. sing.) one face...the other face • **porrō** forward
retrō backward • **intus** inward • **extrā*** outward
diēs (nom.) day • **mēnsis** (nom. and gen.) month • **pācis**
of peace • **bellum...gerunt** wage war • **abest** is absent
mīlitēs (acc.) soldiers • **pācem** (acc.) peace • **clausae**
closed

UNIT VIII

Hercules struggles with a lion in this painting on a Greek vase.

The Nemaean Valley where Hercules overcame the lion, as it appears today

XXX

HERCULES AND THE LION

In silvīs Graeciae ōlim leō° validus habitābat. Noctū leō
magnum equōrum numerum interficiēbat; saepe incolās
interficere temptābat. Dēnique malus leō fīlium agricolae
interfēcit. Incolae vīcī ubi agricola habitābat leōnem° interficere temptāvērunt. Leō autem in dēnsam silvam fūgit.   5

Agricola clāmāvit, "Leō in silvīs nostrīs habitāre nōn
poterit; nūllus leō fīliōs et equōs nostrōs interficiet."

"Herculēs vir validissimus est. Mitte statim nūntiōs ad
Herculem!" dīxit alius agricola.

Statim incolae vīcī nūntiōs ad Herculem mīsērunt. "Audī 10
perīculum agricolārum!" dīxērunt. "Leō agricolās interficit.
Venī ad nostrum vīcum! Interfice leōnem ferum!"

Mox Herculēs in vīcum agricolārum pervēnit ubi leō equōs

°**le′ō** (nom. sing.); **leō′nem** (acc. sing.) lion

170

et virum interfēcerat.° Herculēs magnam clāvam, sed neque arcum° neque sagittās portābat. Quamquam nox° erat, statim 15 ad silvam dēnsam properāvit.

Prīmō Herculēs lentē prōcessit quod silva obscūra erat. Subitō autem parvum sonum audīvit; tum lūna clāra Herculī magnum mōnstrāvit leōnem. Celeriter Herculēs leōnem cēpit et suffōcāre° temptāvit. Ita vir et leō diū pugnāvērunt. 20 Dēnique Herculēs magnā clāvā bēstiam interfēcit. Tum in vīcum properāvit, ubi incolīs leōnem mortuum mōnstrāvit.

Herculēs clāmāvit, "Clāvā meā leōnem interfēcī! Nōn jam leō fīliōs aut equōs agricolārum interficiet."

Posteā Herculēs semper pellem° leōnis° gerēbat et clāvam 25 portābat.

°**interfē′cerat** had killed • **ar′cum** (acc. sing.) bow • **nox** (nom. sing.) night • **suffōcā′re*** to choke • **pel′lem** (acc. sing.) skin, pelt • **leō′nis** (gen. sing.) lion's

*nu′merus, -ī	M., number
fe′rus, -a, -um	wild, fierce
fu′giō, -ere, fū′gī	flee, escape
*prōcē′dō, -ere, -ces′sī	advance, proceed

CONJUGATIONS III AND IV IN PERFECT TENSE

III	III-**iō**	IV	Perfect Endings
Singular	Singular	Singular	Singular
1 **dīx′ī**	**cē′pī**	**audī′vī**	-ī
2 **dīxis′tī**	**cēpis′tī**	**audīvis′tī**	-istī
3 **dīx′it**	**cē′pit**	**audī′vit**	-it
Plural	Plural	Plural	Plural
1 **dīx′imus**	**cē′pimus**	**audī′vimus**	-imus
2 **dīxis′tis**	**cēpis′tis**	**audīvis′tis**	-istis
3 **dīxē′runt**	**cēpē′runt**	**audīvē′runt**	-ērunt

Conjugations III and IV have the same person endings in the perfect as Conjugations I and II, since these endings (used only in the perfect) are the same for all conjugations.

171

TRANSLATION OF VERBS IN PERFECT

TENSE Like **portāvī** (I) and **monuī** (II), the perfect tense of Conjugations III and IV is usually equivalent to a simple past tense in English and may be so translated. Occasionally the translation of a Latin perfect may include "have" or "has," or "did."

III	(dīcō)	dīxī	I said, I have said, I did say[1]
	(capiō)	cēpī	I took, I have taken, I did take
IV	(audiō)	audīvī	I heard, I have heard, I did hear

I With the two forms as clues, give the first three principal parts of each verb.

1 mittam, mīsistī   6 pūniēbāmus, pūnīvistis
2 aedificābant, aedificābō   7 regit, rēxit
3 custōdītis, custōdiam   8 dīcite, dīximus
4 ascendunt, ascendistī   9 dēbēbunt, dēbuit
5 ārdeō, ārsērunt   10 nōmināmus, nōmināvērunt

II Select pairs of words which have something in common, and give the reason for your choice. Example: 6 and 13 are prepositions.

1 aedificium   5 atque   9 laurus   13 praeter
3 agricola   6 circum   10 magister   14 quod
3 apertās   7 columba   11 paucās   15 rēgia
4 appellābam   8 igitur   12 posteā   16 regam

SCRAMBLED SENTENCES

1 **dīxit nautīs "altissimās nōlīte aquās nāvigāre prope" ōrāculum.**
2 **virī patriam dēfendēbant puerīque.**

SOME INTERESTING PERFECTS

Vēnī, vīdī, vīcī! I came, I saw, I conquered! (Julius Caesar said it; Suetonius recorded it.)

Quod dedit recēpit! He got what he deserved! (Comedy writer Terence used this in a play.)

Fuit!/Vīxit! He is dead (has been/has lived)! (common usage)

---

[1]In questions: "Did I say?" or "Have I said?"

The island of Aegina now shows no evidence of having been peopled by ants.

XXXI

PEOPLE FOR A KING

Rēx Aeacus erat vir bonus; semper populum suum° juvāre dēsīderābat. Populus Aeacum benignum amābat et laudābat. Incolae rēgnī, quamquam minimam pecūniam habēbant, tamen bene labōrābant et laetī erant.

Subitō magna pestilentia terram invāsit. Incolae aegrī in 5 agrīs labōrāre nōn jam poterant. Dēnique pestilentia magna virōs, fēminās, puerōs puellāsque occīdit. Oppida rēgnī incolās nōn jam habēbant.

Aeacus benignus multum dolēbat. Sine morā ad templum Jovis prōcessit. 10

Ante āram ita ōrāvit, "Ō Juppiter, magna pestilentia populum meum dēlēvit. Incolās rēgnī meī āmīsī. Aut dā mihi populum novum aut interfice mē quoque!"

Prope templum erat altissima quercus.° Multae formīcae in rāmīs erant; cibum portābant. Aeacus formīcās diū 15

°**su′um** his (own) • **quer′cus** (nom. sing.); F., oak

173

spectāvit, tum dīxit, "Quercus incolās multōs habet! Oppida mea autem nūllōs incolās habent."

Tum rēx lentē ad rēgiam prōcessit. Noctū Aeacus in somniō quercum° vīdit. Iterum formīcās vīdit, sed jam formīcae cibum nōn portābant; ā rāmīs quercūs° cadēbant. 20 In terrā nōn jam formīcae, sed virī et fēminae erant.

Postrīdiē rēx sonum novum audīvit et statim ē rēgiā properāvit. Ante tēctum multī virī et multae fēminae clāmāvērunt, "Erimus tuī incolae novī. Rēx noster eris!"

°**quer′cum** (acc. sing.); **quer′cūs** (gen. sing.) oak

formi′ca, -ae	F., ant
som′nium, -ī	N., dream
tēc′tum, -ī	N., roof; dwelling, house
dē′leō, -ēre, -ē′vī	destroy
āmit′tō, -ere, -mī′sī	lose, let go
ca′dō, -ere, ce′cidī	fall
*__invā′dō, -ere, -vā′sī__	enter, invade
occi′dō, -ere, -ci′dī	cut down, kill
+**mul′tum**	much, deeply
postri′diē	the next day
ta′men	nevertheless, still

SUMMARY AND REVIEW OF VERBS IN PERFECT TENSE according to patterns of perfect stems described on pages 118-119.

1) Perfect ending in **-vī**

   I **portāvī (portō)** and most other Conjugation I verbs
   II **dēlēvī (dēleō)**
   III **cupīvī (cupiō); cognōvī (cognōscō)**
   IV **audīvī (audiō); custōdīvī (custōdiō); dormīvī (dormiō); pūnīvī (pūniō)**

2) Perfect ending in **-uī**

   II **appāruī (appāreō); habuī (habeō); monuī (moneō); pertinuī (pertineō); timuī (timeō); valuī (valeō)**
   III **posuī (pōnō)**
   IV **aperuī (aperiō)**

174

3) Perfect ending in -sī/xī (x = cs or gs)

II   **ārsī (ārdeō); mānsī (maneō)**

III   **āmīsī (āmittō); ēmīsī (ēmittō); mīsī (mittō);**
      dīvīsī (dīvidō); invāsī (invādō)
      gessī (gerō); discessī (discēdō); prōcessī (prōcēdō)
      dīxī (dīcō); dūxī (dūcō); rēxī (regō)

IV   **sēnsī (sentiō)**

4) Perfect ending in -ī (with reduplication of verb stem)

I   **dedī (dō); stetī (stō)**

III   **didicī (discō); cecidī (cadō)**

5) Perfect ending in ī (with lengthened vowel of stem)

I   **jūvī (juvō)**

II   **mōvī (moveō); sēdī (sedeō)**
      vīdī (videō)

III   **accēpī (accipiō); cēpī (capiō); collēgī (colligō);**
      dēlēgī (dēligō); ēdī (edō); fēcī (faciō); fūgī (fugiō)
  interfēcī (interficiō); vīcī (vincō)

IV   **pervēnī (perveniō); vēnī (veniō)**

6) Perfect ending in -ī (with unchanged verb stem)

II **respondī (respondeō)**

III **ascendī (ascendō); dēscendī (dēscendō);**
  dēfendī (dēfendō); occīdī (occīdō)

7) Perfect ending in -ī (with miscellaneous changes)

III **cōnspexī (cōnspiciō); flūxī (fluō)**

I Supply Latin for words underlined. Translate each sentence.
1 Rōmānī <u>placed</u> statuam Jūnōnis in templō.
2 <u>Did you</u> (sing.) <u>kill</u> bēstiam?
3 Fīlia <u>grieved</u> per multōs annōs.
4 Prīmō lentē <u>we proceeded</u>.
5 <u>I sent</u> fīdissimum nūntium ad oppidum propinquum.

II Give the infinitive of each verb. Translate each verb form as given, supplying a pronoun subject, if needed.

1 cecidī	5 dolēbat	9 occīdit
2 gessistis	6 edent	10 posuimus
3 dā	7 jūvērunt	11 stābant
4 dēlēvit	8 invāsit	12 vīcistī

III Choose the translation [a), b), or c)] of each Latin verb and supply a pronoun subject to fit the Latin ending, if needed.

1	aedificāvērunt	a) build	b) will build	c) built
2	āmittēs	a) lose	b) will lose	c) have lost
3	dormīmus	a) are sleeping	b) were sleeping	c) have slept
4	faciētis	a) make	b) were making	c) will do
5	poterat	a) has been able	b) could	c) can
6	prōcēde	a) go forth	b) will go forth	c) went forth
7	rēgnātis	a) do rule	b) did rule	c) will reign
8	tenuistī	a) were holding	b) will hold	c) held

XXXII

KING AND WOODPECKER

Pīcus, rēx Latiī antīquī, magnam rēgiam in mediō campō habēbat. Circē, maga clāra, prope rēgiam Pīcī habitābat. Magnam et malam potentiam habēbat; saepe virōs aut in bēstiās aut in avēs° mūtābat.

Ōlim Circē Pīcum vīdit et statim amāvit. Rēx Pīcus 5 autem Circam nōn amāvit; nympham pulchram in mātrimōnium dūxit.

Circē invidiōsa dīxit, "Pīcum superbum pūniam. Corōnam Pīcus nōn geret; cristam avis° habēbit."

Postrīdiē rēx populum ad magnam cēnam convocāvit. 10 Ante cēnam autem Pīcus cum paucīs amīcīs propinquā in silvā ambulābat. Circē quoque in silvam sēcrētō prōcessit et sub altā arbore° stetit. Tum amīcī rēgis° spectāculum mīrum vīdērunt. Maga invidiōsa fōrmam Pīcī mūtāvit.

Nōn jam corōnam gerēbat Pīcus; cristam habēbat. Jam 15 manūs° Pīcī erant ālae; pedēs° erant pedēs avis; oculī erant parvī oculī avis. Etiam rōstrum avis Pīcus habēbat. Pennae multōrum colōrum° et corpus° et ālās adōrnābant.

°**a'vēs** (nom., acc. pl.) birds • **a'vis** (nom., gen. sing.) bird
ar'bore* (abl. sing.) F., tree • **rē'gis** (gen. sing.) king
ma'nūs* (nom., acc. pl.) hands • **pe'dēs*** (nom., acc. pl.) feet
colō'rum* (gen. pl.) of colors • **cor'pus*** (nom., acc. sing.) body

Hōra cēnae fuit; populus aderat; rēgīna aderat; sōlus Pīcus
aberat.   Subitō per apertam jānuam rēgiae avis pulchra 20
volāvit.   Per magnum ātrium errāvit; tum ē fenestrā rēgiae
celeriter Pīcus volāvit.

Jam Pīcus avis aut in silvīs aut in hortīs habitat. Semper
clāmat, "Ōlim rēx eram et corōnam gerēbam. Jam avis sum
et rōstrō meō cibum in silvīs et in hortīs inveniō."   25

cris'ta, -ae	F., crest
*ma'ga, -ae	F., sorceress
*pen'na, -ae	F., feather
*poten'tia, -ae	F., power, might, potency
*cam'pus, -ī	M., field
*o'culus, -ī	M., eye
rōs'trum, -ī	N., beak
*ab'sum, -esse, ā'fuī	be absent
ad'sum, -esse, ad'fuī	be present
*inve'niō, -īre, -vē'nī	come upon, find
in mātrimō'nium dū'cere	marry

T A B L E   O F   T E N S E S   The following table summarizes all
third-person singular forms of all conjugations in the four
tenses that have been taught.

	Present	Imperfect	Future	Perfect
		Present System		
I	portat	portābat	portābit	portāvit
II	monet	monēbat	monēbit	monuit
III	dīcit	dīcēbat	dīcet	dīxit
III-iō	capit	capiēbat	capiet	cēpit
IV	audit	audiēbat	audiet	audīvit
(sum)	est	erat	erit	fuit
(possum)	potest	poterat	poterit	potuit

I In "King and Woodpecker" find the Latin word for each of
these English expressions.

1 the middle of   4 a few
2 on the next day   5 (she) was present
3 I am going to punish   6 (he) was absent

II For each verb stem choose all endings directly opposite which combine with it to make correct verb forms; then translate each completed verb form.

Stems	Endings			
1 dūx-	a) -am	b) -ērunt	c) -unt	d) -ī
2 capi-	a) -t	b) -mus	c) -bant	d) -tis
3 audi-	a) -ent	b) -unt	c) -bis	d) -et
4 habu-	a) -tis	b) -it	c) -ēmus	d) -ērunt
5 amāv-	a) -istī	b) -itis	c) -ērunt	d) -imus
6 rēx-	a) -am	b) -ī	c) -unt	d) -it
7 pot-	a) -eram	b) -istis	c) -erunt	d) -es
8 pūnīv-	a) -it	b) -bant	c) -ēs	d) -istī

REVIEW OF UNIT VIII

LESSONS XXX—XXXII

Nouns	Adjective	Adverbs
crista, -ae	ferus, -a, -um	multum
formīca, -ae	Verbs	postrīdiē
*maga, -ae	*absum, -esse	tamen
*penna, -ae	adsum, -esse	
*potentia, -ae	dēleō, -ēre	Idiom
*campus, -ī	cadō, -ere	in mātrimōnium
*numerus, -ī	āmittō, -ere	dūcere
*oculus, -ī	fugiō, -ere	
rōstrum, -ī	*invādō, -ere	
somnium, -ī	occīdō, -ere	
tēctum, -ī	*prōcēdō, -ere	
	*inveniō, -īre	

I Supply the missing principal parts of each verb in usual order and give the meaning of the verb.

1 dēleō, dēlēvī		6 errō	
2 occīdō, occīdere		7 fūgī	
3 habēre		8 absum	
4 cadō, cadere		9 habitāre	
5 prōcēdō, prōcessī		10 invāsī	

178

II Supply the two forms of each verb needed to complete a synopsis (summary) of the tenses learned so far in the person and number given.

1 adestis, aderitis
2 dabāmus, dedimus
3 cadēbam, cadam
4 dīcētis, dīxistis

5 invenīs, inveniēbās
6 mittet, mīsit
7 occīdunt, occīdērunt
8 revideō, revidēbam

III Distinguish between the expressions in each group in respect to use and/or meaning.

1 aliquandō/aliter
2 diū/interdiū
3 nōn/nōnne
4 autem/etiam
5 inter/apud
6 jam/nunc
7 interim/iterum/interdum

8 dum/tum
9 hīc/ibi
10 līber/libenter
11 postrīdiē/hodiē
12 procul/propinquus
13 propter/praeter/prope
14 neque . . . neque/aut . . . aut

IV Change all singular verbs to plural and all plural verbs to singular, and make other changes necessary.

1 Rēx cēnam postulāvit.
2 Virī arma valida portābunt.
3 Ante templum multās statuās vidēbitis.
4 Deus oppidum nōmināre nōn poterit.
5 Dum virī casās faciunt, fīliī aquam portant.
6 In agrō lātissimō stābat rēgia splendida.
7 Ursam amīcam nōn necābō.

V Select the word in each group which has no connection in sense with the other words. Explain your choice.

1 māter, amita, socius, fīlia, pater
2 folium, rāmus, silva, flamma, laurus
3 sēmita, arma, scūtum, gladius, hasta
4 morbus, medicus, pestilentia, medicīna, sonus
5 vir, statua, ursa, columba, equus
6 rōstrum, oculus, penna, stella, āla
7 tēctum, rēgia, casa, crista, aedificium
8 rēmus, vēlum, nauta, umbra, nāvicula
9 rēx, signum, rēgīna, regō, corōna
10 somnus, jānua, fenestra, focus, ātrium

ROMAN BATHS

Until our own day, very few people anywhere have maintained the standard of personal cleanliness set by the ancient Romans. Running water for private bathing was piped into the better homes. The majority of Romans, however, patronized the many elaborate but inexpensive public baths. Such baths became recreational centers, providing space and equipment for exercise, reading, and conversation. They were regularly patronized before the evening dinner.

The area for bathing in a public bath consisted of at least four rooms—a warm room (tepidarium) for undressing and working up perspiration, a hot room (caldarium) for the hot bath, a cold room (frigidarium) for the cold plunge, and an anointing room (unctorium), where the patron was given a rubdown with linen towels and anointed with oil. The oil, which might be applied before or after either the hot or cold bath, was essential because soap was not used. Oil was removed by scraping with strigils.

Cities and larger towns in all parts of the Roman world had bathing establishments with provision for heating the rooms and the large amounts of hot water needed. Although women sometimes had separate bathing facilities, the same building was generally used by both men and women, with special hours for each.

Right: Caldarium (hot bath) of the bathing establishment for women in Herculaneum.

Below: The model represents the Baths of Diocletian in Rome, reconstructed from the ruins and from descriptions in literature. What now remains of the extensive structure was embodied in a Christian church.

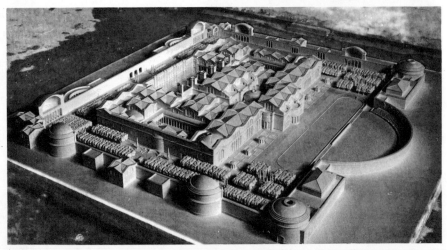

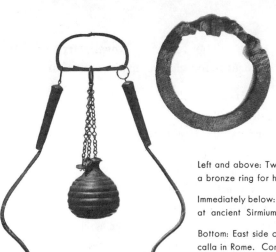

Left and above: Two scrapers and a flask for oil, beside a bronze ring for hanging objects on the wall of a bath.

Immediately below: Remains of a bath recently discovered at ancient Sirmium (now Mitrovica, Yugoslavia).

Bottom: East side of ruins of the massive Baths of Caracalla in Rome. Concerts and performances of opera are now given inside the entrance of the huge building, of which New York's Pennsylvania Station is a counterpart.

SAY IT IN LATIN! The following vocabulary of Latin expressions will be useful for classroom conversation.

Heus!	Hello! (Hi! Hey!)
Salvēte, discipulī!	Good morning (Greetings), pupils!
Salvē, magistra/magister!	Good morning (Greetings), teacher!
Adsum!	Present! (I am here!)
Ubi est Virginia?	Where is Virginia?
Abest; aegra est.	She is absent; she is ill.
Ubi est Paulus?	Where is Paul?
Abest; aeger est.	He is absent; he is ill.
Cōnsīde/Cōnsīdite!	Sit down (be seated)!
Surge/Surgite!	Stand up (rise)!
Claude fenestram/jānuam!	Close the window/door!
Aperī fenestram/jānuam!	Open the window/door!
Aperīte librōs!	Open your books!
Claudite librōs!	Close your books!
Pōnite librōs!	Lay aside your books!
Audī/Audīte!	Listen!
Spectā/Spectāte!	Look! Watch!
Lege/Legite Anglicē/Latīne!	Read in English/Latin!
Verte/Vertite Anglicē!	Change to English!
Verte/Vertite Latīne!	Change to Latin!
Scrībe/Scrībite in tabulā!	Write on the (chalk)board!
Crētam mihi dā!	Give me the chalk!
Sūmite chartam et stilōs!	Take paper and pencils!
Chartās in mēnsā pōnite!	Put your papers on the table!
Chartam tuam dā!	Give me your paper!
Chartās vestrās date!	Give me your papers!
Rēctē (lēgistī/lēgistis)!	Right! (You have read correctly!)
Bene!	Good!
Optimē!	Very good! Excellent!
[1]Errāstī/Errāstis!	You have made a mistake!
Iterum! or Repete/Repetite!	Again! (Repeat!)
Quaesō! or [1]Sīs/Sultis!	Please! (If you please!)
Grātiās tibi/vōbīs agō!	Thanks! (I thank you!)
Ignōsce/Ignōscite mihi!	Pardon me! (I beg your pardon!)
Valēte, . discipulī!	Good-by, pupils!
Valē, magistra/magister!	Good-by, teacher!

[1]Errāstī = Errāvistī; Errāstis = Errāvistis.   Sīs = Sī vīs; Sultis = Sī vultis.

Probably the most famous representation of Perseus is this statue by Benvenuto Cellini (1500-1571), which stands in the Loggia dei Lanzi of Florence, Italy.

XXXIII

PERSEUS AND THE GORGON

Medūsa erat Gorgō. Quamquam fōrmam puellae pulchrae habēbat, Medūsa serpentēs locō comae habēbat.

Gorgō in saxum mūtābat eōs quī° faciem° ejus spectābant. Mox populus Medūsam propter malam ejus potentiam timēbat.

In rēgiā rēgnī vīcīnī Perseus habitābat. Rēx invidiōsus 5 erat et Perseum dīmittere dēsīderābat.

Rēx igitur Perseum vocāvit et eī dīxit, "Pete Medūsam; necā id mōnstrum. Maximum erit perīculum, sed maximam habēbis glōriam."

Statim Perseus Medūsam petere et necāre cōnstituit. 10 Prīmō autem auxilium deōrum ōrāvit.

Plūtō Perseō galeam dedit magicam. "Sī eam galeam magicam gerēs," dīxit deus, "nūllus tē vidēre poterit."

°**quī** M. (nom. sing., pl.) who • **fa′ciem*** (acc. sing.) face

This head of Medusa is in the Capitoline Museum of Rome.

184

Mercurius dedit eī soleās ālātās et gladium magicum. "Sī
eās soleās gerēs," is dīxit, "nūllus tē dēprehendere poterit. 15
Gladiō magicō autem mōnstrum sine perīculō interficiēs."

Minerva Perseō scūtum splendidum dedit. "Scūtum
clārum est speculum," ea dīxit. "In eō speculō Medūsam
vidēre poteris. Ea autem tē in saxum mūtāre nōn poterit,
quod faciem ejus tantum in speculō spectābis." 20

Perseus deīs grātiās ēgit. Tum ad terram longinquam ubi
Medūsa habitābat volāvit. Ibi mōnstrum in scūtō clārō
spectāvit. Celeriter gladiō magicō Medūsam interfēcit.

Deinde Perseus ad rēgiam caput° Medūsae reportāvit. Rēx
invidiōsus caput avidē spectāvit; statim faciēs° mōnstrī in 25
saxum eum mūtāvit.

°**ca′put** (nom., acc. sing.) head • **fa′ciēs*** (nom. sing.) face

spe′culum, -ī	N., mirror
ālā′tus, -a, -um	winged
a′gō, -ere, ē′gī	(with **grā′tiās**) thank, be grateful
cōnsti′tuō, -ere, -sti′tuī	decide
dēprehen′dō, -ere, -hen′dī	seize, catch
*dīmit′tō, -ere, -mī′sī	send away, dismiss
pe′tō, -ere, -ī′vī	pursue, seek
*a′vidē	eagerly, avidly
tan′tum	only, merely

T H E   D E M O N S T R A T I V E **is, ea, id** this, that; he, she, it

	Singular			Plural		
	Masculine	Feminine	Neuter	Masculine	Feminine	Neuter
Nom.	is	ea	id	eī	eae	ea
Gen.	ejus	ejus	ejus	eōrum	eārum	eōrum
Dat.	eī	eī	eī	eīs	eīs	eīs
Acc.	eum	eam	id	eōs	eās	ea
Abl.	eō	eā	eō	eīs	eīs	eīs

Each of these forms has two different uses in Latin—as an
adjective and as a pronoun.

185

**ADJECTIVE USE OF THE DEMONSTRA-
TIVE** When used as an adjective, **is, ea, id** agrees in gender, number, and case with the word it modifies.

Necā id mōnstrum. Kill this monster.

Four English words (this, these; that, those) translate all forms of the Latin demonstrative adjective. Any singular form of **is, ea, id** may be translated by "this" or "that"; any plural form by "these" or "those."

Like "this" and "that" in English, forms of **is, ea, id** are often used to refer to a person or thing mentioned just before.

Scūtum clārum est speculum. In eō speculō Medūsam vidēre poteris. The bright shield is a mirror. In this mirror you will be able to see Medusa.

PRONOUN USE OF THE DEMONSTRATIVE

Nautīs cibum dabunt. They will give the sailors food.
Eī nautīs cibum dabunt. They (these men) will give the sailors food.

Although personal pronouns occur much less frequently in Latin than in English, forms of **is, ea, id** are sometimes used as third-person pronouns (he, she, it, etc.).

When a demonstrative is used as a pronoun, it agrees with its antecedent (the noun to which it refers) in gender and number, but its case depends on its use in the sentence.

Īnsula est pulchra. Vidēsne eam? The island is beautiful. Do you see it?

Here **eam** points to a feminine antecedent (**Īnsula**). The feminine singular **eam** is translated "it," because in English we refer to an island as "it." **Eam** is accusative because it is the object of **vidēs**.

I Replace each underlined noun with a suitable demonstrative pronoun; then translate the entire sentence.
1 Agricola īrātissimus fīliōs incolārum expectābat.
1 Puer nautās ē somnō excitāvit.
3 Pecūniam aurumque in arcā cēlābāmus.
4 Virī sonum rēmōrum nōn audīvērunt.

5 Per apertam jānuam templum vidēre poteram.

6 Dea nymphīs inimīca erat.

7 Nūntiī sagittās nōn jam gerent.

II For each demonstrative adjective in group A find the Latin noun or nouns in group B which it could modify; then translate.

A

1 ea 4 eum

2 eī 5 id

3 ejus 6 is

B

a) agricola e) perīculum

b) gladiī f) praemiō

c) nautam g) puer

d) populum h) specula

III For each word in group A select the word of opposite meaning in group B.

A

1 amīcus

2 beāta

3 propinquus

4 lentē

5 clārus

6 plūrimī

B

a) celeriter

b) obscūrus

c) nūllī

d) inimīcus

e) longinquus

f) maesta

USEFUL LATIN PHRASES often find their way into business and literary writing of modern times.

ad infinītum	to infinity; endlessly
ante bellum	before the war
cum grānō salis	with a grain of salt
dē novō	anew; afresh
ex animō	from the heart; sincerely
ex librīs	from the books (of)
ex officiō	by virtue of official position
in tōtō	entirely; in the whole
multum in parvō	much in little
per annum	annually; by the year
prō bonō pūblicō	for the public good
prō tempore	temporarily; for the time (being)
summum bonum	the supreme (highest) good
via media	a middle course (way)
vice versā	the other way around; conversely

Djerba Island, off the coast of Tunisia, North Africa, was the home of the lotus-eaters, according to Greek historian Herodotus.

XXXIV

THE LAND OF FORGETFULNESS

Graecī, postquam Trōjam cēpērunt, uxōrēs,° līberōs, patri-amque iterum vidēre dēsīderābant.

Inter prīmōs Ulīxēs cum sociīs suīs ōrās Trōjānās relīquit. Prīmō ventī erant secundī; deinde Juppiter magnam tem-pestātem mīsit et nāvēs° eōrum ad īnsulam longinquam ēgit. ₅

Ulīxēs et nautae maritimam ad ōram vēnērunt. Nauta dīxit, "Īnsula pulcherrima est, sed neque oppida neque casās neque incolās videō."

Ulīxēs respondit, "Incolae quidem in rīpīs fluviōrum sunt. Fortasse oppida eōrum in interiōre parte° īnsulae sunt." ₁₀

Ulīxēs trēs° virōs in partem interiōrem° īnsulae mīsit. Eī virī per silvam prōcessērunt; dēnique in vīcum vēnērunt. Incolae ejus vīcī pōma mīra edēbant. Virī nautās benignē accēpērunt et eīs pōma sua dedērunt.

°uxō'rēs (nom., acc. pl.) wives • nā'vēs* (nom., acc. pl.) ships
in interiō're* par'te* in the interior (part) • trēs M., F.
(nom., acc.) three • in par'tem interiō'rem into the interior (part)

"Haec sunt pōma lōtī; magnum dant gaudium."

Nautae pōma avidē gustāvērunt; statim memoriam patriae sociōrumque āmīsērunt. In terrā beātā manēre et cibum amoenum edere dēsīderābant.

Interim sociī eōrum prope ōram maritimam expectābant. Post multās hōrās Ulīxēs iterum nautās in partem interiōrem 20 īnsulae mīsit. Eīs dīxit, "Petite sociōs et eōs redūcite!"

Eī nautae trēs sociōs mox invēnērunt. Sociī autem neque patriam neque uxōrēs neque amīcōs memoriā tenēbant. Nautae vī° sociōs suōs ad nāvēs eōrum redūxērunt.

Ulīxēs statim ab eā īnsulā nāvigāvit. Post multās hōrās 25 trēs nautae memoriam recēpērunt. Tamen sēcrētō saepe dīcēbant, "Aliquandō ad īnsulam lōtī reveniēmus."

°vī (abl. sing.) by force

li′berī, -ōrum	M. pl., children
pō′mum, -ī	N., fruit
amoe′nus, -a, -um	pleasant
+secun′dus, -a, -um	favorable
gus′tō, -āre, -ā′vī	taste
te′neō, -ēre, -uī	hold
+a′gō, -ere, ē′gī	drive, act, do
***reci′piō, -ere, -cē′pī**	take, get or bring back
***redū′cō, -ere, -dūx′ī**	lead back, bring back
***relin′quō, -ere, -lī′quī**	leave, abandon
***benig′nē**	kindly, generously
fortas′se	perhaps
qui′dem	indeed; even
post′quam	(with perfect) after

REFLEXIVE ADJECTIVE suus, -a, -um

Vir casam suam amat. The man likes his (own) house.

Fēmina casam suam amat. The woman likes her (own) house.

Fēminae casās suās amant. The women like their (own) houses.

The possessive modifier **suus, -a, -um** (his, her, its, their) is called a reflexive adjective, because it always refers to the

189

subject of a sentence or clause; that is, the possessor and the subject are the same. A reflexive is like other adjectives in agreeing in gender, number, and case with the noun it modifies. Its declension is like that of **bonus, -a, -um.**

POSSESSIVES suus, -a, -um/ejus, eōrum, eārum

Nautae sociōs suōs ad nāvēs eōrum redūxērunt. The sailors brought their comrades back to their ships.

While in the English sentence the possessive "their" leaves doubt as to the possessor, in Latin, there is no doubt. **Suōs** indicates that the subject **(Nautae)** is the possessor; **eōrum** indicates a different possessor **(sociōs).** Since **ejus, eōrum, eārum** are pronouns in the genitive case, their forms are not affected by the nouns they modify.

OMISSION OF POSSESSIVE IN LATIN

Fēmina fīliam amat. The woman loves her daughter.

A possessive adjective seldom appears in Latin when the meaning is clear without it. A possessive may be supplied in translation when necessary.

I Wherever a possessive is necessary in order to make the meaning of a sentence clear, select an appropriate word from the list; then translate each sentence.

1 Virī līberōs their iterum vidēre cupiēbant.
2 Ulīxēs cum his amīcīs ōrās Trōjae relīquit.
3 Nautae amīcōs your mox invenient.
4 Fīliam their amāmus.
5 Virī in vīcum our fugiunt.
6 Amīcī your memoriam their āmīsērunt.

eārum	suīs
ejus	suōs
eōrum	suum
nostrās	tuī
nostrum	tuum
sua	vestram
suam	vestrōs

II Translate.

1 The men love their daughters.
2 The farmer is calling his sons.
3 The queen lives in her palace.
4 Hercules carries his own club.
5 The sailors see their friends.
6 We saw their friends.

190

III Distinguish between the pairs of look-alike Latin words by finding in the list of English words the meaning of each Latin word.

1 deinde/dēnique	a) after	i) never	
2 interim/iterum	b) again	j) now	
3 ita/itaque	c) finally	k) sometimes	
4 ubi/ibi	d) for	l) then	
5 nunc/numquam	e) in the daytime	m) there	
6 prō/prope	f) later	n) therefore	
7 posteā/post	g) meanwhile	o) thus	
8 interdum/interdiū	h) near	p) where	

WORD MASTERY 8

When a prefix was added to a word, changes sometimes occurred affecting the prefix, the original word, or both.

ob + pugnō = oppugnō   in + portō = importō   ad + capiō = accipiō

The change from **obpugnō** to **oppugnō** is called assimilation; that is, "a making alike." (The **-b** of the prefix **ob** is made like the **p-** of **pugnō**.)

The verb **accipiō** also illustrates another kind of change. Verbs containing short **-a-** or **-e-** in their first syllable often changed that short **-a-** or **-e-** to **-i-** when a prefix was added.

faciō/interficiō   statuō/cōnstituō   teneō/pertineō

Similarly words containing the diphthong **-ae-** in the first syllable changed the diphthong to **-ī-** when a prefix was added.

ob + caedō = occidō   cut down, kill   **in + quaerō = inquīrō**
dē + caedō = dēcidō   cut off, decide   **re + quaerō = requīrō**

This vowel change explains the spelling of such English words as "decide," "inquire," and "require," and of the "-cide" suffix in words meaning "the killing of . . . ." Look up any you do not know from your study of Latin.

fratricide	germicide	homicide	infanticide	suicide
insecticide	regicide	sororicide	tyrannicide	genocide[1]

[1]This new word, which was coined in 1944 to describe the killing of a whole race, was derived in part from Greek (**genos,** race) and in part from Latin (**caedō**).

Arachne is being changed into a spider in this painting by Paolo Veronese.

XXXV

ARACHNE

Arachnē, puella pulchra, pallās mīrās texēbat. Eīs in pallīs erant pictūrae multae.

Ōlim nymphae eās pictūrās spectāvērunt et dīxērunt, "Certē Minerva tibi auxilium dat. Es puella beāta."

Arachnē autem superba hīs respondit verbīs, "Auxilium ab 5 illā deā nōn accipiō. Minervam facile superāre possum. Eam ad certāmen° prōvocābō."

Minerva verba puellae forte audīvit. "Arachnē mē timēre dēbet," Minerva īrāta dīxit, "quod dea sum. Ad tēctum hujus puellae superbae properābō et cōnsilium ejus mūtāre 10 temptābō."

Jam Minerva ante jānuam tēctī stetit. Arachnē autem nōn deam, sed fēminam miseram vīdit.

°**certā′men** (nom., acc. sing.) contest

"Deam prōvocāre nōn dēbēs; Minerva erit īrāta," dīxit fēmina. Arachnē autem respondit, "Illa dea mē nōn terret. 15 Populus hās pallās et hās pictūrās laudat. Laudatne deam Minervam et pallās illīus populus?"

Tum Minerva fōrmam suam in fōrmam deae vēram mūtāvit. "Minerva dea sum," dēclārāvit.

Superba Arachnē tamen nōn erat territa, sed Minervam ad 20 certāmen temerē prōvocāvit.

Pallās texuērunt et puella et dea. In pallā deae erant pictūrae pulchrae beneficiōrum deōrum et deārum; Arachnē in pallā suā pictūrās maleficiōrum deōrum et deārum texuit.

Minerva īrātissima dīxit, "Palla tua est pulchra, sed tū 25 mala es; tē in arāneam° mūtābō."

Miseram puellam in arāneam dea mūtāvit. Nōn jam Arachnē pallam mīram sed tēlam mīram arāneae texuit. Etiam hodiē arāneae semper tēlās suās texunt.

°arā'nea, -ae F. spider

tē'la, -ae	F., web, texture
benefi'cium, -ī	N., good deed, benefit
malefi'cium, -ī	N., evil deed, crime
*vē'rus, -a, -um	true, genuine
*prō'vocō, -āre, -āvī	challenge, provoke
*ter'reō, -ēre, -uī	frighten, terrify
tex'ō, -ere, -uī	weave
*cer'tē	surely, certainly
*fa'cile	easily
for'te	by chance
te'merē	rashly

DEMONSTRATIVES hic AND ille IN USE

In hāc pallā sunt pictūrae maleficiōrum; in illā pallā sunt pictūrae beneficiōrum. On this robe are pictures of evil deeds; on that robe are pictures of good deeds.

The demonstratives **hic** and **ille** both point out persons or things. Usually **hic** refers to a person or thing near the

193

speaker, while **ille** indicates a person or thing farther away. **Is,** meaning "this" or "that," merely refers to a person or thing already mentioned.

Like **is,** both **hic** and **ille** are used not only as adjectives, but also as pronouns—**hic** (this man); **illa** (those things).

THE DEMONSTRATIVE **hic, haec, hoc** this

	Singular			Plural		
	Masculine	Feminine	Neuter	Masculine	Feminine	Neuter
Nom.	hic	haec	hoc	hī	hae	haec
Gen.	hujus	hujus	hujus	hōrum	hārum	hōrum
Dat.	huic	huic	huic	hīs	hīs	hīs
Acc.	hunc	hanc	hoc	hōs	hās	haec
Abl.	hōc	hāc	hōc	hīs	hīs	hīs

The English demonstrative "this" has only two forms: "this" (singular) and "these" (plural). The Latin demonstrative **hic** (this) has different forms for various cases and genders.

THE DEMONSTRATIVE **ille, illa, illud** that

	Singular			Plural		
	Masculine	Feminine	Neuter	Masculine	Feminine	Neuter
Nom.	ille	illa	illud	illī	illae	illa
Gen.	illīus	illīus	illīus	illōrum	illārum	illōrum
Dat.	illī	illī	illī	illīs	illīs	illīs
Acc.	illum	illam	illud	illōs	illās	illa
Abl.	illō	illā	illō	illīs	illīs	illīs

The English demonstrative "that" has only two forms: "that" (singular) and "those" (plural). The Latin demonstrative **ille** (that) has different forms for various cases and genders.

I Translate each phrase, giving special attention to the demonstratives.

1 in eīs casīs
2 huic deae
3 eam vocābō
4 tēctum hujus formīcae
5 eās puellās
6 haec mōnstra
7 cōnsilium ejus
8 illa porta
9 in hāc ārā
10 eī dabit
11 suō scūtō
12 illīus populī

II Translate the sentences and tell whether the word underlined is an adjective or pronoun.

1 Rēx huic fēminae multa praemia dedit.
2 Pīcus illam magam in mātrimōnium dūcere nōn cupit.
3 Nympha verba sua audīre nōn potuit.
4 Jūnō fābulās ejus nōn amābat.
5 Hī virī sunt agricolae, illī sunt nautae.
6 Hīc sunt saxa; ea invēnī.

III Select the most appropriate expression for each word or phrase underlined, and translate each sentence completely.

1 Arachnē autem hīs verbīs respondit. (for these words/because of these words/with these words)
2 Auxilium ab illā deā nōn accipiō. (from that goddess/by that goddess/from this goddess)
3 Minervam superāre nōn possum. (conquer/rise above/surpass)
4 Laudatne deam et fīliās illīus populus? (of that one/her/that one's)
5 Deam prōvocāre nōn dēbēs. (don't have to/should not/must)

LATIN LIVES TODAY in the names of the months of our year.

January	from **Jānus,** god of beginnings
February	from **Februa,** a ceremony of purification held on the fifteenth of this month
March	from **Mārs,** god of war
April	from **aperiō,** since the buds open at this time
May	from **Māia,** mother of Mercury
June	from **Jūnō,** queen of the gods, wife of Jupiter
July	from **Jūlius,** in honor of Julius Caesar
August	from **Augustus,** in honor of the first emperor of Rome, Caesar Augustus
September	from **septem** (seven)
October	from **octō** (eight)
November	from **novem** (nine)
December	from **decem** (ten)

The last four months were correctly numbered in the old Roman calendar, in which March was the first month.

195

In this painting by Caravaggio Narcissus peers at his reflection in the pool.

XXXVI

ECHO AND NARCISSUS

In silvā cum cēterīs Diānae nymphīs Ēchō habitābat. Ēchō laeta et beāta Diānae et cēterīs nymphīs cāra erat.

Jūnō autem, rēgīna deārum, eam nōn amābat. Ōlim nympham vocāvit et eī dīxit, "Posteā verba reddere poteris, sed tū ipsa colloquium incipere nōn jam poteris."

5

196

In silvīs miserrima Ēchō errābat sōla et tacita inter saxa.
Ōlim vīdit in locō apertō silvae juvenem° fōrmōsissimum.
Erat Narcissus quī° cum amīcīs bēstiās petēbat.

Diū Ēchō Narcissum spectābat; ille autem eam nōn vīdit.
Nympha eum appellāre temptāvit. Injūstam propter poenam 10
Jūnōnis Ēchō nihil dīcere poterat. Narcissus ipse nymphae
nihil dīxit; ea igitur verba reddere nōn poterat.

Dēnique Narcissus amīcōs suōs appellāvit. "Heus! Heus!"
clāmāvit. "Ubi estis? Ipse adsum."

"Ipsa adsum!" cum audāciā Ēchō respondit. 15

"Ubi ades?" Narcissus circumspectāvit et iterum clāmāvit,
"Properā! Tē cupiō."

"Tē cupiō!" statim respondit Ēchō.

Tum Narcissus puellam ipsam cōnspexit. Illa verbīs eum
salūtāre nōn poterat; tamen oculīs et manibus° eī signa amī- 20
citiae dedit. Ille autem amīcitiam ejus recūsāvit.

"Tē nōn appellāvī," dīxit. "Nōn tibi dīxī, 'Tē cupiō!' Nōn
tē amō."

"Tē amō," Ēchō misera respondit.

Deinde Narcissus fūgit. Posteā noctū et interdiū Ēchō 25
lacrimābat; mox lacrimae fōrmam ejus vāstāvērunt. Dēnique
nympha ipsa nōn jam fuit; sōla mānsit vōx°—Ēchō.

°ju'venem* (acc. sing.) young man • quī M., who • ma'-
nibus (abl. pl.) with hands • vōx (nom. sing.) F., voice

*amīci'tia, -ae	F., friendship
*audā'cia, -ae	F., boldness, audacity
poe'na, -ae	F., punishment, penalty
*collo'quium, -ī	N., conversation, talk
ni'hil	N. (indeclinable), nothing
cē'terī, -ae, -a	pl., other, remaining; (as noun) the others
fōrmō'sus, -a, -um	handsome
*ta'citus, -a, -um	silent, tacit
*circumspec'tō, -āre, -ā'vī	look around
la'crimō, -āre, -ā'vī	weep, cry
inci'piō, -ere, -cē'pī	begin
red'dō, -ere, red'didī	give back, return
heus!	hello! hi there!

THE INTENSIVE ipse, ipsa, ipsum is declined like **ille** (p. 194), except that the neuter singular ends in **-um** in nominative and accusative. The complete declension is found in the Summary of Grammar.

Nympha ipsa nōn jam fuit. The nymph herself no longer existed.

In this sentence **ipsa** is feminine nominative singular to agree with **Nympha**. The forms of **ipse** are translated "myself," "yourself," "himself," "herself," "itself," or "ourselves," "yourselves," "themselves," according to person, gender, and number of the word with which the form is used. An intensive simply adds emphasis.

I Supply a form of **ipse** for each blank. Translate.
1 Rēgīnam _____ in mātrimōnium dūcet.
2 Tēcta incolārum stābant _____ in rīpīs fluviī.
3 Praemium puerō _____ dedī.
4 Portae rēgiae _____ erant aureae.
5 Nautās _____ in oppidō hodiē vīdimus.
6 Cēpistisne, virī, scūtum _____ ā magā?

II Choose from the list a suitable demonstrative pronoun to replace each word underlined in the sentences.

1 Ōlim Echō nympha erat.	a) eam	h) huic
2 Diānae cārissima erat; cum nymphīs deae in silvā habitābat.	b) eās	i) id
	c) eīs	j) illa
3 Nymphīs quoque Ēchō grāta erat, quod fābulās nārrābat.	d) eōs	k) ille
	e) eum	l) illī
4 Jūnō autem puellae dīxit, "Nōn jam fābulās nārrābis."	f) hāc	m) illīus
	g) haec	n) illud ·
5 Puella puerum in silvā vīdit.		
6 Narcissus comam auream habēbat.		
7 Narcissus amīcōs appellāre temptāvit.		

III Which of these forms may be neuter only? Masculine only? Feminine only? If any forms are used for more than one gender, tell which genders they are.
hic, illī, hanc, id, eum, illud, eō, ipse, hujus, eās, ejus, haec, ille, ipsum, hōs, illum, ipsam, illārum, ipsīus, ipsa, illōs, illam, ipsīs, ipsās, ipsōrum, illā

XXXVII

A NEW RACE ON EARTH

Ōlim virī malī et fēminae malae in terrā habitābant. Templa deōrum nōn cūrābant; deōs ipsōs nōn adōrābant.

Tum Juppiter deōs convocāvit et dīxit, "Quamquam virōs et fēminās monuimus, tamen bonī nōn sunt; eadem verba iterum nōn dīcam. Nōn jam eīdem incolae malī in terrā 5 manēre dēbent; eōs pūniam."

Tum Juppiter multam aquam in terram mīsit, ubi diū manēbat et agrōs cēlābat; in agrīs nūllī virī erant. Aqua alta oppida ipsa quoque cēlāvit; in oppidīs nūllī virī et nūllae fēminae erant. Incolae malī erant mortuī. 10

Deucaliōn sōlus erat vir bonus et pius, atque Pyrrha sōla erat fēmina bona et pia. Dī igitur hunc virum bonum et hanc fēminam bonam in altō locō servāvērunt.

"In eādem terrā, sed nōn jam cum eīsdem incolīs, habitā-bunt," dīxērunt dī. 15

Dēnique aqua alta nōn jam terram cēlāvit, sed Deucaliōn et Pyrrha nūllōs virōs, nūllās fēminās in terrā vidēbant. Caelum et aquam spectābant. Aquam altam timēbant et auxilium dēsīderābant.

Templum erat propinquum et Deucaliōn dīxit, "In templum 20 ipsum properābimus. Hīc manēbimus, hīc dī certē nōs juvābunt."

The early stages of the flood which only Deucalion and Pyrrha survived are pictured in this painting.

Ōrāvērunt, "Ō dī, juvāte nōs. Quid faciēmus?"

Ōrāculum eīs dīxit, "Jacite ossa° mātris° post terga."

Quamquam Pyrrha ōrāculum timēbat, tamen Deucaliōn 25
dīxit, "Dī benignī sunt. Terra est māter nostra. Saxa sunt
ossa mātris nostrae."

Statim Pyrrha saxa post tergum jēcit; haec saxa dī in
fēminās mūtāvērunt.

Deucaliōn quoque saxa post tergum jēcit; illa saxa dī in 30
virōs mūtāvērunt.

Nōn jam erat Deucaliōn sōlus vir; nōn jam Pyrrha fēmina
sōla. Ita terra iterum multōs habēbat incolās.

°os'sa (nom., acc. pl.) bones • mā'tris (gen. sing.) mother's

ter'gum, -ī	N., back
*pi'us, -a, -um	dutiful, reverent, pious
ja'ciō, -ere, jē'cī	throw, hurl

DECLENSION AND USE OF idem, eadem, idem
the same

	Singular			Plural		
	Masculine	Feminine	Neuter	Masculine	Feminine	Neuter
Nom.	īdem	eadem	idem	eīdem	eaedem	eadem
Gen.	ejusdem	ejusdem	ejusdem	eōrundem	eārundem	eōrundem
Dat.	eīdem	eīdem	eīdem	eīsdem	eīsdem	eīsdem
Acc.	eundem	eandem	idem	eōsdem	eāsdem	eadem
Abl.	eōdem	eādem	eōdem	eīsdem	eīsdem	eīsdem

The forms of the adjective idem are almost identical with
the forms of is, plus -dem. In the accusative singular (masculine and feminine) and in the genitive plural, -ndem appears
instead of -mdem: eundem, eandem; eōrundem, eārundem.
The neuter nominative and accusative singular is idem
(not iddem).

These forms changed because -nd- is easier to pronounce
than -md-, as are īdem (for isdem) and idem (for iddem).

Like the demonstratives, idem is also used as a pronoun,
meaning "the same (one)."

I Translate each word or phrase underlined.

1 portae <u>of their town</u>
2 <u>the same</u> tēcta
3 <u>those girls'</u> praemia
4 <u>his own</u> vīllam
5 oppidum <u>itself</u>

6 <u>her</u> studium
7 <u>that slave's</u> dominō
8 <u>these men's</u> sapientia
9 <u>his</u> inimīcīs
10 <u>the same</u> puer

II Choose the adjective or pronoun which completes each sentence; then translate.

1 Cum sociīs (suīs/meīs/ipsōrum) in hortō puerum cēlābō.
2 Servus dominum (hoc/ejus/suum) timet.
3 (Haec/Illae/Hae) scūta clārissima sunt.
4 (Illās/Illōs/Illīs) fēminās ē somnō excitāvimus.
5 (Hujus/Ipsīs/Īdem) vir puellam servāre temptāvit.

III For each noun select an adjective which could be used with it.

Noun: cōnsiliī corōnam perīculum sociō agricola laurus oculum

Adjective: eōsdem eandem idem eadem īdem ejusdem eīdem eundem

USEFUL LATIN is sometimes disguised in common abbreviations.

A.D.	**Annō Dominī**	in the year of Our Lord
A.M.	**ante merīdiem**	morning (before midday)
P.M.	**post merīdiem**	afternoon
B.A.	**Baccalaureus Artium**	Bachelor of Arts
M.A.	**Magister Artium**	Master of Arts
Ph.D.	**Philosophiae Doctor**	Doctor of Philosophy
D.D.	**Dīvīnitātis Doctor**	Doctor of Divinity
M.D.	**Medicīnae Doctor**	Doctor of Medicine
N.B.	**notā bene**	note well
P.S.	**post scrīptum**	written afterthought
D.V.	**deō volente**	God willing
e.g.	**exemplī grātiā**	for example
i.e.	**id est**	that is
ad lib.	**ad libitum**	at pleasure
pro tem.	**prō tempore**	temporarily; for the time
et al.	**et aliī**	and others
etc.	**et cētera**	and other things

REVIEW OF UNIT IX

LESSONS XXXIII—XXXVII

Nouns	Verbs	Adverbs
*amīcitia, -ae	*circumspectō, -āre	*avidē
*audācia, -ae	gustō, -āre	*benignē
poena, -ae	lacrimō, -āre	*certē
tēla, -ae	*prōvocō, -āre	*facile
līberī, -ōrum	teneō, -ēre	fortasse
beneficium, -ī	*terreō, -ēre	forte
*colloquium, -ī	agō, -ere	quidem
maleficium, -ī	cōnstituō, -ere	tantum
pōmum, -ī	dēprehendō, -ere	temerē
speculum, -ī	*dīmittō, -ere	Conjunction
tergum, -ī	incipiō, -ere	postquam
nihil	jaciō, -ere	Interjection
Adjectives	petō, -ere	heus!
ālātus, -a, -um	*recipiō, -ere	Idioms
amoenus, -a, -um	reddō, -ere	grātiās agere
cēterī, -ae, -a	*redūcō, -ere	nāvēs agere
fōrmōsus, -a, -um	*relinquō, -ere	
*pius, -a, -um	texō, -ere	
+secundus, -a, -um		
*tacitus, -a, -um		
*vērus, -a, -um		

I Substitute a pronoun from the list for each underlined expression. Translate.

1 Amīcus puerī impigerrimus est.
2 Grātiās incolae agēmus quod nos juvat.
3 In pallā Arachnē pictūrās texuit.
4 Propter speculum Gorgō puerum in saxum nōn mūtābit.
5 Deae īrātissimae colloquium habēbant.
6 Memoriam nōn āmīsī, quamquam ipse pōma gustāvī.

eā	illud
eam	id
eae	eō
ejus	haec
eōrum	huic
illīs	hunc

II Select all the demonstrative adjectives which agree in gender, number, and case with each noun.

1 agricolae	a) ea		h) hoc
2 maleficium	b) eī		i) hōc
3 audācia	c) ejus		j) huic
4 colloquia	d) eōrum		k) hujus
5 sociō	e) hāc		l) hunc
6 poenārum	f) haec		m) illud
7 amīcitiā	g) hārum		n) is

III Choose from the list an appropriate verb form to replace each English verb. Then translate the completed Latin sentences.

1 Rēx Perseō dīxit, "<u>Seek</u> eam; necā id mōnstrum."

2 Prīmō ille autem auxilium deōrum <u>begged</u>.

3 "Sī galeam magicam <u>wear</u>," dīxit is, "nūllus tē vidēre poterit."

4 Hic dīxit, "Sī eās soleās gerēs, nūllus tē <u>catch</u> poterit."

5 In eō speculō illam vidēre <u>we can</u>.

6 Is deīs grātiās <u>thanked</u>.

7 Sociī illīus memoriam <u>lost</u>.

8 Haec pallās mīrās <u>wove</u>.

9 Puella superba illam ad certāmen temerē <u>challenged</u>.

10 Jūnō eī dīxit, "Ipsa colloquium <u>begin</u> nōn jam poteris."

āmīsērunt
dabat
dēprehendere
ēgit
gerēs
incipere
jacite
lacrimat
ōrāvit
pete
portās
possumus
prōvocāvit
recūsāvit
texuit

IV Change all singular verbs to third person singular, and all plural verbs to third person plural. Make all other changes as needed. Caution: Watch the possessives.

1 Cum fīliīs meīs ōrās Trōjānās relīquī.

2 Nōnne memoriam sociōrum tuōrum statim āmīsistī?

3 Ad tēcta vestra properābāmus.

4 Fortasse oppidum vestrum procul ā silvā inveniam.

5 Redūcisne sociōs tuōs ad nāvēs?

6 Cōnsilium tuum mūtāre temptābō.

7 In tuā pallā beneficia deārum texēbās.

8 Amīcitiam tuam recūsāmus.

203

THE ROMAN EMPIRE

According to legend, Rome began as a village established by Romulus in 753 B.C. Later, as a republic, Rome dominated all of Italy and extended its power into North Africa, Asia Minor, and northward into Europe. Under Augustus, Rome became an empire and extended its power even farther. Eventually, much of France, Spain, Germany, Britain, and even parts of Russia were included in the Roman Empire. Since their provinces encircled the Mediterranean, the Romans called the world "orbis terrarum" (the circle of lands). Wherever the Romans went they carried their language, their laws, and their roads; and wherever they went they brought prosperity based on flourishing trade.

Above: Part of Hadrian's Wall, which protected Roman boundaries in northern Britain.

Below: Cameo, Gemma Augustea, celebrating triumph of Tiberius, seen stepping from chariot. Augustus is seated beside the goddess Roma; soldiers and prisoners are below.

Kunsthistorisches Museum of Vienna

Above: Signet ring from Syria, with its impression, probably a head of Mark Antony, member of triumvirate which preceded the Empire.

Right: Signet ring with sphinx, used by first Roman Emperor, Augustus.

Above: Imposing columns still stand near the entrance gate (Decumana) as the only reminders of the buildings which were part of the once busy Roman city of Timgad in North Africa.

Below: This Roman aqueduct, until recently, carried water to Segovia, Spain, adding to the evidence that from Spain and Portugal in the west to Syria in the east, and from Britain in the north to Egypt in the south, the influence of Rome persists even to our day.

IMPERIUM ROMANUM

HIBERNIA

OCEANUS ATLANTICUS

BRITANNIA

GERMANIA

Albis

Rhenus

Sequana

Rhodanus

GALLIA

HISPANIA

CORSICA

SARDINIA

EUROPA

SARMATIA (RUSSIA)

Danuvius

ALPES

Padus

ETRURIA

Veii

Roma

Ostia

LATIUM

Tiberis

ITALIA

MONS VESUVIUS

Herculaneum

Pompeii

Tarentum

AEOLIA

Carthago

AFRICA

MELITA

SICILIA

MONS AETNA

MARE INTERNUM (Mediterranean Sea)

MARE

Mare Adriaticum

THRACIA

MACEDONIA

MONS OLYMPUS

EPIRUS

THESSALIA

Troja

Hellespontus

Aulis

Athenae

ACHAIA

Olympia

Sparta

ARCADIA

ITHACA

IONS IDA

DELOS

Strymon

PONTUS EUXINUS (Black Sea)

COLCHIS

Phasis

MARE CASPIUM (Caspian Sea)

Tigris

Euphrates

BABYLONIA

ARABIA

PHOENICIA

ASIA

CYPRUS

CRETA

LIBYA

AEGYP

ARABIA

Sin

Arab

CARTHAGO

MARE

MELITA

•COLOR KEY•

TO 396 B.C.	
TO 264 B.C.	
TO 133 B.C.	
TO 44 B.C.	
TO A.D. 177	

0   100   200   300   400   500   1000

Ivory carving of animals in an arena, from the Hermitage Museum in Leningrad.

Painting by Rembrandt (in Museum Dahlem, Berlin) shows Daniel being comforted by an angel. Already in poor condition, it was further damaged in storage during World War II.

XXXVIII

A MAN WHO WAS NOT AFRAID

Ōlim rēx Babylōnicus cum Isrāēlītīs pugnāvit, quōs facile vīcit. Deinde ad rēgiam paucōs puerōs Isrāēlītārum captīvōs dūxit, inter quōs erat Daniēl.

Daniēlī, quī propter sapientiam ēgregius erat, rēx dedit multa praemia et multōs honōrēs.°   5

°**honō′rēs*** (acc. pl.) honors

Sociī rēgis autem, quī invidiōsī erant, dīxērunt, "Ō rēx, Daniēl neque deōs Babylōnicōs neque tē° ipsum, rēgem hujus terrae, adōrat. Lēge° Babylōnicā Daniēl perīre dēbet."

Propter haec verba sociōrum, rēx miserrimus Daniēlem in spēluncam ubi erant multī leōnēs° jēcit. 10

Daniēl autem nōn erat territus; clāmāvit, "Deus quem adōrō mē servābit!"

Rēx dīxit, "Es fīdus, Daniēl; deus tuus, quem semper adōrās, tē servābit."

Postrīdiē rēx māne ad spēluncam properāvit et magnā 15 vōce Daniēlem vocāvit, "Ō Daniēl, servāvitne tē deus quem adōrās?"

Ex spēluncā Daniēl respondit, "Ō rēx, angelus vēnit, quī apud mē in hāc spēluncā mānsit. Leōnēs mē nōn vulnerāvērunt. Deus mē servāvit!" 20

Tum rēx populō dīxit, "Studium et scientia et sapientia sunt in hōc virō. Deus quī Daniēlem servāvit deus vērus est. Capite illōs quī eum accūsāvērunt! Illōs jacite in eandem spēluncam ubi leōnēs sunt!"

°**tē** (acc. sing.) you • **lē′ge** (abl. sing.) by law • **leō′nēs** (nom. pl.) lions

spēlun′ca, -ae	F., cave, cavern
quī, quae, quod	(relative pronoun) who, which, that
*****fī′dus, -a, -um**	faithful, loyal
*****per′eō, -īre, -īvī**	perish, die
mā′ne	early; in the morning
mag′nā vō′ce	(abl. sing.) in a loud voice

DECLENSION OF RELATIVE PRONOUN

	Singular			Plural		
	Masc.	Fem.	Neut.	Masc.	Fem.	Neut.
Nom.	quī	quae	quod	quī	quae	quae
Gen.	cujus	cujus	cujus	quōrum	quārum	quōrum
Dat.	cui	cui	cui	quibus	quibus	quibus
Acc.	quem	quam	quod	quōs	quās	quae
Abl.	quō	quā	quō	quibus	quibus	quibus

209

RELATIVE PRONOUN IN USE   In both Latin and English the case of a relative pronoun depends on its use.

Deus quem semper adōrās tē juvābit. The god whom you always worship will help you.

In this sentence, **quem** (direct object of **adōrās**) is in the accusative case; likewise, "whom" (direct object of "worship") is in the objective case.

The case of a Latin relative pronoun depends on its use within its own clause, but its gender and number are determined by its antecedent. Thus, **quem** is masculine singular to agree with **deus.**

TRANSLATION OF RELATIVE PRONOUNS

In the nominative, a Latin relative pronoun is translated by "who," "which," or "that"; in the genitive, by "whose," "of whom," or "of which"; and in other cases by "whom," "which," or "that."

"Who," "whose," and "whom" refer to persons; "which" refers to things; and "that" to either persons or things. The same form is used for both singular and plural in English.

RELATIVE PRONOUN WITH cum   The preposition **cum** with a relative pronoun is not a separate word, but is added to the ablative of the pronoun as a final syllable; e.g., **quōcum, quācum, quibuscum,** with whom, with which.

Ubi sunt puerī quibuscum Daniēl ad rēgiam vēnit? Where are the boys with whom Daniel came to the palace?

I From the list supply the appropriate relative pronoun, and translate.

1 Puer nautās ＿＿＿ ad oppidum reveniēbant dē perīculō monuit.
2 Fēmina ＿＿＿ māne in silvā ambulābō līberīs amīca erit.
3 Templum ＿＿＿ vidēre nunc potestis dēlēbimus.
4 Pīrātās malōs virī ＿＿＿ tēcta ārdent vincent.

a) cui
b) cujus
c) quācum
d) quae
e) quās
f) quem
g) quī
h) quibuscum
i) quod
j) quōrum
k) quōs

II Translate the sentences and justify the form of each relative pronoun.

1 Praemium quod fīliō suō dedit est pulchrum.
2 Verba quae dīxistī sunt pauca.
3 Captīvus quem laudās fīdissimus est.
4 In spēluncā quam hodiē invēnī aurum est.
5 Fēminae quibuscum puellae ambulant Graecae sunt.
6 Virī quōs servābimus bonī sunt.

III For each relative pronoun find a suitable antecedent in the list to complete each sentence. Translate the completed sentences.

1 Āmīsistīne ＿＿＿ quae vōbīs dedimus?
2 Nōlīte vulnerāre ＿＿＿ quōcum fugere temptāvī.
3 ＿＿＿ quod aedificāvistī ārdet.
4 Nōnne ＿＿＿ timent quae rēgem in pīcum mūtāvit?
5 Ille vir ＿＿＿ quās parāmus semper vītat.
6 Incolae vīcī ad ＿＿＿ properant in quibus ursae habitant.
7 Illī cum ＿＿＿ pugnant quōs facile superābunt.

a) amīcitia
b) captīvum
c) cēnās
d) dōna
e) hortīs
f) magam
g) magistrō
h) oculōrum
i) pīrātīs
j) spēluncās
k) tēctum

USEFUL LATIN may be found in phrases, proverbs, and other sayings still frequently quoted because their message is timeless.

Bis dat qui cito dat. He gives twice who gives quickly.
Bonus vir nemo est nisi qui bonus est omnibus. No one is a good man who is not good to everybody.
Ei vivunt qui ex corporum vinculis evolaverunt. They are living who have flown from the bondage of the body.
Natura abhorret a vacuo. Nature abhors a vacuum.
Qui docet, discet. He who teaches, learns.
Sic transit gloria mundi. So passes away the glory of the world.
Causa sine qua non. An indispensable condition.
Status quo. The state in which (a thing is or was).
Urbem quam statuo vestra est. The city that I am building is yours.
Verbum sapienti sat est. A word to the wise is sufficient.

211

STREETS, ROADS, AND WATER SUPPLY

Roads built by the Romans in all parts of the Empire were better than any other roads ever made until recent times. City streets were of the same durable construction. Stretches of Roman streets and highways are still used in many places. Constructed with a deep and solid fill, they had a surface of stone, cut, fitted, and set in concrete. Many bridges, an essential part of the ancient road system, survive. Roman roads were built primarily for moving troops and military supplies, but they also contributed greatly to commerce by making overland transport feasible.

The engineering genius that created the network of Roman roads also developed water and drainage systems, without which large cities could not have existed. The Romans used masonry to bring water into the city, since they did not have metal pipes of sufficient strength to bear the heavy load of water. Stone aqueducts carried the water channels over low ground. Remains of such aqueducts can be seen in all parts of the Roman world, and some have continued in use until modern times.

Lacking adequate pipes, ancient sewers were not so extensive nor so effective as modern sewage systems. The old sewers of Rome were masonry channels which emptied into the Tiber.

Above left: The well-preserved arch over a nearly obliterated fragment of Roman road is evidence of the fact that even the outposts of Roman territory had a network of roads to facilitate movements of troops, supplies, and trade goods.

Above right: Present remains of Cloaca Maxima, the outlet into the Tiber River for the sewers of Rome. Originally more than twelve feet high, the lower third of the arch is now filled with silt.

Left: The towers mark the eastern terminus of the Appian Way in Brindisi (ancient Brundisium), the port from which Romans sailed to Greece and the East. In Italian "Brindisi!" is used as a farewell toast to a friend.

Right: Crossroads on one of the main streets of Pompeii. The narrow raised path for pedestrians and the stepping stones to keep their feet out of mud and water are evident. Though much narrower than highways, city streets were made with the same care for durability.

Below: Model of a surveyor's instrument for measuring to find a level, and part of a large reconstruction of the Appian Way demonstrating materials and methods used in building it.

Right: Bridge at Rimini in northern Italy, built in the time of Augustus or his successor Tiberius.
Below left: The great height and remarkable state of preservation of the Roman aqueduct in Segovia, Spain, are evident. It helped to carry the city's water supply well into the twentieth century.
Below right: Careful inspection of the bridge at Alcántara, another Spanish city, shows modern alterations constructed on piers built in the days of ancient Rome.

XXXIX

ANDROCLES AND THE LION

Androclēs erat servus dominī Rōmānī in Āfricā. Ā dominō
malō in loca dēserta fūgit, ubi in spēluncā obscūrā latēbat.

Ōlim in spēluncam vēnit leō° ferus, quī fugitīvum magnopere terruit. Androclēs tamen sē nōn mōvit. Leō lentē ad
servum appropinquāvit et eī mōnstrāvit pedem,° quem spīna 5
longa vulnerāverat.° Androclēs celeriter spīnam remōvit.

Jam leō servum benignum amābat; apud amīcum manēbat.
Diū vir et leō in spēluncā habitābant.

Dēnique mīlitēs° Rōmānī fugitīvum procul ā spēluncā
vīdērunt. Androclēs sē servāre temptāvit, sed mīlitēs eum 10
vulnerāvērunt. Tum mīlitēs servum ad dominum dūxērunt.

°**leō** (nom. sing.) lion • **pe′dem** (acc. sing.) paw • **vul-
nerā′verat** had wounded • **mī′litēs*** (nom. pl.) soldiers

This bronze statuette of lions, dating from the second century A.D., was found in
Rome, and is now in the Metropolitan Museum, New York.

Dominus cum servō in Ītaliam nāvigāvit. Ille vir dīxit, "Crās in arēnā bēstiīs tē dabō; leōnēs ferī tē necābunt. Imperātor° ipse aderit."

Androclēs sē līberāre nōn potuit; postrīdiē mīlitēs eum in 15 arēnam dūxērunt. Statim ūnus ē leōnibus° ad servum appropinquāvit. Subitō autem stetit, ad servum vēnit, pedem mōnstrāvit. Nōn jam leō erat ferus; Androclēs erat amīcus. Erat īdem leō quōcum Androclēs tam diū in spēluncā habitāverat.° 20

Prīmō populus īrātus erat quod leō servum nōn necāvit. Sed imperātor, ubi vērum cognōvit, et Androclem et leōnem° līberāvit.

°imperā'tor (nom. sing.) emperor • ū'nus ē leō'nibus one of the lions • habitā'verat had lived • leō'nem (acc. sing.) lion

*spī'na, -ae	F., thorn
*do'minus, -ī	M., master
*vē'rum, -ī	N., truth
appropin'quō, -āre, -āvī	approach
*la'teō, -ēre, -uī	hide, lie hidden
*crās	tomorrow
magno'pere	greatly, very much

DECLENSION OF THIRD-PERSON REFLEXIVE PRONOUN

	Nom.	Gen.	Dat.	Acc.	Abl.
Singular Plural	—	suī	sibi	sē	sē

The reflexive pronoun sometimes appears as a double form (sēsē) in accusative and ablative.

REFLEXIVE PRONOUN IN USE

Androclēs sē līberāre nōn potuit. Androcles could not free himself.

The direct object sē (himself) refers to the same person as the subject Androclēs. A pronoun used in this way is called a reflexive pronoun.

215

Since a reflexive pronoun always refers to the subject of the sentence or clause in which it stands, there is no nominative form.

Fēminae sē servant. The women save themselves.
Leō sē servat. The lion saves itself.
Puer sē servat. The boy saves himself.

The same form is used for both singular and plural, and for all three genders.

I From the alternatives given select the appropriate word, and translate the sentences.
1 Fugitīvus miser ipsōs/meus/sē servāre temptāvit.
2 Androclēs dīxit, "Quis est amīcus tuum/meus/ipsa?"
3 Vir ipse/hoc/eum est mortuus; gladium suum/eī/ejus habeō.
4 Fugitīvus dominum suum/ipse/sē timet.
5 Servus amīcōs ipsās/suōs/sibi līberāre nōn potest.
6 Agricola bēstiās in spēluncā eōrum/suā/suō vīdit.

II For each phrase select from the list a word of similar meaning.
1 in hōc locō   a) certē
2 in illō locō   b) dormīre
3 sē cēlāre   c) fugere
4 sē līberāre   d) hīc
5 somnō sē dare   e) ibi
6 auxilium dare   f) juvāre
7 sine dubiō   g) latēre

III For each underlined word that would be expressed by a reflexive pronoun or adjective in Latin, supply the correct form. Explain disqualification of any word.
1 The boy gave <u>his</u> friend a gift.
2 The wild beasts could not defend <u>themselves</u>.
3 The slave freed <u>himself</u> from <u>his</u> master.
4 The queen gave <u>herself</u> a gift.
5 Jupiter <u>himself</u> was not able to overcome the Titans.
6 Which <u>man</u> could not help <u>himself</u>?

M O T T O   of Constantine, first Christian emperor of Rome:
In hōc signō vincēs. In this sign (the cross) you will conquer.

XL

MANLIUS AND THE GEESE SAVE ROME

Gallī barbarī et ferī ā portīs Rōmae nōn longē aberant.
Magnum propter perīculum multī Rōmānī ad oppida propinqua fūgērunt.

Senātus Rōmānus tamen in arce° Capitōliī mānsit. In
Capitōliō Juppiter et Jūnō et Minerva templa habēbant. In 5
templō Jūnōnis erant ānserēs° sacrī.

Portae Rōmae erant apertae, et mox Gallī tēcta dēserta
dēlēvērunt. Rōmānī tamen, inter quōs erat Mānlius, dēfendēbant Capitōlium.

Dēnique Gallī viam sēcrētam et angustam et dūram invēn- 10
ērunt, quae ad mūrum arcis° dūcēbat. Noctū ad Capitōlium
Gallī sēcrētō ascendērunt.

Quamquam Rōmānī ipsī nihil audīvērunt, tamen in templō
Jūnōnis ānserēs sacrī strepuērunt° et Mānlium excitāvērunt.
Statim ille cēterōs Rōmānōs vocāvit.   15

"Gallī adsunt! Servāte vōs! Properāte ad mūrum!" clāmāvit Mānlius.

Prīmus Gallus jam in mūrō stābat. Sē servāre temptāvit,
sed celeriter Mānlius eum gladiō interfēcit. Multī sociī ejus
post prīmum Gallum ascendēbant, sed statim corpus° mortuī 20
illōs dē viā angustā dēpulit. Sē servāre nōn potuērunt. Mox
hōs Gallōs Rōmānī interfēcērunt. Capitōlium prō sē et cēterīs
Rōmānīs servāvērunt.

°**ar′ce** (abl. sing.); **ar′cis** (gen. sing.) citadel • **ān′serēs** (nom·
pl.) geese • **strepuē′runt** made a noise • **cor′pus**
(nom. sing.) N., body, corpse

*__mū′rus, -ī__	M., wall
*__bar′barus, -a, -um__	uncivilized, strange; (as noun) M., foreigner, barbarian; M. pl., the barbarians (all who were non-Roman)
*__dū′rus, -a, -um__	hard, difficult
__dēpel′lō, -ere, -pulī__	dislodge, drive away
*__lon′gē__	far (away)

Section of old Roman paving on the Capitoline Hill

DECLENSION OF ego AND tū

	Singular		Plural		Singular		Plural	
Nom.	**ego**	I	**nōs**	we	**tū**	you	**vōs**	you
Gen.	**meī**[1]	of me	**nostrī**[1]	of us	**tuī**[1]	of you	**vestrī**[1]	of you
Dat.	**mihi**	to me	**nōbīs**	to us	**tibi**	to you	**vōbīs**	to you
Acc.	**mē**	me	**nōs**	us	**tē**	you	**vōs**	you
Abl.	**mē**	me	**nōbīs**	us	**tē**	you	**vōbīs**	you

USE OF PERSONAL PRONOUNS OF FIRST AND SECOND PERSONS

Latin usually indicates first and second persons by verb endings (**-ō, -s; -mus, -tis**) where English uses "I," "you," or "we" as subject of a verb. However, for emphasis or contrast, **ego, tū, nōs, vōs** are often used in addition to the person endings of a Latin verb.

Tū dormīs; ego labōrō. You sleep; I work.

Vōs fūgistis; nōs mānsimus. You fled; we stayed.

[1]The genitive forms **meī, tuī, nostrī,** and **vestrī** are not used to show possession. The possessive adjectives **meus, -a, -um; tuus, -a, -um; noster, -tra, -trum;** and **vester, -tra, -trum** are used for this purpose. The uses of the genitive forms of the personal pronouns **ego** and **tū** do not occur in this book.

REFLEXIVE PRONOUNS OF FIRST AND SECOND PERSONS

Like third-person **sē,** a first- or second-person reflexive pronoun always refers to the subject of the sentence or clause in which it stands.

Mē nōn laudō. I do not praise myself.
Nōs nōn laudāmus. We do not praise ourselves.
Tē nōn laudās. You do not praise yourself.
Vōs nōn laudātis. You do not praise yourselves.

PRONOUNS WITH cum

When **mē, tē, nōbīs,** or **vōbīs** is used as the object of **cum,** the preposition is attached to the pronoun as a final syllable.

mēcum	with me	**nōbīscum**	with us
tēcum	with you	**vōbīscum**	with you

Cum appears also as a final syllable attached to an ablative form of a reflexive, interrogative, or relative pronoun: **sēcum; quōcum, quibuscum; quōcum, quācum, quibuscum.**

I Complete the sentences with appropriate pronouns selected from the list. The same pronoun may be used more than once. Translate.

1 _____ fugiam, quamquam _____ manēs.
2 _____ servāre dēbētis; _____ juvāre nōn possum.
3 _____ gladiōs nostrōs invēnērunt.
4 Captīvus _____ cēlāre nōn poterat.
5 Quamquam cēterī _____ nōn laudant, tamen saepe _____ laudās.
6 Ambulā _____ ; mōnstrā _____ viam.
7 Hodiē _____ in silvā ambulābimus.

ego
illī
mēcum
mihi
sē
tē
tū
vōs
vōbīscum

II In each group below, four of the five words are in the same case. Identify the one word which is in a different case.

1 hunc, illud, nōbīs, quem, vōs
2 ipsīus, id, cujus, quārum, hōrum
3 ille, hic, ipse, hāc, ego
4 quae, cui, huic, mihi, tibi
5 idem, quis, tuīs, quī, hī

XLI

DECEIVING THE ENEMY

Anna erat puella Rōmāna, quae apud avunculum caecum in Britanniā prope magna castra Rōmāna habitābat. Quamquam haec īnsula erat prōvincia Rōmāna, tamen multī Britannī Rōmānīs amīcī nōn erant. Jam sēcrētō bellum parābant, eīsque Gallī quī trāns aquam angustam habitābant 5 auxilium dabant.

Ōlim Anna rāmōs ex silvā portābat. Avunculus, quamquam caecus erat, tamen eam juvābat. Sonum armōrum subitō audīvērunt. Deinde Anna vīdit multōs virōs armātōs quōrum arma erant nova et mīra. Prīmō virī neque puellam 10 neque avunculum vīdērunt.

Avunculus parvā vōce quaesīvit, "Quid est, Anna? Quī sunt illī virī? Quid faciunt?"

Puella respondit, "Illī virī arma nova portant; sine dubiō sunt Gallī, inimīcī nostrī." 15

Jam dux° virōrum Annam et avunculum vīdit, et eīs dīxit,

°**dux** (nom. sing.) leader

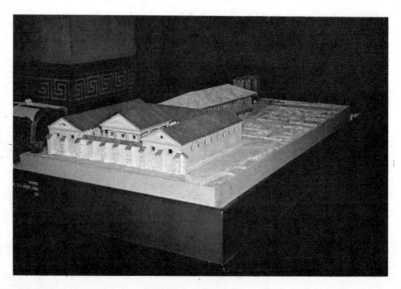

Model of a Roman camp

"Ad oppidum propinquum properāmus, cujus cum incolīs negōtia habēmus. Nōs juvāre dēbētis. Vōbīs praemia dabimus, sī ad hoc oppidum nōs dūcētis."

Avunculus respondit, "Caecus sum, sed haec puella tibi [20] viam mōnstrābit."

Anna, quae timida nōn erat, Gallōs nōn ad oppidum, sed ad castra Rōmāna dūxit, ubi Rōmānī Gallōs cēpērunt.

avun'culus, -ī	M., mother's brother, uncle
cas'tra, -ōrum	N. pl., camp
***du'bium, -ī**	N., doubt
***negō'tium, -ī**	N., business, occupation
quis, quid	(interrog. pron.) who, what
***armā'tus, -a, -um**	armed, equipped
cae'cus, -a, -um	blind
quae'rō, -ere, quaesī'vī	seek, search for
par'vā vō'ce	(abl. sing.) in a low voice

DECLENSION OF THE INTERROGATIVE PRONOUN

	Singular			Plural		
	Masc.	Fem.	Neut.	Masc.	Fem.	Neut.
Nom.	**quis**	**quis**	**quid**			
Gen.	**cujus**	**cujus**	**cujus**	All plural forms are like		
Dat.	**cui**	**cui**	**cui**	those of the relative pro-		
Acc.	**quem**	**quem**	**quid**	noun (see p. 209).		
Abl.	**quō**	**quō**	**quō**			

Singular forms of the interrogative pronoun are the same for all genders except neuter nominative and accusative.

INTERROGATIVE PRONOUN IN USE The
case of an interrogative pronoun is determined by its use in the sentence.

Quid faciunt? What are they doing?
Quī sunt illī virī? Who are those men?

In the first sentence, **Quid** is accusative because it is the direct object of **faciunt.** İn the second, **Quī** is nominative because it is the subject of the sentence.

TRANSLATION OF INTERROGATIVE PRO-NOUNS

In the nominative, a Latin interrogative pronoun is translated by "who" or "what"; in the genitive by "whose," "of what"; and in other cases by "whom" or "what."

"Who," "whose," and "whom" refer to persons; "what" refers to things. The same form is used for both singular and plural of interrogative pronouns in English.

I Select the interrogative pronoun which completes each sentence, and translate.

1 Quid/quī/quā/cui in spēluncā cēlāvērunt?
2 Quibus/quem/quis/quō hōc in oppidō vidēbō?
3 Quae/cujus/quem/quōrum ille vir caecus in mātrimōnium dūxit?
4 Quī/quās/quae/quōrum illa scūta faciunt?
5 Quōs/quis/quī/cui mē cum puellā pulchrā vīdit?

II Translate each sentence and justify the form of each relative or interrogative pronoun.

1 Nōnne puella quae in hāc casā habitat caeca est?
2 Cujus negōtia meus avunculus cūrābat?
3 Arma quae portant capere dēbēmus.
4 Quis mē juvābit?
5 Cui captīvī fābulam suam nārrāvērunt?

III Use each preposition from the list only once to complete the sentences.

1 Puellae _____ silvam ad templum saepe ambulant.   ad
2 Avunculus meus _____ templum habitābat.   apud
3 _____ dubiō incolae oppidī inimīcī erunt.   ex
4 Nautae _____ aquam ad īnsulam nāvigābunt.   in
5 Captīvī _____ castrīs fūgērunt.   per
6 _____ spēluncam mox appropinquābis.   prope
7 Ille fēminam _____ mātrimōnium dūcere dēsīderat.   sine
8 Puella parva _____ nōs nōn jam manet.   trāns

XLII

Plīnius sum; apud avunculum habitābam, cujus vīlla erat in
locō altō inter oppidum Misēnum et ōram maritimam.

Ōlim māter mea in hortō vīllae ambulābat. Subitō clāmāvit, "Spectā flammās clārās! Spectā caelum obscūrum!
Quod perīculum est propinquum?"

Caelum spectāvī. Circum Vesuvium flammae erant clārae
et fūmus erat dēnsus. Statim Plīnium avunculum meum
vocāvī.

Avunculus Vesuvium spectāvit. Tum ad locum altum
extrā mūrōs hortī properāvit.

Mox revēnit et dīxit, "Vocā servōs! Nostrī amīcī, quī vīllās
Vesuviō proximās habent, magnō in perīculō sunt; eōs juvāre
dēbeō. Quī servī mē juvābunt?"

Statim paucīs cum servīs ad ōram maritimam properāvit.
In hortō mānsimus; diū eum expectāvimus, sed nōn revēnit.

Postrīdiē erat magnus mōtus terrae.° Vesuvius fūmum et
cinerēs° dēnsōs in hortum et circum mūrōs mittēbat. Perīculum maximum erat.

Dēnique ā vīllā per viās Misēnī fūgimus. Multī incolae
territī per viās obscūrās et angustās currēbant. Multās post
hōrās ad vīllam lentē revēnimus et ibi avunculum iterum
expectābāmus.

Postrīdiē nūntius vēnit, quī dīxit, "Vesuvius Pompeiōs et
Herculāneum dēlēvit. Avunculus tuus, quī multōs servāvit,
mortuus est."

°**mō'tus ter'rae** (nom. sing.) earthquake • **cinerēs** (acc. pl.)
ashes

*****fū'mus, -ī**	M., smoke
quī, quae, quod	(interrog. adj.) which, what
*****prox'imus, -a, -um**	nearest, very near
*****cur'rō, -ere, cucur'rī**	run
*****ex'trā**	(with acc.) beyond, outside

View of a peaceful Vesuvius from a point southwest of Pompeii. At times the volcano still shows signs of activity, although its recent eruptions have fallen far short of the disaster of A.D. 79, which buried Pompeii and Herculaneum.

THE DECLENSION OF INTERROGATIVE ADJECTIVES is exactly the same as that of relative pronouns (see p. 209).

Quī servī mē juvābunt? Which slaves will help me?
Quod oppidum mōtus terrae dēlēvit? What town did the earth-quake destroy?

An interrogative adjective always agrees in number, gender, and case with the noun it modifies.

A Latin interrogative adjective is translated by "which" or "what."

The same form is used for both singular and plural of interrogative adjectives in English.

I Distinguish between the usage of relative pronouns, interrogative pronouns and interrogative adjectives.

1 Quod templum est pulcherrimum?
2 Quis ad oppidum hodiē vēnit?
3 Quī captīvī fūgērunt ad templum quod vidētis?
4 Virī quī oppidum cēpērunt Rōmānī sunt.
5 Cui nautae fugitīvum mōnstrābō?
6 Dea quam vīdistī Diāna est.
7 Quī servus pīrātam videt cujus gemmās cēpimus?

II 1 Upon what does the case of a Latin relative pronoun depend? Of an interrogative pronoun?
2 What determines the gender and number of a relative pronoun?
3 In what respect does an interrogative adjective agree with the noun that it modifies?

SCRAMBLED SENTENCES

1 servī mē quī juvābunt?
2 quā ā ad fūgistis vīllā oppidum?
3 puerī magnum habet cujus hortum avunculus?
4 incolae dēlēvit quōrum casās territī tempestās sunt.
5 villam quī nūntius ad nostram vēnit?
6 timēbant quod perīculum vīcīnī?
7 quācum est vēnistī quis fēmina?

FIDES OBLIGATA

Fidem meam obligō	I pledge allegiance
vexillō	to the flag
Cīvitātum Ūnitārum	of the United States
Americae	of America
et reī pūblicae	and to the republic
prō quā stat,	for which it stands,
ūnī nātiōnī	one nation
sub Deō	under God,
nōn dīvidendae	indivisible,
cum lībertāte	with liberty
jūstitiāque	and justice
omnibus.	for all.

REVIEW OF UNIT X

Nouns	Adjectives	Adverbs
spēlunca, -ae	*armātus, -a, -um	*crās
*spīna, -ae	*barbarus, -a, -um	*longē
avunculus, -ī	caecus, -a, -um	magnopere
*dominus, -ī	*dūrus, -a, -um	māne
*fūmus, -ī	*fīdus, -a, -um	
*mūrus, -ī	*proximus, -a, -um	Preposition
castra, -ōrum	quī, quae, quod	*extrā
*dubium, -ī	Verbs	
negōtium, -ī	appropinquō, -āre	Idioms
*vērum, -ī	*lateō, -ēre	magnā vōce
Pronouns	*currō, -ere	parvā vōce
quī, quae, quod	dēpellō, -ere	
quis, quid	quaerō, -ere	
	*pereō, -īre	

I Give the infinitive and meaning of each verb as you select
   a) pairs which have similar meanings
   b) pairs which sometimes have similar meanings
   c) look-alikes which may be mistaken for each other
   d) pairs which have contrasting meanings.

1 appellō/dēpellō
2 accūsō/recūsō
3 adōrō/adōrnō
4 cadō/occīdō
5 cupiō/dēsīderō
6 currō/cūrō
7 dō/agō
8 doceō/discō

9 doleō/dēleō
10 gerō/portō
11 jactō/jaciō
12 lateō/cēlō
13 parō/appāreō
14 quaerō/rogō
15 revocō/prōvocō
16 terreō/timeō

II Translate each sentence and justify the form of every Latin pronoun.

1 Incolae oppidōrum, quōs facile vīcimus, tēcta sua dēlent.
2 Daniēl, cui grāta erant pōma, avidē ēdit.
3 Avunculus apud quem manēbāmus nōbīscum ambulāvit.
4 Spēlunca in quā fugitīvus latēbat nōn longē ā vīllā abest.

5 Quid puerī in arcā invenient quam in ōrā maritimā spectant?

6 Sociī rēgis, quī invidiōsī erant, captīvum accūsābant.

7 Quibus servī grātiās ēgērunt?

8 Ipsī nihil dē hīs virīs aut dominō eōrum audīvērunt.

9 Sociōs quibuscum ad īnsulam nāvigāvērunt petunt.

10 Prō cujus ārā scūta posuistis?

III By using a pronoun from the list, combine each pair of separate sentences so as to make a single sentence. Make as few changes as possible.

1 Fēminās fīdās prō templō vīdimus. Eae āram custōdiēbant.

2 Servī ā dominō malō jam fugient. Ille eōs saepe pūnit.

3 Verba sociōrum rēgis audīvī. Haec captīvum accūsāvērunt.

4 Agisne negōtia cum incolīs oppidī? Illud vidēre nunc possumus.

5 Puerīne ursam parvam vulnerāvērunt? Cum eīs per silvam ambulābātis.

6 Virī barbarī incolās oppidī occīdent. Tēcta eōrum jam ārsērunt.

cui
quācum
quae
quārum
quās
quem
quī
quibuscum
quod
quōrum

IV Change each statement to a question by substituting an appropriate interrogative pronoun or interrogative adjective for the word or words underlined.

1 Hoc signum vidēs.

2 Magister discipulōs in viīs relīquit.

3 Cum magā ad cēnam vēnērunt multī virī ferī.

4 Illa castra prōvinciae ā fluviīs nōn longē aberant.

5 Eīdem sonī puellās semper terrent.

6 Sociī fīdī equum ligneum faciunt.

LATIN LIVES TODAY For each of these common English expressions find one or more words in the list on page 226 giving a clue to the meaning of the phrase.

spelunkers' club

exhaust fumes

dubious statement

negotiable check

latent talent

current events

habitual procrastinator

extra-mural competition

ROMAN TRADE

A flourishing international trade was created by the need to import foreign goods for a large population at Rome and by the demand in the provinces for Roman and Italian products. Concentration of wealth in Rome and an increasing taste for luxury stimulated trade with India, China, and Africa. From these distant lands came silks, fine woods, ivory, and other luxurious materials. In turn, Rome and Italy exported manufactured goods to all parts of the empire and even beyond. Overland trade made use of good roads to some extent, but shipping carried most of the trade. With large warehouses and a crowded harbor, Rome's seaport, Ostia, was a busy place.

Above right: Market of Cuicul (modern Djemila) in Roman North Africa, with table (center rear) defining standard measures of grain and wine sold commercially or paid as taxes to Rome.
Above left: Bronze pitcher, an example of goods that were stored in and shipped from Roman warehouses.
Below: Warehouse at Ostia, seaport of Rome. Such storage was vital to Rome's vast shipping trade.

Above left: Mosaic showing square-rigged ship, with oars to be manned by slaves. Such ships carried all kinds of merchandise.

Right: Glassware and (above right) silver bowl, examples of merchandise shipped to all parts of the Roman world. Cargo ships laden with such wares have been found in recent years at the bottom of the Mediterranean, as deep-sea archaeology continues to increase our knowledge of Roman life.

Above left: Air view of extensive ruins of Ostia, and the Tiber River connecting Rome and its seaport.

Below: Roman pottery bowls and (above right) jug found in Britain—probably some of the trade goods of the Roman Empire.

5

A TRICK OF WAR

Ōlim Isrāēlītae cum Midianītīs pugnābant. Midianītae erant multī, sed Isrāēlītae magnās cōpiās nōn habēbant. Isrāēlītae bonōs gladiōs et scūta valida habēbant et bene pugnābant, sed cōnsilia bellī nōn satis bona cēpērunt.

Dēnique Gideōn Isrāēlītās ad cōnsilium convocāvit et 5 dīxit, "Cōnsilia proeliī nostra nōn sunt bona. Dolum autem in animō ēgregium habeō. Hodiē, quod vōs bene pugnāvistis, fessī estis. Midianītae quoque bene pugnāvērunt et jam fessī sunt; proelium noctū nōn expectābunt. Deus noster cōpiās nostrās dūcet et nōbīs splendidam dabit victōriam." 10

Ubi Gideōn cōnsilium nārrāvit, Isrāēlītae ejus cōnsilium statim laudāvērunt. Virī erant fessī, sed erant laetī quod dolus erat ēgregius.

Gideōn virīs tubās et urnās et lucernās dedit. Noctū cum virīs fessīs ē tabernāculīs properāvit. Virī lucernās in urnīs 15 portābant. Nūllus Midianīta Isrāēlītās vīdit, quod nox erat obscūra. Subitō Gideōn tubam īnflāvit et clāmāvit. Virī tubās īnflāvērunt, clāmāvērunt, urnās frēgērunt. Tum lūmina mōnstrāvērunt. Cōpiae Isrāēlītārum nōn erant magnae, sed lūmina erant multa et clāra. Midianītae cōnfūsī 20 et territī celeriter fūgērunt.

Itaque Isrāēlītae oppida et agrōs pulchrōs Midianītārum miserōrum occupāvērunt.

cōpiae, -ārum F. pl., troops • **satis** sufficiently • **proe-lium, -ī** N., battle • **dolus, -ī** M., craft, trick • **fessus, -a, -um** tired • ***tuba** trumpet • ***urna** urn • ***taber-nāculum, -ī** N., tent • **nox** (nom.) night • ***īnflāvit** blew into • **frēgērunt** broke • **lūmina** (nom., acc. pl.) lights • ***cōnfūsus, -a, -um** confused

The Palatine portion of Rome as seen from the air. In antiquity this was the choice
residential area, where the important and the wealthy built their palatial homes.

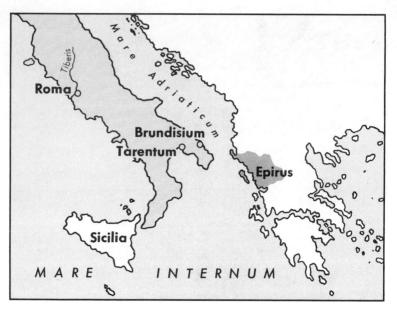

The map shows the relative positions of Rome and Epirus, the native land of Pyrrhus.

XLIII

SMALL BEGINNING OF A GREAT WAR

Prīmō Rōma erat parva urbs. Paulātim autem Rōmānī urbēs fīnitimās vincēbant et terrās suās augēbant; mox magnam partem Ītaliae tenēbant.

Multī incolae quoque ē Graeciā in Ītaliam migrāvērunt. Rōmānī colōniās eōrum appellābant "Magnam Graeciam." Maximum oppidum Magnae Graeciae erat Tarentum. Cum 5 Tarentīnīs Rōmānī pācem fēcērunt.

Per lēgātōs Rōmānī Tarentīnīs dīxērunt, "Nostrae nāvēs longae numquam prope vestram ōram maritimam nāvigābunt; vōbīscum amīcitiam pācemque habēbimus perpetuam gerēmusque negōtia." 10

Ōlim autem decem nāvēs longae Rōmānōrum prope oppidum Tarentum nāvigāvērunt. Rōmānī nōn petīvērunt bellum, sed negōtia pācis. Tarentīnī autem īrātissimī proelium commīsērunt et quīnque nāvēs Rōmānās dēlēvērunt.

Rōma statim bellum parāre incēpit. Tarentīnī ducēs, quod 15
parvās cōpiās habēbant, auxilium ā Graecīs fīnitimīs petīvērunt. Graecī autem satis magnās cōpiās nōn habēbant.

Forte erat in īnsulā Siciliā Pyrrhus, rēx Ēpīrī, quī in animō
habēbat rēgnum īnsulae obtinēre. Pyrrhus, ubi dē ducibus
Tarentīnīs īrātīs audīvit, magnīs cum cōpiīs in Ītaliam 20
prōcessit. Initium vērō bellī fuit!

+**cōpiae,**[1] **-ārum**	F. pl., troops, forces
lēgātus, -ī	M., representative; staff officer, lieutenant
proelium, -ī	N., battle
dux, ducis	M., leader
*__nāvis, nāvis (-ium)__	F., ship; (with **longa**) warship
*__pars, partis (-ium)__	F., part, portion
pāx, pācis	F., peace
*__urbs, urbis (-ium)__	F., city
fīnitimus, -a, -um	neighboring, adjacent; (as noun) M. pl., neighbors
*__decem__	ten
*__quīnque__	five
*__augeō, -ēre, auxī__	increase, enlarge
*__obtineō, -ēre, -tinuī__	possess, occupy, obtain
*__committō, -ere, -mīsī__	commit, entrust; (with **proelium**) begin
numquam	never
paulātim	little by little
satis	enough
*__vērō__	truly, surely, in fact

THIRD-DECLENSION NOUNS have many kinds
of endings in nominative singular. The declension to which
a Latin noun belongs, however, can always be determined
from the genitive singular ending, which is different for each
declension.

All Declension III nouns have genitive singular ending in
-is. (Declension I nouns have **-ae;** Declension II nouns
have **-ī.**)

---

[1]Beginning with this lesson the accented syllables of vocabulary words will not be indicated. For help with accent and syllabication see page 398.

233

ALL THREE GENDERS occur in Declension III nouns. Words for males are naturally masculine; for females, feminine: **rēx**, king (M.); **māter**, mother (F.).

Other nouns may be masculine, feminine, or neuter: **honor**, honor (M.); **pāx**, peace (F.); **caput**, head (N.).

As with nouns of other declensions, the ending of the nominative singular sometimes gives a clue to gender. The most practical way to remember the gender of Declension III nouns is to memorize a phrase in which a modifying adjective clearly indicates gender. For example, in "Small Beginning of a Great War" we find **parva urbs, magnam partem, nostrae nāvēs, pācem perpetuam.**

DECLENSION OF MASCULINE/FEMININE NOUNS OF THIRD DECLENSION

	Singular	Singular	Endings		Singular	Singular	Endings
Nom.	**lēx** (F.)	**dux** (M.)	—		**arx** (F.)	**urbs** (F.)	—
Gen.	**lē′gis**	**du′cis**	-is		**ar′cis**	**ur′bis**	-is
Dat.	**lē′gī**	**du′cī**	-ī		**ar′cī**	**ur′bī**	-ī
Acc.	**lē′gem**	**du′cem**	-em		**ar′cem**	**ur′bem**	-em
Abl.	**lē′ge**	**du′ce**	-e		**ar′ce**	**ur′be**	-e
	Plural	Plural			Plural	Plural	
Nom.	**lē′gēs**	**du′cēs**	-ēs		**ar′cēs**	**ur′bēs**	-ēs
Gen.	**lē′gum**	**du′cum**	-um		**ar′cium**	**ur′bium**	-ium
Dat.	**lē′gibus**	**du′cibus**	-ibus		**ar′cibus**	**ur′bibus**	-ibus
Acc.	**lē′gēs**	**du′cēs**	-ēs		**ar′cēs**	**ur′bēs**	-ēs
Abl.	**lē′gibus**	**du′cibus**	-ibus		**ar′cibus**	**ur′bibus**	-ibus

MOST CASE ENDINGS are the same for all Declension III masculine and feminine nouns, except in nominative singular and genitive plural. Genitive plural ends usually in **-um**, less frequently in **-ium**. Whenever **-ium** occurs, it will be indicated in the vocabulary listing of the noun.

	Singular (M./F.)	Plural (M./F.)
Nom.	(varied)	-ēs
Gen.	-is	-um/-ium
Dat.	-ī	-ibus
Acc.	-em	-ēs
Abl.	-e	-ibus

NOUNS OF ONE SYLLABLE ENDING IN

-x are mostly feminine.

lēx, lēgis (F.), law	**arx, arcis** (F.), citadel

Exceptions are nouns referring to males or male occupations.

dux, ducis (M.), leader	**rēx, rēgis** (M.), king

NOUNS OF ONE SYLLABLE ENDING IN

-s, when final **-s** is preceded by a consonant, are mostly feminine.[1]

pars, partis (F.), part	**urbs, urbis** (F.), city

Only four exceptions are masculine.

fōns, fontis (M.), fountain	**pōns, pontis** (M.), bridge
mōns, montis (M.), mountain	**dēns, dentis** (M.), tooth

All Declension III nouns should be memorized with the genitive singular. English derivatives can be useful in learning the genitive singular; e.g., dental (**dēns, dentis**); legal (**lēx, lēgis**).

I Change singulars to plurals in the same cases.

1 magna urbs
2 bonī ducis
3 altae arcis
4 longae nāvī
5 cum bonō duce
6 bonam lēgem

II Translate each English phrase into Latin; then give an English translation of each complete sentence.

1 Into a neighboring city migrāvimus.
2 A few ships armātae sunt.
3 With faithful leaders appropinquant.
4 Aquam of the clear fountain bibam.
5 A large part agrī arida est.
6 Fugitīvī across the bridge cucurrērunt.
7 Ā ducibus just laws petimus.
8 Rēx on the high citadel stat.

---

[1]When final **-s** is preceded by a vowel in a monosyllabic noun, the gender is usually neuter; e.g., **jūs, jūris** (N.), law, right. A few such nouns are masculine.

III Add appropriate endings to the incomplete words; then translate the sentences. When either singular or plural ending
is correct, complete the word both ways.

1 Incolae urb- magnopere pāc- dēsīderābant.
2 Pont- in fluviō lātissimō fēcimus.
3 Agricola ursam timidam in obscūrā part- cavernae vīdit.
4 Pōns ab alt- arc- ad proxim- mont- pertinet.
5 Optim- duc- praemia splendida dedī.
6 Lēg- jūstae rēg- benign- incolīs grātae sunt.

SCRAMBLED SENTENCE Rearrange the words of this
sentence and translate.

amīcitiamque   urbēs   cum   habēbant   insulīsque
Graeciae   pācem   oppidīs   multae   fīnitimīs.

XLIV

A PYRRHIC VICTORY

Mox Pyrrhus cum cōpiīs Graecīs in Ītaliam vēnit, ubi
bellum gerere incēpit.

Mīlitēs Graecī gladiōs longōs, hastās longissimās, clipeōs°
habēbant; galeās validās in capitibus gerēbant.

Praetereā Pyrrhus multōs elephantōs habēbat. Elephantī 5
erant maxima animālia; in tergīs elephantōrum erant parva
tēcta, ubi mīlitēs armātī stābant.

Inter cōpiās Rōmānās erant multī peditēs equitēsque. Eō
tempore Rōmānī quoque valida arma—hastās, gladiōs, galeās,
scūta—habēbant. Nōn satis longī autem erant eōrum gladiī 10
et hastae.

Prīmō Rōmānī firmiter stetērunt; tum Pyrrhus elephantōs
in proelium mīsit. Hī elephantī nova atque mīra animālia
erant; tamen Rōmānī sē nōn recēpērunt.

°**clipeus, -ī** M., round shield (as opposed to the Roman **scūtum,** an
oblong shield)

Equī autem Rōmānōrum timēbant elephantōs. Fūgērunt 15
et dominōs suōs interfēcērunt et per aciem° Rōmānām cucurrērunt. Quā dē causā Graecī prīmō proeliō Rōmānōs
vīcērunt.

Tamen victōria Pyrrhī pretiōsissima erat; nam in campō
proeliī corpora optimōrum mīlitum Graecōrum jacēbant. 20

°**aciem** (acc. sing.) battle line

*caput, capitis	N., head
*corpus, corporis	N., body
*eques, equitis	M., horseman; pl., cavalry
*miles, militis	M., soldier
*pedes, peditis	M., foot soldier; pl., infantry
*tempus, temporis	N., time
*pretiōsus, -a, -um	costly, precious, expensive
*jaceō, -ēre, -uī	lie, recline
*firmiter	firmly
praetereā	besides
nam	for (introduces an explanation)
bellum gerere	to wage war
sē recipere	to retreat

NEUTER NOUNS OF THIRD DECLENSION

follow "the Neuter Law"; as in all neuter nouns, nominative
and accusative are identical, and in the plural, nominative
and accusative end in **-a.**

Like other Declension III nouns, most neuters have **-um**
in genitive plural.

Exceptions are neuter nouns ending in **-e, -al,** or **-ar,** which
have **-ium** in genitive plural. These same nouns also have **-ī**
in ablative singular and **-ia** in nominative and accusative
plural.

Neuter nouns may cause confusion if they are not recog-
nized as such. A useful practice is to make a list of Declension III neuters as you meet them. They are not numerous.

DECLENSION OF NEUTER NOUNS

	Declension III	Declension III	Declension II
	Singular	Singular	Singular
Nom.	ca'put	a'nimal	bel'lum
Gen.	ca'pitis	animā'lis	bel'lī
Dat.	ca'pitī	animā'lī	bel'lō
Acc.	ca'put	a'nimal	bel'lum
Abl.	ca'pite	animā'lī	bel'lō
	Plural	Plural	Plural
Nom.	ca'pita	animā'lia	bel'la
Gen.	ca'pitum	animā'lium	bellō'rum
Dat.	capi'tibus	animā'libus	bel'līs
Acc.	ca'pita	animā'lia	bel'la
Abl.	capi'tibus	animā'libus	bel'līs

This decorated pottery plate dates from the time of the war with Pyrrhus, and bears testimony to the sensation Pyrrhus' elephants caused among the Romans.

NEUTER CASE ENDINGS COMPARED

	Declension III Nouns		Declension II Nouns	
	Singular	Plural	Singular	Plural
Nom.	(varied)	**-a/-ia**	**-um**	**-a**
Gen.	**-is**	**-um/-ium**	**-ī**	**-ōrum**
Dat.	**-ī**	**-ibus**	**-ō**	**-īs**
Acc.	(varied)	**-a/-ia**	**-um**	**-a**
Abl.	**-e/-ī**	**-ibus**	**-ō**	**-īs**

LOOK AND THINK about other Declension III nouns in "A Pyrrhic Victory." What clues can you find as to the form and use of each of these words?

peditēs (line 8)
equitēs (line 8)

mīlitēs (lines 3, 7)
mīlitum (line 20)

I Supply the ending of the noun or adjective in each phrase so that the adjective is in agreement with its noun.

1 magna animāl___
2 tacitus mīl___
3 eōdem tempor___
4 peditēs armāt___
5 benignī duc___

6 pulchram urb___
7 magn___ caput
8 multās part___
9 parvōs dent___
10 magn___ corpus

II In the sentences below substitute for each underlined word or phrase a Declension III noun of similar meaning. Make other necessary changes and translate both versions.

1 Māne mīlitēs <u>oppidum</u> dēlēre incēpērunt.
2 Rēx prō populō <u>vītam quiētam</u> cupīvit.
3 Nautae <u>nāviculam</u> validam aedificāvērunt.
4 Dux <u>armātōs virōs</u> pugnāre docuit.

XLV

A ROMAN STATESMAN

Post prīmum proelium magnum Pyrrhus pācem dēsīderāvit et ad Rōmānōs nūntium mīsit. Oppida Rōmāna Magnae

The meeting place of the Italian Senate is decorated with frescoes of scenes from Roman history by Cesare Maccari. Appius Claudius is pictured in one of these.

Graeciae postulāvit. Multī ducēs Rōmānī Pyrrhō illa oppida dare cupiēbant.

Ēgregius senātor et cōnsul erat Appius Claudius, quī cōn-struxerat° longum aquaeductum—Aquam Appiam. Viam Appiam Appius Claudius quoque mūnīvit. 5

Appius, jam senex° caecusque, vītam agēbat quiētam et in senātū° nōn saepe aderat.

Appius, quamquam ā senātū aberat, tamen ex amīcīs verba nūntiī audīvit. Statim auxiliō servōrum in senātum pro-perāvit. 10

Ibi Appius dīxit, "Interdum amīcī meī dolent quod sum caecus. Sed hodiē sum laetus, quod hunc Graecum superbum in senātū Rōmānō vidēre nōn possum. Hodiē mihi dolōrem dant amīcī meī. Quam caecī vōs estis, Rōmānī! Rōma erit 15 tūta; illa oppida erunt tūta; nēmō° in fīnibus nostrīs nōs vincet."

°cōnstrūxerat had built • senex (nom. sing.) aged, old
senātū* (abl. sing.) senate • nēmō (nom.) no one

240

Propter haec verba senātōrēs pācem cum hostibus nōn fēcērunt. Posteā cōpiae Rōmānae ācriter pugnāvērunt; 20 dēnique Pyrrhus cum cōpiīs suīs Ītaliam relīquit.

*dolor, -ōris	M., grief, sorrow
*fīnis, -is (-ium)	M. or F., limit, end; M. pl., boundaries, territory
mūniō, -īre, -īvī	fortify, build; (with **viam**) build a road
ācriter	fiercely
quam	how
vītam agere	live

WORD MASTERY 9

Many Latin nouns ending in **-or** have the same form and meaning as in English.

actor   color   furor   janitor   odor   tutor   victor

Some Latin words in **-or** are closely related to verbs you have already learned and denote the result of the action expressed in the verb.

ārdor/ārdeō   clāmor/clāmō   error/errō   terror/terreō

Other Latin nouns in **-tor** designate the agent of the act expressed by the verb to which they are related.

agitātor/agitō   creātor/creō   liberātor/līberō   monitor/moneō

Give the meaning of the English equivalents of these Latin nouns in **-tor**.

dēbitor   crēditor   cūrātor   nārrātor   spectātor

From these familiar verbs form Latin nouns and give the English derivative of each.

audiō   cantō   doceō   faciō   inveniō   nāvigō

LOOK AND THINK   Some English nouns in **-tor** have a vowel before the suffix; others do not.

NOUNS IN -tor/-or are mostly masculine. In these nouns, as in many other Declension III nouns, nominative singular is the same as the base, to which regular endings of other cases are added.

senātor, senātōris (M.), senator   **dolor, dolōris** (M.), grief

Three **-or** nouns are feminine, and a few are neuter.

soror, sorōris (F.), sister   **arbor, arbŏris** (F.), tree
uxor, uxōris (F.), wife   **aequor, aequŏris** (N.), surface

GENITIVE PLURAL ENDING IN -ium is found with most Declension III nouns which have two consonants before the ending of genitive singular **(urbs, urbis)**; also with most nouns which have the same number of syllables in genitive singular as in nominative singular **(finis, finis).**

Many of these nouns end in **-is** or **-ēs** and are sometimes masculine, sometimes feminine. Some nouns obviously may be either masculine or feminine.

hostis, hostis (M.), enemy   **nāvis, nāvis** (F.), ship
cīvis, cīvis (M. or F.), citizen   **nūbēs, nūbis** (F.), cloud

Exceptions to these two keys to the **-ium** form of genitive plural are **frāter, frātris** (M.), brother; **māter, mātris** (F.), mother; **pater, patris** (M.), father; **canis, canis** (M. or F.), dog, and **juvenis, juvenis** (M.), young man. All of these have **-um** in genitive plural.

I From the endings select all those which may appear in other cases of each Latin word in the numbered list.

-a	-um	1 animal	6 dēns
-e	-is	2 arbor	7 dolor
-ī	-em	3 canis	8 fīnis
-ium	-ia	4 caput	9 sōl
-ō	-ibus	5 corpus	10 urbs
-īs	-ēs		

II Translate the following sentences.
1 Peditēs, dum in ōrā maritimā jacent, animal ferum vīdērunt.
2 Mīlitēs arcem occupāvērunt et cōnsulēs in exilium ēgērunt.

242

3 Paucī senātōrēs in urbe manēbant.
4 Dolor multārum uxōrum lēgātum mōvit.
5 Canis Cerberus portās Orcī custōdit.
6 Cōnsul equitēs trāns pontem mittit.

WORD MASTERY 10

We add certain suffixes in English to indicate a smaller size of something. A cigarette, for instance, is a small cigar. We find this same suffix in the noun drum majorette (a person smaller than a drum major, and feminine, too). A booklet is a little book, and a lambkin, a little lamb. "Jenkins" is Welsh for "little John." "Armadillo" is Spanish for a "little armed (animal)", from Latin **armātus**. Such words are called diminutives.

Latin diminutives often end in **-ulus, -a, -um** (English -le, -ule) or **-culus, -a, -um** (English -cle, -cule). **Calx, calcis** means "stone, pebble." **Calculus** means "a little stone." People used stones for reckoning; therefore, they "calculated." **Corpusculum** means "a little body." **Avunculus** came from **avus** (grandfather) and meant literally "little grandfather" before the meaning shifted to "uncle."

Diminutives are also used to express affection or endearment. **Filiola** therefore means "(dear) little daughter." **Tulliola** was Cicero's pet name for his daughter Tullia. At a later time, Roman soldiers affectionately called their emperor Caligula (from **caliga,** boot).

The sword-shaped leaves of a certain flower inspired a Roman naturalist (Pliny) to name that flower **gladiolus** (little sword).

The diminutive of **puer** is **puerulus;** the feminine form **puerula** is the origin of **puella.**

Look up the origin and development in meaning of these English words: rivulet, formula, ventricle.

With what familiar Latin nouns do you associate these diminutives? What does each one mean?

capitulum	nāvicula	oppidulum	rēgulus

What is the meaning of **particula (pars)**? What is the corresponding English word? To what does a particular refer? Why might a person be called "particular"?

ROMAN INDUSTRIES

The only industry a freeborn Roman could properly engage in was agriculture. Small farms were tilled by the owner and his family; large estates were worked by slaves. Such farms often produced wood and stone for building, but their chief products were oil, wine, and grain.

Most of the industrial work of Rome was done by slaves or by former slaves who had earned or been given their freedom. In towns and cities brick and pottery industries flourished, as did also shipbuilding and metalworking. A large commercial business, carried on by fullers, was the cleaning of clothes, although clothing and the cloth from which it was made were usually produced at home.

Bread, which was seldom baked at home, was made and sold by bakers, who were also millers. Other foods, including prepared hot food, were sold in open-air markets. In fact, almost every large house had small rooms fronting on the street which were rented to various shopkeepers.

Above: Fuller's vats in a Pompeian shop.
Left: Baker's shop pictured on a Pompeian wall.

Below: Holes in the counter held pots of hot food for sale in an open-air food stall in Herculaneum.

Above: A famous mosaic from North Africa shows buildings and activities of a Roman farm—plowing, sowing, pumping water, feeding animals, hunting, and netting birds.

Below left: Factory for pressing olive oil and purifying it by gravity flow.
Right: Mills where grain was ground into flour for a bakery in Ostia.
Bottom: Amphorae lie in the racks of a wine shop as when in use.

Family relationships of the Romans are indicated by these commonly used terms.

avus, -ī	M., grandfather		**fīlius, -ī**	M., son
avia, -ae	F., grandmother		**fīlia, -ae**[1]	F., daughter
pater, -tris	M., father		**frāter, -tris**	M., brother
māter, -tris	F., mother		**soror, -ōris**	F., sister

The relationship of father to mother (**pater/māter**) is that of husband to wife (**marītus/uxor**).

marītus, -ī M., husband   **uxor, -ōris** F., wife

Like "spouse" in English, the Latin word **conjūnx, -jugis** means either "husband" or "wife." In Latin the gender of an accompanying adjective helps to determine the meaning.

conjūnx altus M., tall husband   **conjūnx pulchra** F., pretty wife

The English words "uncle" and "aunt" do not reveal whether the relationship is on the father's or mother's side. The Romans had two words for "uncle" and two for "aunt."

Father's brother:	**patruus,**	**-ī**	M., uncle
Mother's brother:	**avunculus, -ī**		M., uncle
Father's sister:	**amita,**	**-ae**	F., aunt
Mother's sister:	**mātertera, -ae**		F., aunt

The Latin words for "first cousin" make a similar distinction.

Father's side:	**patruēlis,**	**-is**	M. or F., first cousin
Mother's side:	**cōnsōbrīnus, -ī**		M., first cousin
	cōnsōbrīna, -ae		F., first cousin

The English words "niece" and "nephew" make no distinction between a brother's child and a sister's child. Latin terms for brother's son, sister's son, brother's daughter, and sister's daughter leave no doubt as to the relationship.

fīlius frātris	M., nephew	**fīlia frātris**	F., niece
fīlius sorōris	M., nephew	**fīlia sorōris**	F., niece

---

[1]Dative and ablative plural forms are **fīliābus** to distinguish them from corresponding forms of **fīlius.**

With Clio, the Muse of history (left), are Melpomene, who presided over tragedy (indicated by the theatrical mask), and Thalia, Muse of comedy, playing a rustic flute. The nine Muses of Greek and Roman mythology were under the protection of Apollo, and inspired mortals in poetry, arts, and sciences. The painting by Eustache Le Seuer (1616-1655) is in the Louvre.

XLVI

THE TWELVE TABLES

Initiō Rōmānī lēgēs scrīptās nōn habēbant. Tandem vērō cīvēs lēgēs scrīptās° postulāvērunt.

Senātōrēs igitur trēs° lēgātōs ad urbem Athēnās mīsērunt. Hī lēgātī lēgēs Solōnis sapientissimī° explōrāvērunt et ad urbem Rōmam revēnērunt. 5

°**lēgēs scrīptae** written laws • **trēs** (nom., acc.) three
sapientissimus, -a, -um wisest, very wise

Ollie Atkins, The Saturday Evening Post

A panel of the bronze door of the Supreme Court Building in Washington, D.C., bears the inscription "Justinian Code," with the figure of the emperor who commissioned the revision of the Roman law code called Corpus Juris. The whole design acknowledges the debt of our law codes to Roman law.

Cīvēs Rōmānī tum cōnstituērunt, "Decem virōs dēligēmus quī summum imperium habēbunt dum lēgēs novās parant."

Deinde cīvēs prō cōnsulibus decemvirōs dēlēgērunt, inter quōs erant illī trēs lēgātī. Post ūnum annum° decemvirī decem tabulās lēgum in forō posuērunt. Cīvēs lēgēs magnā 10 cum cūrā lēgērunt et probāvērunt.

Decemvirī autem labōrem nōndum perfēcerant.° Iterum dēlēgērunt cīvēs Rōmānī aliōs decemvirōs.

Eī decemvirī autem, potestātis cupidī, neque lēgēs cēterās parāvērunt neque imperium dēposuērunt. Quasi° paucī ty- 15 rannī multitūdinem cīvium rēgnābant.

Senātōrēs tandem decemvirōs imperium dēpōnere co- ēgērunt. Cīvēs iterum dēlēgērunt cōnsulēs, quī mox duās° tabulās lēgum parāvērunt.

Jam erant cōnsulēs jūstī; jam erant lēgēs bonae duodecim° 20 tabulārum.

°**post ūnum annum** one year later; after one year • **perfē- cerant** had completed • **quasi*** as if, as though • **duās** (acc.) two • **duodecim** twelve

***tyrannus, -ī**	M., tyrant, absolute ruler
decemvirī, -ōrum	M. pl., magistrates who drew up the XII tables; group of ten magistrates
***imperium, -ī**	N., government, authority; empire
***cīvis, -is (-ium)**	M. or F., citizen
***lēx, lēgis**	F., law
potestās, -ātis	F., power, control
cupidus, -a, -um	desirous, eager
summus, -a, -um	highest, greatest, utmost; top of, highest part of
***probō, -āre, -āvī**	test, try, prove
***rēgnō, -āre, -āvī**	rule, reign
cōgō, -ere, coēgī	compel, force
***dēpōnō, -ere, -posuī**	lay down, put aside
legō, -ere, lēgī	collect; gather together; read
perficiō, -ere, -fēcī	finish, accomplish
nōndum	not yet
tandem	at last, at length

249

are feminine. These nouns have regular case endings, with
-um in genitive plural.

potestās, potestātis (F.), power
multitūdō, multitūdinis (F.), multitude

Similarly, nouns in **-tūs** (gen., **-tūtis**) and **-ūs** (gen., **-ūtis**)
are also mostly feminine.

virtūs, virtūtis (F.), courage   **salūs, salūtis** (F.), greeting

I Add endings (both singular and plural, when sensible) to the
incomplete words, and make necessary changes to suit singular
and plural endings. Translate.

1 Cōnsul labōr- mīlit- castrōrum auxit.
2 Fīdus can- prope pedit- jacēbat.
3 Nūb- ātra fūmī urb- cēlāvit.
4 Multitūdō nautārum īrātōrum cīv- amīca nōn erat.
5 Cum uxōr- senātōr- ad forum properat.
6 Partēs nāv- longae dēlēbimus.

II Combine each noun from the numbered list with an adjective
from the lettered list to form a sensible phrase.

1 sorōrēs	6 mīlitis	a) albī	g) validōrum
2 pācem	7 uxōre	b) tacitī	h) dūrī
3 nāvibus	8 corporum	c) altus	i) summae
4 eques	9 potestātī	d) cārā	j) aeternam
5 mōns	10 labōrēs	e) geminae	k) pulchrōs
		f) longīs	l) perītus

XLVII

THE TIBER

Flūmen Tiberis dē montibus per urbem Rōmam fluit. Inter-
dum flāvum est quod flāvam arēnam et lutum flāvum dēportat.
Hoc flūmen Jāniculum ā cēterīs regiōnibus Rōmae sēparat.
Hostēs autem fīnitimī flūmen facile trānsīre nōn poterant.
Rōmānī Jāniculum quoque mūrīs validīs mūnīvērunt.   5

250

Rēx Ancus antīquitus prīmum pontem, Pontem Sublicium, ex lignō cōnstrūxit. Posteā custōdēs pontem custōdiēbant. Dē illō ponte Rōmānī hanc fābulam nārrābant.

Ōlim rēx Etrūriae cum Rōmānīs pugnābat. Magnīs cōpiīs cēpit Jāniculum. Statim ad Pontem Sublicium properāvit; 10 flūmen Tiberim trānsīre in animō habuit.

Permōtī custōdēs fugere incēpērunt, sed Horātius, Rōmānus ēgregius et firmus, clāmāvit, "Dēlēte pontem! Aliter Rōmam dēfendere nōn poterimus!"

Duo° ex hominibus quidem cum Horātiō firmiter stetērunt, 15 dum aliī cīvēs pontem dēlent. Ubi pōns tremere incēpit, illī hominēs fūgērunt. Horātius sōlus pontem angustum dēfendit. Subitō in flūmen pōns cecidit, sed Horātius armātus in Tiberim dēsiluit, et ad alteram rīpam natāvit ubi cēterī Rōmānī eum expectābant. 20

Jam Rōma tūta erat, quod sine ponte hostēs urbem Rōmam capere nōn poterant. Hostēs flūmen Tiberim trānsīre nōn poterant.

°**duo*** two

lignum, -ī	N., wọod
lutum, -ī	N., mud, dirt
***custōs, -ōdis**	M., guard, watchman
flūmen, -inis	N., river
homō, -inis	M., man, human being
***hostis, -is (-ium)**	M., enemy
***mōns, montis (-ium)**	M., mountain
***pōns, pontis (-ium)**	M., bridge
[1]**alter, altera, alterum**	other, the other
flāvus, -a, -um	yellow
permōtus, -a, -um	alarmed, moved
***dēportō, -āre, -āvī**	carry away, remove
natō, -āre, -āvī	swim
***cōnstruō, -ere, -strūxī**	build, construct
***tremō, -ere, -uī**	tremble, quake
dēsiliō, -īre, -uī	leap down
***trānseō, -īre, -iī**	go across, cross over

[1]The declension of this adjective is irregular in genitive and dative singular. (See page 428.)

251

NOUNS ENDING IN -iō (-iōnis) or -ō (-inis) are mostly feminine.

regiō, regiōnis (F.), region   **virgō, virginis** (F.), maiden

Exceptions are **-iō** words designating males and male occupations, and a few **-ō** words with genitive singular **-inis** (including some proper names), which are masculine.

centūriō, centūriōnis (M.),   **homō, hominis** (M.), man, human being
centurion   **Apollō, Apollinis** (M.), Apollo

NOUNS ENDING IN -ō (-ōnis) are masculine.

leō, leōnis (M.), lion   **sermō, sermōnis** (M.), talk, speech

NOUNS ENDING IN -en (-inis) are mostly neuter.

flūmen, flūminis (N.), river   **carmen, carminis** (N.), song

A painting of the Tiber in the eighteenth century by the Italian artist Vanvitelli (1653-1736). Many of the buildings and the bridge look much the same today. The round edifice on the right was the tomb of the Emperor Hadrian, and through much of the time since has served as a fortress and a prison. It is the setting of Puccini's opera *Tosca*, and is now called Castel Sant' Angelo.

Feminine nouns are formed in Latin from certain adjectives by adding the suffix **-tūdō.** Their English derivatives end in -tude.

altitūdō   **lātitūdō**   **longitūdō**   **magnitūdō**

Form Latin nouns and their English derivatives from these adjectives, and use each derivative in a sentence.

sōlus   **multus**   **pulcher**   **quiētus**

Other feminine nouns are formed from Latin adjectives by adding **-tās.** Their English derivatives end in -ty.

antīquitās   **dignitās**   **lībertās**   **timiditās**

Form Latin nouns and their English derivatives from these adjectives; then use each derivative in a sentence.

benignus   **cūriōsus**   **ūnus**   **propinquus**   **vīcīnus**

Action nouns in Latin are formed by the hundreds from Latin verbs. They appear with the suffix **-tiō/-siō,** and corresponding English words end in -tion/-sion.

explōrātiō   **missiō**   **inventiō**   **petītiō**   **vīsiō**

With what verbs can you associate the preceding nouns? Form Latin nouns and English derivatives from these verbs.

dēleō   **faciō**   **mūniō**   **occupō**   **redūcō**   **vocō**

Many other Latin nouns ending in **-iō** have English derivatives ending in -ion.

centūriō   **legiō**   **nātiō**   **optiō**   **ratiō**   **regiō**

Latin nouns in **-iō/-tiō/-siō** are nearly all feminine. Exceptions are a few (like **centūriō**) that refer to males or male occupations.

LOOK AND THINK   Give the Latin nouns that correspond to the English nouns of these phrases.

application for a position   faculty of the university
dignity in the community   security of the multitude

253

I Translate.

1 Flūmen Tiberis per urbem Rōmam fluit.

2 Hostēs multa flūmina in regiōnibus montium trānsībunt.

3 Rōmānī centuriōnēs mīlitēsque legiōnis Rōmānae vītam perīculōsam agēbant.

4 Lēgēs Solōnis, virī Athēnārum, bonae et jūstae sunt.

5 Trēs ex nāvibus longīs ad pontem paulātim appropinquābant.

6 Graecī magnō cum labōre equum ex lignō cōnstrūxērunt.

II Translate each underlined word with a Declension III noun, supplying the ending appropriate to its use in the sentence. Give the nominative and genitive plural of each.

1 There was no spring near the river.

2 The shouts of the citizens approved the new laws.

3 Between the two mountains is a narrow region of fields.

4 The soldiers' helmets protect their heads.

5 The man took the food from the animal.

6 The other tree stood near the end of the road.

7 The citizens are very unfriendly to the senator.

8 We shall attack the cavalry and infantry of the enemy at the same time.

XLVIII

A LETTER FROM THE FRONT

Mārcus Sextō salūtem dīcit. Sī valēs, bene est; valeō. Sumus prope parvum oppidum Haeduōrum, et legiō nostra castra posuit in rīpā flūminis quod lātum et altum est.

Hodiē mīlitēs nostrī, quī bene labōrāvērunt, circum castra mūrum aedificāvērunt. Magnā cum difficultāte multī rāmōs 5 et saxa ē silvā portābant; multī equōs cūrābant; multī tabernācula parābant, sed cum illīs mīlitibus nōn labōrābam. Cum paucīs explōrātōribus cibum in dēnsā silvā petēbam. In hāc regiōne sunt multa genera animālium. Nūllī autem leōnēs in hāc parte Galliae, sed ursae paucae sunt. Multōs cervōs 10 necāvimus, quōrum corpora ad castra portāvimus.

Hodiē paucīs cum sociīs in silvā ambulābam. Silvam circumspectāvimus, sed nūllōs vīdimus Helvētiōs. In mediō flūmine erat magnum saxum ad quod cum sociīs meīs natāvī. In saxō diū sedēbāmus et mīlitēs in alterā rīpā spectābāmus. 15 Paucī in flūmine natābant; capita eōrum in aquā vīdimus. Laetus sum, quod hāc in regiōne diū manēbimus.

Explōrātōrēs nostrī dīxērunt, "Helvētiī, quī magnās cōpiās trāns flūmen habent, castra nostra vāstāre parant, sed eōs nōn timēmus. Gallī Helvētiōs timent, quod corpora valida 20 habent et sunt barbarī. Dux Helvētiōrum est perfidus, sed bona cōnsilia bellī capiunt magnamque fortitūdinem ducēs nostrī habent. Imperātor Caesar multās legiōnēs in hāc regiōne habet, sed legiō nostra est optima."

Nōnne legiō tua mox veniet in Galliam? Tum tē vidēbō et 25 tibi multa hāc dē regiōne nārrābō. Venī ante fīnem bellī! Valē.

cervus, -ī	M., stag, deer
*tabernāculum, -ī	N., tent
*explōrātor, -ōris	M., scout, explorer
*genus, -eris	N., kind, sort
imperātor, -ōris	M., commander, leader
*legiō, -ōnis	F., legion, division of the Roman army (4000-6000 men)
*leō, -ōnis	M., lion
*perfidus, -a, -um	faithless, perfidious
castra pōnere	pitch camp, set up camp
salūtem dīcere	greet

I Whenever practical, change Declension III nouns from singular to plural or from plural to singular, and change other forms as needed for correct construction.

Explōrātōrēs nostrī dīxērunt, "Ducēs Helvetiōrum, quī magnās cōpiās trāns flūmen habent, castra nostra vāstāre parant. Cōnsulēs ducēs Helvetiōrum timent, quod corpora fortia habent et magnam fortitūdinem mōnstrant. Bona autem cōnsilia bellī et virtūtem centuriōnēs nostrī habent, et legiōnēs nostrae optimae sunt. Imperātor Rōmānus difficultātem nōn habēbit."

255

REVIEW OF UNITS XI-XII

LESSONS XLIII–XLVIII

Nouns	Adjectives (cont.)	Adverbs
+cōpiae, -ārum	decem	ācriter
cervus, -ī	quīnque	*firmiter
decemvirī, -ōrum	Verbs	nōndum
lēgātus, -ī	*dēportō, -āre	numquam
*tyrannus, -ī	natō, -āre	paulātim
*imperium, -ī	*probō, -āre	praetereā
lignum, -ī	*rēgnō, -āre	quam
lutum, -ī	*augeō, -ēre	satis
proelium, -ī	*jaceō, -ēre	tandem
*tabernāculum, -ī	*obtineō, -ēre	*vērō
Adjectives	cōgō, -ere	Conjunction
alter, altera, alterum	*committō, -ere	nam
cupidus, -a, -um	*cōnstruō, -ere	Idioms
fīnitimus, -a, -um	dēpōnō, -ere	bellum gerere
flāvus, -a, -um	legō, -ere	castra pōnere
perfidus, -a, -um	perficiō, -ere	proelium committere
permōtus, -a, -um	*tremō, -ere	salūtem dīcere
*pretiōsus, -a, -um	dēsiliō, -īre	sē recipere
summus, -a, -um	mūniō, -īre	viam mūnīre
	trānseō, -īre	vītam agere

I Complete the sentences and translate.

1 Cīv- ex urb- fugere nōn poterunt; temp- nōn est.
2 Fīn- hostium mox pertinēbunt ad flūmin-.
3 Juven- vītam perīculōsam agēbat.
4 Duc- cum paucīs pedit- pont- trānsībant.
5 Senātōr- Rōmānōs et lēg- Rōmānās memoriā tenēre temptāmus.

II Change all underlined words from singular to plural or vice versa, and make other necessary changes. Translate.

1 Peditēs galeās in capitibus gerent.
2 Mīles armātus prope flūmen stābat.
3 Nāvem longam procul ab ōrā maritimā frātrēs meī vīdērunt.
4 Quā dē causā custōs ex arce sē nōn recipit?
5 In locō proeliī corpora mīlitum mortuōrum jacēbant.

Masculine		Feminine		Neuter	
*dolor,	-ōris	*arbor,	-ŏris	*corpus,	-oris
*explōrātor,	-ōris	*soror,	-ōris	*tempus,	-oris
imperātor,	-ōris	uxor,	-ōris	*genus,	-eris
*senātor,	-ōris				
*eques,	-itis			*caput,	-itis
*mīles,	-itis	potestās,	-ātis		
*pedes,	-itis				
*custōs,	-ōdis				
homō,	-inis	*multitūdō,	-inis	flūmen, -inis	
*leō,	-ōnis	*legiō,	-ōnis		
dux,	ducis	pāx,	pācis		
rēx,	rēgis	*lēx,	lēgis		
*dēns,	dentis	arx,	arcis	*animal, -ālis	
*fōns,	fontis	*pars,	partis		
*mōns,	montis	*urbs,	urbis		
*pōns,	pontis				
*hostis,	hostis	*nāvis,	nāvis		
*cīvis,	cīvis (M./F.)				
*fīnis,	fīnis (M./F.)				
*canis,	canis (M./F.)				
*juvenis,	juvenis				
*pater,	patris	*māter, mātris			
*frāter,	frātris				

LOOK AND THINK The patterns formed by the groups of nouns listed above can help to increase your vocabulary. Compare these English words with related Latin nouns.

dolorous	military	custody	juvenile	patrimony	corporal
general	capital	legion	sorority	partisan	matrimony

How do the English words help with the Latin spelling?

Point out the nouns with two consonants before the genitive singular ending. Point out those with the same number of syllables in nominative and genitive singular. What do most of the words in these two groups have in common?

257

ROMAN THEATERS AND PLAYS

The form of the Roman theater itself, as well as the plays presented there, was adapted from the earlier Greek theater and drama. Stage settings were stereotyped, representing a street in front of two or more houses. The first Roman theaters were wooden structures, erected for specific occasions. Later, permanent semicircular auditoriums were built of stone. Since these theaters were outdoors without means of artificial lighting, all plays were presented by day. The curtain, if there was one, was lowered into a slot at the front of the stage instead of being raised as is done in modern indoor theaters.

For both comic and tragic rôles, actors wore costumes, wigs, and masks that identified them as stock characters—old men, young men, slaves, girls, and old women. Since no respectable woman could appear on the stage, feminine rôles were regularly taken by men. Ancient plays resemble our musical comedy or opera in having part of the action disclosed by a chorus, which chanted the lines.

The only Roman stage plays that have survived in complete form are the comedies written by Plautus and Terence, who imitated Greek comic writers.

Margin: Theatrical masks.

Below: Fresco of an actor viewing a mask held up before him.

Right: Scene from a puppet performance of a comedy by Plautus—*Menaechmi.* Shakespeare probably borrowed the plot for his *Comedy of Errors* (a story of the confusion caused by identical twins) from this play.

Below right: Remains of the stage of a Roman theater in Mérida, Spain.

Right: Greek theater at Taormina, in Sicily, which is similar to Roman theaters in the two pictures below.

Below left: Both the Roman theater and the arena in the heart of the modern city of Arles in southern France are well preserved. These ancient structures are still in use, although the arena is now the scene of bull fights instead of gladiatorial combats.

Below right: The smaller theater at Pompeii, with entrance to the stage at the left.

Below: In the theater of Sabratha in North Africa both the semicircular tiers of seats and the back of the stage are in a fair state of preservation. Arrangement of the columns to represent houses, and to provide recesses between them where characters could hide, was essential to working out the plot of a Roman play.

6

THE TARPEIAN ROCK

Servius, amīcus Lūciī, in parvō vīcō Etrūriae habitat, sed nunc in urbe Rōmā apud Lūcium amīcum est.

Lūcius. Quid, amīce, in urbe nostrā prīmum vidēre dēsīderās?

Servius. Capitōlium est in magnō saxō. Maximē dēsīderō 5 saxum vidēre Tarpeium.

Lūcius. Ita. Saxum Tarpeium est clārum. Nārrābō tibi dē Tarpeiā, dum in Capitōliō sumus.

Mox puerī stant in Capitōliō.

Lūcius. Vidē! In hōc locō Tatius, rēx Sabīnōrum, dolō 10 Capitōlium occupāvit. Tarpeius, pater Tarpeiae, castellum cum sociīs dēfendēbat. Cotīdiē Tarpeia aquam ab fonte sub saxō magnō portābat. Ōlim autem in sēmitā sēcrētā prope fontem virōs incognitōs vīdit. Virī armillās aureās et ānulōs aureōs habuērunt. Tarpeia stulta armillās et 15 ānulōs dēsīderābat. Itaque Tatius, dux virōrum, dīxit, "Mōnstrā nōbīs sēmitam et dabimus tibi ea quae gerimus in bracchiīs nostrīs." Tarpeia stulta noctū Tatium et virōs ad Capitōlium dūxit, et . . .

Servius. Tatiusne Tarpeiae armillās dedit?
20
Lūcius. Minimē. Tatius sociīque, postquam Capitōlium. occupāvērunt, dē bracchiīs scūta ēripuērunt et miseram puellam interfēcērunt.

Servius. Ita Tarpeia recēpit ea quae advenae gerēbant in bracchiīs! Neque armillās neque ānulōs, sed scūta virī 25 Tarpeiae miserae dedērunt.

---

dolus, -ī M., trick • **castellum***, -ī N., castle, fortress
cotīdiē daily • **incognitus, -a, -um** unknown • **armilla, -ae** bracelet • **ānulus, -ī** ring • **stultus, -a, -um** stupid, foolish • **ēripuērunt** took off • **advena, -ae** M. or F., stranger

A bronze statuette representing a warrior of the Etruscans or an allied people of Italy. Such groups were eventually conquered and absorbed by the Romans.

XLIX

A MAN WHO PANICKED

Locus est parva urbs Hispāniae, prōvinciae Rōmānae. In viā brevī virī, fēminae, puerī, puellae aut stant aut ambulant. Ā sinistrā stant duo virī—Galba et Titus. Ā dextrā celeriter occurrit puer in viam.

Galba. Quis est ille juvenis? Quid portat? Estne nūntius? 5 Audīsne ejus vōcem ācrem?

Titus. Ille est Pūblius, cujus pater Sextus in Galliā pugnat.

Pūblius. Epistulās ē Galliā portō. Ad omnēs incolās hujus urbis pater meus hās mittit epistulās. Barbarī ācrēs Galliam oppugnant. Fortūna bellī est dubia. Perīculum est maximum! 10

Galba. Quī sunt sociī Gallōrum?

Pūblius. Britannī sunt sociī eōrum.

Titus. Nōnne Gallī auxilia ā suīs sociīs postulāvērunt?

In Evora, Portugal, stands this Roman temple. Portugal was part of the province of Hispania (Spain), and Evora, then Ebora, was an important military station.

Pūblius. Ita, Gallī auxilia postulāvērunt, sed potentēs sociōs nōn habent Gallī. Britannī pauca auxilia mīsērunt. 15

Galba. Quae oppida Gallōrum ācrēs barbarī occupāvērunt?

Pūblius. Plūrima oppida Gallōrum barbarī occupāvērunt.

Titus. Timentne Britannī barbarōs?

Pūblius. Minimē, nam aqua Britanniam ā Galliā sēparat. Via facilis autem hostēs in Hispāniam dūcet. Brevī tempore 20 barbarī oppida nostra fortasse oppugnābunt!

Galba. Heu! Barbarōs timeō ācrēs! Vīta mea brevis erit! Nihil tūtum erit! Hostēs nostrōs timeō! Omnēs timeō!

*epistula, -ae	F., letter
⁺auxilia, -ōrum	N. pl., auxiliary troops, reinforcements
*juvenis, -is	M., young man, youth
vōx, vōcis	F., voice
*dexter, -tra, -trum	right; **ā dextrā,** on the right
*dubius, -a, -um	doubtful, uncertain
*sinister, -tra, -trum	left; **ā sinistrā,** on the left
ācer, ācris, ācre	sharp, shrill, fierce
*brevis, -e	short; **brevī tempore,** in a short time
*facilis, -e	easy
*fēlīx, gen., -īcis	happy, fortunate
omnis, -e	every; pl., all
*potēns, gen., potentis	powerful, strong
oppugnō, -āre, -āvī	attack, besiege
*occurrō, -ere, -currī	run against, run to meet
heu!	alas!

ADJECTIVES OF THIRD DECLENSION

Three Endings:	**ācer** (M.)	**ācris** (F.)	**ācre** (N.)
Two Endings:	**facilis** (M., F.)	**facile** (N.)	
One Ending:	**fēlīx** (M., F., N.)		

Some third-declension adjectives have three different forms in nominative singular, one for each gender.

Some have the same form for masculine and feminine in nominative singular, but a different form for neuter.

In a few third-declension adjectives, nominative singular is the same for all three genders.

	Three Endings	Two Endings	One Ending
	Singular	Singular	Singular
Nom.	ācer/ācris/ācre	facilis/facile	fēlix
Gen.	ācris	facilis	fēlicis
Dat.	ācrī	facilī	fēlicī
Acc.	ācrem/ācre	facilem/facile	fēlicem/fēlix
Abl.	ācrī	facilī	fēlicī
	Plural	Plural	Plural
Nom.	ācrēs/ācria	facilēs/facilia	fēlicēs/fēlicia
Gen.	ācrium	facilium	fēlicium
Dat.	ācribus	facilibus	fēlicibus
Acc.	ācrēs/ācria	facilēs/facilia	fēlicēs/fēlicia
Abl.	ācribus	facilibus	fēlicibus

Declension III adjectives resemble Declension III nouns that have -ium in genitive plural and -ī in ablative singular.

Like neuter nouns of this type, neuter adjectives of Declension III have -ia in nominative and accusative plural. Likewise in nominative and accusative singular, neuter adjectives of Declension III have the same form, following the "Neuter Law."

Masculine and feminine adjectives of Declension III have -em in accusative singular and -ēs in nominative and accusative plural.

I Complete each adjective and translate the sentences.
1 Medūsa mōnstrum ācr- erat.
2 Equitēs facil- proelium gerunt.
3 Dī incolās mortāl- orbis terrārum dēlēre possunt.
4 Brev- tempore nōmina victōrum fēlīc- audiēmus.
5 Potent- ducēs nautae praemia grāta dedērunt.

II Group adjectives in the list according to number of endings in nominative singular (3, 2, 1). Then give all forms of nominative and ablative singular, genitive and accusative plural of one adjective in each group.

1 ācris	3 fēlīcī	5 facilium
2 brevibus	4 omnēs	6 potentem

L

Antīquitus pīrātae ācrēs incolās Siciliae Ītaliaeque vexābant. Sextus, cīvis Siciliae, hanc saepe nārrābat fābulam.

Ōlim pīrātae magna castra in locō sēcrētō īnsulae nostrae posuērunt; frūmentum aurumque petēbant. In castrīs erat Seleucus, dux potēns malusque pīrātārum.   5

Haec castra autem vidēre nōn poterāmus. In tantīs perīculīs puerī puellaeque vigilābant, dum agrōs colimus.

Subitō fīlia mea pīrātās ācrēs vīdit et clāmāvit, "Pīrātās videō! Dux eōrum venit; est altior atque ferōcior quam reliquī pīrātae. Currite, puerī, ad agrōs; vocāte agricolās! 10 Properāte, puellae, ad oppidum! Vocāte ad arma incolās!"

Sine morā omnēs convēnērunt. Incolae oppidī bona arma gerēbant; sed nōs habuimus nihil praeter gladiōs.

Ego vērō nōn territus eram. Clāmāvī, "Ubi est Seleucus? Ego sōlus Seleucum prōvocō!"   15

Seleucus, quamquam vir maximus, tamen erat territus. Fūgit ille; sē servāre temptāvit. Sine duce reliquī male pugnāvērunt; brevissimō tempore eōs facile vīcimus.

Ego potentior fortiorque quam sociī eram; nam sōlus vīgintī interfēcī pīrātās. Deinde in mediīs castrīs Seleucum 20 ipsum dēprehendī, quem gladiō interfēcī.

Omnēs dīxērunt, "Vir fortissimus, Sexte, es; oppidum nostrum fēlīcissimum est."

reliquus, -a, -um	remaining; rest
tantus, -a, -um	so great; pl., so many
***ferōx**, gen., **-ōcis**	wild, ferocious
***fortis, -e**	brave
vīgintī	twenty
***vexō, -āre, -āvī**	harass, annoy, vex
+**vigilō, -āre, -āvī**	be awake, be vigilant; be on guard
colō, -ere, -uī	till, cultivate
***male**	badly; unsuccessfully
+**quam**	than

A wall decoration from Pompeii shows Roman ships moored alongside a seaside villa.

COMPARISON OF ADJECTIVES

Positive	Comparative	Superlative
M. F. N.	M., F. N.	M. F. N.
altus, -a, -um	**altior, altius**	**altissimus, -a, -um**
(high, tall)	(higher, taller)	(highest, tallest)

In addition to positive, most adjectives have comparative and superlative forms. Each indicates a degree of comparison, and each has a separate declension. Some positives, like **altus,** belong to Declension I-II; others, like **fortis,** belong to Declension III of adjectives.

A superlative indicates the greatest or an extremely great degree: **altissimus** (highest, very high). All superlatives are declined like Declension I-II adjectives: **longissimus, -a, -um.**

A comparative indicates a greater degree than a positive and a lesser degree than a superlative. **Altior** (higher) is more than **altus** (high), and less than **altissimus** (highest).

DECLENSION OF A COMPARATIVE ADJECTIVE is like that of a regular Declension III noun (not adjective).

	Singular	Plural
Nom.	**altior/altius**	**altiōrēs/altiōra**
Gen.	**altiōris**	**altiōrum**
Dat.	**altiōrī**	**altiōribus**
Acc.	**altiōrem/altius**	**altiōrēs/altiōra**
Abl.	**altiōre**	**altiōribus**

Nominative singular ending of a comparative adjective is either **-ior** (M., F.) or **-ius** (N.). Both nominative and accusative plural of a neuter comparative end in **-a,** and neuter accusative singular ends in **-ius** like the nominative, in accordance with the "Neuter Law."

Since all comparative adjectives have regular noun endings, ablative singular always ends in **-e** and genitive plural in **-um.**

TRANSLATION OF COMPARATIVES AND SUPERLATIVES

	Positive	Comparative	Superlative
M.	**fortis vir**	**fortior vir**	**fortissimus vir**
	(brave man)	(braver man)	(bravest man)
F.	**fēlix puella**	**fēlicior puella**	**fēlicissima puella**
	(happy girl)	(happier girl)	(happiest girl)
N.	**altum templum**	**altius templum**	**altissimum templum**
	(high temple)	(higher temple)	(highest temple)

The comparative of many English adjectives is indicated by the suffix "-er"; the superlative, by "-est." Sometimes "more" and "most" show degrees of comparison in English: "more powerful" (comparative); "most powerful" (superlative).

Comparative	Superlative
coma longior	**aqua frīgidissima**
(quite long hair)	(very cold water)
flūmen lātius	**mōns altissimus**
(rather wide river)	(extremely high mountain)

Sometimes a comparative may be better translated by modifying the English adjective with "quite," "rather," or "somewhat" than with "-er" or "more."

Likewise, a superlative may sometimes be translated with "extremely" or "very" instead of with "-est" or "most."

"Too" with an adjective sometimes indicates a comparative: "too high"; that is, "higher" (than it ought to be). "Too" may also (in colloquial speech) indicate a superlative: "too kind"; that is, "very kind" or "extremely kind."

I (A) Give corresponding comparative and superlative forms of each adjective and translate.

puella fortis   **oppidum tūtum**

(B) Give corresponding positive and superlative forms of each adjective and translate.

inimīcus potentior   **ferōcius animal**

(C) Give corresponding positive and comparative forms of each adjective and translate.

juvenis fēlīcissimus   **templum novissimum**

II Select the most appropriate meaning from the three given for each word underlined, and translate the entire sentence.

1. Mīlitēs pontem longiōrem trānsīre cupīvērunt.
   a rather long   too long   longer
2. Aqua flūminis frīgidissima erat.
   coldest   extremely cold   too cold
3. In hoc forum angustius populum convocāre nōn dēsīderō.
   too narrow   narrower   very narrow
4. Uxor fēlīcissima deīs grātiās ēgit.
   rather fortunate   luckiest   very happy
5. Dōna nōn sōlum pretiōsissima sed etiam deae grāta sunt.
   dearest   very costly   most precious
6. Arma virō quam fēminae grātiōra sunt.
   more pleasing   rather pleasing   too grateful

LI

EXPENSIVE BOOKS

Septimus et ultimus[1] rēx Rōmae fuit Tarquinius Superbus, quem populus Rōmānus nōn amābat.

---

[1] **Ultimus, -a, -um** (farthest, last) is a superlative adjective without corresponding positive. Its comparative is **ulterior, -ius** (farther).

Ōlim Rēx Tarquinius fēminam sōlam prō rēgiā vīdit. Ea rēgiam spectābat.

Rēx sibi dīxit, "Quis est illa fēmina?"   5

Vesperī eadem fēmina in rēgiā subitō appāruit. Jam novem librōs rēgī mōnstrāvit, prō quibus magnum pretium postulāvit.

Rīsit rēx. "Librī tuī sunt pretiōsiōrēs!" clāmāvit. "Tibi tantum pretium nōn dabō."   10

Statim fēmina trēs° librōs dēlēvit et ē rēgiā properāvit.

Postrīdiē iterum in rēgiam vēnit et rēgī sex librōs mōnstrāvit et dīxit, "Dā mihi pretium novem librōrum; tibi reliquōs dabō librōs."

Tarquinius iterum rīsit; iterum fēmina īrātissima trēs 15 librōs dēlēvit et discessit.

Tertiō diē° revēnit. Trēs librōs mōnstrāvit. "Ecce reliquī librī!" inquit. "Aut dabis mihi idem pretium aut trēs hōs librōs quoque jam dēlēbō."

Rēx sibi dīxit, "Dī eam mīsērunt. Īnfēlīx malumque 20 jūdicium fēcī."

Itaque fēminae pretium novem librōrum dedit et trēs librōs pretiōsissimōs accēpit.

Fēmina erat Sibylla; librī erant Sibyllīnī. Librōs, quī arcāna° multa mōnstrābant, Rōmānī sub ārā templī in arcā 25 aureā posuērunt. Posteā illī librī Rōmam saepe ex perīculō servābant.

°**trēs** (nom., acc.) three • **diē** (abl. sing.) day • **arcānum, -ī** N., secret

*liber, -brī	M., book
*jūdicium, -ī	N., judgment
pretium, -ī	N., price
novem	nine
septimus, -a, -um	seventh
sex	six
tertius, -a, -um	third
*ultimus, -a, -um	last
infēlix, gen., -īcis	unhappy
*rīdeō, -ēre, rīsī	laugh

269

The Cumaean Sibyl decorates the Convent of Sant' Apollonia in Florence, Italy.

ADJECTIVES IRREGULARLY COMPARED

Positive	Comparative	Superlative
bonus, -a, -um (good)	**melior, melius** (better)	**optimus, -a, -um** (best)
malus, -a, -um (bad)	**pejor, pejus** (worse)	**pessimus, -a, -um** (worst)
magnus, -a, -um (large)	**major, majus** (larger)	**maximus, -a, -um** (largest)
parvus, -a, -um (small)	**minor, minus** (smaller)	**minimus, -a, -um** (smallest)
multus, -a, -um (much)	——, **plūs** (more)	**plūrimus, -a, -um** (most)

The singular comparative of **multus,** which occurs only as a neuter, is used as a noun, not an adjective; e.g., **plūs pecūniae,** more (of) money; but **plūrēs hominēs,** more men.

Certain adjectives with irregular superlatives have already appeared in this book. These same adjectives have irregular comparative forms.

An irregular comparative is declined like the comparative of any other adjective (see p. 266), just as an irregular superlative is declined like any other superlative (see p. 153).

I Supply two forms which will complete the comparison of each adjective.

Example: **tūtus, tūtior, tūtissimus**

1 altissimus   3 fēlīcius   5 minus   7 pejor

2 brevior   4 maximus   6 optimus   8 pessimus

II Select the most appropriate form of the adjective and translate the entire sentence.

1 Cōnstituistīne illōs librōs pretiōsus/pretiōsissimī/pretiōsiōrēs esse?

2 Itinera longius/longa/longissimus saepe grātissima erant.

3 Jūdicium bonōrum/melius/optimus fēcimus.

4 Majōrēs/Maximīs/Magnam cōpiās statim postulō.

5 Hostēs omnēs ducēs fortis/fortiōrī/fortissimōs in proelium mittunt.

6 Reliquī mīlitēs castra sub monte alta/altiōre/altissimī pōnēbant.

7 Tertiō diē tabulae decem lēgum jūstiōrem/jūstārum/jūstissimum in forō apparēbunt.

USEFUL LATIN

Ad majōrem Deī glōriam. To the greater glory of God. (Motto of the Jesuits)

Nihil tibi dulcius esse dēbet quam patria. Nothing ought to be dearer (sweeter) to you than your country. (Cicero)

Ūtilius/satius fuit. It would have been better.

Sapientior quam fortior fuit. He was wiser than he was brave.

Ē plūribus ūnum. One out of many. (Motto on United States coins)

CIRCUSES AND RACING

Everybody in Rome watched chariot races at the circuses. The oldest, largest, and most famous circus was the Circus Maximus, which in time was enlarged to seat nearly two hundred thousand spectators.

The arena (so called because it was covered with sand to protect the horses' unshod feet) for about two thirds its length was divided by a fence or wall called spina, with the track on either side. A gesture from the consul or other presiding officer was the signal for the race to begin. At either end of the spina stood a pedestal, one holding seven large marble eggs, the other seven dolphins. One of each was removed to mark the completion of every lap.

Excitement for spectators was caused not so much by speed as by the danger of the race, with its sharp turns and confusion of teams, and by the fact that unlimited betting was legal. Drivers' attempts to foul their competitors added to the excitement. Four-horse teams were generally used, with each charioteer wearing the color—red, white, blue, or green—of one of the four racing companies which controlled the supply of drivers and horses. The sponsor of a racing program contracted with these companies for teams and charioteers. Drivers who were frequent winners acquired great wealth and were idolized by their public.

Right: On pedestal, ova to mark the laps in the race.

Bottom left: Marble statue of auriga with palms of victory, wearing a protective corselet.

Center: Lamp with racing horse and attendants.

Right: Famous mosaic of aurigae.

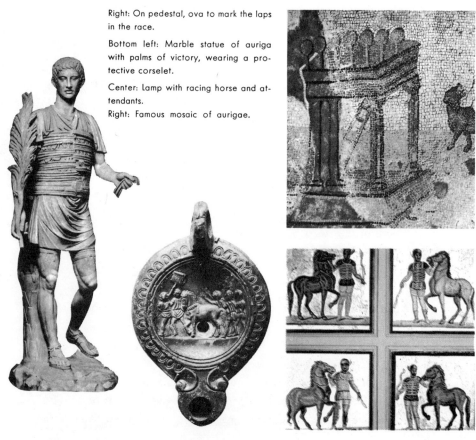

Top left: The "Colchester Vase" with four-horse team and chariot (quadriga).

Above: Mosaic of race, from a villa in Sicily.

Center left: The consul on his curule chair prepares to start the race by dropping the cloth from his hand.

Below: Remains of the Circus Maximus today.

Bottom: Marble statue of a two-horse chariot (biga).

LII

Cum Etrūscīs Rōmānī saepe bellum gerēbant. Etrūscī Rōmānīs dissimilēs erant. Nōn longē ab urbe Rōmā erant Veiī, oppidum Etrūscōrum. Mūrī oppidī erant altī et validissimī; nātūra locī erat difficillima; itaque incolae diū erant tūtī. Per decem annōs Rōmānī Veiōs frūstrā oppugnābant. 5

Dēnique vir Etrūscus in mūrō urbis stetit. Superbē dīxit, "Haec sunt verba ōrāculī! Dum aqua est in lacū° Albānō, dī nōs dēfendent! Numquam nōs vincētis!"

Dux Rōmānus, Camillus, cēpit cōnsilium bonum. "Labor difficillimus erit," inquit, "sed cunīculum° fodere° dēbēmus. 10 Aqua per cunīculum ē lacū fluet." Haec omnēs probāvērunt.

Tum sēcrētō Rōmānī cunīculum sub terrā fōdērunt.° Per hunc cunīculum aqua ē lacū trāns campōs flūxit. Jam nūlla erat aqua in lacū.

Mox ācrī proeliō Rōmānī Etrūscōs vīcērunt et Veiōs occu- 15 pāvērunt. Verba ōrāculī vēra erant.

°**lacū*** (abl. sing.) lake • **cunīculus, -i** M., tunnel • **fodere** to dig • **fōdērunt** dug

*difficilis, -e	difficult, hard, not easy
*dissimilis, -e	dissimilar, unlike, not like
*frūstrā	in vain
*superbē	proudly

COMPARISON OF ADJECTIVES IN -lis

Positive	Comparative		Superlative
facilis, -e	facilior,	facilius	facillimus, -a, -um
difficilis, -e	difficilior,	difficilius	difficillimus, -a, -um
similis, -e	similior,	similius	simillimus, -a, -um
dissimilis, -e	dissimilior,	dissimilius	dissimillimus, -a, -um
humilis, -e	humilior,	humilius	humillimus, -a, -um
gracilis, -e	gracilior,	gracilius	gracillimus, -a, -um

Superlatives of six Declension III adjectives ending in -lis have -limus, -a, -um added to the base of the positive.

Comparative forms are regular, with **-ior** or **-ius** added to the base of the positive.

COMPARISON OF ADJECTIVES IN -er

Positive	Comparative	Superlative
pulcher, -chra, -chrum	**pulchrior, -chrius**	**pulcherrimus, -a, -um**
miser, -era, -erum	**miserior, -erius**	**miserrimus, -a, -um**
ācer, ācris, ācre	**ācrior, ācrius**	**ācerrimus, -a, -um**

Like other **-er** adjectives, Declension III adjectives in **-er** have **-errimus, -a, -um** as the superlative ending. Comparative forms are regular, with **-ior** or **-ius** added to the base.

I Give superlatives only for the adjectives in the list which have some irregularity of comparison.

1 difficilis 3 ferōx 5 bonus 7 piger 9 līber
2 malus 4 ēgregius 6 parvus 8 multī 10 fortis

The Alban Lake as it is today. The summer residence of the Popes, Castel Gandolfo, is located on this small lake, about five miles in circumference. Since it is the crater of an extinct volcano it is very deep. The channel which the Romans bored in the rock during the siege of Veii still exists.

II For each form in A select from the forms in B the other two
corresponding degrees of comparison.

A B

1 ācerrimī ācris, ācria, ācrius, ācriōris, ācrī
2 plūrima multa, plūrēs, plūs, plūra, multae
3 altius altum, altior, altē, altissimum, altiōrem
4 majōrēs maximae, majus, major, magnae, maximōs
5 similēs similior, similī, simillimī, simillimīs, similiōrēs

III For each Latin word in the numbered list, find a matching
English expression in the lettered list.

1 fortiōris	6 facilia	a) very talkative	g) safest
2 potēns	7 pulchriōrum	b) too short	h) braver
3 maximī	8 tūtissimae	c) most ferocious	i) powerful
4 brevius	9 fēlīciōrem	d) more beautiful	j) best
5 ferōcissima	10 plūrima	e) happier	k) most
		f) very large	l) easy

LIII

A LIFE FOR A FRIEND

Trōjānī erant in magnō perīculō. Aenēās ex castrīs suīs
paucīs cum virīs discessit et auxilium ab urbibus propinquīs
petīvit. Ascanius, fīlius ejus, in castrīs mānsit.

Tum Rutulī castra Trōjāna vehementer oppugnāvērunt.
Trōjānī hoc perīculum Aenēae nūntiāre cupiēbant. Undique 5
autem mīlitēs hostium portās ācerrimē oppugnābant.

Nīsus, amīcus Ascaniī, dīxit, "Ego cum Euryalō comite
per castra hostium nūntium portābō. Hoc iter difficillimum
temptābimus, quod nihil est melius quam glōria."

Omnēs Trōjānī dīxērunt, "Tuum cōnsilium optimum est." 10

Ascanius laetus hīs amīcīs bona arma dedit; ducēs eīs
epistulās dedērunt. Noctū Nīsus et Euryalus ad castra hostium
sēcrētō appropinquāvērunt, et multōs mīlitēs facile necāvērunt. Hīc galeās aureās, pulchriōrēs et splendidiōrēs quam
galeās suās, invēnērunt. Statim illās galeās cēpērunt; tum 15
ex castrīs hostium discessērunt.

Subitō agmina hostium novōrum vīdērunt; sociī Rutulōrum auxilia addūcēbant. Amīcī inter arborēs latēre temptāvērunt, sed lūce lūnae hostēs galeās aureās facillimē vīdērunt.

Nīsus celerius currere poterat; itaque in silvam fūgit. 20
Ex silvā Nīsus perīculum amīcī vīdit et ad Euryalum properāvit. Euryalum autem dux ipse hostium interfēcit.

Prō amīcō mortuō fortissimē pugnāvit; dēnique gladiō
ducem interfēcit. Comitēs hujus ducis autem mīlitem sōlum
facillimē superāvērunt. Mox capita amīcōrum sociī Rutu- 25
lōrum in hastīs prope castra Trōjāna superbē portābant.

agmen, -inis	N., marching army, marching column
***arbor, -oris**	F., tree
comes, -itis	M. or F., companion, associate
***iter, itineris**	N., way, journey, trip
***lūx, lūcis**	F., light
***nūntiō, -āre, -āvī**	announce
addūcō, -ere, -dūxī	lead or bring to, lead against, influence
undique	from or on all sides, everywhere
***vehementer**	vehemently, violently

Fourth century illustration of the Roman camp which Aeneas left in Ascanius' care

ADVERBS COMPARED REGULARLY Many adverbs are formed from adjectives. With some exceptions, adverbs related to Declension I-II adjectives end in **-ē**[1] in positive; those related to Declension III adjectives, in **-iter**.[1] The comparative of any adverb is the same as neuter accusative singular of the corresponding comparative adjective. The superlative adverb is like the superlative adjective except for the ending, which is **-ē** instead of **-us**.

	Positive	Comparative	Superlative
(lātus)	**lātē**	**lātius**	**lātissimē**
(pulcher)	**pulchrē**	**pulchrius**	**pulcherrimē**
(ācer)	**ācriter**	**ācrius**	**ācerrimē**
(brevis)	**breviter**	**brevius**	**brevissimē**

In English, the corresponding degrees of comparison are shown thus: **lātē**, widely; **lātius**, more widely; **lātissimē**, most (or very) widely.

ADVERBS THAT ARE IRREGULAR either in formation or in comparison have comparative and superlative forms similar to those of corresponding irregular adjectives.

	Positive		Comparative		Superlative	
(bonus)	**benĕ**	well	**melius**	better	**optimē**	best
(malus)	**malĕ**	badly	**pejus**	worse	**pessimē**	worst
(magnus)	**magnopere**	greatly	**magis**	more	**maximē**	most
(multus)	**multum**	much	**plūs**	more	**plūrimum**	most
(parvus)	**parum**	little	**minus**	less	**minimē**	least

I (A) Find the words in the list used only as adverbs.

(B) Find those which can be used only as adjectives.

(C) Point out the forms that may be used as either adverbs or adjectives and give an explanation.

1 ācerrimē	6 lentius	11 plūrimum
2 facile	7 fortiter	12 minus
3 similior	8 hīc	13 plūrēs
4 facillimum	9 lentior	14 aegerrimum
5 libenter	10 avidē	15 magis

[1]Exceptions include **primō** (from **primus**), **antīquitus** (from **antīquus**), and **facilĕ** (accusative singular neuter of **facilis**).

II Select the appropriate form of adjective or adverb and translate the entire sentence.

1 Agmen longē/longius/longissimus hostium ad mūrōs illīus oppidī facilī/facilior/facillimē appropinquāvit.
2 Peditēs celerius/celeriter/celerrimē quam equitēs currēbant.
3 In castrīs bene/melior/optimus jam labōrāre dēbēmus.
4 Ducēs eōrum iter brevissimus/breve/breviōrem faciunt.
5 Facile flūmen lātē/lātius/lātissimē trānsīre poteritis.

III Translate each phrase, with special attention to the adverbs.

1 crūdēliter agere
2 lentē ambulāre
3 vehementer oppugnāre
4 libenter accipere
5 frūstrā fugere
6 hūc venīre
7 diū tenēre
8 facile vincere
9 breviter dīcere
10 magnopere timēre

WORDS TO REMEMBER (UNIT XIII)

Nouns	Adjectives (cont.)	Verbs (cont.)
*epistula, -ae	*sinister, -tra, -trum	*vexō, -āre
*liber, -brī	tantus, -a, -um	+vigilō, -āre
+auxilia, -ōrum	tertius, -a, -um	*rīdeō, -ēre
*jūdicium, -ī	*ultimus, -a, -um	addūcō, -ere
pretium, -ī	vīgintī	colō, -ere
agmen, -inis	ācer, ācris, ācre	*occurrō, -ere
*arbor, -oris	*brevis, -e	Adverbs
comes, -itis	*difficilis, -e	*frūstrā
*iter, itineris	*dissimilis, -e	*male
*juvenis, -is	*facilis, -e	+quam
*lūx, lūcis	*fēlīx, gen., -īcis	*superbē
*vōx, vōcis	*ferōx, gen., -ōcis	undique
Adjectives	*fortis, -e	*vehementer
*dexter, -tra, -trum	īnfēlīx, gen., -īcis	Interjection
*dubius, -a, -um	omnis, -e	heu!
novem	*potēns, gen., -entis	Phrases
reliquus, -a, -um	Verbs	ā dextrā
septimus, -a, -um	*nūntiō, -āre	ā sinistrā
sex	oppugnō, -āre	brevī tempore

MOTTO: **Citius, Altius, Fortius** (Theme of Modern Olympic Games)

The Latin suffix **-īnus** appears as -ine in such English words as canine (dog-like) or equine (pertaining to a horse). Look up those which you do not know in this list.

aquiline	bovine	feline	tigrine
asinine	elephantine	leonine	vulpine

Observe that strange things may happen as the meanings of words develop or as new words are made. An example is the word "vaccine," formed the same way as those in the list above, and derived from Latin **vacca** (cow). Yet its meaning is quite different, even though it basically means "pertaining to a cow."

Further examples are alimony (**alere,** feed), money paid for support; testimony (**testis,** witness), what a witness says; parsimony (**parcere,** spare), sparing use of money. On the other hand, patrimony (**pater**) means "money inherited from a father," while in sharp contrast, matrimony (**māter**) means "state of being married."

Latin **sinister** (left hand, left, left-handed) gave rise to other unforeseeable developments in meaning. English "sinister" now carries the idea of evil, wrong. The opposite of this sinister association of left hand with evil is the association of **dexter** (right hand, right, right-handed) with good. A dexterous person may also be ambidexterous. French **droit** (right), together with a prefix, produced adroit, which we have taken into English directly from French.

The Latin suffix **-ōsus,** meaning "full of" appears as English -ous/-ose. For example, copious from **cōpiōsus.** Give the meaning of the following English derivatives of this type.

furious	curious	invidious	numerous	**verbose**	glorious

At least one such word is derived from a diminutive: ridiculous.

CHANGING TIMES often bring about illogical changes in the meanings of words, as in these phrases.

typewritten manuscript	dilapidated <u>wooden</u> building
manufacture by <u>machine</u>	afternoon matinee

UNIT XIV

At Locri, in Calabria, where Ceres and Proserpina were worshiped, this relief of Pluto and Proserpina enthroned in Hades was recently found.

LIV

Nūlla puella uxor Plūtōnis esse dēsīderābat quod ille erat rēx mortuōrum et in Orcō habitābat.

Ōlim autem Plūtō, quī in terrā equōs suōs agēbat, Prōserpinam fīliam Cereris cōnspexit. Statim rēx potēns puellam pulchram amāvit et eam capere cōnstituit.   5

Celeriter Prōserpinam īnfēlīcem Plūtō cēpit et sub terram in Orcum, rēgnum mortuōrum, portāvit. Vēstīgia nūlla in terrā puella misera relīquit.

Jam Plūtō uxōrem habēbat. Jam Prōserpina erat rēgīna mortuōrum, sed erat rēgīna īnfēlīx. Semper magnopere 10 dolēbat quod mātrem vidēre cupiēbat. Lūcem autem dēsīderābat in Orcō obscūrō, ubi neque sōl neque lūna erat.

Diū māter maesta Prōserpinam fīliam in terrā petēbat. Mox neque frūmentum in agrīs neque folia in arboribus erant. Cerēs, dea agricultūrae, quod per multās terrās 15 errābat, agricultūram neglegēbat.

Dēnique Cerēs dē Plūtōne et dē uxōre īnfēlīcī audīvit. Dea īrāta ad Jovem properāvit, ā quō auxilium postulāvit.

Juppiter respondit, "Fīliam tuam tibi reddere cupiō, sed Prōserpina in Orcō manēre dēbet quod in rēgnō mortuōrum 20 cibum gustāvit. Illa est lēx deōrum."

Propter Cereris lacrimās autem Juppiter benignus cōnsilium bonum cēpit.

"Annum dīvidam," dīxit. "Per sex mēnsēs Prōserpina in terrā apud mātrem habitābit; tum in Orcō cum Plūtōne 25 per sex mēnsēs manēbit."

Itaque aestāte, dum Prōserpina est in terrā, Cerēs est fēlīx et hominibus frūmentum dat. Hieme autem dum Prōserpina est in Orcō, Cerēs īnfēlīx hominibus nihil dat.

lacrima, -ae	F., tear
*vēstīgium, -ī	N., footprint, trace
mēnsis, -is (-ium)	M., month
*sōl, sōlis	M., sun
*neglegō, -ere, -lēxī	disregard, neglect

The abduction of Proserpina by Pluto. Proserpina's companions are clinging to the chariot in a desperate attempt to prevent the kidnaping.

A B L A T I V E   O F   T I M E answers the question, "When?"

Aestāte Cerēs fēlix est. In summer Ceres is happy.
Iter duābus hōrīs perfĭciam. I shall finish the trip in two hours.

The time at which or within which something happens is usually expressed in Latin by a noun or pronoun in ablative case without a preposition.

In English, expressions of time usually have a preposition such as "in," "on," or "at"; for example, "in that year"; "on the same day"; "at the appointed time."

LATIN NUMBERS from one to ten are **ūnus, duo, trēs, quattuor, quīnque, sex, septem, octō, novem, decem.**

Only the first three of these are declined. **Ūnus** (one) is declined like the singular of **bonus** except in genitive and dative. **Duo** (two) and **trēs** (three) are naturally always plural.

DECLENSION OF ūnus, duo, trēs

	M.	F.	N.	M.	F.	N.	M.,F.	N.
Nom.	**ūnus/ūna/ūnum**			**duo**	**duae**	**duo**	**trēs/tria**	
Gen.	**ūnīus**			**duōrum**	**duārum**	**duōrum**	**trium**	
Dat.	**ūnī**			**duōbus**	**duābus**	**duōbus**	**tribus**	
Acc.	**ūnum/ūnam/ūnum**			**duōs**	**duās**	**duo**	**trēs/tria**	
Abl.	**ūnō/ūnā/ūnō**			**duōbus**	**duābus**	**duōbus**	**tribus**	

I Select the adjective or adjectives to complete each phrase correctly, and translate. (In 7 and 8 two adjectives apply.)

1 duōbus/duōs/duo mēnsibus
2 aliōs/ācrem/nūllā hieme
3 trēs/tria/trium annōs
4 tertiō/illī/tribus hōrīs
5 septima/septem/septimī folia
6 decem/ūnus/secundum rēgem
7 ūna/ūnum/ūnus conjūnx
8 novārum/novem/novum epistulārum

II Replace each underlined name with the word or phrase that fits the case and meaning. Translate both versions.

1 Ōlim Plūtō Prōserpinam cēpit quam esse rēgīnam Orcī dēsīderāvit.
2 Haec puella fīlia Cereris erat.
3 Cerēs maximē dolēbat, quod Prōserpinam vidēre cupiēbat.
4 Dēnique dea dē Plūtōne et dē Prōserpinā audīvit.
5 Dea īrāta auxilium ā Jove postulāvit.
6 Lacrimae Cereris Jovem mōvērunt.
7 Juppiter cōnsilium sapiēns cēpit.
8 Prōserpina apud Plūtōnem per sex mēnsēs, tum per sex mēnsēs apud Cererem manēbat.

deae agricultūrae	**mātris dolentis**	**rēgem mortuōrum**
filiam	**puellam pulcherrimam**	**rēgnī subterrāneī**
īnfēlīx rēgīna	**rēge deōrum**	**rēx deōrum**
māter puellae	**rēgem deōrum**	**rēx mortuōrum**
mātrem	**rēge mortuōrum**	**uxōre īnfēlīcī**

LV

FOUR IMPOSSIBLE TASKS

Venus, Cupid, and Psyche are the central figures in this centerpiece of fine Meissen china, made by the famous designer of Meissen porcelain figures, Johann Joachim Kändler, who worked in the eighteenth century.

Venus, dea invidiōsissima, erat crūdēlis in Psȳchēn, quod illam puellam pulcherrimam multī laudābant, quī autem deam nōn laudābant.

Ōlim Venus Psȳchae dīxit, "Sunt mīlia sēminum in illō acervō; dīvide ea et rēctē dispōne ante vesperum°; aliter tē 5 pūniam."

Psȳchē, quod hic labor erat gravissimus, ācerrimē lacrimābat. Cupīdō autem, fīlius Veneris, plūrimīs hujus regiōnis formīcīs dīxit, "Juvāte eam ın hōc labōre."

Mox formīcae omnēs convēnērunt et tōtum acervum 10 celeriter dīvīsērunt; tum fūgērunt.

Venus, ubi sēmina vīdit, īrāta dīxit, "Hoc ipsa nōn fēcistī; est labor multōrum servōrum!"

Postrīdiē dea crūdēlis dīxit, "In agrō fīnitimō sunt mīlle ovēs. Portā mihi floccum° eōrum vellerum." 15

Deus flūminum benignus puellam īnfēlīcem monuit, "Difficillimum est floccum capere dum ovēs in agrō stant. Sine perīculō autem floccōs dē rāmīs humilibus arborum carpere° poteris dum omnēs ovēs sē somnō dant."

Hōc modō Psȳchē floccōs cēpit et ad Venerem portāvit. 20

Venus īrātior dīxit, "Cape hanc urnam et portā ad mē aquam fontis parvī dē illō monte altō."

Psȳchē urnam cēpit et ad montem prōcessit. Saevae serpentēs erant in sēmitā. Aquila autem urnam cēpit et suprā capita serpentium volāvit. Sine difficultāte avis urnam aquae 25 plēnam ad Psȳchēn reportāvit.

Venus, cui Psȳchē urnam plēnam dedit, ācerrimē dīxit, "Nunc tibi majōrem labōrem dabō. Sūme hanc pyxidem° et dēscende in Orcum. Dīc Prōserpinae, 'Venus paulum° tuī fūcī° dēsīderat.' Pyxidem aperīre nōn dēbēs; sine morā mihi 30 reportā fūcum in pyxide!"

Maximā cum difficultāte Psȳchē iter in Orcum fēcit. Libenter autem Prōserpina eī fūcum suum dedit. Sed Psȳchē cūriōsissima in itinere pyxidem aperuit. Statim puella īnfēlīx cecidit et jacēbat quasi° mortua. 35

°**ante vesperum** before evening • **floccus, -ī** M., a tuft of wool • **carpere** to pluck • **pyxis, -idis** F., cosmetic box **paulum, -ī** N., a little • **fūcus, -ī** M., rouge • **quasi** as if, just as

Dēnique Cupīdō Psychēn invēnit et eam ā morte servāvit. Sed Psychē erat mortālis; Cupīdō dēsīderābat eam esse immortālem. Juppiter igitur Psychae ambrosiam° dedit, quae eam ēdit. Posteā Psychē pulchra erat immortālis, et Cupīdō eam in mātrimōnium dūxit. 40

°**ambrosia, -ae***   F., food of the gods, ambrosia

*****aquila, -ae**	F., eagle
acervus, -ī	M., heap, pile
*****modus, -ī**	M., way, manner, mode
*****avis, avis (-ium)**	F., bird
*****fōns, fontis (-ium)**	M., fountain, spring
*****mors, mortis (-ium)**	F., death
ovis, ovis (-ium)	F., sheep
*****sēmen, -inis**	N., seed
vellus, -eris	N., fleece
plēnus, -a, -um	full
saevus, -a, -um	savage, fierce
*****tōtus, -a, -um**	whole, entire
*****crūdēlis, -e**	cruel
*****gravis, -e**	heavy, serious, hard
mille	(indecl.) thousand; N. pl. as noun, **mīlia, -ium**
*****dispōnō, -ere, -posuī**	arrange, distribute
*****efficiō, -ere, -fēcī**	finish, accomplish, effect
*****sūmō, -ere, sūmpsī**	take, lay hold of
rēctē	in a straight line; rightly
suprā	(adv. and prep. with acc.) above, over

m i l l e   A N D   m i l i a

In agrō sunt mille ovēs. There are a thousand sheep in the field.
Sunt mīlia sēminum in illō acervō. There are thousands of seeds in that pile.

The Latin word meaning "thousand" is **mille,** an indeclinable adjective; that is, it has the same form in all cases and genders.

On the other hand, **mīlia** (thousands) is a neuter plural noun, declined like **animālia** (plural of **animal**).

287

I Select the appropriate preposition to complete each sentence, and translate.

1 Puella īnfēlīx cum/prope/in/sine sorōrēs suās in cavernā stābat.
2 Līberī in/ē/per/dē silvā fūgērunt.
3 Ventus īnfantem cum/ante/sub/ab undās portāvit.
4 Virī fortiōrēs inter/propter/post/trāns agrum cucurrērunt.
5 Duo frātrēs cum/apud/ad/ante patre iter facient.
6 Ūnus ē/cum/inter/suprā mīlitibus vōs juvābit.
7 Propter/Sub/Post/Ex āram, puerī, stāre nōn dēbētis.

II Translate the phrases underlined.

1 The leader gave gifts to thousands of soldiers.
2 Thousands of citizens were killed.
3 A thousand houses were destroyed.
4 The men captured thousands of slaves.
5 Sicily was attacked by a thousand ships.

LVI

PANDORA'S BOX

Ōlim in terrā sōla fēmina erat uxor Epimētheī. Haec fēmina nōn sōlum pulcherrima, sed etiam cūriōsissima erat. Nōmen ejus erat Pandōra, significāns "omnia dōna." Multa dōna deōrum habēbat, inter quae erat arca, dōnum Jovis.

"Haec arca," Juppiter dīxit, "magnum sēcrētum tenet. 5 Eam aperīre nōn dēbēs; aliter perīcula gravia in terrā aderunt. Dā arcam tuō conjugī."

Epimētheus arcam libenter cēpit; sed eam nōn aperuit. Nōn satis sapiēns autem erat conjūnx Pandōrae cūriōsae. Arcam nōn cēlāvit. 10

Cotīdiē Pandōra arcam spectābat, cupiēns eam aperīre. Timēns autem perīcula gravia, ab arcā procul sē tenēre temptāvit.

Ōlim Pandōra sōla erat in hortō ubi arca erat. Fēmina cūriōsa eam diū spectāvit. Scrīpta° in arcā haec verba vīdit: 15 "Teneō omnia gaudia deōrum. Aperī mē."

288

Haec gaudia habēre maximē cupiēns, Pandōra arcam mox
aperuit. Subitō mala, nōn gaudia, ex arcā volāvērunt. Prīmō
duo mala, deinde tria alia ex arcā vēnērunt. Dēnique omnia
mala hominum per terrās volābant. Pandōra territa celeriter 20
arcam clausit.

Mox autem Pandōra īnfēlīx audīvit vōcem dīcentem,
"Aperī iterum arcam. Summum bonum in arcā relīquistī.
Hominēs juvābō. Līberā mē!"

Itaque Pandōra parvam arcam iterum aperuit. Ex arcā 25
vēnit dōnum deōrum optimum, Spēs.°

°scrīptus, -a, -um* written • **Spēs** (nom. sing.) Hope

*conjūnx, -jugis	M. or F., husband; wife; spouse
*nōmen, nōminis	N., name
sapiēns, gen., -ientis	wise
*significō, -āre, -āvī	mean, signify
*claudō, -ere, clausī	shut, close
cotīdiē	daily

Pandora holding the box which was the source of both trouble and help

A **PRESENT ACTIVE PARTICIPLE** is declined like a Declension III adjective of one ending. It agrees in gender, number, and case with the noun or pronoun which it modifies.

DECLENSION OF PRESENT PARTICIPLES

	portāns carrying	**monēns** warning	**audiēns** hearing
	Singular (M., F., N.)	Singular (M., F., N.)	Singular (M., F., N.)
Nom.	**portāns**	**monēns**	**audiēns**
Gen.	**portantis**	**monentis**	**audientis**
Dat.	**portantī**	**monentī**	**audientī**
Acc.	**portantem/portāns**	**monentem/monēns**	**audientem/audiēns**
Abl.	**portante, -ī** [1]	**monente, -ī** [1]	**audiente, -ī** [1]
	Plural (M., F./N.)	Plural (M., F./N.)	Plural (M., F./N.)
Nom.	**portantēs/portantia**	**monentēs/monentia**	**audientēs/audientia**
Gen.	**portantium**	**monentium**	**audientium**
Dat.	**portantibus**	**monentibus**	**audientibus**
Acc.	**portantēs/portantia**	**monentēs/monentia**	**audientēs/audientia**
Abl.	**portantibus**	**monentibus**	**audientibus**

Present participles of all first-conjugation verbs follow the pattern of **portāns**. All other present participles are like **monēns**. However, -iō verbs (III-iō and IV) have -i- before the -ē- throughout: **capiēns, audiēns**.

PRESENT PARTICIPLES IN USE

Vehiculum movēns eum interfēcit. A moving vehicle killed him.

In this sentence **movēns** serves only as an adjective. Another adjective could replace it without changing the structure of the sentence: **vehiculum magnum.**

However, since the present active participle is a verb form, it may have a direct object.

Perīcula timēns, ab arcā procul manēre temptāvit. Fearing dangers, she tried to stay away from the box.

[1]In the ablative singular the ending **-ī** occurs when the participle is used simply as an adjective modifier; when it also functions as a verb the ending is **-e.**

TRANSLATION OF A PRESENT PARTI-CIPLE can be literal, but a phrase or clause often expresses an idea more naturally and more effectively.

Arcam nōn cēlāns, sapienter nōn ēgit. Since he did not hide (not hiding) the box, he did not act wisely.

Haec gaudia habēre maximē cupiēns, Pandōra arcam aperuit. Because she wanted very much to have these joys, Pandora opened the box.

The English suffix "-ing" equals **-nt- (-ns)**, the Latin sign of a present participle.

I Supply missing endings of participles and adjectives, and translate the complete sentences. Complete each participle in sentences 8 and 10 with two different endings, and show the difference by your translation.

1 Suō arcam custōdien- conjugī fēmina nūllās grātiās ēgit.
2 Vōcēs mātrum suārum līberī curren- nōn audiunt.
3 Nautam spectān- sēmitam sēcrētam inveniō.
4 Satis dīligentēs nōn erant labōrēs hominum īnfantem ab aquilā servāre temptan-.
5 Ovēs in agrum agen-, puerī animal novum vīdērunt.
6 Majōra mala timēn-, puella arcam clausit.
7 Ducem sapien- dēlēgistī.
8 Cum patre urbem relinquen- fīliae ad portam ambulant.
9 Avēs suprā montēs volan- mīlia sēminum reportābunt.
10 Paucīs mēnsibus illī fīnitimī poten- nostrōrum sociōrum bellum incipient.

II Translate.

1 Nōmen puellae Pandōra erat, significāns "omnia dōna."
2 Conjūnx, perīculum nōn petēns, arcam libenter cēpit.
3 Tamen, difficultātēs majōrēs timēns, fēmina arcam nōn cēlāvit.
4 Dēnique, gaudia deōrum cupiēns, Pandōra arcam aperuit.
5 Mox uxor īnfēlīx verba monentia audīvit.

LOOK AND THINK How does a knowledge of Latin present participles help you to spell these words correctly?

convenient   current   efficient   latent   significant

LVII

A LOST WIFE

Per silvam sonum amoenum lyra ēmittēbat. Avēs, ubi sonum amoenum audīvērunt, cantāre dēstitērunt. Bēstiae ferae quidem stetērunt neque hominēs necāre temptāvērunt. Orpheus, fīlius Apollinis, lyrā cantābat.

Eurydicē quoque Orpheum cantantem audīvit. Eum 5 vidēre cupiēns, virgō pulchra ad eum properāvit. Orpheus eam venientem vīdit et statim amāvit. Posteā Eurydicēn in mātrimōnium dūxit.

Ōlim serpēns pedem Eurydicēs in agrō ambulantis mo-mordit.° Illa statim ē vītā dēcessit et sub terram in Orcum, 10 locum mortuōrum, dēscendit.

Orpheus, dē uxōre dolēns, eam etiam in Orcō petere cōn-stituit. Multa mīlia passuum iter fēcit; dēnique per cavernam sub terram dēscendit.

Ubi Orpheus ad flūmen Stygem vēnit, portitor° Charōn 15 eum vīventem trāns flūmen portāre recūsāvit. Orpheus autem lyram cēpit et cantāvit; tum Charōn libenter eum trāns flūmen portāvit. Ibi Cerberus, magnus canis, eum terrēre temptāvit. Orpheus autem iterum cantāvit et canis statim dormīvit. 20

Ita post multa perīcula Orpheus ad rēgiam Plūtōnis vēnit, ā quō uxōrem petīvit. Plūtō autem Eurydicēn āmittere recūsāvit. Tum Orpheus lyram cēpit et cantāvit.

Dēnique Plūtō maestus eī Eurydicēn dedit hāc condi-ciōne: "Orpheus ad terram prōcēdet; uxōrem post sē veni- 25 entem nōn respiciet. Sī Orpheus respiciet, Eurydicēn in Orcum redūcam."

Orpheus laetus ad terram ascendere incēpit. Prīmō Orpheus nōn respexit. Subitō prope portam cavernae re-spexit et uxōrem vīdit. 30

Eurydicē misera clāmāvit, "Valē, conjūnx cāre! Valē!" Tum Plūtō eam ad Orcum revenīre jussit.

Orpheus maestissimus breve tempus vīvēbat; mox in Orcō uxōrem cāram iterum invēnit.

°**momordit** bit • **portitor, -ōris** M., ferryman

While strolling in a field with her companions Eurydice was stung by a serpent.

*condiciō, -ōnis	F., condition
+mīlia, -ium	N. pl. (with **passuum**) miles
*pēs, pedis	M., foot
*serpēns, -entis	M. or F., snake, serpent
*cantō, -āre, -āvī	sing; play (an instrument)
jubeō, -ēre, jussī	order, command
*dēcēdō, -ere, -cessī	depart, leave; **ē vītā dēcēdere,** die
*dēsistō, -ere, dēstitī	stop, cease, desist
respiciō, -ere, -spexī	look back
*vīvō, -ere, vīxī	live

ACCUSATIVE OF EXTENT OF SPACE, in effect, answers the question, "How far?"

Multa mīlia passuum iter fēcit. He traveled many miles.

An accusative without a preposition may express distance (extent of space).

ACCUSATIVE OF EXTENT OF TIME answers the question, "How long?"

Orpheus breve tempus vīvēbat. Orpheus lived a short time.

An accusative without a preposition may express duration (extent or length) of time. For emphasis, the preposition **per** may precede an accusative of extent.

Per multōs mēnsēs captīvus fuit. For many months he was a captive.

I Translate the following phrases or words.

1 breve tempus
2 centum annōs
3 paucās hōrās
4 vīgintī mīlia passuum
5 eōdem tempore
6 illā hōrā ipsā
7 tribus mēnsibus
8 tertiō hieme
9 hodiē
10 māne
11 noctū
12 vesperī

II For each of the expressions in I select the term which best describes the function it would serve in a sentence.
a) time when
b) extent of space
c) extent of time
d) time within which

III Add suitable endings to incomplete words; then translate the sentences, using each word or phrase in the lettered list at least once.

1 Avēs, ubi sonum amoenum audīvērunt, cantā- dēstitērunt.
2 Bēstiae ferae quidem stet-.
3 Orpheus Eurydicēn venien- vīdit.
4 Fīlius Apollinis puellam pulchram amāv-.
5 Virgō statim ē vītā excess-.

a) coming
b) fell in love with
c) died
d) singing
e) stood still

294

LESSONS XLIX-LVII

Nouns	Nouns (cont.)	Verbs (cont.)
*aquila, -ae	*serpēns, -entis	*dēcēdō, -ere
lacrima, -ae	*sōl, sōlis	*dēsistō, -ere
acervus, -ī	vellus, -eris	*dispōnō, -ere
*modus, -ī	Adjectives	*efficiō, -ere
*vēstīgium, -ī	plēnus, -a, -um	*neglegō, -ere
*avis, avis (-ium)	saevus, -a, -um	respiciō, -ere
*condiciō, -ōnis	*tōtus, -a, -um	*sūmō, -ere
*conjūnx, -jugis	*crūdēlis, -e	*vīvō, -ere
*fōns, fontis (-ium)	*gravis, -e	Adverbs
mēnsis, -is (-um/-ium)	sapiēns, gen., -ientis	cotīdiē
+mīlia, -ium	mille	rēctē
*mors, mortis (-ium)	Verbs	suprā
*nōmen, -inis	*cantō, -āre	Idioms
ovis, -ovis (-ium)	*significō, -āre	mīlia passuum
*pēs, pedis	jubeō, -ēre	ē vītā dēcēdere
*sēmen, -inis	*claudō, -ere	

(For review vocabulary of Unit XIII, see page 279.)

I Change all adjectives and adverbs from superlative to positive or vice versa. Translate both versions.

1 Juvenī fēlīcī comes optimus epistulam longam mīsit.
2 Vir sapientissimus iter difficile fēcit.
3 Mīlitēs fortēs urbem ācriter oppugnābant.
4 Brevī tempore avēs pulcherrimae cantābunt.
5 Arborem altam facile vidēre possumus.
6 Ea nūntiāvit, "Conjūnx meus cārissimus est aeger."
7 Rēx crūdēlis rīsit et dīxit, "Librī sunt pretiōsī."
8 Lūx clāra et vōx magna aquilam ferōcem terruērunt.
9 Hostēs Rōmānōrum fortium auxilia potentissima habent.
10 Multīs cum lacrimīs māter mortem conjugis patrisque līberīs īnfēlīcissimīs nūntiāvit.

II Give the comparative form of each adjective and adverb in the sentences of I.

The common Latin suffixes **-ālis** and **-ilis,** meaning "pertaining to," appear as -al and -il/-ile in many English words.

civil   natural   fatal   legal   manual   mural   hostile

The suffix **-ālis** when added to a Latin word that contains an **-l-** in either of the two syllables preceding the suffix, takes the form **-āris** (English -ar/-ary).

familiar   consular   lunar   military   salutary   popular

What English adjectives came from these Latin adjectives?

servīlis   auxiliāris   liberālis   prīncipālis   singulāris

Latin can help you with a pair of words whose spelling is often confused. Capital **(capitālis,** pertaining to the head) often means "the head city." Montgomery is the capital of Alabama. When the spelling is -ol, however, capitol means "the official building of the government," and gets its spelling from **Capitōlium,** the temple of Jupiter on the Capitoline Hill in Rome.

The suffixes **-ārium/-ōrium** were added to Latin nouns or perfect participles. The former indicates "a place where the thing mentioned (by the noun) is found." The latter, "a place where verbal action (expressed by the participle) takes place."

Librārium (library) is a place where **librī** (books) are found. Explain granary, mortuary, aquarium, aviary.

A sanatorium is a place where people go to regain their health **(sānāre,** to heal). Another form of this word is sanitarium, a place where health **(sānitās)** is found. Explain auditorium, factory, laboratory, purgatory.

In many cases the English -ary/-ory suffix (Latin **-ārius/-ōrius)** forms adjectives indicating a rather vague relationship, such as "having to do with" or "pertaining to." From your knowledge of Latin give the meaning of these English words.

sedentary   ambulatory   temporary   honorary   declamatory

Use each of the following phrases correctly in a sentence.

solar system	transitory life	pedal extremities
criminal negligence	military service	interplanetary space

This terra cotta plaque in the British Museum pictures the building of Jason's ship, the Argo, while Minerva looks on.

LVIII

Ōlim in terrā longinquā habitābant frāter et soror, Phrixus et Hellē. Hī līberī autem crūdēliter agēbantur. Dī Olympī igitur frātrem sorōremque servāre in animō habēbant.

Mercurius in conciliō deōrum dīxit, "Hōs līberōs ex patriā ad locum tūtum trānsportābō, sed iter perīculōsum erit." 5

Frāter sororque in magnō agrō ubi ovēs erant saepe lūdēbant. Ovēs eīs nūllam injūriam faciēbant.

Ōlim autem līberī lūdentēs arietem aureum inter ovēs vīdērunt. Is ariēs nōn erat saevus. Rē vērā placidissimus erat, dum corōnīs adōrnātur. Dēnique et frāter et soror in 10 tergum arietis ascendērunt. Subitō ariēs volāre incēpit, et līberī territī in caelum celeriter portābantur.

Ariēs trāns montēs, flūmina, maria volāvit. Dēnique Hellē fessa dē tergō arietis in mare angustum cecidit. Quam ob rem Phrixus maximē dolēbat. 15

Post multās hōrās ariēs Phrixum tūtum dēposuit in Colchide, terrā cujus rēx benignissimus erat.

Ibi vōx Phrixō dīxit, "Sacrificā hunc arietem in ārā, sed servā vellus. Pōne vellus in arbore sacrā. Sum Mercurius; dracō mittētur quī noctū et interdiū arborem custōdiet." 20

A Roman mosaic pictures the moment when Helle grew so tired that she fell off the golden ram into the sea which now bears the name Hellespont.

Posteā Phrixus vellus ad rēgiam portāvit. Rēx, ubi fābulam arietis aureī audīvit, dīxit, "Tū eris fīlius meus. Vellus aureum saepe quaerētur. Magnus honor ad rēgnum meum veniet."

ariēs, -etis	M., ram
dracō, -ōnis	M., dragon
***mare, maris (-ium)**	N., sea
***soror, -ōris**	F., sister
fessus, -a, -um	weary, tired
***placidus, -a, -um**	calm, placid
⁺agō, -ere, ēgī	(with adv.) treat
***lūdō, -ere, lūsī**	play
***crūdēliter**	cruelly
ob	(with acc.) because of
quam ob rem	therefore; for this reason
rē vērā	in truth

ACTIVE AND PASSIVE VOICES Latin verbs have two voices, active and passive.

Ariēs līberōs in tergō portābat. The ram carried the children on his back.
Līberī in tergō arietis portābantur. The children were carried on the back of the ram.

A verb in active voice denotes something the subject does; a verb in passive voice denotes something done to the subject.

The endings of verbs in passive voice are different from those in active voice, but passive endings show person and number just as active endings do.

ACTIVE AND PASSIVE ENDINGS are the same for all regular conjugations in the present system (present, imperfect, future tenses).

	Singular			Plural		
	Active	Passive		Active	Passive	
First Person:	**-ō**	**-or**	I	**-mus**	**-mur**	we
Second Person:	**-s**	**-ris**	you	**-tis**	**-minī**	you
Third Person:	**-t**	**-tur**	he (she, it)	**-nt**	**-ntur**	they

SUMMARY OF PRESENT SYSTEM IN PASSIVE VOICE

	Present Passive	Imperfect Passive	Future Passive
	Singular	Singular	Singular
I	portātur	portābātur	portābitur
II	monētur	monēbātur	monēbitur
III	dūcitur	dūcēbātur	dūcētur
III-iō	capitur	capiēbātur	capiētur
IV	audītur	audiēbātur	audiētur
	Plural	Plural	Plural
I	portantur	portābantur	portābuntur
II	monentur	monēbantur	monēbuntur
III	dūcuntur	dūcēbantur	dūcentur
III-iō	capiuntur	capiēbantur	capientur
IV	audiuntur	audiēbantur	audientur

A complete conjugation of the present system in passive voice is in the Summary of Grammar included in the reference materials at the end of this book.

TRANSLATION OF PRESENT SYSTEM IN PASSIVE VOICE

Present: **Liberī crūdēliter aguntur.** The children are being cruelly treated.

Imperfect. **Liberī crūdēliter agēbantur.** The children were being cruelly treated.

Future: **Liberī crūdēliter agentur.** The children will be cruelly treated.

A verb in present passive denotes something that is being done to the subject; a verb in imperfect passive, something that was being done to the subject; and a verb in future passive, something that will be done to the subject.

A PREDICATE NOUN may occur with passive forms of **appellō** and other words of naming and calling. Like the predicate noun which may be found with a form of **sum,** it means the same thing as the subject.

Puer Phrixus appellābātur. The boy was called Phrixus.
Puella est soror Phrixī. The girl is the sister of Phrixus.

I Using an appropriate word from the lettered list, complete each sentence. Then translate.

1 Saepe Phrixus et Hellē, frāter sororque, crūdēliter _____ .

2 Itaque dī potentēs eōs servāre in animō _____ .

3 Mox līberī, in agrō _____ , arietem vidē-bunt.

4 Ariēs eīs nūllam injūriam _____ .

5 Puer et puella in tergum ejus _____ .

6 Dēnique Hellē fessa dē tergō arietis _____ .

7 Post multās hōrās Phrixus in terrā _____ .

8 Vōx dīcet, "_____ vellus in arbore sacrā."

a) **agētur**
b) **aguntur**
c) **ascendent**
d) **cadet**
e) **dēpōnētur**
f) **faciet**
g) **habent**
h) **lūdent**
i) **lūdentēs**
j) **pōne**
k) **portābuntur**

II Change active verbs to passive, and passive to active, in the same person, number, and tense. Translate both forms.

1 accipiunt	5 juvor	9 inveniēminī
2 augētur	6 aperit	10 servantur
3 agimus	7 mūtāmus	11 moneō
4 vidētis	8 regeris	12 pūnīs

LIX

Per multōs annōs Jāsōn in scholā Centaurōrum manēbat.

Dēnique Chīrōn magister dīxit, "Ōlim pater tuus fuit rēx Thessaliae. Peliās, frāter ejus, autem rēgnum cēpit et patrem tuum in exilium ēgit. Jam prīdem pater tuus est mortuus; Thessalia ab avunculō tuō tenētur. Cūr in Thessaliam 5 nōn contendis? Rēgnum patris recipe!"

Interim ōrāculum rēgem ita monuit, "Virum ūnum calceum gerentem cavē!"

Brevī tempore Jāsōn, dum iter in Thessaliam facit, ad flūmen lātum pervēnit. Nusquam autem pontem vīdit. 10 Jāsōn, dum in rīpā flūminis rapidī stat, subitō aniculam vīdit. Anicula perterrita aquam spūmōsam spectābat. Jāsōn benignīs verbīs auxilium dare temptābat.

Fresco of Jason appearing before Pelias, his uncle, wearing only one shoe

Anicula eī dīxit, "Dēbeō trānsīre hoc flūmen, sed flūmen est altum et rapidum." 15

Jāsōn respondit, "Ascende in tergum meum. Tū incolumis trānsportāberis."

In mediō flūmine Jāsōn ūnum calceum āmīsit. Ille, postquam aniculam in alterā rīpā dēposuit, calceum petere incēpit. Subitō in aniculae locō dea splendida in rīpā stetit. 20

Dea Jāsonī attonitō dīxit, "Sum Jūnō, rēgīna deōrum! Nōlī petere calceum tuum; prōcēde sine morā ad rēgiam avunculī tuī. Stā audācter prō soliō; postulā ab avunculō rēgnum tuum!"

Itaque Jāsōn, gerēns ūnum calceum, ad rēgiam avunculī 25 prōcessit. Audācter stetit prō soliō rēgis, quī ūnum pedem nūdum juvenis statim vīdit. Rēx territus in animō verba ōrāculī habuit, "Virum ūnum calceum gerentem cavē!"

anicula, -ae	F., little old woman
calceus, -ī	M., shoe
solium, -ī	N., throne
attonitus, -a, -um	thunderstruck, stunned
***perterritus, -a, -um**	terrified
spūmōsus, -a, -um	foamy
incolumis, -e	safe, unharmed
caveō, -ēre, cāvī	beware
***contendō, -ere, -tendī**	hurry; insist, contend
***perveniō, -īre, -vēnī**	arrive at, reach
***audācter**	boldly
nusquam	nowhere
prīdem	long ago; (with **jam**) for a long time now
⁺ā, ab	(with abl.), by

ABLATIVE OF AGENT

Thessalia ab avunculō tuō tenētur. Thessaly is held by your uncle.

A word in the ablative case with preposition **ā (ab)** frequently occurs with a passive verb to show the agent (person by whom the act is done).

Ab ariete līberī portābantur. The children were carried by a ram.

In addition to persons, animals may be regarded as agents.

I In each pair, complete the second sentence by supplying the passive form of the verb of the first sentence. Translate both sentences.

1 Ipse vōs māne excitābō. Ā mē ipsō māne _____ .
2 Mātrēs fīliōs monent. Fīliī ā mātribus _____ .
3 Puer saxum jaciēbat. Saxum ā puerō _____ .
4 Cīvēs ducem sapientem dēligunt. Dux sapiēns ā cīvibus _____ .
5 Pīrātī vōs captīvōs diū tenēbant. Captīvī ā pīrātīs diū _____ .
6 Libenter amīcī tē accipient. Libenter ab amīcīs _____ .
7 Jānuam templī aperiam. Jānua templī ā mē _____ .
8 Fīnitimī inimīcī nōs agitābant. Nōs ā fīnitimīs inimīcīs _____ .
9 Rēx rosās hortī negleget. Rosae hortī ā rēge _____ .
10 Mē dīligenter custōdīs. Ā tē dīligenter _____ .

II Change all verbs from active to passive and make other necessary changes. Translate both versions.

1 Magister Jāsonem dē perīculō monēbit.
2 Tuus pater rēgnum nōn jam tenet.
3 Tuus avunculus populum jam regit.
4 Avunculus Jāsonem nōn amat.
5 Vir benignus aniculae auxilium dat.
6 Juvenis aniculam trāns flūmen portābat.
7 Jāsōn ūnum calceum āmittet.
8 Dea calceum nōn petit.
9 Verba ōrāculī rēgem terrent.
10 Argus nāvem validam aedificābit.

LX

A CRUEL PLOT

Rēx Peliās, quī Jāsonem timēbat, interficere juvenem in
animō habēbat. Cēlāvit autem suam invidiam atque laudāvit
audāciam juvenis. Post multōs mēnsēs fābulam velleris aureī
nārrāvit Jāsonī quī invidiam rēgis sēnsit.

Statim Jāsōn dīxit, "Sum validus; sociī meī sunt validī. 5
Nōs nāvigābimus ad terram Colchidem; capiēmus vellus."

Sed Peliās dīxit, "Colchis est terra longinqua; nūlla nāvis
poterit nāvigāre trāns maria perīculōsa."

Jāsōn respondit, "In hōc rēgnō habitat Argus, quī summam
scientiam nāvium habet. Is aedificābit nāvem validam." 10

Brevissimō tempore igitur Argus maximam nāvem aedificāvit. Nāvis, appellāta Argō, erat longa et angusta. Aedificāta ex rōbore,° nāvis poterat resistere magnīs tempestātibus
et altissimīs undīs.

Jāsōn per nūntiōs iter perīculōsum nūntiāvit. Statim ex 15
omnibus regiōnibus Graeciae multī juvenēs convēnērunt. In
hōc numerō erant Herculēs, Orpheus, Thēseus, et multī aliī
quōrum nōmina sunt nōtissima.

°rōbur, -oris N., oak wood

Itaque nāvis Argō nāvigāvit per maria perīculōsa. Nautae
nāvis validae neque tempestātēs neque undās timēbant.　20

Dēnique Argō ad Symplēgadēs perīculōsās pervēnit. Hae
erant duo saxa maxima, quae parvō intervāllō° in marī natābant. Sī quid° in medium spatium vēnerat, saxa incrēdibilī
celeritāte concurrēbant.

Jāsōn autem cōnsilium optimum cēpit; nōn territus erat. 25
Stāns in prōrā columbam ēmīsit, quae rēctā viā per medium
spatium celeriter volāvit et priusquam saxa cōnflīxērunt
incolumis ēvāsit. Columba autem caudam āmīsit.

Tum saxa utrimque discessērunt. Saxa cōnflīgere nōn
poterant priusquam Argō inter ea nāvigāvit.　30

°**parvō intervāllō*** . . . **natābant** were floating . . . a short distance
apart　•　**sī quid** . . . **vēnerat** if anything had come

cauda, -ae	F., tail
invidia, -ae	F., envy, hatred, jealousy
prōra, -ae	F., bow (of a ship)
*spatium, -ī	N., space
*celeritās, -ātis	F., quickness, swiftness
rēctus, -a, -um	straight
*concurrō, -ere, -currī, -cursum	run together, dash together
*cōnflīgō, -ere, -flīxī, -flīctum	strike together, bring together
*ēvādō, -ere, -vāsī, -vāsum	evade, escape
*resistō, -ere, -stitī, ——	withstand, resist (with dative)
*sentiō, -īre, sēnsī, sēnsum	feel, be aware of, sense
utrimque	from both sides
priusquam	before

A **PERFECT PARTICIPLE** agrees in gender, number, and case with the noun or pronoun it modifies. Such a
participle is declined like **bonus, -a, -um.**

I	**portātus, -a, -um**	carried, having been carried
II	**monitus, -a, -um**	warned, having been warned
III	**dictus, -a, -um**	said, having been said
IV	**audītus, -a, -um**	heard, having been heard

A painting by Francesco Peselino (1422-1457) showing the Argo drawn up in a bay, where it stands ready for boarding

PERFECT PARTICIPLE IN USE

Aedificāta ex rōbore, nāvis erat valida. Built of oak, the ship was strong.

As a verb form, **aedificāta** shows something done to the subject **(nāvis)** in the past. As an adjective, it agrees in number, gender, and case with **nāvis,** which it modifies.

Perfect participles are sometimes called "perfect passive participles" because of their passive function.

TRANSLATION OF A PERFECT PARTI-
CIPLE, like the translation of a present participle, may often be literal. Sometimes, however, a phrase or clause expresses the idea more naturally and more effectively.

Aedificāta ex rōbore, nāvis erat valida. Since it was built of oak, the ship was strong.   or   The ship, which was built of oak, was strong.

A FOURTH PRINCIPAL PART, that is, nominative singular neuter of the perfect participle, will be in-

cluded hereafter in the vocabulary listing of any verb which has a perfect participle.

	Present	Infinitive	Perfect	Perf. Part.
I	portō	portāre	portāvī	portātum
II	moneō	monēre	monuī	monitum
III	dīcō	dīcere	dīxī	dictum
IV	audiō	audīre	audīvī	audītum

The fourth principal part of many verbs ends in **-sum** instead of **-tum**; e.g., **āmissum**, perfect participle of **āmittō**.

II	III	IV
jubeō (jūssum)	**claudō (clausum)**	**sentiō (sēnsum)**
respondeō (respōnsum)	**dīvidō (dīvīsum)**	
videō (vīsum)	**mittō (missum)**	

Some verbs have no perfect participle; e.g., **sum, esse, fuī,**
————; **stō, stāre, stetī,** ————; **timeō, timēre, timuī,** ————;
fugiō, fugere, fūgī, ————.

I Match each past participle in the numbered list with an infinitive of the same verb or of a related verb in the lettered list. Tell the conjugation and give meaning of each verb.

1 aperta
2 audītōs
3 dēpulsī
4 doctus
5 ducta
6 excitātus
7 monitus
8 mūtātam
9 perfectum
10 permōtī
11 posita
12 receptōrum
13 rēctae
14 territās

a) docēre
b) regere
c) excitāre
d) pōnere
e) audīre
f) dūcere
g) aperīre
h) facere
i) monēre
j) terrēre
k) mūtāre
l) dēpellere
m) capere
n) movēre

II Translate the sentences, using a clause as the equivalent of each participle underlined.

1 Juvenis rēgnum ā frātre rēgis <u>captum</u> postulāvit.
2 Anicula incolumis <u>trānsportāta</u> Jāsonī grātiās ēgit.
3 Calceum in flūmine <u>āmissum</u> invenīre nōn potuī.
4 Auxilium ā mīlite ad jānuam <u>vocātō</u> petīvī.
5 Avēs <u>perterritae</u> cantāre dēstitērunt.
6 Bracchia nymphae in arborem <u>mūtātae</u> rāmī erant.
7 Itinera ā comitibus meīs <u>suscepta</u> longa et perīculōsa erant.
8 Vellera ovium <u>interfectārum</u> in arbore pōnēmus.

GLADIATORS AND AMPHITHEATERS

Most cities of the Roman Empire had at least one amphitheater where gladiators fought with each other or with wild animals. The most famous amphitheater is the Colosseum in Rome.

Gladiators, in spite of their name, fought not only with swords but also with spears, daggers, nets, and even bare fists. Each type of combat had its special armor or protective uniform. The alleged greeting of professional gladiators— "Morituri te salutant" (Those about to die salute you)—given to the presiding official, reflects the desperate nature of their occupation.

Originally gladiators were prisoners of war, who often preferred death to slavery. As the demand outgrew the supply, slaves were trained in special schools for gladiators. In the early days of the Empire, criminals were sentenced to combat fighting— later "to the lions." Under some emperors petty offenders and even innocents, including women and children, were sent to slaughter in the arena.

Pompeian gladiators were housed in the barracks at the rear of their enclosed exercise ground.
The elaborate metal helmet, embossed with fighting figures, protected the entire head and the back of the neck, but may have been for show rather than for use.
Below: Mosaics show (left) a hunt for wild animals for the arena and (right) gladiators fighting.

Top: Ancient Thysdrus (now El Djem) in North Africa had a handsome arena.
Above: Interior of Rome's huge Colosseum shows the ravages of time more than the Amphitheater at Capua (below), where elaborate arrangements under the arena floor can be seen.
Bottom right: The successful career of a gladiator is memorialized by the wreaths of victory on his tombstone.

LXI

THE GOLDEN FLEECE

Dēnique post multa perīcula terrā marīque Argonautae ad terram Colchidem vēnērunt. Jāsōn et comitēs ad rēgem illīus terrae appropinquāvērunt, ā quō vellus aureum postulāvērunt.

Rēx respondit, "Sī vellus aureum cupis, haec facere 5 necesse est. In meō agrō sunt duo taurī. Prīmō junge taurōs. Eī taurī sunt ācrēs, ignem expīrantēs.

"Deinde, agrum magnum arā. Cum agrum arāveris, dentēs dracōnis serēs. Ē dentibus virī armātī venient, quī tē necāre temptābunt.   10

"Dēnique, cum omnēs virōs interfēceris, mōnstrum ācre superāre vellusque capere poteris."

The ancient Greek ships pictured on this bowl are rigged like Roman ships, but differ from them in some details. The rudder is clearly visible on the left-hand ship, which does not show arrangements for rowing. The second ship has one bank of oars. Roman ships (bireme and trireme) usually had two or three banks of oars.

Haec facta perīculosa Jāsonī fortī grāta erant, et mox hōra certāminis aderat. Jāsōn in agrō stābat. Perīculum nōn timēbat, quod Mēdēa, fīlia rēgis, eī unguentum magicum 15 dederat. Tamen rēx populusque mortem juvenis fortis expectābant.

Taurī in agrum vēnērunt et ad Jāsonem ācriter appropinquāvērunt. Ignem expīrābant, sed Jāsonem unguentō magicō prōtēctum nōn vulnerāvērunt. Jāsōn, postquam taurōs 20 jūnxit, sine morā agrum arāvit dentēsque dracōnis serere incēpit.

Post paucās hōrās virī armātī ē dentibus ēvēnērunt. Jāsōn magnum saxum (ita enim praecēperat Mēdēa) inter hominēs ācrēs jēcit. Mox hominēs stupidī inter sē ācriter pugnābant 25 neque juvenem necāre temptābant.

Post hoc certāmen Mēdēa Jāsonem in silvam dēnsam dūxit, ubi vellus aureum ab ingentī dracōne custōdiēbātur. Celeriter Mēdēa in mōnstrum venēnum jēcit; statim somnus dracōnem oppressit. Tum Jāsōn vellus cēpit et cum Mēdēā fūgit. 30

taurus, -ī	M., bull
*factum, -ī	N., deed, act, event
*unguentum, -ī	N., ointment
*venēnum, -ī	N., poison
certāmen, -inis	N., struggle, fight, contest
*dēns, dentis (-ium)	M., tooth
*ignis, ignis (-ium)	M., fire
ingēns, gen., ingentis	huge, enormous
*necesse	(indecl. adj.) necessary
arō, -āre, -āvī, -ātum	plow
*expirō, -āre, -āvī, -ātum	breathe out, expire
*jungō, -ere, jūnxī, jūnctum	yoke, join
*opprimō, -ere, -pressī, -pressum	press down, oppress
*praecipiō, -ere, -cēpī, -ceptum	teach, instruct
*prōtegō, -ere, -tēxī, -tēctum	protect; cover
serō, -ere, sēvī, satum	sow, plant
*ēveniō, -īre, -vēnī, -ventum	come forth; happen
enim	for

PAST PERFECT TENSE of a Latin verb represents action which took place before a specified or suggested time in the past. The translation of this tense usually contains the verb "had."

Mēdēa eī unguentum magicum dederat. Medea had given him a magic ointment.

FUTURE PERFECT TENSE indicates action completed before a given time in the future. This tense does not often appear in Latin. It is even rarer in English, where the future aspect of the perfect tense is usually not expressed.

Cum agrum arāveris, dentēs dracōnis serēs. When you (will) have plowed the field, you will sow the dragon's teeth.

PAST PERFECT ACTIVE AND FUTURE PERFECT ACTIVE are formed in the same way for all four conjugations, and for **sum** and **possum.**

Past Perfect Active

Perfect Stem	+	Tense Sign	+	Person Endings (like imperfect)
portāv-	+	**-erā- (-era)**	+	**-m, -s, -t; -mus, -tis, -nt**

Future Perfect Active

Perfect Stem	+	Tense Sign	+	Person Endings (like present)
portāv-	+	**-eri-**[1]	+	**-ō,**[1] **-s, -t; -mus, -tis, -nt**

I	II	III	IV	**sum**	**possum**
portāv-	**monu-**	**dix-**	**audīv-**	**fu-**	**potu-**

Past Perfect Active

portāveram	**monueram**	**dīxeram**	**audīveram**	**fueram**	**potueram**
portāverās	**monuerās**	**dīxerās**	**audīverās**	**fuerās**	**potuerās**
etc.	etc.	etc.	etc.	etc.	etc.

Future Perfect Active

portāverō[1]	**monuerō**	**dīxerō**	**audīverō**	**fuerō**	**potuerō**
portāveris	**monueris**	**dīxeris**	**audīveris**	**fueris**	**potueris**
etc.	etc.	etc.	etc.	etc.	etc.

[1]Before **-ō** the **-i-** of the tense sign is dropped.

SUMMARY OF PAST PERFECT ACTIVE AND FUTURE PERFECT ACTIVE

	Past Perfect Active	Future Perfect Active
	Singular	Singular
I	portāverat	portāverit
II	monuerat	monuerit
III	dīxerat	dīxerit
IV	audīverat	audīverit
sum	fuerat	fuerit
possum	potuerat	potuerit
	Plural	Plural
I	portāverant	portāverint
II	monuerant	monuerint
III	dīxerant	dīxerint
IV	audīverant	audīverint
sum	fuerant	fuerint
possum	potuerant	potuerint

A complete conjugation of past perfect active and future perfect active is in the Summary of Grammar included in the reference materials at the end of this book.

I Translate.
1 Ōlim erat vellus aureum ab ingentī mōnstrō dēfēnsum.
2 Jāsōn id invenīre in animō habuit.
3 Juvenis cum paucīs comitibus dēlēctīs nāvigābit.
4 Sī vellus cupiēs, haec facere necesse erit.
5 Eī taurī, ignem expīrantēs, ācrēs sunt.
6 Cum agrum arāveris, dentēs dracōnis serēs.
7 Jāsōn nōn sōlum taurōs jūnxerat, sed etiam agrum arāverat.
8 Vellus ā dracōne custōdītur.

II In the sentences of I, find one example of as many of the following items as possible.
a) present passive tense
b) imperfect tense
c) future active tense
d) perfect active tense
e) past perfect active tense
f) future perfect active tense
g) present participle
h) ablative of agent
i) perfect participle used as an adjective
j) perfect participle used in place of clause

313

LXII

JASON'S RETURN

Intereā comitēs Jāsonis nāvem custōdiēbant; animō ānxiō ducem expectābant. Postquam sōl occidit, dē ejus salūte dēspērāre incēpērunt. Subitō autem, dum ducem petere parant, lūmen clārum cōnspexērunt. Quae causa lūminis fuit?

Fuit vellus aureum, quod ā Jāsone reportātum erat. Nōn jam 5 territī, comitēs ducem et Mēdēam magnō cum gaudiō recēpērunt. Sine morā omnēs nāvem cōnscendērunt, ad Graeciam nāvigāvērunt.

Tandem, post plūra perīcula, Jāsōn ad Thessaliam pervēnit. Statim ad rēgiam Peliae properāvit, quī rēgnum adhūc obtinē- 10 bat. Jāsōn vellus aureum mōnstrāvit et rēgnum prō sē postulāvit.

Peliās prīmum nihil respondit. Dēnique dīxit, "Relinque mihi paulisper hanc potentiam. Jam aetāte cōnfectus sum. Sine dubiō hoc rēgnum mox ā tē obtinēbitur." 15

Head of Ulysses found in a cave at Sperlonga, Italy, depicting horror at sight of the monsters Scylla and Charybdis which menaced his ship

Jāsōn, misericordiā mōtus, respondit, "Retinē rēgnum usque ad vītae fīnem tuae."

Post paucōs annōs Jāsōn rēgnum Peliae mortuī obtinuit, et diū rēgnābat. Ōlim sub umbrā nāvis suae, quae in ōram subducta erat, Jāsōn senex° dormiēbat. At nāvis, quae adhūc ₂₀ ērēcta steterat, subitō cecidit et Jāsonem īnfēlīcem oppressit.

°**senex,** gen., **senis** old, aged; (as noun) old man, old woman

misericordia, -ae	F., pity
aetās, -ātis	F., age
***lūmen, -inis**	N., light
***dēspērō, -āre, -āvī, -ātum**	despair
***retineō, -ēre, -uī, -tentum**	hold or keep back, retain
cōnficiō, -ere, -fēcī, -fectum	finish, accomplish; weaken
cōnscendō, -ere, -scendī, -scēnsum	embark, go aboard ship
occidō, -ere, -cidī, -cāsum	fall, fall down; (of sun) set
***subdūcō, -ere, -dūxī, -ductum**	haul up, draw up
adhūc	till now
intereā	meanwhile
paulisper	a little while
usque ad	(with acc.) till
at	but; yet

IN PERFECT SYSTEM IN PASSIVE VOICE each verb form consists of two separate words: a perfect passive participle and a form of **sum.**

Puer dīxit, "Monitus sum." The boy said, "I have been warned."
Monitae erātis, puellae! You had been warned, girls!
Oppidum monitum erit. The town will have been warned.

AGREEMENT The participle in a passive verb form agrees with the subject in gender and number and has the appropriate adjective ending: **-us, -a, -um; -ī, -ae, -a.**

The form of **sum** used with the participle agrees with the subject in person as well as in number. Its tense varies with the tense of the passive verb; that is, present forms (**sum,** etc.) occur in perfect passive; imperfect (**eram,** etc.), in past perfect passive; future (**erō,** etc.), in future perfect passive.

315

SUMMARY OF PERFECT SYSTEM IN PASSIVE VOICE

	Perfect Passive	Past Perfect Passive	Future Perfect Passive
	Singular	Singular	Singular
I	portātus est	portātus erat	portātus erit
II	monitus est	monitus erat	monitus erit
III	ductus est	ductus erat	ductus erit
IV	audītus est	audītus erat	audītus erit
	Plural	Plural	Plural
I	portātī sunt	portātī erant	portātī erunt
II	monitī sunt	monitī erant	monitī erunt
III	ductī sunt	ductī erant	ductī erunt
IV	audītī sunt	audītī erant	audītī erunt

A complete conjugation of the perfect system in passive voice is in Summary of Grammar near the end of this book.

TRANSLATION OF PASSIVE VERBS IN THE PERFECT SYSTEM

Verbs in perfect passive (like those in perfect active) represent a single act completed in past time.

portātum est it was carried, it has been carried

Verbs in past perfect passive (like those in past perfect active) represent action which took place before a specified or suggested time in the past.

portātum erat it had been carried

Verbs in future perfect passive (like those in future perfect active) represent action completed before a given time in the future.

portātum erit it will have been carried

I (A) For each active verb in the numbered list, select from the lettered list a passive verb in the same tense that also has the same person and number.

(B) For each passive verb select an active verb in the same tense, person, and number.

(C) Translate each pair of verbs.

1 vīsa est	8 mūtāvimus	a) auxerant	h) accēpit
2 ēgeritis	9 crēdita erant	b) terrēbiminī	i) arābimus
3 custōdiēs	10 prōtegeris	c) coāctī erātis	j) dēlēbantur
4 audiar	11 juvābor	d) dabō	k) tenēberis
5 fēcistī	12 pūnītī estis	e) jūnctī sumus	l) relictī eritis
6 obtinēbitis	13 cōnfēcerātis	f) laudāta es	m) invēnistis
7 cupiēbant	14 agēmur	g) perveniam	n) vincis

II Select from the list an appropriate verb to complete each sentence, and translate the entire sentence.

1 Jam prīdem servī male ā dominīs ____.	a) ācta est
2 Līberī ____, "Ubi māter est?"	b) āctī erant
3 Dēnique ursa ex oppidō ____.	c) agēbāmur
4 Hōc proeliō nōbīs maxima injūria ____.	d) agentibus
5 Virī patriam memoriā nōn ____.	e) agētur
6 Jam puer benignē ____.	f) ēgī
7 Meō comitī fortī grātiās ____.	g) facta est
8 Fīliae ā mātribus ____.	h) fēcimus
9 Dracō ā Jāsone ____.	i) necātus est
10 Terrā marīque itinera multa ____.	j) quaerent
11 Nusquam crūdēliter ____.	k) quaesītae sunt
12 Virīs taurōs ____ grātiās ēgimus.	l) tenuērunt

REVIEW OF UNIT XV

LESSONS LVIII-LXII

Nouns	Nouns (cont.)	Nouns (cont.)
anicula, -ae	*unguentum, -ī	*mare, maris (-ium)
cauda, -ae	*venēnum, -ī	*soror, -ōris
invidia, -ae	aetās, -ātis	Adjectives
misericordia, -ae	ariēs, -etis	attonitus, -a, -um
prōra, -ae	*celeritās, -ātis	fessus, -a, -um
calceus, -ī	certāmen, -inis	*perterritus, -a, -um
taurus, -ī	*dēns, dentis (-ium)	*placidus, -a, -um
*factum, -ī	dracō, -ōnis	rēctus, -a, -um
solium, -ī	*ignis, -is (-ium)	spūmōsus, -a, -um
*spatium, -ī	*lūmen, -inis	incolumis, -e

317

Adjectives (cont.)	Verbs (cont.)	Adverbs (cont.)
ingēns, gen., ingentis	*lūdō, -ere	nusquam
*necesse	occidō, -ere	paulisper
Verbs	*opprimō, -ere	prīdem
*arō, -āre	*praecipiō, -ere	utrimque
*dēspērō, -āre	*prōtegō, -ere	Conjunctions
*expīrō, -āre	*resistō, -ere	at
caveō, -ēre	serō, -ere	enim
*retineō, -ēre	*subdūcō, -ere	priusquam
+agō, -ere	*ēveniō, -īre	Prepositions
*concurrō, -ere	*perveniō, -īre	+ā, ab
cōnficiō, -ere	*sentiō, -īre	ob
*cōnflīgō, -ere	Adverbs	usque ad
cōnscendō, -ere	adhūc	Phrases
*contendō, -ere	*audācter	quam ob rem
*ēvādō, -ere	*crūdēliter	rē vērā
*jungō, -ere	intereā	

I Change active verbs to passive and vice versa, making other necessary changes. Translate both versions.

1 Virī nāvem in ōram subdūxērunt.
2 Ignis ā taurīs expīrābātur.
3 Juvenis agrōs arāverat.
4 Līberī ovēs benignē agunt.
5 Vellus aureum ā dracōne semper custōdiētur.
6 Dentēs dracōnis ā Jāsone seruntur.
7 Rēx crūdēlis cīvēs perterritōs oppressit.
8 Jāsōn calceum āmīsit.
9 Ille taurōs magnā cum difficultāte jūnxerit.
10 Hostēs contrā sociōs nostrōs bellum gessērunt.

II Give the corresponding active form of each passive verb in the list.

appellātur	capiēbantur	jubeor	positum est
audientur	cēlābitur	monēberis	probātī sumus

III Give the corresponding passive form of each active verb in the list.

coluerint	habēbās	mūniēbant	prōtegō
cupiet	jūverātis	pellam	pūnīvimus

318

The English artist George Frederick Watts (1817-1904) whimsically pictured the Minotaur as a realistic bull looking hopefully out to sea for the ship which each year brought boys and girls to be sacrificed to him. The painting is in the Tate Gallery in London.

7

A RECKLESS DRIVER

Phaëthōn, fīlius Apollinis, nōn in caelō, sed in terrā
habitābat. Erat puer audācissimus quī suam glōriam augēre
dēsīderābat.

Ōlim sibi dīxit, "Currus sōlis ā patre meō per caelum agitur.
Equī sōlis sunt optimī et ācerrimī. Ego, patrī meō similis, 5
illum currum facile regere possum. Omnēs, cum mē agentem
equōs sōlis vidēbunt, dīcent, 'Certē Phaëthōn est fīlius
Apollinis!' "

Itaque puer audāx in rēgiam splendidam sōlis sēcrētō
ascendit. Ibi Apollō tamen fīlium ad sē vocāvit et benignē 10
recēpit.

"Juvā mē!" puer dīxit. "Omnēs rīdent cum dīcō, 'Apollō
meus pater est.' "

Apollō quaesīvit, "Quid dēsīderās? Dabō! Per aquās
Stygiās jūrō!" 15

Phaëthōn petīvit, "Dēsīderō agere currum sōlis."

Apollō erat attonitus. "Hoc est difficillimum!" dīxit.
"Ego sōlus illōs equōs regere possum."

Fīlius autem dīxit, "Mentem meam nōn mūtābō. Dī ipsī
illō jūre jūrandō tenentur." 20

Deinde pater maestus puerum dē viā perīculōsā docuit et
dē equīs ācerrimīs monuit.

Jam diēs erat; jam audāx puer iter suscēpit. Currus levior
erat; itaque equī dē viā cucurrērunt. Nunc in summās
regiōnēs caelī, nunc in humillimās, contendērunt. Omnis 25
terra ārdēbat.

Dēnique Juppiter īrātus dīxit, "Plūrima loca, urbēs, montēs,
silvae, ignibus dēlentur! Aquae terrārum siccantur."

Sine morā Juppiter fulmine īnfēlīcem puerum—etiam
fīlium deī—interfēcit. 30

---

*audāx, gen., audācis bold • currus chariot • jūrō,
-āre, -āvī, -ātum take an oath, swear • mēns, mentis F., mind
jūre jūrandō by an oath • diēs (nom.) day • suscēpit
he undertook • levior lighter, too light • siccō, -āre, -āvī,
-ātum dry (up) • fulmen, fulminis N., lightning

8

THE FIRST AVIATOR

Daedalus, Graecus incrēdibilī ingeniō, et fīlius Īcarus captīvī in īnsulā Crētā habitābant. Suam ad urbem Athēnās redīre magnopere cupiēbant. Nūllam viam salūtis autem invenīre poterant.

Tum Daedalus sibi dīxit, "Neque terra neque mare quidem 5 nōbīs auxilium dēsīderātum dat, sed caelum certē patet! Ex pennīs avium ālās faciam; hōc modō fugiēmus."

Diū avēs spectābat. Deinde sagittīs multās avēs Daedalus fīliusque necāvērunt et eārum pennās servāvērunt. Ex hīs pennīs cērā ligātīs ālās vir callidus fēcit. 10

Dēnique ālae parātae erant. Hae ālīs avium similēs erant, sed majōrēs et potentiōrēs quam illae.

Daedalus puerō ālās dāns eum monuit, "Sī volābis altius, pennae propter sōlem cēram āmittent. Mediō itinere tūtissimī volābimus. Audī et accipe cōnsilium bonum!" 15

Ipse levissimīs ventīs sē commīsit; item fīlius. Prīmō Īcarus docta verba patris memoriā tenuit; tum haec verba neglēxit. In altiōrēs regiōnēs caelī puer iter fēcit.

Propter radiōs sōlis cēra ālārum inūtilis jam erat. Subitō Īcarus ālās āmīsit, et in mare cecidit. Diū frūstrā pater fīlium 20 quaesīvit, sed pennās sōlās in undīs vīdit. Ab illō puerō hae aquae nōmen habent—mare Īcarium.

*ingenium, -ī N., talent, ability • patet is open • cēra, -ae F., wax • ligō, -āre, -āvī, -ātum tie, bind • callidus, -a, -um skillful, shrewd • levis, -e light • item likewise

Panels from door in memorial to the Wright brothers, at Kitty Hawk, North Carolina

9

THESEUS MEETS THE MINOTAUR

Crēta, īnsula nōta, ā Graeciā nōn longē abest. In Crētā labyrinthus clārus ab architectō nōtō, Daedalō, aedificātus erat. Hīc in sēcrētō locō Mīnōtaurus habitābat. Hoc mōnstrum virōs, fēminās, puerōs, puellās dēvorābat.

Ōlim forte in lūdīs sacrīs fīlius rēgis Crētae ā virō Athē- 5 niēnsī interfectus est.

Populus Crētae dīxit, "Factum est malum; itaque necesse erit dare sacrificium. Dī sacrificium hūmānum postulant."

Quotannīs puerī et puellae Athēnārum portābantur ad hunc labyrinthum, ubi ā mōnstrō necābantur. Cum puerī 10 et puellae ad īnsulam Crētam nāvigābant, semper vēla nāvis erant ātra.

Thēseus, fīlius rēgis Athēnārum, juvenis ēgregius et validus, maximē dolēbat.

Dēnique patrī suō dīxit, "Satis est! Populus puerōs et 15 puellās Mīnōtaurō dare nōn dēbet. Sum validus; Mīnōtaurum superābō. Hodiē cum puerīs et puellīs ad Crētam nāvigābō. Priusquam reveniam, vēla nāvis meae mūtābō; nōn jam ātra erunt!"

Quamquam perīculum magnum sentiēbat, Thēseus cēterīs 20 cum juvenibus ad Crētam nāvigāvit. Ibi ab Ariadnā, fīliā rēgis Crētae, jūtus est. Ea juvenī fīlum longum dedit. Noctū Thēseus fīlum ad jānuam labyrinthī sēcrētō alligāvit.

Mīnōtaurus, ubi Thēseum vīdit, juvenem interficere temptāvit. Thēseus autem erat parātus; gladiō mōnstrum necāvit. 25 Deinde jānuam obscūram labyrinthī fīlō facile invēnit. Sine perīculō juvenēs cēterī līberātī sunt.

Tum Thēseus cēterīs cum comitibus celerrimē nāvem cōnscendērunt. Jam ad Graeciam nāvigāvērunt.

Quamquam puellae puerīque servātī erant, tamen vēla 30 nāvis ātra manēbant. Thēseus memoriā nōn tenēbat ea quae patrī ōlim prōmīserat. Pater vidēns vēla ātra sē interfēcit et Thēseus jam appellātus rēx est.

lūdus, -ī M., game, sport • quotannīs yearly • juvenis, juvenis M., young man • fīlum, -ī N., thread • alligō, -āre, -āvī, -ātum tie or fasten (to)

Paris escorts Helen to the ship that will take them to Troy.

THE TROJAN WAR

In the late nineteenth century, Heinrich Schliemann, a
retired German businessman and amateur archaeologist,
excavated a hill in Asia Minor. What he found there proved
that a legend many hundreds of years old is based on history.

Working at his own expense, Schliemann uncovered a
series of buried cities. One on top of the other, nine cities
were located on the site of legendary Troy, made famous by
the *Iliad* and the *Odyssey* of Homer and by the *Aeneid* of
Vergil. Archaeologists are still not sure which of the many

323

strata excavated by Schliemann was Homeric Troy, but continued excavations show that the legendary city probably was at one of the levels near the surface. Thus, through archaeology, the Trojan War becomes a page of history.

Units XVI-XVIII of this book tell some of the tales that developed around the siege of Troy. According to legend, the Trojan War had its origin in a beauty contest among the goddesses of Olympus. The real prize went not to one of the contestants but to the judge, Paris, a Trojan prince. He won as his bride "the most beautiful woman in the world"—Helen of Greece, who, after her escapade with Paris, was known as Helen of Troy.

Unfortunately Helen was already married to Menelaus, king of Sparta, who, with other Greek chieftains, sailed to Troy to recover his queen. The Greeks declared war on the Trojans, and after a ten-year siege Troy was destroyed. Through a trick the Greeks had at last got within the walls of the city. The story of this trick is the story of "the Wooden Horse" (sometimes called "the Trojan Horse"), which has become a symbol of treachery, particularly among nations.

Many Trojans perished, but one of them, Aeneas, escaped with his young son from the burning city. He was destined to become the father of the Roman state (see Units XVII and XVIII).

Unit G is a flash back to events which occurred while the Greeks were assembling men and ships in preparation for the war with Troy and while they were awaiting favorable weather for the voyage. King Menelaus' niece, Iphigenia, is the central figure in the stories of this unit.

Unit H describes the return of one of the most famous of the Greek chieftains to his home and family. This chieftain is Ulysses (also known as Odysseus), the hero of Homer's Odyssey.

Even today professional archaeologists continue to find, throughout the ancient world, evidences indicating that the men and women of the Trojan legends were real people. Playwrights and poets may have embroidered the truth somewhat, but the fact remains that Paris and Helen, Agamemnon and Clytemnestra, Ulysses and Aeneas were more than mere characters in a play or figures in a legend.

Collections of Corning Museum of Glass

This glass bowl found in Roman Syria dates from the late Roman Empire. Paris is shown selecting Venus as more beautiful than Minerva and Juno.

LXIII

A GIFT FOR THE FAIREST

Ōlim erat magna cēna in Graeciā. Omnēs dī deaeque
praeter deam Discordiam invītātī erant. Ea dea īrātissima
tamen ad cēnam vēnit, ubi jēcit inter deōs deāsque mālum
aureum in quō erat hoc verbum, "Pulcherrimae."

Statim dē hōc mālō deae Jūnō et Minerva et Venus inter sē 5
disputāre incēpērunt. Omnēs mālum aureum habēre cupiēbant.

Juppiter, quī contrōversiam audīverat, dīxit, "Hujus certāminis jūdex esse nōn cupiō. In monte Īdā autem habitat
pāstor, cujus nōmen est Paris. Hanc contrōversiam fīnīre 10
dēbet. Is deae pulcherrimae dabit hoc mālum, signum
victōriae."

Deae igitur in montem Īdam convēnērunt. Mercuriī
auxiliō Paridem invēnērunt.

Mercurius pāstōrī Paridī mālum aureum mōnstrāvit, 15
dīcēns, "In hōc mālō quod teneō est ūnum verbum, 'Pulcherrimae.' Magna est contrōversia inter hās deās quibuscum vēnī. Quis est pulcherrima dea? Juppiter tē jūdicem
hujus contrōversiae dēlēgit."

Paris, magnopere agitātus, dīxit, "Jūdicium est dif- 20
ficillimum."

Prīmō Jūnō dīxit, "Rēgīna deōrum sum. Dā mihi mālum
aureum, Paris; dīvitiās potentiamque tibi dabō."

Deinde Minerva jūdicī dīxit, "Dea sapientiae sum. Dā
mihi mālum aureum; magnam sapientiam et cōnsilia bona 25
tibi dabō."

Dēnique Venus prō jūdice stetit. "Fīnem hujus contrōversiae facile faciam," dīxit. "Dea amōris sum. Dā mihi
mālum aureum; pulcherrima fēmina orbis terrārum tua
conjūnx erit!" 30

Paris autem jūdicium facile facere nōn potuit. Dīvitiae
potentiaque, sapientia cōnsiliaque bona—haec omnia juvenī
grāta erant. Tamen conjugem pulcherrimam ā deā amōris
prōmissam maximē cupiēbat.

Itaque Paris dīxit, "Venus, tū es dea pulcherrima; tibi 35
mālum aureum dabō."

326

dīvitiae, -ārum	F. pl., riches, wealth
mālum, -ī	N., apple
***amor, -ōris**	M., love
***jūdex, -icis**	M., judge
***orbis, -is (-ium)**	M., circle, orb
***agitō, -āre, -āvī, -ātum**	drive, agitate, disturb
***prōmittō, -ere, -mīsī, -missum**	promise
***fīniō, -īre, -īvī, -ītum**	finish, put an end to

PRESENT ACTIVE INFINITIVES have already appeared many times in the stories of this book. In this story there are five.

I	II	III	IV	(sum)
disputāre	**habēre**	**facere**	**fīnīre**	**esse**
to argue	to have	to make	to finish	to be

Deae inter sē disputāre incēpērunt. The goddesses began to quarrel among themselves.

PRESENT PASSIVE INFINITIVES of the four conjugations are patterned after these.

I	II	III	IV
portārī	**monērī**	**dūcī**	**audīrī**
to be carried	to be warned	to be led	to be heard

In Conjugations I, II, and IV, passive infinitives are like active, except the final letter is -ī instead of -e. In Conjugation III also, the final letter of the passive infinitive is -ī, but in this conjugation alone the preceding syllable (-er-) of the active infinitive is dropped.

I Supply the correct infinitives of verbs in parentheses, and translate the completed sentences.
1 (Errō) hūmānum est.
2 Urbs (dēleō) nōn potuit.
3 Bellō patriam (dēfendō) necesse est.
4 Nōn omnēs prīmī (sum) possunt.
5 Nātūra ipsa nōs parentibus grātiās (agō) jubet.
6 Melius est ab hominibus bonīs (amō) quam ā malīs (timeō).

In this rendition of Paris' kidnaping of Helen, all the figures except Cupid and the boatman are in medieval dress, and the ship is also of medieval design. The picture, which is now commonly attributed to a follower of Fra Angelico (1387-1455), is in the National Gallery, London.

II Match English meanings with Latin verb forms, and supply suitable pronoun subjects.

<table>
<tr><td>1 vincēbāris</td><td>a) tasted</td></tr>
<tr><td>2 gustāvistis</td><td>b) are being driven</td></tr>
<tr><td>3 respiciunt</td><td>c) shall lie</td></tr>
<tr><td>4 audiēmur</td><td>d) were being overcome</td></tr>
<tr><td>5 dormīs</td><td>e) are sleeping</td></tr>
<tr><td>6 timēbāmus</td><td>f) shall be heard</td></tr>
<tr><td>7 geritur</td><td>g) is being worn</td></tr>
<tr><td>8 jacēbō</td><td>h) will be present</td></tr>
<tr><td>9 aderis</td><td>i) were feared</td></tr>
<tr><td>10 agiminī</td><td>j) are looking back</td></tr>
<tr><td></td><td>k) used to fear</td></tr>
</table>

LXIV

PARIS GETS HIS REWARD

Venus, postquam mālum accēpit aureum, Paridī dīxit, "Fēmina pulcherrima in Graeciā habitat. Nōmen ejus est Helena; Helena erit tua conjūnx."

Dea quoque dīxit Paridem ipsum nōn esse fīlium pāstōris; patrem et mātrem esse rēgem et rēgīnam Trōjae. "Monitus 5 ōrāculō," inquit, "pater tuus mortem tuam cupiēbat; tē in silvīs relīquit. Pāstor benignus autem tē ā perīculīs silvārum servāvit."

Deinde dea dīxit Hectorem, frātrem Paridis, in rēgiā Trōjānā habitāre et ab omnibus Trōjānīs propter magnam audā- 10 ciam laudārī.

Statim Paris invidiōsus īrātusque ad urbem Trōjam prōcessit. Priamus, rēx Trōjānus, ubi pāstōrem vīdit, statim sēnsit eum esse fīlium suum. Nōn jam mortem Paridis cupiēbat. Laetus quod Paris vīvēbat, Priamus juvenem 15 libenter in rēgiam invītāvit.

Posteā Paris sēcrētō ad Graeciam nāvigāvit. Pater autem crēdidit eum ad aliam terram iter factūrum esse.[1] In Graeciā juvenis audīvit Helenam, fēminam ā Venere prōmissam, Spartae rēgīnam et uxōrem Menelāī rēgis esse. 20

Paris autem sōlus ad urbem Spartam prōcessit. Rēgina perfida, Helena, Paridem vīdit et eum fōrmōsissimum esse putāvit. Suā voluntāte Helena sēcrētō ē rēgiā discessit et ad urbem Trōjam cum Paride fūgit.

Multum agitātus, rēx Menelāus prīncipēs Graeciae convo- 25 cāvit. Propter amōrem Helenae, Menelāus in animō bellum in Trōjānōs gerere habuit.

*prīnceps, -ipis	M., leader, chief; as adj., first, chief
*voluntās, -ātis	F., will, wish, inclination
*putō, -āre, -āvī, -ātum	consider, think, suppose
*crēdō, -ere, crēdidī, -itum	trust (in), believe (with dative)

[1] **eum . . . iter factūrum esse,** that he would travel. **Factūrum esse** (future active infinitive) indicates action that is to take place after the time of the main verb.

A DIRECT QUOTATION repeats the exact words of a speaker. In writing, we enclose the exact words of a speaker in quotation marks.

Dīcit, "Frāter tuus in rēgiā habitat." She says, "Your brother is living in the palace."

AN INDIRECT QUOTATION repeats the thought, but not the exact words of the original speaker. In writing there are no quotation marks.

Dīcit frātrem tuum in rēgiā habitāre. She says (that) your brother is living in the palace.

The name "indirect statement" is given to this kind of indirect quotation. The verb of indirect statement in Latin is an infinitive and its subject is in the accusative.

In English an indirect statement is often introduced by the conjunction "that"; sometimes the conjunction is omitted. In Latin no conjunction is used to introduce an indirect statement.

INDIRECT STATEMENTS occur in Latin not only with verbs that mean "say," but also with verbs that mean "hear," "know," "believe," "see," "think," and the like.

Dīcit tē errāre. He says (that) you are wrong.
Priamus sēnsit filium vīvere. Priam realized his son was alive.
Paris audīvit Helenam in Graeciā habitāre. Paris heard that Helen was living in Greece.

When the subject of an infinitive is the same as the subject of the main verb, the accusative of a reflexive pronoun is used as the subject of the indirect statement.

Putat sē errāre. He thinks (that) he is wrong.

PREDICATE NOUN OR ADJECTIVE IN INDIRECT STATEMENT is in the accusative to agree with the subject of the infinitive.

Dea dīxit patrem ejus esse rēgem Trōjae. The goddess said his father was the king of Troy.

**P R E S E N T   I N F I N I T I V E   I N   I N D I R E C T
S T A T E M E N T** represents an act as occurring at the
time shown by the tense of the main verb.

In these examples **timēre** means "fears" with **dīcit**, but
"feared" with **dīxit**.

Dīcit sē perīculum timēre. He says that he fears danger.
Dīxit sē perīculum timēre. He said that he feared danger.

P R A C T I C E Study the seven Latin sentences on this page and
the facing page that are used as examples of indirect statement. Change each one into a direct statement in Latin, and
then translate.

Example: **Dīcit tē errāre.** He says that you are wrong.
Change to: **Dīcit, "(Tū) errās."** He says, "You are wrong."

I Change each direct quotation to indirect, using one of the
infinitives listed, and make all other necessary changes.
Translate both versions.

1 Pater Paridis dīxit, "Fīlius meus iter longum facit."
2 Paris sibi dīcit, "Fēminam ā Venere prōmissam invenīre
cupiō."
3 Helena dīcit, "Juvenis fōrmōsissimus est."
4 Menelāus prīncipibus suīs nūntiāvit, "Propter amōrem
Helenae bellum in Trōjānōs geritur."
5 Helena dīxit, "Meā voluntāte ā rēgiā discēdō."

cupere	discēdī	esse	gessī
cupī	facere	gerere	invenīre
discēdere	fēcī	gerī	invenīrī

II Change each indirect quotation to direct, making all necessary changes to form complete sentences. Translate both
versions.

Venus Paridī dīcit:
1 fēminam pulcherrimam in Graeciā habitāre.
2 nōmen ejus Helenam esse.
3 ibi patrem ejus, rēgem, invenīrī posse.
4 eum deinde ad Graeciam nāvigāre dēbēre.
5 Graecōs bellum in Trōjānōs gerere.

331

LXV

ULYSSES' TRICK

Convocātī ā Menelāō, multī prīncipēs Graeciae convēnērunt. Jam magnus exercitus° parātus ad urbem Trōjam
nāvigāre erat.

Aberant autem duo ducēs, Ulīxēs et Achillēs.

Ulīxēs uxōrem fīliumque relinquere nōn dēsīderābat. 5
Fīlius īnfāns jam erat. Ulīxēs igitur jūnxit equum bovemque
et ōram maritimam arāre incēpit. Nūntius ā Menelāō missus
prīmō crēdidit Ulīxem esse īnsānum.

Dēnique autem nūntius sēnsit hoc esse dolum Ulīxis.

°**exercitus** (nom. sing.) army

Achilles betraying his masculine nature by inspecting the peddler's sword rather
than the jewels, is the main figure in "Achilles at the Court of Lycomedes." This
painting by Pompeo Girolamo Batoni (1708-1787) is in the Uffizi Gallery, Florence.

Celeriter īnfantem cēpit et prō animālibus jūnctīs posuit. 10
Ulīxēs, fīlium suum interficere nōn dēsīderāns, puerum
vītāvit. Tum nūntius scīvit Ulīxem sānum esse; Ulīxēs
igitur sē cum cēterīs Graecīs jūnxit.

Interim māter Achillis, Thetis, quae fīlium bellum gerere
nōn dēsīderābat, Achillem ad rēgiam amīcī mīsit. Thetis 15
nēminī dīxit sē fīlium apud amīcum cēlāvisse. Nēmō scīvit
Achillem ā mātre ad rēgnum longinquum missum esse.

Ibi Achillēs vestēs fēminae gerēbat et inter fēminās familiae
rēgis habitābat. Thetis crēdēbat juvenem, inter fēminās cēlā-
tum, tūtum esse. 20

Tum multī ad illam rēgiam vēnērunt bellum nūntiantēs.
Nūllōs autem virōs vīdērunt. Tamen Ulīxēs quī cum nūntiīs
iter fēcerat dolum latēre sēnsit.

Itaque novum dolum parāvit; ubi iterum ad rēgiam vēnit,
vestem mercātōris gerēbat. Fēminīs puellīsque gemmās et 25
vestēs pulchrās et urnās aureās ostendit. Gladium pulchrum
quoque ostendit. Fēminīs gemmae et vestēs grātae erant, sed
Achillēs gladium statim cēpit.

Tum Ulīxēs clāmāvit, "Achillēs es! Cum cēterīs ducibus
ad urbem Trōjam nāvigāre dēbēs!" 30

Hīs verbīs Ulīxis mōtus, Achillēs libenter arma cēpit et
cum eō discessit.

Itaque duo prīncipēs quī pugnāre nōn dēsīderāverant sē
cēterīs ducibus jūnxērunt.

dolus, -ī	M., trick, deceit, fraud
*bōs, bovis	M., ox; F., cow
mercātor, -ōris	M., merchant, trader
nēmō, dat., **nēminī**	M. or F., no one (no gen. or abl.)
vestis, -is (-ium)	F., clothing, garment
ostendō, -ere, -tendī, -tentum	show, display
*sciō, -īre, -īvī, -ītum	know, understand

A PERFECT ACTIVE INFINITIVE consists of
the perfect stem of a verb and the ending -isse.

I	II	III	IV
portāvisse	**monuisse**	**dūxisse**	**audīvisse**
to have carried	to have warned	to have led	to have heard

A PERFECT PASSIVE INFINITIVE consists of the perfect participle with **esse**.

portātum esse	monitum esse	ductum esse	audītum esse
to have been carried	to have been warned	to have been led	to have been heard

TENSE OF INFINITIVE IN INDIRECT STATEMENT An infinitive expresses relative time. It merely shows the time relationship of its own action to the action of the main verb.

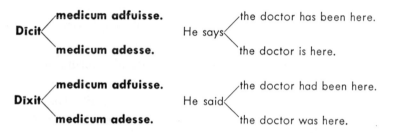

Here, two Latin infinitives may each be translated in two ways in English, depending on the tense of the main verb.

A Latin perfect infinitive always represents an act as completed before the time shown by the tense of the main verb; a present infinitive represents an act as occurring at the same time as that shown by the tense of the main verb.

These principles apply also to passive infinitives.

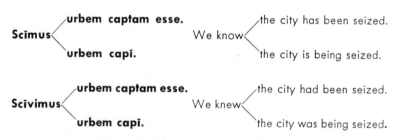

I Change each direct quotation to indirect, and each indirect quotation to direct. Translate both versions.

1 Menelāus Graecīs dīcit Trōjam dēlērī.
2 Imperātor sē plūrimōs hostēs cēpisse dīxit.
3 Trōjānus nūntiāvit, "Equus ligneus in urbem ductus est."
4 Priamus respondit, "Graecī dolum parāvērunt."

LXVI

Postquam Paris et Hector ā Graecīs interfectī sunt, magnus dolor animōs populī Trōjānī occupāvit. In viās urbis Helena exīre nōn audēbat, quod fēminae Trōjānae clāmābant, "Propter tē, fēmina pessima, dī nōs nōn jam amant."

In templīs sacerdōtēs dīcēbant, "Deōs, Trōjānī, ōrāte; in ārīs sacrificia pōnite. Ōmina sunt mala. Fāta nōs dēlēbunt." 5

Trōjānī sciēbant sē ducēs bonōs nōn jam habēre. Quamquam bellum Trōjānum diū gerēbātur, tamen mīlitēs Graecī urbem Trōjam nōn cēpērunt.

Jam Helena ad Graecōs trānsīre cupiēbat. Tamen nōn 10 sōlum īram Menelāī timēbat, sed etiam ex urbe exīre nōn poterat, quod portae clausae erant. Helena Graecōs juvāre dēsīderāvit; Trōjānī autem eam prohibuērunt.

Ōlim Helena in urbe mendīcum vīdit. Multī līberī, clāmantēs et lapidēs jacientēs, ad eum ībant. Helena subitō 15 sēnsit hunc mendīcum esse Ulīxem, ducem clārum Graecum.

Itaque servō suō dīxit, "Vocā mendīcum in rēgiam; dā eī cibum et aquam."

Deinde Helena servōs expulit suōs et parvā vōce mendīcō dīxit, "Tē recognōscō; tū es Ulīxēs. Quid in hāc urbe facis? 20 Nōnne ad Graecōs redībis?"

Ulīxēs respondit sē portās et viās urbis spectāre; Graecōs novum cōnsilium inīre. "Certē," dīxit, "Trōja dēlēbitur."

Tum Helena dīxit, "Tē juvābō; tibi viam in mediam urbem mōnstrābō. Ita meō auxiliō Graecī Trōjam dēlēbunt." 25

*īra, -ae	F., wrath, anger, ire
*mendīcus, -ī	M., beggar, mendicant
*lapis, lapidis	M., stone
*ōmen, ōminis	N., omen, sign
sacerdōs, -dōtis	M. or F., priest, priestess
audeō, -ēre	dare
*prohibeō, -ēre, -hibuī, -itum	restrain, hinder, prohibit
*expellō, -ere, -pulī, -pulsum	drive out, expel
*recognōscō, -ere, -cognōvī, -cognitum	recognize

335

CONJUGATION OF eō, like that of English "go," is irregular. Its principal parts are **eō, īre, iī (īvī), itum.**

	Present		Imperfect		Future	
	Singular		Singular		Singular	
1	**e'ō**	I go	**i'bam**	I went	**i'bō**	I'll go
2	**īs**	you go	**i'bās**	you went	**i'bis**	you'll go
3	**it**	he, she goes	**i'bat**	he, she went	**i'bit**	he'll, she'll go
	Plural		Plural		Plural	
1	**i'mus**	we go	**ibā'mus**	we went	**i'bimus**	we'll go
2	**i'tis**	you go	**ibā'tis**	you went	**i'bitis**	you'll go
3	**e'unt**	they go	**i'bant**	they went	**i'bunt**	they'll go

In the perfect, eō is conjugated like any other Latin verb (perfect stem + perfect endings): **iī (īvī), iistī (īvistī), iit (īvit); iimus (īvimus), iistis (īvistis), iērunt (īvērunt).**

So also in past perfect: **ieram (īveram), ierās (īverās),** etc.; and in future perfect: **ierō (īverō), ieris (īveris),** etc.

IN TRANSLATING FORMS OF eō in present tense, "I am going," "you are going," "he is going," etc., are often more natural than "I go," etc.

Likewise, in the imperfect, "I was going," "you were going," "he was going," etc., sometimes are preferable to "I went," etc.

Forms of eō in future tense may be translated "I shall go," "you will go," "he will go," etc., contractions of which are given above. They may also be translated "I am going," "you are going," etc.

In English, "I am going," "you are going," etc., may be either present or future, depending upon the context. In Latin, the form of the verb eō indicates its tense.

Anna ad Eurōpam it. Anna is going (is on the way) to Europe.
Anna ad Eurōpam ibit. Anna is going (intends to go) to Europe.

INFINITIVES OF eō

Present: **īre** to go   Perfect: **isse (iisse)** to have gone

IMPERATIVES OF eō

Singular: **ī** go   Plural: **īte** go

COMPOUNDS OF eō are conjugated like eō, with a prefixed syllable (ab-, ad-, ex-, in-, sub-, trāns-, etc.). There are
many compounds of eō; e.g., abeō, adeō, exeō, ineō, subeō,
trānseō. The meaning of these compounds is clear, because
each prefix is already familiar as a preposition. The first
(abeō) means "go away." What do the others mean?

Another compound of eō (redeō) has the syllable red-
(for re-, "back" or "again") prefixed.

I Supply the correct form of each verb in parentheses to complete the sentence it follows.
1 Mīlitēs ab hostibus ——— recūsāvērunt. **(dēprehendō)**
2 In rīpā flūminis lātissimī castra ——— cōnstituimus. **(pōnō)**
3 Vītam quiētissimam in īnsulā ——— temptābās. **(agō)**
4 Vir fortis sē in perīculum maximum ——— crēdidit. **(dūcō)**
5 Vōs ———poteritis, sī mē juvābitis. **(servō)**

II Change each direct statement to indirect, and each indirect
statement to direct.
1 Menelāus, ad urbem Trōjam nāvigāre parāns, nūntiāvit,
"Absunt duo ducēs."
2 Ulīxēs sē uxōrem fīliumque relinquere nōn dēsīderāre dīxit.
3 Nūntius ā rēge missus prīmō Ulīxem īnsānem esse putāvit.
4 Posteā autem nūntius rēgī dīxit, "Hic fuit dolus Ulīxis."
5 Māter Achillem monuit, "Bellum gerere nōn dēbēs."
6 Thetis Achillem ad rēgiam amīcī sēcrētō missum esse
nārrāvit.

LXVII

THE WOODEN HORSE

Auxiliō Helenae, quae ex urbe Trōjā exīre jam dēsīderābat,
Graecī dolum parāvērunt. Magnum equum ligneum īn-
strūxērunt in quō numerum virōrum fortium cēlāvērunt.
Noctū cēterī Graecī equum in cōnspectū° Trōjānōrum relīquērunt et ad īnsulam propinquam discessērunt. Ūnus 5

°**cōnspectū** (abl. sing.) sight, view

ex comitibus, cujus nōmen erat Sinōn, prope urbem sē cēlāvit.

Māne Trōjānī ex urbe magnō cum gaudiō exiērunt et in castra Graecōrum dēserta convēnērunt. Equum spectā- vērunt. Aliī, quī dolum Graecōrum nōn sēnsērunt hunc equum esse, in urbem equum trahere dēsīderāvērunt. Aliī, quī autem equum timuērunt, eum dēlēre dēsīderāvērunt. Rēx et magistrātūs° dēnique equum intrā mūrōs urbis intrō- dūxērunt.

Deinde Lāocoōn, sacerdōs, clāmāvit, "In equō latet dolus. Timeō Graecōs et dōna ferentēs°."

Statim Lāocoōn hastam in equum jēcit. Subitō autem duo serpentēs ex marī vēnērunt, quī Lāocoontem et ejus duōs fīliōs interfēcērunt.

Interim Sinōn inventus et ad rēgem ductus est.

Is dīxit sē Graecum esse; aliōs Graecōs sē ipsum inter- ficere temptāvisse; sē autem fūgisse et latuisse; jam exercitūs° Graecōs in patriam suam reditūrōs esse.

"Hic equus Minervae sacer est," dīxit. "Pōne equum in arce; ita urbs semper erit tūta."

°**magistrātūs*** (nom. pl.) magistrates • **et dōna ferentēs** even when they are bringing gifts • **exercitūs** (nom., acc. pl.) armies

This painting by Giovanni Battista Tiepoli (1696-1770) represents the moment when the decision has been made to move the wooden horse into the city.

Postquam equus in arce positus est, deīs sacrificia Trōjānī
fēcērunt. In tōtā urbe magnum erat gaudium.

Mediā nocte Sinōn ad equum vēnit. Ille jānuam parvam
in corpore equī aperuit; Graecī dēscendērunt et portās urbis
aperuērunt. Jam omnēs exercitūs Graecī adfuērunt. 30

Signum proeliī datum est; impetus° in Trōjānōs factus est.
Urbs, equī ligneī auxiliō capta, jam ā Trōjānīs dēserta,
vāstāta est.

°impetus* (nom. sing.) attack

arx, arcis (-ium)	F., citadel
nox, noctis (-ium)	F., night
aliī . . . aliī	some . . . others
*dēserō, -ere, -seruī, -sertum	abandon, forsake, desert
*īnstruō, -ere, -strūxī, -strūctum	build up, construct, equip
*intrōdūcō, -ere, -dūxī, -ductum	lead into, introduce
*trahō, -ere, trāxī, tractum	draw, drag, pull
intrā	(with acc.) within, inside, into

A FUTURE ACTIVE PARTICIPLE in Latin is
like a perfect participle in form, except that it has **-ūr-** before
the case ending.

portātūrus, -a, -um	about to carry	or	going to carry
monitūrus, -a, -um	about to warn	or	going to warn
dictūrus, -a, -um	about to say	or	going to say
audītūrus, -a, -um	about to hear	or	going to hear

Some verbs which have no perfect participle have a future
active participle. The future active participle of such verbs
is often given as the fourth principal part: **sum, esse, fuī,
futūrus; stō, stāre, stetī, stātūrus.**

The future active participle of a Latin verb is often combined with a form of **sum** to refer to something which the
subject intends to do or is about to do.

Mānsūrus eram.	I was about to remain.	or	I intended to remain.
Laudātūrus est.	He is about to praise.	or	He intends to praise.

339

A FUTURE ACTIVE INFINITIVE also has two parts—a future active participle and infinitive **esse** (to be): **portātūrum esse** to be about to carry.

Putō mē mānsūrum esse. I think I shall stay.
Putāvit sē mānsūram esse. She thought she would stay.

In indirect statement, a future active infinitive is translated with "shall" or "will" after a main verb in present or future tense and with "should" or "would" after a main verb in any past tense.

I Use idiomatic English in translating each sentence, giving special attention to verb forms.
1 Ūnus ē comitibus sē in equō cēlātūrus erat.
2 Magnō cum gaudiō in dēserta Graecōrum castra ventūrī Trōjānī sunt.
3 Aliī equum in urbem trahere cupiēbant, aliī dolum timēbant.
4 In equō latet dolus.
5 Mediā nocte vir fortis ad arcem vēnit.
6 Urbs jam ā Trōjānīs dēserta est.
7 Helena ex urbe discessūra erat.

II Change each underlined expression to a relative clause, choosing the proper relative and verb from the lists below.
1 Auxiliō Helenae ex urbe exīre dēsīderantis equum ligneum aperuit.
2 Trōjānī magnō cum gaudiō in castra ā Graecīs dēserta iērunt.
3 Paucī autem incolae equum mīlitēs cēlantem timēbant.
4 Lāocoōn cum duōbus fīliīs ā serpentibus ē marī venientibus interfectus est.
5 Ille jānuam parvam positam in equī corpore Graecōs tenentis aperuit.

quae quam quās quem quī quibus quō quod quārum

cēlābat	**dēsīderābat**	**dēserta erant**	**posita erat**	**vēnerant**
cēlāvērunt	**dēsīderat**	**dēseruērunt**	**posuerat**	**venient**

LATIN LIVES TODAY in English word families whose ancestry may be traced to the verbs listed on page 339. Below is one word from each family. Consult a dictionary for others.

desertion   instructor   introduction   tractor

REVIEW OF UNIT XVI

LESSONS LXIII—LXVII

Nouns	Nouns (cont.)	Verbs (cont.)
dīvitiae, -ārum	*orbis, orbis (-ium)	*dēserō, -ere
*īra, -ae	*prīnceps, prīncipis	*expellō, -ere
dolus, -ī	sacerdōs, -dōtis	*īnstruō, -ere
*mendīcus, -ī	vestis, vestis (-ium)	*intrōdūcō, -ere
mālum, -ī	*voluntās, -tātis	ostendō, -ere
*amor, -ōris	Adjectives	*prōmittō, -ere
arx, arcis (-ium)	aliī . . . aliī	*recognōscō, -ere
*bōs, bovis	*prīnceps, gen., -cipis	*trahō, -ere
*jūdex, jūdicis	Verbs	*fīniō, -īre
*lapis, lapidis	*agitō, -āre	*sciō, -īre
mercātor, -ōris	*putō, -āre	Preposition
nēmō, —	audeō, -ēre	*intrā
nox, noctis (-ium)	*prohibeō, -ēre	
**ōmen, ōminis	*crēdō, -ere	

I In the numbered list find all possible verb forms which illustrate each descriptive term in the lettered list.

a) present passive infinitive   e) future active participle
b) perfect passive infinitive   f) perfect participle
c) present participle   g) future active infinitive
d) present active infinitive   h) past perfect passive tense

1 fīnīrī   5 posuisse   9 āmissa esse   13 relictus erit
2 augentia   6 coāctī erant   10 posse   14 āctūra
3 adesse   7 vīcī   11 jactūrī   15 jūnctae
4 tractūram esse   8 dīc   12 vincī   16 dēstitī

II Translate each sentence in as many ways as are indicated by the different verb forms each contains. Change 4 and 5 to indirect statement; translate the three versions of each.

1 Crēdidistī mē īre/itūrum esse/īsse ad castra Graecōrum.
2 Scīvimus equum ligneum ā Trōjānīs dūcī/ductum esse.
3 Prōmīsit/Prōmittit mīlitēs mānsūrōs esse in castrīs.
4 "Cōnsilia bona capimus/capiēmus/cēpimus," dīcunt.
5 Nūntiāvī, "Jam hostēs nāvigant/nāvigābunt/nāvigāvērunt."

Many Latin verbs have given us whole families of English derivatives. A particularly large family is that of **cēdō, cēdere, cessī, cessus,** move, yield, give ground.

Most English verbs related to this word family are derived from the first principal part.

accede   antecede   concede   intercede   precede   secede

"Proceed" and "succeed" also belong to this family, but note the difference in spelling.

Most nouns of this family are derived from the fourth principal part.

access	cession	process	secession
accession	concession	procession	success
accessory	intercession	recession	succession

There are also nouns derived from the present participle.

antecedent   decedent   precedence   precedent

Adjectives of this family are also formed from both present and past participles.

antecedent   precedent   excessive   successful

Notice how Latin can help you spell the endings of such words correctly. Derivatives of the present participle of a Conjugation III (or II) verb naturally end in -ent/-ence: antecedent, apparent, permanence.

Derivatives of the present participle of a Conjugation I verb, however, have -ant/-ance, reflecting the spelling of its present participle: errant, ambulance.

Verbs ending in **-iō** (III-**iō** and IV) have corresponding derivatives ending in -ient/-ience: recipient, convenient, audience.

Borrowings from French (whose present active participles all end in -ant) account for certain exceptions: defendant, tenant, tenancy. Occasionally a derivative has more than one spelling: dormient (from **dormiēns**) and dormant (through French).

Make word families based on **portō, moveō, capiō, audiō.**

342

This famous mosaic shows Vergil reading from his long epic poem *The Aeneid* (I, 8). The Muses Clio (history) and Melpomene (tragedy) stand on either side in portions of the mosaic not shown here.

LXVIII

IN SEARCH OF A PROMISED LAND

Trōjā ā Graecīs vāstātā, Aenēās, dux Trōjānus, cum sociīs suīs ad Thrāciam nāvigāvit. Simul atque nāvium ancorae jactae sunt, Aenēās paucīs cum sociīs ad lītus prōcessit.

In lītore erat tumulus arboribus cēlātus. Ex humō Aenēās ūnam ex arboribus fōdit, quod āram adōrnāre dēsīderāvit. 5 Dux fortis, sanguine in rādīcibus vīsō, magnopere ipse territus est.

Tum vōx ā tumulō clāmāvit, "Ō Aenēās, mē miserum vulnerāvistī. Sum Polydōrus Trōjānus. Rēx hujus terrae mē necāvit et sub hōc tumulō corpus cēlāvit meum. Fuge ab 10 hīs lītoribus perīculōsīs sine morā!"

Hīs verbīs audītīs, Aenēās et sociī ā lītoribus Thrāciae fūgērunt. Dēlos, īnsula Apollinī grāta, nōn longē aberat. Hīc Aenēās, patre praesente, auxilium deī rogāvit.

Ita Aenēās ōrāvit, "Ō Apollō, dā Trōjānīs domicilium idō- 15 neum; dā gentem validam et urbem mānsūram; dā nōbīs ōmen bonum."

Vōx deī respondit, "Antīquam exquīrite mātrem vestram. Ibi Aenēās erit rēx, et līberī ejus erunt rēgēs."

Hōc audītō, rogāvērunt sociī Aenēae, "Ubi est māter nostra 20 antīqua?"

Tum sine morā Anchīsēs, pater Aenēae, dīxit, "In īnsulā Crētā initium gentis nostrae fuit. Patrēs nostrī dīxērunt illam īnsulam esse mātrem nostram antīquam."

Itaque, ventō surgente, Trōjānī laetī ad īnsulam Crētam 25 nāvigāvērunt. Posteā, parvā urbe aedificātā, pestilentia multōs Trōjānōs interfēcit.

Tum Aenēās ā deīs suīs ita monitus est, "Crēta nōn est antīqua māter vestra. Longē ab hāc īnsulā in terrā Ītaliā tūtum domicilium vōs expectat." 30

*ancora, -ae	F., anchor
*humus, -ī	F., earth, ground, soil
tumulus, -ī	M., mound, tomb
gēns, gentis (-ium)	F., nation, clan, tribe
lītus, -oris	N., shore, beach

*rādix, -īcis	F., root
sanguis, -inis	M., blood
idōneus, -a, -um	fit, qualified, suitable
*praesēns, -entis	present, at hand
exquīrō, -ere, -quīsīvī, -quīsītum	seek out, search for
fodiō, -ere, fōdī, fossum	dig
*surgō, -ere, surrēxī, surrēctum	rise, arise, stand up
simul atque	as soon as

This Roman fresco represents Neptune, god of the sea, riding in his chariot as he stirs up the waves.

ABLATIVE ABSOLUTE

Trōjā vāstātā, Aenēās ad Thrāciam nāvigāvit. After Troy had been destroyed Aeneas sailed to Thrace.

In this sentence, **Trōjā vāstātā** is an ablative absolute. The word "absolute" here means "free" or "independent." An ablative absolute is independent of the rest of the sentence;

345

that is, it is not connected with it grammatically. **Trōjā vāstātā** gives additional information, but the rest of the sentence is grammatically complete without these words.

An ablative absolute may consist of any one of several combinations of words. **Trōjā vāstātā,** for example, is made up of a noun and perfect participle.

1 Noun and participle

Ventō surgente, Trōjānī ad īnsulam Crētam nāvigāvērunt. Since the wind was rising (with the rising wind), the Trojans sailed to the island of Crete.

2 Pronoun and participle

Hōc vīsō, Aenēās territus erat. When he saw this (having seen this), Aeneas was frightened.

3 Two nouns

Numā rēge, pestilentia erat. When Numa was king (during Numa's reign), there was a plague.

4 Pronoun and noun

Eō cōnsule, Rōmānī multa proelia commīsērunt. When he was consul (during his consulship), the Romans waged many battles.

5 Noun (or pronoun) and adjective

Aenēās, patre praesente, auxilium deī rogāvit. Aeneas, in the presence of his father (with his father present), asked for the god's help.

In English, the use of an absolute phrase is rare. Usually such a phrase is awkward and is therefore avoided.

The danger past, we went home.

The expression "The danger past," which is not connected grammatically to the rest of the sentence, is an absolute phrase.

I Substitute an ablative absolute for the subordinate clause in each sentence without changing the sense. Translate.

1 Juppiter, ubi contrōversiam audīvit, jūdex certāminis esse recūsāvit.
2 Quamquam nāvēs parātae erant, ducēs tamen nāvigāre nōn poterant.
3 Cum paucī virī fortēs in equō cēlātī erunt, cēterī ad īnsulam discēdent.
4 Līberī, cum jānua parva hortī aperta est, in viam currunt.

II For each underlined word substitute from the list a verb form that reverses the meaning of the sentence, and make other necessary changes. Translate both versions.

1. Comitēs, duce praesente, in castrīs <u>mānsērunt</u>.
2. Hostibus vīsīs, dux castra <u>posuit</u>.
3. Brevī tempore custōdēs portās urbis <u>claudent</u>.
4. Cōnsiliō captō, hae gentēs inter sē pugnāre <u>dēstitērunt</u>.
5. Urbe <u>vāstātā</u> mortem <u>accipit</u>.
6. Rēgīna territa fēminās urbis <u>petīvit</u>.
7. Frāter sororque <u>lacrimābant</u>, bonīs calceīs <u>āmissīs</u>.
8. Mīlitēs castra nostra sine morā <u>dēfendunt</u>.

aedificātā
aperient
fūgērunt
incēpērunt
inventīs
mōvit
oppugnant
recūsat
rīdēbant
vītāvit

LXIX

NO PERMANENT HOME

Nāvibus parātīs, Aenēās sociīque iterum trāns mare ab īnsulā Crētā nāvigāvērunt. Eōs, ubi longē ā lītore āfuērunt et caelum undique et undique mare vīdērunt, magna tempestās per undās perīculōsās in vada portāvit. Dēnique Aenēās cum sociīs suīs ad īnsulam sibi ignōtam vēnit. 5

Hīc Trōjānī fessī multa in lītore animālia vīdērunt. Paucīs animālibus necātīs, cēnam et sacrificia parāvērunt. Subitō dē caelō avēs ferae circum eōs volāvērunt. Haec mōnstra, quae habēbant corpora avium, capita fēminārum, Harpyiae appellābantur. Hīs mōnstrīs vīsīs, Trōjānī territī fūgērunt. Posteā, 10 verbīs ducis excitātī, sociī Aenēae contrā Harpyiās pugnāre temptābant, sed terga dūra avium nē gladiīs quidem acūtīs vulnerāre poterant.

Subitō Harpyia fera magnā vōce clāmāvit, "Animālia nostra necāvistis; nōs necāre temptāvistis. In hāc terrā igitur pācem 15 numquam habēbitis. In Italiā urbem dēsīderātam habēbitis."

Trōjānī propter terrōrem mortis in hōc locō manēre nōn jam poterant. Mente mūtātā, ab īnsulā celeriter nāvigāvērunt.

Deinde Aenēās prope ōram Graeciae nāvigāvit; dēnique cum cēterīs Trōjānīs ad terram vēnit ubi Helenus erat rēx 20

atque sacerdōs Apollinis. Helenus, fīlius rēgis Trōjānī, amīcōs vidēns erat laetus eōsque ad rēgiam dūxit. Ibi eīs cibum
et multa dōna dedit.

Tum, auxiliō deī prō Aenēā rogātō, Helenus dīxit, "Magna
erunt perīcula et magnae erunt difficultātēs; per multa maria 25
nāvigābitis; dēnique in Ītaliā domicilium tūtum et idōneum
inveniētis."

vadum, -ī	N., ford, shoal
***mēns, mentis (-ium)**	F., mind, purpose
***terror, -ōris**	M., fear, fright, terror
***acūtus, -a, -um**	sharp, pointed, acute
ignōtus, -a, -um	unknown
nē . . . quidem	not even
***conrrā**	(with acc.) against

**FREE TRANSLATION OF ABLATIVE AB-
SOLUTE** Since there is no English construction exactly like the ablative absolute, such a Latin phrase may often
be translated by a dependent clause introduced by "when,"
"after," "if," "since," or "although." Occasionally an English phrase is a better translation than a complete clause.

A **Nāvibus parātīs, Aenēās ad Thrāciam nāvigāvit.** When the ships
were ready (with the ships ready), Aeneas sailed to Thrace.

B **Paucīs animālibus necātīs, cēnam parāvērunt.** After a few animals had been killed or After killing a few animals (after they had
killed a few animals), they prepared a feast.

C **Ventō surgente, Trōjānī ad Crētam nāvigāvērunt.** Since the wind
was rising (with the rising wind), the Trojans sailed to Crete.

D **Camillō duce, militēs fortiter pugnant.** Under the leadership of
Camillus or When Camillus is the leader, the soldiers fight bravely.

A perfect participle in an ablative absolute phrase indicates
time earlier than that of the main verb, as in sentence B.
A present participle indicates the same time, as in sentence C.

PRACTICE   (I) Give at least two possible translations for each ablative absolute in the following sentences.

1 **Hīs mōnstrīs vīsīs, Trōjānī fūgērunt.**
2 **Mente mūtātā, ab īnsulā nāvigāvērunt.**
3 **Auxiliō rogātō, Helenus dīxit, "Magna erunt perīcula."**

(II) Make five sentences in English, each containing a different phrase or clause that could be expressed in Latin by an ablative absolute.   (Practice II is optional.)

I Change 1 and 2 to direct statement and 3 to indirect.
1 Sacerdōs dēclārāvit in equō latēre dolum; sē Graecōs timēre.
2 Sinōn rēgī dīxit equō in arce positō urbem semper tūtam futūram esse; hunc equum Minervae sacrum esse.
3 Ille dīxit, "Aliī Graecī mē interficere temptāvērunt. Jam mīlitēs Graecī in patriam suam redeunt."

II Translate each Latin sentence, using suitable English conjunctions and pronouns in the list in expressing ablative absolute phrases as clauses in the translation.
1 Venus mālō acceptō aureō Paridī dīxit ejus conjugem Helenam futūram esse.
2 Patre ōrāculō monitō, fīlius in silvā relictus est.
3 Ulīxēs equō et bove jūnctīs ōram maritimam arāre incēpit.
4 Signō proeliī datō, mīlitēs oppidum nōn oppugnāvērunt.
5 Ulīxēs fīliō jam īnfante patriam relinquere nōn dēsīderābat.

| after | as soon as | if | when | while |
| although | because | since | which | who |

LXX

A FATEFUL STORM

Aenēās, terrā Helenī relictā, iterum in Ītaliam pervenīre temptāvit. Jūnō autem magnam tempestātem mīsit, quae nāvēs Trōjānās ad lītus Āfricae pepulit. Inter vada et magna

saxa classis tempestāte paene dēlēta est. Dēnique Trōjānī
tūtī in lītore Āfricae stetērunt.

Frūmentum in nāvibus portātum nōn jam bonum erat,
quod nāvēs multam aquam accēperant. In silvā propinquā
cibum petēns, Aenēās sagittīs septem cervōs occīdit; ita virī
cēnam in ōrā parāre potuērunt.

Postrīdiē Aenēās et sociī in lītore ambulantēs appropinquāvērunt ad magnam et pulchram urbem Carthāginem,
quae ā Phoenīcibus aedificāta erat.

Dīdō, ōlim rēgīna Phoenīciae, post mortem conjugis trāns
Mare Mediterrāneum ad Āfricam cum multīs comitibus
nāvigāverat. Hīc hanc novam urbem aedificāverat Dīdō.

Calamitāte Trōjānōrum ab Aenēā nūntiātā, Dīdō, jam
rēgīna Carthāginis, Trōjānōs cum benignitāte accēpit. Aenēās
et Ascanius, fīlius ejus, cum multīs prīncipibus ad rēgiam
ductī sunt.

Eādem nocte in rēgiā magna cēna parāta est. Cibus et alia
dōna ad cēterōs Trōjānōs missa sunt. Posteā Dīdō dīxit sē
Trōjānō dē bellō audīre cupere. Aenēās, verbīs rēgīnae
mōtus, fābulam maestam Trōjae nārrāvit.

As Queen Dido welcomes Aeneas and Ascanius, the cupids point to the love that will
spring up between Dido and Aeneas. Pietro da Cortona (1596-1669) is the artist.

Dīdō, memoriā tenēns dolōrem suum, Trōjānōs in Africā manēre dēsīderāvit; itaque Aenēae et sociīs domicilia in regnō suō dedit regīna. Brevī tempore Juppiter, hāc morā Aenēae vīsā, Mercurium nūntium ad Aenēam mīsit. ²⁵

Mercurius dīxit, "Carthāgō nōn est illa urbs Trōjānīs ā deīs prōmissa. Trāns mare Italia tē expectat. Ibi urbem aedificābis clāram; ibi Lāvīnia, fīlia regis, erit conjūnx tua. ³⁰ Relinque statim hanc urbem. In Italiā pete domicilium tuum."

Tum Aenēās, verbīs deī āctus, sine morā urbem relīquit et eōdem diē ab ōrīs Āfricae nāvigāvit. Spectāns ē regiā, Dīdō misera nāvēs Trōjānās vīdit. Jam magnō regnō ³⁵ dēspērātō, sibi mortem dēlēgit.

*benignitās, -tātis	F., kindness, courtesy
*calamitās, -tātis	F., disaster, calamity
*classis, -is (-ium)	F., fleet; division, class
*pellō, -ere, pepulī, pulsum	beat, strike; rout, drive away
paene	nearly, almost

I Combine words from groups A and B to form sensible examples of the ablative absolute. Translate them as clauses.

A   B

1 ancorīs   5 morā   a) acceptō   f) praesentibus
2 cibō   6 sacerdōtibus   b) dēlētā   g) rogātā
3 domiciliō   7 tempestāte   c) clāmantibus   h) servātīs
4 līberīs   8 urbe   d) excitātīs   i) surgente
                       e) inventō   j) jactīs

II From the combinations resulting from II, select an appropriate ablative absolute to add to each sentence, and translate.
1 Virī fessī in lītore jacēbant.
2 Classis in saxa pulsa est.
3 Comitēs Aenēae vītās fēlīcēs agent.
4 Dux et sociī ē nāvibus dēscendērunt.
5 Hominēs sacrificia in ārīs pōnunt.
6 Incolae tēcta nova cōnstruere incēpērunt.

LXXI

BY BEES AND FIRE FORETOLD

Ōrīs Āfricae relictīs, Aenēās ad Ītaliam nāvigāvit. In Ītaliā erat domicilium prōmissum; in Ītaliā, conjūnx Aenēae prōmissa—Lāvīnia.

Mediō in hortō rēgiae ubi Lāvīnia cum patre, rēge Latīnō, habitābat arbor sacra stābat. Ōlim multae apēs, super mare 5 Tiberimque volantēs, ad hanc urbem pervēnērunt. Prīmō circum mūrōs urbis volāvērunt; dēnique in hortum vēnērunt et in arbore sacrā sēdērunt.

Comitēs rēgis et populus erant territī. Servī apēs ex hortō agere temptāvērunt, sed apēs in arbore mānsērunt. Signō 10 datō, mīlitēs tubās īnflāre incēpērunt, sed apēs mānsērunt. Rēx Latīnus ipse, quī ex somnō excitātus erat, ducibus ad rēgiam vocātīs, auxilium deōrum ōrāvit.

Vōx magna respondit, "Apēs sunt ōmen. Jam advenae appropinquant. Apēs trāns mare ad urbem tuam volāvērunt, 15 et in summā arbore sēdērunt; advena in summā arce mox sedēbit."

A fourth century codex of the *Aeneid* shows Latinus, Lavinia, attendant, and priest.

Postrīdiē Latīnus vīdit aliud ōmen. Lāvīnia prō ārā stābat, dum Latīnus ignem sacrum incendit. Subitō flammae comam longam Lāvīniae occupāvērunt. Puella territa per rēgiam 20 fūgit. Sed, flammīs subitō extīnctīs, Lāvīnia fuit incolumis.

Latīnus, haec ōmina magnopere timēns, sine morā ad ōrāculum sacrum properāvit. Hīc in silvā mediā nocte rēx Latīnus magnās vōcēs audīvit.

"Ab advenā Lāvīnia in mātrimōnium dūcētur," hae vōcēs 25 dīcēbant. "Advenae erunt fīliī tuī, ō Latīne. Advenae, Trōjānī nunc appellātī, nōmen tuum habēbunt; brevī tempore Latīnī appellābuntur. Ab hīs advenīs nōmen Latīnum ad stellās portābitur; gēns tua erit clārissima."

advena, -ae	M. or F., stranger, foreigner
***tuba, -ae**	F., trumpet
***apis, apis (-ium)**	F., bee
***īnflō, -āre, -āvī, -ātum**	blow (into), inflate
***extinguō, -ere, -tīnxī, -tīnctum**	put out, extinguish
***incendō, -ere, -cendī, -cēnsum**	set fire to, burn, inflame; enrage
***super**	(with acc. or abl.) over, above

"VERSATILE ABLATIVE" is a term that may be aptly used in connection with the ablative case in Latin. The ablative is used in many ways, both with and without a preposition.

ABLATIVE WITH PREPOSITION, in general, supplies additional information which would answer such questions as these.

Questions	Answers
1 **Ā quō?** or **Ā quibus?** By whom? (by what person or persons?)	**Ā mātre, ab amitā, ā puerīs**
2 **Quōmodo?** How? (in what manner?)	**Cum gaudiō; sine morā**
3 **Quōcum? Quibuscum?** With whom? (accompanied by whom?)	**Cum patre, cum sociīs; mēcum**
4 **Ubi?** Where? (in, on, under, in front of what?)	**In arcā; sub aquā; prō ārā**

5 **Unde?** Whence? From what place? **Ā Forō; ex Āfricā; dē monte**
(away, out, down from what?)

In Latin a careful distinction is made between "away
from" **(ā, ab)**, "out from" **(ē, ex)**, and "down from" **(dē)** by
the use of the appropriate preposition with the ablative.

Nāvis ā terrā mōvit. The ship moved (away) from the land.
Ē rēgiā Aenēās properāvit. Aeneas hurried (out) from the palace.
Dē mūrō saxum jēcit. He threw a stone (down) from the wall.

One of these prepositions **(ā, ab)** also means "by" and
introduces agent, that is, the person by whom **(ā quō)** an action is performed. This use occurs only with a passive verb.

Āra ā sacerdōte parāta erat. The altar had been prepared by
the priest.

Another preposition with the ablative which serves a two-
fold purpose is **cum,** which always means "with." Sometimes a prepositional phrase with **cum** tells in what manner
(quōmodo) something is done; sometimes it tells with whom
(quōcum) it is done.

Dīdō Trōjānōs cum benignitāte accēpit. Dido received the Trojans
with kindness.
Dīdō trāns mare cum multīs comitibus nāvigāverat. Dido had
sailed across the sea with many attendants.

ABLATIVE WITHOUT PREPOSITION sup-
plies additional information which would answer such questions as **Quandō?** "When?" (at or within what time?) and
Quō instrūmentō? "How?" (by what means?).

Advenae brevī tempore Latīnī appellābuntur. In a short time
the strangers will be called Latins.
Aenēās sagittīs septem cervōs occīdit. With arrows Aeneas
killed seven stags.

In translating an ablative of time, an English preposition
("at," "in," or "within") is usually supplied.
In translating an ablative of means, "with," "by," or "by
means of" must be supplied.

I Find in the sentences an example of each ablative use mentioned below, and give a free translation of each sentence.

1 Apēs, quae dē monte volāverant, in summā arbore sedēbant.
2 Eādem nocte mīlitēs sonō tubae ex somnō excitātī sunt.
3 Mox serpentēs ingentēs ē marī venient.
4 Corpus nostrī amīcī in lītore jacet.
5 Dux cum comite in rēgiam vēnerat, ubi ā rēgīnā cum benignitāte acceptus est.
6 Juvenis sagittīs acūtīs duōs cervōs necāvit.

a) accompaniment
b) manner
c) means
d) place (down) from which
e) place where
f) place (out) from which
g) personal agent
h) time

THE BEATITUDES (OPTIONAL)

Beātī pauperēs spīritū; quoniam ipsōrum est rēgnum caelōrum.

Beātī quī lūgent; quoniam ipsī cōnsōlābuntur.

Beātī quī sunt mītēs; quoniam ipsī possidēbunt terram.

Beātī quī ēsuriunt et sitiunt jūstitiam; quoniam ipsī 5 saturābuntur.

Beātī quī sunt misericordēs; quoniam ipsīs misericordia tribuētur.

Beātī quī sunt mundī corde; quoniam ipsī Deum vidēbunt.

Beātī quī sunt pācificī; quoniam fīliī Deī vocābuntur.   10

Beātī quī persecūtiōnem patiuntur propter jūstitiam; quoniam ipsōrum est rēgnum caelōrum.

Beātī estis cum maledīxerint vōbīs et persecūtī vōs fuerint et mentientēs dīxerint omne malum adversus vōs, propter mē; gaudēte et exultāte, quoniam mercēs vestra cōpiōsa est 15 in caelīs, sīc enim persecūtī sunt prophētās, quī fuērunt ante vōs.[1]

---

[1]From a Latin translation of the Greek New Testament: Matthew V:3-12. After St. Jerome (A.D. 340-420), a scholarly father of the Church, had spent many years studying Hebrew and Greek, he translated the Bible into Latin. His translation—known as the *Vulgate*—remained the official version for centuries. The version presented here was adapted from the *Vulgate*.

LXXII

Post multās difficultātēs calamitātēsque classis Trōjāna ad
Ītaliam et rēgnum Latīnī pervēnit. Castrīs in lītore positīs,
nūntiī, pācem amīcitiamque prō Trōjānīs petentēs, statim ad
rēgem ab Aenēā missī sunt. Multa dōna pretiōsa rēgī Latīnō
dux Trōjānus dedit.   5

Rēx Latīnus convocātīs comitibus suīs dīxit, "Hic quidem
dux Trōjānus est ille advena ā nōbīs expectātus. Hic nōbilis
Aenēās erit conjūnx fīliae meae. Haec omnia ōminibus
praedicta sunt."

Hīs verbīs dictīs, Lāvīnia, fīlia rēgis, Aenēae conjūnx 10
prōmissa est. Māter autem Lāvīniae Turnum, rēgem Rutulōrum, esse conjugem fīliae suae cupiēbat.

Rēgīna Amāta igitur, Latīnum implōrāns multīs cum
lacrimīs, dīxit, "Lāvīnia ab Aenēā petitur. Territus ōminibus
incertīs, dabisne fīliam nostram huic advenae Trōjānō?" 15

Alia verba saeva dīxit rēgīna īrāta; sed Latīnus, ā deīs
monitus, mentem nōn mūtāvit. Amāta igitur noctū in
montēs altōs cum fīliā Lāvīniā fūgit. Ibi in sēcrētō locō
Lāvīniam cēlāvit.

Interim Turnus in somniō haec verba audīvit, "Rēgnum 20
tuum et conjūnx prōmissa tua ab hōc advenā Trōjānō capien-
tur! Convocā omnēs comitēs fīdōs! Oppugnā parva castra
hostium! Dūc mīlitēs fortēs in hostēs! Pugnā prō Lāvīniā!
Cōnfirmā animum tuum! Dī tē juvābunt; fortūna tibi victōriam dabit." 25

Māne Turnus, populō convocātō, clāmāvit, "Postulō
uxōrem prōmissam, Lāvīniam; omnēs Trōjānī sunt perfidī!
Nōs ā deīs nostrīs dūcimur; victōria nōbīs dabitur!"

*incertus, -a, -um	uncertain, doubtful
*nōbilis, -e	well-known, high-born, noble, of noble birth
*cōnfirmō, -āre, -āvī, -ātum	strengthen, confirm, establish
*implōrō, -āre, -āvī, -ātum	beseech, beg, implore
*praedicō, -ere, -dīxī, -dictum	foretell, predict; advise

I Change each of the selections below from direct quotation to indirect.

1 Vōx magna respondit, "Apēs ōmen sunt; eae trāns mare ad urbem tuam volāvērunt; advena in summā arce mox sedēbit."

2 Ōrāculum dīcit, "Turnus Lāvīniam in mātrimōnium nōn dūcet; advenae nōmen tuum capient; illī nunc Trōjānī appellantur; advenae nōmen Latīnum ad stellās portābunt."

M O T T O E S   such as these are age-old favorites.

Ad astra per aspera. To the stars through difficulties.

Fortūna fortēs adjuvat. Fortune favors the brave.

Mēns sāna in corpore sānō. A sound mind in a sound body.

Omnia vincit amor. Love conquers all.

Aeneas performs a sacrifice while attendants stand behind him.

REVIEW OF UNIT XVII
LESSONS LXVIII-LXXII

Nouns	Nouns (cont.)	Verbs (cont.)
advena, -ae	sanguis, -inis	*extinguō, -ere
*ancora, -ae	*terror, -ōris	fodiō, -ere
*tuba, -ae	Adjectives	*incendō, -ere
*humus, -ī	*acūtus, -a, -um	pellō, -ere
tumulus, -ī	idōneus, -a, -um	*praedicō, -ere
vadum, -ī	ignōtus, -a, -um	*surgō, -ere
*apis, apis (-ium)	*incertus, -a, -um	Adverbs
*benignitās, -tātis	*nōbilis, -e	nē . . . quidem
*calamitās, -tātis	*praesēns, gen., -entis	paene
*classis, -is (-ium)	Verbs	Conjunction
gēns, gentis (-ium)	*cōnfīrmō, -āre	simul atque
litus, -oris	*implōrō, -āre	Prepositions
*mēns, mentis (-ium)	*inflō, -āre	*contrā
*rādix, -īcis	exquīrō, -ere	*super

I For each numbered sentence select from the lettered list a
clause or phrase which may be added as part of a logical sentence. Choose from the list at the right appropriate connecting
words when they are needed. Translate the completed
sentences.

1 Nōx erat
2 Nūntius castra statim relīquit
3 Mīlitēs fessī dormiē-bant
4 Magnam dolōris causam ipse habeō
5 Ventī secundī nōs ad Trōjam portābunt
6 Trōjānōs superābitis

a) epistulā acceptā
b) sacrificiō factō
c) castra quiēta sunt
d) nōbīs juvantibus
e) sacerdōs mē fīliam sacrificāre jussit
f) in ducis tabernācu-lō lūmen nōndum extīnctum erat

atque
cum
et
itaque
quamquam
quae
quī
quod
sed

II In the lettered list of Exercise I point out three ablative
absolute phrases. Translate each ablative absolute in at least
two ways, being careful to use idiomatic English.

358

III Translate each sentence, giving particular attention to the phrases and clauses underlined.

1 Urbe oppugnātā, Paris et Hector interfectī sunt.
2 Helena, timēns fēminās Trōjānās, in viās urbis exīre nōn audēbat.
3 Equō ligneō in urbem tractō, mīlitēs Graecī urbem Trōjam cēpērunt.
4 Mendīcō vīsō, līberī clāmant et lapidēs jaciunt.
5 Īra conjugis timēbātur ab Helenā, quae ad Graecōs trānsīre cupiēbat.
6 Rēgīna subitō sēnsit illum mendīcum esse Ulīxem.
7 Viā sēcrētā mōnstrātā, amīcōs tuōs juvāre poteris.
8 Trōjā dēlētā, novum cōnsilium Ulīxēs cēpit.
9 Cōnscendite in nāvēs, mīlitēs; reditūrī ad Graeciam sumus.
10 Signō datō, vir surrēxit et tubam īnflāvit.

IV Change the underlined clauses to ablative absolute phrases. Translate both versions of each sentence.

1 Trōja dēlēta erat; Aenēās lītora nova petēbat.
2 Haec verba audīvit; tum Anchīsēs dīxit, "In īnsulā Crētā initium gentis nostrae fuit."
3 Animālia necāvērunt; timuērunt Harpyiās quae capita fēminārum et corpora avium habuērunt.
4 Īnsulam relīquērunt; postrīdiē ad terram vēnērunt ubi Helenus sacerdōs Apollinis erat.
5 Tempestās undās excitāvit; Jūnō nāvēs Trōjānōrum ad lītus Āfricae pepulit.
6 Nāvēs in lītus subductae sunt; Aenēās cum sociīs ad urbem Carthāginem appropinquāvit.
7 Auxilium prōmissum est; deinde Dīdō Trōjānōs cum benignitāte accēpit.
8 Soleās ālātās sūmpsit; brevī tempore Mercurius, Jovis nūntius, ad Aenēam vēnit.
9 Urbem Dīdōnis vīdit; tum Mercurius dīxit Ītaliam Aenēam trāns mare expectāre; ibi Lāvīniam conjugem ejus futūram esse.
10 Aenēās mentem mūtāvit; ab Āfricā nāvigāvit.

V In III and IV, find and identify all ablative uses.

A dictionary provides much of interest in showing the origin of words. Look up the following words. All of them have come to us from Latin, and all have acquired special meanings.

arbiter   larva   posse   pupil   quorum   quota   rostrum

Numerous names of places and countries also come from Latin, some direct, others by way of a language such as Spanish or French. A dictionary will give the sources.

Argentina	Ecuador	Formosa	Montevideo	Nigeria
Australia	Florida	Liberia	Nevada	Nova Scotia

In ancient times people believed in astrology, just as some do even today. Because astrology has to do with the supposed influence of the stars on people and events, to those who believe in it, it is important to know the sign of the Zodiac under which one was born.

Aries	Cancer	Libra	Capricornus
Taurus	Leo	Scorpio	Aquarius
Gemini	Virgo	Sagittarius	Pisces

The twelve signs of the Zodiac, however, do not coincide with the twelve months of the year. For instance, the sun enters the sign of Cancer, the Crab, on June 22 and that of Leo, the Lion, on July 23. If you do not already know what the other names mean, look them up in a dictionary.

Do you have a Latin name? You do if yours is one of these. There are many others listed in the dictionary.

Anna	Lucia	Cornelius	Marcus
Clara	Lucretia	Dexter	Rex
Claudia	Paula	Felix	Rufus
Cornelia	Vera	Julius	Silvanus
Diana	Victoria	Leo	Silvester
Julia	Virginia	Lucius	Victor

But, even if your name is Amy or Emily, Florence or Sylvia, Adrian or Anthony, Laurence or Patrick, Paul or Vincent, it is Latin derived. How about yours?

10

THE OLD MAN OF THE SEA

Prōteus erat fīlius Neptūnī, sed in rēgiā Neptūnī nōn habitābat; altīs in cavernīs sub Ōceanō habitābat. Sub sōle altō interdum relinquēbat altās aquās cavernāsque Ōceanī et ad terram natābat. Magnus numerus phōcārum ex undīs cum Prōteō veniēbat. Prōteus, ubi stetit tūtus in ōrā, phōcās ₅ ēnumerābat. Deinde in cavernā somnō sē dabat.

Graecī dē Prōteō nōtam nārrant fābulam.

Nautae multās fābulās dē Prōteī scientiā Ulīxī nārrāverant, quī igitur deum vidēre in animō habuit. Ulīxēs et paucī nautae, ubi ad magna saxa prope Prōteī cavernam vēnērunt, ₁₀ magnō silentiō ad ea saxa natāvērunt. Post saxa sē cēlāvērunt. Prōteus post merīdiem cum phōcīs natāvit ad ōram. Prīmum Prōteus phōcās ēnumerāvit, sed in cavernam nōn intrāvit. Prōteus in ōrā inter phōcās somnō sē dedit.

Deinde Ulīxēs cum nautīs ad locum properāvit, ubi Prōteus ₁₅ phōcaeque jacēbant. Ulīxēs sine morā deum cēpit. Phōcae ad altam aquam Ōceanī fūgērunt, sed Prōteus sē ē somnō excitāvit; fōrmam suam iterum atque iterum mūtāvit; fuit leō, serpēns, aper, aqua, arbor, flammae—sed Ulīxēs deum firmiter semper tenēbat. ₂₀

Dēnique Prōteus fessus vēram fōrmam suam habuit. Nunc Ulīxī multa dē vītā futūrā et perīculīs futūrīs nārrāvit.

11

THE WHITE STAG

In Latiō antīquō cervus albus erat ōmen bonae fortūnae. Ita sine timōre cervus albus per silvās regiōnis errāre

361

"Illa est sagitta Trojana!"

poterat. Vēnātōrēs album cervum numquam necāre audēbant.

In Latiō habitābat agricola Tyrrhus. Ōlim in silvā fīliī
Tyrrhī album cervum vulnerātum invēnērunt. Sine morā 5
cervum ad casam portāvērunt. Mox herbīs cervum cūrāre
poterant. Frātrēs sorōrī Silviae cervum dedērunt.

Aenēās Trōjānus, ubi in Latium pervēnit, castra prope
flūmen Tiberim posuit. Mox mūrōs parvae urbis aedificābat.

Ascanius, fīlius Aenēae, cum sociīs in silvīs errābat. 10
Sagittīs parvīs animālia necāre temptābant.

Subitō puerī cervum album in rīpīs flūminis vīdērunt.
Ascanius, quod sibi magnam glōriam dēsīderābat, necāre
cervum temptāvit. Sagitta cervum vulnerāvit sed nōn interfēcit. Cervus vulnerātus ad casam Tyrrhī fūgit. 15

Tyrrhus, ubi sagittam vīdit, clāmāvit, "Illa est sagitta
Trōjāna! Perfidī Trōjānī! Vōs cervum album sagittīs vul-
nerāvistis; sagittīs nostrīs igitur Trōjānōs vulnerābimus!"

Statim Tyrrhus cum fīliīs et amīcīs eōrum castra Trōjāna
vehementer oppugnāvit; haec erat causa bellī! 20

This imaginative scene, painted by the French artist Charles François Jalabert (1819-1901), shows the reaction of Augustus and his family to Vergil's reading of *Aeneid* VI: 860-866. These verses, which memorialize the death of young Marcellus, nephew of Augustus and husband of Augustus' daughter Julia, apparently have caused the young widow to faint in the arms of her stepmother Livia. Her father gestures sympathetically, as if to interrupt the reading. The man on the left is believed to be Asinius Pollio, a patron of Vergil. Some believe that, instead of Julia, the fainting woman is Octavia, mother of the dead Marcellus and sister of Augustus.

LXXIII

AENEAS SEEKS AID

Turnus sociīque ejus, furōre excitātī, Trōjānōs ex Ītaliā in
mare expellere volēbant. Mīlitibus agricolīsque gentium
propinquārum convocātīs, Turnus cum Trōjānīs pugnāre
parāvit. Trōjānī quoque castra sua vehementer dēfendere
cōnstituērunt. 5

Nox erat, et Aenēās erat fessus. Prope castra Trōjāna
flūmen Tiberis fluēbat; in rīpā ejus flūminis Aenēās jacēbat.

In somniō vōx deī flūminis Aenēae dīxit, "Nōlī timēre
aut Turnum aut ejus sociōs! In hāc terrā erit domicilium
tuum. Haec ā deīs prōmissa sunt. Socius tuus erit Evander, 10

A medieval painting of Evander showing Aeneas the site of Rome amīcus patris tuī. Ante bellum Trōjānum ille in Ītaliam vēnit, et jam parvae urbis rēx est. Haec urbs, in colle aedificāta, ab hōc locō nōn longē abest. Pete auxilium ab Evandrō."

Aenēās paucīs cum nāvibus māne castra relīquit; postrīdiē ad urbem Evandrī appropinquāvit. Incolae urbis, nāvibus Trōjānōrum vīsīs, multum territī erant et statim arma cēpērunt. Pallās, fīlius Evandrī, ad rīpam properāvit.

"Īnsignia armōrum vestrōrum mihi nōta nōn sunt," dīxit. "Quī estis? Cūr ad urbem nostram appropinquātis?"

Aenēās respondit, "Sumus Trōjānī; sum Aenēās, dux Trōjānus. Bellum vōbīscum gerere nōlumus; bellum cum Rutulīs jam gerimus; auxilium ab Evandrō petimus."

Tum Evander ita dīxit, "Populus meus tibi auxilium dabit. Saepe incolae hujus regiōnis cum Rutulīs bellum gerunt. Mīlitēs gentium quoque Etrūriae propinquae vōs juvāre volunt. Etiam nunc eōrum nāvēs sunt parātae; eōrum mīlitēs sunt in armīs. Signō datō, proelium jungent. Tū, Aenēās, omnium eris dux."

collis, -is (-ium)	M., hill, height
***īnsigne, -is (-ium)**	N., mark, badge; pl., insignia

volō, velle, voluī	will, wish, intend
nōlō, nōlle, nōluī	be unwilling, don't wish

THE VERBS volō AND nōlō are conjugated like most other -ō verbs of third conjugation, except for four irregular forms of each verb in present tense.

Nōlō (I do not wish, I am unwilling) combines a negative (**nē**) and **volō** (I wish, I am willing); that is, **nōlō = nōn volō; nōlumus = nōn volumus; nōlunt = nōn volunt.** For the remaining three forms of **nōlō** in present tense **nōn** is used with corresponding forms of **volō**: **nōn vīs, nōn vult, nōn vultis.**

Principal parts of these verbs are **volō, velle, voluī, ——;** **nōlō, nōlle, nōluī, ——.**

USE YOUR EYES What is unusual about the forms **velle** and **nōlle?** Point out three differences between the principal parts of **nōlō** and those of **volō.**

PRESENT TENSE OF volō AND nōlō

Singular

1	**volō**	**nōlō**	
2	**vīs**	**nōn vīs**	
3	**vult**	**nōn vult**	

Plural

1	**volumus**	**nōlumus**	
2	**vultis**	**nōn vultis**	
3	**volunt**	**nōlunt**	

IN OTHER TENSES than present, **volō** and **nōlō** are identical (except for the first two letters) in all persons and numbers.

	Imperfect	Future	Perfect	Past Perfect	Future Perfect
	Singular	Singular	Singular	Singular	Singular
1	**volēbam**	**volam**	**voluī**	**volueram**	**voluerō**
2	**volēbās**	**volēs**	**voluistī**	**voluerās**	**volueris**
3	**volēbat**	**volet**	**voluit**	**voluerat**	**voluerit**
	Plural	Plural	Plural	Plural	Plural
1	**volēbāmus**	**volēmus**	**voluimus**	**voluerāmus**	**voluerimus**
2	**volēbātis**	**volētis**	**voluistis**	**voluerātis**	**volueritis**
3	**volēbant**	**volent**	**voluērunt**	**voluerant**	**voluerint**

COMPLEMENTARY INFINITIVE WITH volō AND nōlō often occurs in Latin, as it does also in English in corresponding expressions.

Hīc manēre volō. I am willing to stay here.
Hīc manēre nōlō. I don't wish to stay here.

The use of an infinitive with imperative **nōlī** (singular) or **nōlīte** (plural) to express a negative command has already been explained on page 159.

Nōlī manēre hīc, Aenēās! Don't stay here, Aeneas!
Nōlīte manēre hīc, Trōjānī! Don't stay here, Trojans!

I Complete each sentence with a suitable form of the appropriate verb of the pair following it. Translate.

1 Tum līberī saxa in aquam jacere ____ . **accipiō/incipiō**
2 Paucae stellae novae duōbus annīs ____ sunt. **inveniō/conveniō**
3 Calceō ____ , ad solium ūnō pede nūdō appropinquāvit. **āmittō/prōmittō**
4 Mīles quī virum fortem ad certāmen ____ pugnāre nōluit, **convocō/prōvocō**

5 Hostibus victīs rēx sine prīncipibus _____ . **redeō/exeō**

6 Tribus deābus pulcherrimīs disputantibus, nēmō jūdex _____ volēbat. **legō/dēligō**

7 Decemvirī potestātis cupidī imperium _____ nōlēbant. **impōnō/dēpōnō**

8 Dea, quamquam ad cēnam invītāta nōn erat, tamen _____ . **absum/adsum**

9 Ulixēs cum comitibus nāvēs māne _____ . **dēscendō/cōnscendō**

10 Dux mīlitibus dīxit sē condiciōnēs pācis cum hostibus _____ velle. **perficiō/interficiō**

LXXIV

THE WAR IS ON

Brevī tempore aliae gentēs Rutulīs, aliae gentēs Trōjānīs sē conjūnxērunt. Sonō cornūs audītō, duo exercitūs tum in acerbō bellō ācriter pugnāvērunt. Plūrimī mīlitēs vulnerātī sunt; plūrimī interfectī sunt.

Dēnique rēx Latīnus, magnā caede permōtus, bellum 5

Latinus' kingdom was not far from this hill, known as Mons Sacer.

diūtius gerere nōluit. Itaque Trōjānī prope urbem Latīnī castra posuērunt.

Rutulī quoque castra posuērunt lātō in campō per quem flūmen Tiberis fluēbat. Fessī mīlitēs aut in grāmine campī aut in rīpīs flūminis dormiēbant.

Mediā nocte Turnus ad rēgiam Latīnī prōcessit. "Māne," Turnus rēgī dīxit, "Aenēam prōvocābō ad certāmen. Aut hāc dextrā ducem Trōjānōrum interficiam aut Aenēās Lāvīniam conjugem habēbit."

Latīnus respondit, "In Latiō sunt multae virginēs; dēlige conjugem ex aliīs virginibus. Dī mē jussērunt Aenēae Lāvīniam in mātrimōnium dare; imperāta deōrum facere volō.

"Jam Latīnī in proeliō superātī sunt, quamquam moenia adhūc mūniuntur et vehementer dēfenduntur. Multī sociī, ā Trōjānīs necātī, in campīs in cōnspectū meō jacent. Tū magnam glōriam jam cēpistī; pete pācem ā Trōjānīs."

Turnus respondit, "Mortem nōn timeō sed vītam sine glōriā tolerāre nōlō. Aut gladiō meō Aenēam vincam aut vītam meam āmittam."

Illa verba ā rēgīnā audīta sunt, quae territā vōce clāmāvit, "Tū, Turne, fortūnam bellī temptāre nōn dēbēs. Quis tibi auxilium dabit? Nōnne meae lacrimae tē movent?"

Turnus autem ācriter respondit, "Ō rēgīna, lacrimae tuae sunt ōmen malum! Mē nōn vincunt. Mēns mea mūtāta nōn est. Neque Trōjānī neque Rutulī iterum impetum facient. Ego sōlus cum Aenēā sōlō pugnābō; victor Lāvīniam habēbit!"

*dextra, -ae	F., right hand
imperātum, -ī	N., order, command
caedēs, caedis (-ium)	F., slaughter, blood-shed
grāmen, -inis	N., grass, plant
moenia, -ium	N. pl., city walls, fortifications
*virgō, -inis	F., maiden, unmarried woman
*cōnspectus, -ūs	M., sight, view
*impetus, -ūs	M., attack
cornū, -ūs	N., horn; wing of an army, flank
acerbus, -a, -um	harsh, biting, severe
*tolerō, -āre, -āvī, -ātum	bear, sustain, tolerate
*conjungō, -ere, -jūnxī, -jūnctum	join together, unite

FOURTH-DECLENSION NOUNS have genitive

singular ending in **-ūs.** Nominative singular of masculine
and feminine nouns ends in **-us;** of neuter nouns, in **-ū.**

	exercitus (M.) army			**cornū** (N.) horn	
	Singular	Plural		Singular	Plural
Nom.	**exercitus**	**exercitūs**		**cornū**	**cornua**
Gen.	**exercitūs**	**exercituum**		**cornūs**	**cornuum**
Dat.	**exercituī**	**exercitibus**		**cornū**	**cornibus**
Acc.	**exercitum**	**exercitūs**		**cornū**	**cornua**
Abl.	**exercitū**	**exercitibus**		**cornū**	**cornibus**

Most fourth-declension nouns are masculine; a few are
neuter. The most common feminine noun of this declension
is **manus** ("hand" or "band").

FOURTH-DECLENSION ENDINGS

	Masculine or Feminine			Neuter	
	Singular	Plural		Singular	Plural
Nom.	**-us**	**-ūs**		**-ū**	**-ua**
Gen.	**-ūs**	**-uum**		**-ūs**	**-uum**
Dat.	**-uī**	**-ibus**		**-ū**	**-ibus**
Acc.	**-um**	**-ūs**		**-ū**	**-ua**
Abl.	**-ū**	**-ibus**		**-ū**	**-ibus**

I Each group below is made up of endings of the same case and
number for the various declensions of nouns. Give the case
and number represented by each group and identify the
declension or declensions in which each occurs.
Example: 3 dative and ablative plural: **-ibus** (III, IV); **-īs**
(I, II)

1 **-am, -um, -em, -al, -ū, -e, -en**

2 **-ī, -ae, -ūs, -is**

3 **-ibus, -īs**

4 **-ae, -ō, -uī, -ī, -ū**

5 **-al, -is, -a, -e, -um, -us, -er, -r, -or, -tor, -tās, -tūdō, -en**

6 **-ēs, -a, -ua, -ōs, -ūs, -ās**

7 **-um, -ōrum, -ium, -uum, -ārum**

8 **-ā, -ō, -ī, -ū, -e**

9 **-ēs, -ī, -a, -ae, -ūs, -ia**

LXXV

A BROKEN TREATY

Aenēās prōvocātiōnem Turnī accēpit. Itaque posterō diē exercitūs Rutulōrum et Trōjānōrum, castrīs relictīs, sub moenia urbis prōcessērunt, ubi locum certāminis parāvērunt. Prope locum dēsignātum erant magna āra et sella rēgia.

Tempore cōnstitūtō Latīnus et Turnus cum paucīs prīn- 5 cipibus suīs in medium campum prōcessērunt. Ad eōs Aenēās et fīlius ejus, Ascanius, paucīs cum comitibus lentē appropinquāvērunt. Virī silentēs circum campum stābant.

Prīmō Aenēās prō soliō magnā vōce clāmāvit, "Hōc certā- mine foedus petimus aeternum; hoc foedus bellum prohibēbit. 10 Rēx Latīnus arcem suam, urbem suam, rēgnum suum, omnēs suās rēs habēbit. Turnō victōre, Trōjānī numquam hoc rēgnum oppugnābunt; sed, mē victōre, Latīnī sub potestāte Trōjānōrum numquam erunt. Trōjānī urbem suam aedificā- bunt, et Lāvīnia huic urbī novae nōmen suum dabit." 15

Deinde Latīnus dē soliō altō ita dīxit, "Hās rēs probō; hoc foedus semper erit sacrum. Pāx aeterna erit inter nōs."

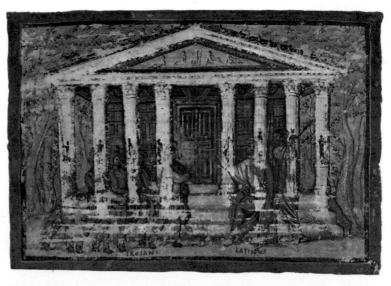

Latinus and the Trojans confronting one another in front of a temple

His rēbus ab Aeneā Latīnōque probātīs, tamen furor mentēs Rutulōrum occupāvit. Eīs hoc foedus nōn erat grātum; bellum, nōn pācem facere volēbant. 20

Nunc Turnus sōlus et tacitus ad āram prōcēdēbat. Subitō silentium frāctum est.

Jūturna, soror Turnī atque sacerdōs Jūnōnis, clāmāvit, "Ubi est honor? Ubi est fāma? Capite arma, Rutulī! Pugnāte prō patriā vestrā! Vultisne Turnum sōlum pugnāre? Eum 25 juvāre dēbēmus!"

Verbīs Jūturnae audītīs, Turnus spē novā occupātus est. Etiam mēns ejus jam mūtāta est. Itaque Rutulī foedus frēgērunt. Arma petīvērunt; hastae jactae sunt. Foedere frāctō, mīlitēs cum mīlitibus iterum pugnābant. 30

sella, -ae	F., seat, chair, stool
*silentium, -ī	N., silence
*foedus, -eris	N., agreement, treaty, league
*prōvocātiō, -ōnis	F., challenge, appeal, provocation
spēs, speī	F., hope, expectation
*dēsignātus, -a, -um	pointed out, designated, elect
*posterus, -a, -um	following, next
*rēgius, -a, -um	royal, regal
*silēns, gen., -entis	quiet, silent
*frangō, -ere, frēgī, frāctum	break

FIFTH-DECLENSION NOUNS always end in **-ēs** in the nominative singular. The genitive singular ends in **-ēī (-eī** after a consonant).

Rēs (thing) and **diēs** (day) are the only fifth-declension nouns with forms for all cases. The few other nouns of this declension are used mostly in the singular.

rēs (F.) thing

	Singular	Plural
Nom.	rēs	rēs
Gen.	reī	rērum
Dat.	reī	rēbus
Acc.	rem	rēs
Abl.	rē	rēbus

diēs (M. or F.) day

	Singular	Plural
Nom.	diēs	diēs
Gen.	diēī	diērum
Dat.	diēī	diēbus
Acc.	diem	diēs
Abl.	diē	diēbus

371

Diēs in the singular is sometimes masculine and sometimes feminine; in the plural it is always masculine. Most other nouns of fifth declension are feminine.

I For each underlined expression choose from the list a word to convey a similar idea and supply proper endings, if necessary.

1 <u>Posterō diē</u> exercitus castra sua relīquit.
2 <u>Hās rēs</u> probō.
3 Sub <u>mūrōs</u> urbis ambulābāmus.
4 Prope locum <u>dēsignātum</u> solium rēgis erat.
5 Tempore cōnstitūtō cum <u>prīncipibus</u> in medium <u>campum</u> perveniam.
6 Hominēs <u>silentēs</u> circum solium stābant.
7 Mē <u>superante</u> sub potestāte ejus numquam eritis.
8 Furor <u>animōs</u> sociōrum <u>cēpit</u>.

a) **ager**   c) **haec**   e) **lēgātus**   g) **occupō**   i) **tacitus**

b) **dēligō**   d) **mēns**   f) **moenia**   h) **postrīdiē**   j) **victor**

II In the sentences find a Latin word or phrase that corresponds to each English expression.

1 Hōc certāmine foedus petimus aeternum.   a) everlasting
2 Lāvīnia huic urbī novae nōmen suum dabit.   b) her own
3 Eīs hoc foedus grātum erat.   c) priestess
4 Turnus sōlus ad āram cum silentiō prōcessit.   d) silently
5 Jūturna soror rēgis atque sacerdōs Jūnōnis erat.   e) they liked
     f) violated
6 Turnus spē novā occupātus est.   g) was filled
7 Rutulī foedus frēgērunt.   h) our aim is

LXXVI

RENEWED CONFLICT

Foedere frāctō, Aenēās, īrā excitātus, magnā vōce clāmāvit, "Nōlīte pugnāre, Trōjānī. Dēpōnite tēla! Cūr bellum iterum geritis? Foedus frāctum est, sed ego huic foederī fīdus erō! Ego sōlus cum Turnō pugnāre volō!"

372

Neque Trōjānī neque Rutulī autem ā proeliō recēdere 5 voluērunt.

Paucīs hōrīs magnus numerus Trōjānōrum sociōrumque in terrā jacēbat, ā Rutulīs perfidīs necātus. Multī Rutulī quoque necātī sunt.

Latīnus cum comitibus suīs ad urbem fūgit; portae sunt 10 clausae.

Sociīs mortuīs vīsīs, Aenēās magnopere agitātus est. Undique multās hōrās Turnum petēbat. Proelium prope portās urbis conjūnctum est. Hōc vīsō, mēns Aenēae mūtāta est.   15

"Oppugnāte moenia! Haec est diēs victōriae nostrae," Aenēās, cum tribus comitibus in tumulō stāns, clāmāvit. "Vultisne hanc urbem, causam bellī, manēre? Nostrī in proeliō injūstō interficiuntur."

Hōc tempore Trōjānī moenia ascendēbant et portās expugnā- 20 bant. Nōn sōlum hastae, sed etiam taedae in urbem jaciē- bantur. Magnus erat terror cīvium; urbs et domicilia eōrum flammīs dēlēbantur.

"Ubi est Turnus?" clāmāvit rēgīna Amāta, furōre agitāta. "Urbs nostra vincitur. Turnus sōlus nōs servāre poterit; sine 25 eō superābimur. Heu! Ego sum causa calamitātis; propter mē Turnus interficiētur. Nōn jam vīvere volō!"

Hīs verbīs dictīs, Amāta dēmēns sē interfēcit. Latīnus, dolōre affectus, brevī tempore mortuus est. Lāvīnia cum aliīs puellīs ad āram Jūnōnis fūgit.   30

Clāmōre audītō, Turnus, quī extrā moenia pugnāverat, ad urbem fūmō flammīsque paene cēlātam cucurrit.

"Ō Rutulī et Latīnī!" clāmāvit Turnus, "nōlīte pugnāre diūtius. Ego sōlus Aenēam in certāmine petītūrus sum."

Cīvēs, jam morte rēgis rēgīnaeque stupefactī, maximīs 35 clāmōribus per multōs diēs dolēbant.

tēlum, -ī	N., weapon
*dēmēns, gen., dēmentis	out of one's mind, insane
expugnō, -āre, -āvī, -ātum	take by storm, overcome, capture
*afficiō, -ere, -fēcī, -fectum	influence, afflict, affect
*recēdō, -ere, -cessī, -cessum	retreat, recede, withdraw
*stupefaciō, -ere, -fēcī, -factum	stun, stupefy

LXXVII

Vōce Turnī audītā, Aenēās urbem relīquit et ad certāmen avidē prōcessit. Jam et Latīnī et Trōjānī ē locō recesserant et silentiō certāmen spectābant.

Prīmō Aenēās hastam suam in hostem jēcit, sed hasta suprā Turnī caput volāvit et in arbore propinquā stetit. 5 Turnus deinde hastam jēcit suam, quae, umbōne° scūtī Trō- jānī dēclīnāta, in terram cecidit.

Deinde gladiīs Aenēās et Turnus vehementer pugnābant. Sed subitō avis fera, ā Jove ad terram missa, volāvit circum Turnī umerōs et scūtum ejus ālīs pulsāvit. Turnus hoc 10 ōmen mortis recognōvit.

Jūturna hanc avem procul vīdit et clāmāvit, "Haec avis quidem missa est, quod dī Turnum interficī et Rutulōs vincī volunt. Frātre meō interfectō Rutulīsque victīs, ego nōn jam vīvere dēsīderō." 15

Itaque Jūturna mortem in undīs Tiberis petīvit.

Nunc Aenēās Turnum agitāre incēpit.

"Cūr recēdis, Turne?" clāmāvit ille. "Cūr mortem tuam fugere temptās? Mēcum pugnāre nōn vīs?"

Turnus respondit, "Verba tua mē nōn terrent. Dī et odium 20 deōrum mē terrent. Juppiter est mihi inimīcus."

Tum Aenēās, spē victōriae excitātus, ictū gladiī magnō Turnum trānsfīxit; Turnus, graviter vulnerātus, cecidit.

Turnus victus dīxit, "Vītam meam āmittere prō patriā jam diū parātus sum. Satis pugnāvī; nunc mē vīcistī. Lāvīnia 25 erit conjūnx tua. Vītam nōn ōrō, sed certē prō patre miserō meīs amīcīs corpus meum dabis."

°**umbō, -ōnis**   M., boss (in center of shield)

umerus, -ī	M., shoulder
***odium, -ī**	N., hatred
ictus, -ūs	M., thrust, blow
***dēclīnō, -āre, -āvī, -ātum**	turn aside; deviate; shun
***pulsō, -āre, -āvī, -ātum**	beat, knock (on)
***trānsfīgō, -ere, -fīxī, -fīxum**	thrust or pierce through; transfix

374

REVIEW OF UNIT XVIII

LESSONS LXXIII-LXXVII

Nouns	Nouns (cont.)	Verbs
*dextra, -ae	*cōnspectus, -ūs	*dēclīnō, -āre
sella, -ae	*exercitus, -ūs	expugnō, -āre
umerus, -ī	ictus, -ūs	*pulsō, -āre
*odium, -ī	*impetus, -ūs	tolerō, -āre
imperātum, -ī	cornū, -ūs	*afficiō, -ere
*silentium, -ī	diēs, diēī	*conjungō, -ere
tēlum, -ī	rēs, reī	*frangō, -ere
caedēs, -is (-ium)	spēs, speī	*recēdō, -ere
collis, -is (-ium)	Adjectives	*stupefaciō, -ere
*foedus, -eris	acerbus, -a, -um	*trānsfīgō, -ere
grāmen, -inis	*dēsignātus, -a, -um	nōlō, nōlle
*insigne, -is (-ium)	*posterus, -a, -um	volō, velle
moenia, -ium	*rēgius, -a, -um	
*prōvocātiō, -ōnis	*dēmēns, gen., -entis	
*virgō, -inis	*silēns, gen., -entis	

I Supply the proper form of each verb in parentheses and translate the completed sentences.

1 Puer equōs suī patris (agō) cupiēbat.
2 Mātrēs līberōs suōs (pūniō) nōn amant.
3 Hominēs auxilium ab amīcīs (postulō) cōnstituērunt.
4 Nūlla vēstīgia in hortō ejus (relinquō) temptābimus.
5 Apud avunculum meum trēs mensēs (maneō) nōn dēbeō.
6 Hieme in flūmine (natō) nōn potestis.
7 Nōnne cibum amoenum īnsulae (gustō) dēsīderāvistī?

II Substitute the corresponding form of **nōlō** for each under-lined verb in Exercise I with which **nōn** appears. For the remaining underlined verbs substitute corresponding forms of **volō**.

III Translate.

1 Posterō diē in cōnspectū exercitūs Turnus foedus frēgit.
2 Rē vērā pāx est spēs hominum omnium.

375

IPHIGENIA

The Greeks were fond of stories portraying struggles of mortals against a fate which the gods had arranged for them. Such is the story of "Iphigenia"—a famous classic in world literature.

In this legend, the gods opposed the Greeks' leaving their camp at Aulis and sailing to Troy to recover Helen. At least, weather unsuitable for sailing had been interpreted by the Greeks as evidence of divine displeasure. They believed that some important person must be sacrificed to gain the favor of the gods and with it a favorable wind that would take them to Troy.

Iphigenia, daughter of King Agamemnon and his wife Clytemnestra, was considered worthy for such a sacrifice. She was also Helen's niece, since King Menelaus (Helen's husband) and King Agamemnon were brothers.

The stories of this unit tell of Iphigenia's being tricked into coming to the Greek camp through a letter from her own father; Agamemnon's frustrated attempt to save his daughter; her last-minute rescue by the goddess Diana, after sacrificial ceremonies were under way; and of the dramatic reunion between Iphigenia and her brother Orestes after many years.

Between the intended sacrifice of Iphigenia and her reunion with Orestes were the ten long years of the Trojan War and a tragic postwar period which saw the murder of Agamemnon by his wife, who in turn was murdered by her son Orestes. In remorse for his crime, Orestes lost his mind. After years of insanity and suffering, he was sent by the gods to the land of the Taurians, on the promise that he would regain his sanity if he fulfilled certain obligations.

It was there, in this faraway land of the Taurians, that Orestes found his sister Iphigenia, whom he and the rest of the Greeks had believed dead. For it was to this place that Iphigenia had been carried by Diana, in whose temple she was serving as priestess when Orestes discovered her.

The tragic theme based on the experiences of Agamemnon and his family was used by each of the three great writers of Greek tragedy, Aeschylus, Sophocles, and Euripides.

Giovacchino Agricola painted Iphigenia's rescue by Diana. Calchas is staring in unbelief at Iphigenia and the goddess. The weeping Clytemnestra is still unaware of her daughter's unexpected rescue, while the attendants bow their heads in awe. The deer is going to be a substitute sacrifice.

12

Nox est, et castra Graecōrum, prope urbem Aulidem posita, silent. In tabernāculō Agamemnonis, ducis Graecī, lūmen clārum nōndum extīnctum est. Subitō rēx ad portam tabernāculī venit servumque ad sē vocat.

Servus. Ō domine, vocāvistīne mē? 5

Agamemnōn. Ita; ego dēsīderō hanc epistulam ad uxōrem Clytemnestram sine morā portārī.

Servus. Ego tibi semper fīdus sum. Cūr, domine, per tōtam noctem tū numquam dormīvistī?

Agamemnōn. Magnam causam dolōris habeō. Ventī ad- 10 versī per trēs mēnsēs nāvēs nostrās nāvigāre prohibent. Cotīdiē sacerdōs Calchās mihi nūntiat Diānam esse īrā-tam, magnaque sacrificia postulāre. Meam fīliam, Īphi-genīam, sacrificāre jussus sum.

Servus. Certē Calchās est vir malus. Īphigenīa nōbīs 15 cārissima est.

Agamemnōn. Sed Menelāus, frāter meus, dīxit, "Hōc sacri-ficiō ā tē factō, ventī secundī nōs ad urbem Trōjam portā-bunt. Exercitū nostrō et auxiliō deōrum nōs Trōjānōs superābimus." 20

Servus. Cūr Menelāus fīliam suam nōn dat? Tū tē tuamque familiam dēfendere dēbēs.

Agamemnōn. Dī fīliam ejus nōn postulāvērunt. Itaque maestus ad uxōrem meam jam mīsī epistulam in quā scrīpsī, "Achillēs fīliam nostram, Īphigenīam, in mātri- 25 mōnium dūcere dēsīderat. Mitte eam sine morā ad castra nostra."

Servus. Cūr, domine, nunc aliam epistulam mittis?

Agamemnōn. Mentem meam mūtāvī. Hāc in epistulā quam tibi dō scrīpsī, "Ō conjūnx amāta, servā tē et fīliam nos- 30 tram; perīculum est maximum; tenē Īphigenīam domī. Nōlī venīre ad hoc locum! Nōlī dūcere fīliam Īphigenīam ad castra!"

Servus fīdus, epistulā receptā, ē tabernāculō in noctem properat. 35

378

13

Servus, portāns epistulam Agamemnonis, ā custōdibus captus est, sed Agamemnōn hoc nescit. Audiēns igitur uxōrem Clytemnestram cum fīliā Īphigeniā ad castra appropinquāre, graviter movētur. Scit sine dubiō fīliam amātam ad mortem dūcī. Itaque Agamemnōn ad frātrem Menelāum 5 properat.

Agamemnōn. Heu! Mox uxor mea fīliam nostram ad mē dūcet. Dī puellam juvent! Ego, rēx potēns sapiēnsque, ad mortem fīliam meam mittō! Jam in vincula Īphigenīa conjiciētur. Numquam fēlīx laetusque erō. Hanc timēbam 10 calamitātem, sed Fāta mē regunt.

Menelāus. Dīc Clytemnestrae Achillem ā castrīs abesse. Calchās in tabernāculō manēbit fīliamque tuam nōn vidēbit.

Agamemnōn. Sed Ulīxēs, vir sapiēns, voluntātem deōrum 15 scit. Ego sciō hunc virum potentem cum inimīcīs meīs sē jungere.

Interim Clytemnestra et Īphigenīa, ā mīlite ductae, ad Agamemnonem appropinquant.

Clytemnestra. Ecce, Īphigenīa, pater tuus! Laeta, Aga- 20 memnōn, tē videō. Propter imperāta tua ad castra pervēnimus.

Īphigenīa. Ō pater, iter erat dūrum. Heu! Tū es maestus! Nōnne putās Achillem mē in mātrimōnium dūcere velle? Putō Achillem esse virum fortem, sapientem, fēlīcem. 25 Fēlīx erō, uxor ducis clārī. Tū quoque fēlīx sīs!

Agamemnōn. Ita, Achillēs vir fortis est. Sed Trōja est longinqua.

Īphigenīa. Sciō iter esse longum; bene sciō omne bellum esse ācre. Ubi est Achillēs? Cūr ad mē nōn venit? Cūr 30 nōs nōn salūtat?

Agamemnōn. Achillēs cum cōpiīs suīs in lītore nunc est. Mox aderit. Eāmus in tabernāculum.

Hōc dictō, Agamemnōn fēminās in tabernāculum dūcit.

Agamemnōn (tabernāculum relinquēns). Heu! Jam miser ₃₅
vīvō! Certē servus meus epistulam ad Clytemnestram nōn
portāvit. Quid faciam?

THE TERM ''MOOD'' is used to describe the manner
in which a verb functions in a sentence. There are three
moods: indicative, imperative, subjunctive.[1] To these may
be added infinitive and participle, sometimes referred to as
moods.

Indicative is used in making a statement or asking a question. Imperative is used to give a command.

Indicative: **Librōs portat.** He is carrying the books.
Imperative: **Portā librōs!** Carry the books!

Indicative: **Mūsicam audiunt.** They hear music.
Imperative: **Audīte mūsicam!** Hear the music!

Indicative: **Cūr jacēs?** Why are you lying down?
Imperative: **Jacē!** Lie down!

[1]Only the present subjunctive is introduced in this book, and only its use in an independent clause.

This cameo shows Iphigenia seated in a chair, flanked by Orestes and Pylades. The
attendant in the back is holding a small statue of Diana.

SUBJUNCTIVE IN PRESENT TENSE often expresses a wish, hope, possibility, or mild command.

Indicative		Subjunctive	
I	**portat** = he is carrying	**portet** = let him carry
II	**habēs** = you have	**habeās** = may you have, I hope you have
III	**vīvimus** = we live	**vīvāmus** = let us live, may we live
IV	**audiunt** = they hear	**audiant** = may they hear

Although subjunctive is often found in Latin, it has almost disappeared from English usage. It survives in a few set phrases: "So be it." "Thy kingdom come." "Come what may."

PRESENT SUBJUNCTIVE FORMS are easy to recognize. In Conjugation I, **-a-** of the indicative is replaced by **-e-**. In Conjugations II, III, IV, and **eō** and its compounds, an **-a-** precedes the person ending in present tense.

I	II	III	III-iō	IV	eō
portem	moneam	dūcam	capiam	audiam	eam
portēs	moneās	dūcās	capiās	audiās	eās
portet	moneat	dūcat	capiat	audiat	eat

Corresponding plural forms end thus: (I) **-ēmus, -ētis, -ent**; (II) **-eāmus, -eātis, -eant**; (III) **-āmus, -ātis, -ant**; (III-iō/IV) **-iāmus, -iātis, -iant**; (eō) **eāmus, eātis, eant**.

Passive forms of present subjunctive are like the active except for addition of regular passive endings: **porter, portēris,** etc.; **monear, moneāris,** etc.

Sum and its compounds and **volō** and **nōlō** have **-i-** before the person ending. **Volō** has another change; its first vowel appears as **-e-**.

sim/possim	sīmus/possīmus	velim/nōlim	velīmus/nōlīmus
sīs/possīs	sītis/possītis	velīs/nōlīs	velītis/nōlītis
sit/possit	sint/possint	velit/nōlit	velint/nōlint

I Express in English as wishes.

1 Fāta nōs dēfendant!
2 Dormiās bene!
3 Mittāmus eīs paucōs librōs!
4 Possītis expellere apēs!
5 Dominī servīs benignī sint!
6 Ad scholam eāmus!

14

ACHILLES DISCOVERS THE PLOT

Māne Achillēs, quī nōn intellegit Clytemnestram in castra pervēnisse, prō tabernāculō Agamemnonis stat.

Achillēs (magnā vōce). Ubi est Agamemnōn quī exercitūs Graecōs agit? Dīc eī Achillem prō tabernāculō stāre. Omnēs sciunt mē ad hoc bellum ā Menelāō arcessītum esse. 5 Jam pugnāre parātus, exercitus meus propter moram longam graviter dolet.

Clytemnestra ē tabernāculō venit. Achillēs cōnfūsus eam diū spectat.

Achillēs. Quem videō? Certē tū fēmina nōbilis es. 10

Clytemnestra. Sum Clytemnestra, conjūnx Agamemnonis. Laeta sum quod tū Īphigenīam, fīliam meam, in mātrimōnium dūcēs.

Achillēs. Quid dīcis? Ego sum Achillēs. Quis dīcit mē fīliam tuam in mātrimōnium dūcere velle? Numquam hoc 15 dīxī!

Clytemnestra. Quid? Agamemnōn mē jussit ad castra cum fīliā nostrā venīre, quod tū eam in mātrimōnium dūcere vīs.

Achillēs. Ego fīliam tuam numquam arcessīvī. 20

Servus territus ad Clytemnestram currit.

Servus. Ō rēgīna, mala sunt ōmina! Agamemnōn in animō magnum scelus habet. In animō habet fīliam suam occīdere. Nōn sōlum āram parātam et gladium sed etiam sacerdōtem vīdī. Jam Calchās sacrificium parāvit; nunc 25 virī animālia ad āram dūcunt. Tum fīlia quoque sacrificābitur.

Clytemnestra. Crēdō conjugem meum īnsānum esse! Quis hoc scelus parāvit? Achillēs, juvā mē! Servā fīliam meam! Ab omnī perīculō Īphigenīa dēfendātur! 30

Achillēs (graviter excitātus). Ō Clytemnestra, ego fīliam tuam dēfendam! Meōs mīlitēs contrā Agamemnonem agam!

15

SACRIFICE OF IPHIGENIA

Adventū Clytemnestrae rēx Agamemnōn nescīvit servum epistulam portantem ā custōdibus captum esse. Is fīliam suam servāre dēsīderābat; nōn jam putābat deōs per Calcham mortem Īphigenīae jussisse.

Diē sacrificiī mīlitēs omnium exercituum Graecōrum in 5 lītore jussa ducum expectābant. Inter sē dīxērunt, "Sacrificiō datō, deī mittent ventōs secundōs."

Achillēs autem mīlitēs suōs ad tabernācula redīre subitō jussit. Ulīxēs et Menelāus multum mōtī sunt, quod Achillēs hoc sacrificium nōn probābat. 10

Clytemnestra, clāmōribus hominum audītīs, sēnsit hōram sacrificiī adesse. Agamemnōn tōtam noctem doluerat, sed fīliam suam ē tabernāculō ad āram dūcere parābat.

Īphigenīa, sine lacrimīs, mātrī maestae dīxit, "Māter amāta, pater meus mē sacrificāre nōluit; injūriam nōn facit; 15 est voluntās deōrum. Nōn erō ignāva; cupiō mīlitēs nostrōs ā fortūnā malā dēfendī. Venī! Eāmus ad āram. Fēlīx ōmen sit mors mea! Victōriam habeant Graecī!"

Omnia ā sacerdōte parāta erant et puella in ārā posita est. Subitō magnus clāmor audītus est; clārum lūmen in caelō 20 appāruit. Dea Diāna aderat. Dea corpus cervae prō corpore Īphigenīae in ārā posuit. Graecī, lūmine caecī, hoc esse corpus Īphigenīae crēdidērunt.

Diāna autem virginem, nūbe dēnsā tēctam, per caelum ad locum longinquum portābat. 25

16

A FATEFUL MEETING

Graecī crēdidērunt, Īphigenīā sacrificātā, animum deōrum mūtātum esse. Brevī tempore nāvēs igitur ad lītora Trōjae nāvigāverant. Decem annōs cum Trōjānīs pugnāverant.

Tandem Trōja expugnāta erat victōrēsque Graecī ad patriam redierant.

Agamemnonem, quod imperāta dīvīna ēvādere temptāverat, dī magnā cum crūdēlitāte pūnīvērunt. Rēx miser ab uxōre occīsus est, quod Clytemnestra crēdidit eum fuisse causam Īphigenīae mortis. Deinde Orestēs, fīlius eōrum, lēgibus Fātōrum mātrem suam occīdere coāctus est. Propter hoc scelus diū erat īnsānus.

Dēnique sacerdōtēs eī dīxērunt, "In terrā Taurōrum est parva statua Diānae. Nāvigā ad illam terram. Haec statua capiātur; ea ad templum Apollinis portētur. Hōc factō, iterum eris sānus."

Terra Taurōrum longē aberat. Orestēs scīvit neque sorōrem vīvere suam Īphigenīam, ā Diānā ad hanc terram portātam, neque eam jam sacerdōtem Diānae diū esse.

Orestēs cum amīcō nāvigāvit; dēnique post multōs mēnsēs in portum hujus terrae vēnērunt. In locō sēcrētō juvenēs nāvem cēlāvērunt. Duo advenae autem, ā pāstōribus captī, ad Īphigenīam ductī sunt. Lēgibus crūdēlibus terrae omnēs advenae deīs sacrificābantur.

Statim sacerdōs Īphigenīa advenās sacrificāre parāvit. Orestēs et socius, catēnīs vīnctī, ad āram conductī sunt. Ubi juvenēs prope āram stetērunt, Īphigenīa Orestem frātrem recognōvit.

"Nōnne es Orestēs, frāter meus?" quaesīvit. "Sum soror tua, Īphigenīa, ā Diānā servāta. Multa perīcula sunt in saevā terrā Taurōrum. Sine morā fugiāmus!"

Orestēs, verbīs sorōris permōtus, respondit, "Prīmō necesse est mē capere parvam statuam Diānae prope āram; sine statuā nōn poterimus redīre in Graeciam!"

Hāc statuā captā, Orestēs cum suō amīcō atque sorōre Īphigenīā ad nāvem fūgit. Orestēs nōn jam īnsānus erat.

Ventīs secundīs portātī, ex portū Taurōrum nāvigāvērunt; brevī tempore ad Graeciam pervēnērunt. Ibi magnō cum gaudiō ā populō attonitō acceptī sunt.

SAY IT IN LATIN

Prīmās partēs agō. I play the leading rôle.

Fābula ad scaenam composita est. It's a stage play.

Actor/Scaenicus est. He is an actor/a stage hero.

This statue of Ulysses wearing the peaked Phrygian cap is in the Vatican.

17

RETURN OF ULYSSES

Decem annōs Ulīxēs circum mūrōs Trōjae pugnāverat. Posteā decem annōs propter īram deōrum in multīs terrīs errāre coāctus erat, quamquam dea Athēna prōmīserat eum ad patriam tūtum reditūrum esse.

Dēnique autem post multōs cāsūs Ulīxēs ad Ithacam per- 5 vēnit. Nēmō eum recognōvit, quod dea Athēna vestēs et faciem ejus mūtāverat. Omnēs crēdidērunt eum esse mendīcum.

Ulīxēs casam Eumaeī, pāstōris fidēlis, petīvit, sed subitō canēs ferī impetum in eum fēcērunt. Magnā cum difficultāte 10

Pinturicchio (1454-1513) painted "The Return of Ulysses" in a setting and with the clothing of the Italian Renaissance. Some of the startled suitors watch Ulysses approaching Penelope at her loom. The ship that brought Ulysses home can be seen through the window.

Eumaeus canēs lapidibus reppulit Ulīxemque servāvit. Celeriter eum in casam dūxit et eī cibum vīnumque dedit.

Ulīxēs, accipiēns haec dōna, dīxit, "Cūr es mihi, hominī miserō, benignus? Nūllam pecūniam habeō, sed mihi cibum vīnumque dedistī. Dominus tuus erit īrātus; tē culpābit." 15

Eumaeus autem respondit, "Dominus benignus erat et semper mendīcōs juvābat; tamen nōn jam domī adest. Vīgintī annōs dominum nostrum expectāmus. Ejus uxor et fīlius Tēlemachus crēdunt eum ad tēctum suum reditūrum esse." 20

Tum Ulīxēs dīxit, "Suntne Tēlemachus et rēgīna in rēgiā?"

Eumaeus respondit, "Tēlemachus Ithacam relīquit; dīxit sē patrem suum petītūrum esse. Pēnelopē Ulīxem expectat. Cotīdiē in rēgiā texit. Pallā factā, conjugem alium accipere cōgētur. Itaque interdiū texit; noctū pallam textam retexit. 25

"Cotīdiē procī hūc veniunt et animālia, frūmentum, vīnum dominī meī cōnsūmunt, sed mihi pecūniam nōn dant. Jam Pēnelopē territa est, quod procī dīcunt ūnum ē numerō suō brevī tempore eam in mātrimōnium ductūrum esse."

18

REUNION OF FATHER AND SON

Tēlemachus quidem per omnēs urbēs Graeciae iter fēcerat, sed nēmō prō certō dīcere potuerat patrem Ulīxem vīvere. Dēnique dea Athēna somniō Tēlemachum dē perīculō mātris Pēnelopae monuerat; itemque dīxerat procōs malōs in animō eum interficere habēre. 5

Ita monitus Tēlemachus ad patriam suam statim redīre cōnstituit. Sciēns autem procōs adventum ejus expectāre et eōrum dolōs timēns, in portum nōn intrāvit. Nāve relictā, ante prīmam lūcem sōlus ad casam Eumaeī, pāstōris fidēlis, prōcessit. 10

Hīc Eumaeus et mendīcus, igne accēnsō, cibum parābant. Vōce hominis audītā, Eumaeus ad portam properāvit.

Ubi Tēlemachum vīdit, magnō cum gaudiō juvenem nōmine appellāvit. Tēlemachus dē mātre et dē procīs atque

387

dē rēgnō et dē multīs rēbus aliīs rogāvit, dolēbatque quod 15
pater ad Ithacam nōn redierat.

Dēnique dīxit, "Ego propter suspīciōnem procōrum in
casā tuā tōtum diem manēbō; tū, Eumaee, ī ad tēctum meum
et dīc mātrī meae mē tūtum rediisse."

Eumaeus haec omnia fēcit. Interim Athēna iterum vestem 20
et faciem Ulīxis mūtāvit.

Tēlemachus quidem clāmāvit ubi hominem tam mūtātum
vīdit, "Tū es deus! Tū nōs juvāre potes! Nōlī nōs
relinquere!"

Ulīxēs fīliō suō respondit, "Nōlī timēre! Nōn deus sum; 25
sum pater tuus, quī post multōs cāsūs rediī. Tempus est
breve; necesse est nōs procōs interficere et mātrem tuam
līberāre. Tū, Tēlemache, ad rēgiam redī; explōrā omnia; es
fortis!

"Paucīs hōrīs ego mendīcus ad tēctum veniam. Tum tibi 30
signum dabō. Hōc signō vīsō, ī sēcrētō et portā omnia arma
ex ātriō. Relinque autem prope portam duo scūta valida,
duās hastās, duōs gladiōs; hīs armīs impetum mēcum facere
poteris; hodiē procōs occīdāmus!"

19

RECOGNITION OF ULYSSES

Ulīxēs veste iterum mūtātā, mendīcus, ad rēgiam vēnit.
Jussū patris Tēlemachus arma parāverat. Ulīxēs ipse in
ātriō cum servīs mānsit, sciēns Pēnelopam brevī tempore
adfutūram esse.

Pēnelopē, ubi in ātrium intrāvit, omnēs servōs servāsque 5
dīmīsit praeter nūtrīcem longaevam, cui dīxit, "Cāra nūtrīx,
cum omnēs servī discesserint, dūc ad mē mendīcum. Certē
iter fēcit in regiōnibus ubi conjūnx meus errābat."

Jussū nūtrīcis Ulīxēs ad rēgīnam appropinquāvit. Pēnelopē
sine suspīciōne eī dīxit, "Noctū et interdiū doleō quod 10
Ulīxēs, conjūnx amātus meus, ā terrā Trōjānā nōn rediit.
Certē in longinquīs terrīs errāvistī. Vīdistīne eum?"

Ulīxēs Pēnelopae respondit, "Ōlim in Crētā virum quī ā

comitibus Ulīxēs appellābātur vīdī. Vestem purpuream cum fībulā aureā gerēbat. In hāc fībulā erant figūrae canis et 15 cervī parvī."

Pēnelopē lacrimāns dīxit, "Certē conjugem meum ipsum vīdistī. Illam vestem et illam fībulam Ulīxī ipsa dedī."

Ulīxēs respondit, "Sciō Ulīxem hōc annō ad patriam reventūrum esse." 20

Pēnelopē, magnō gaudiō mōta, jussit nūtrīcem pedēs mendīcī lavāre. Nūtrīx fīda, ubi pedēs Ulīxis lavāre incēpit, lātam cicātrīcem recognōvit.

Magnopere excitāta, parvā vōce eī dīxit, "Rediistī, Ulīxēs."

Ulīxēs quidem celeriter respondit, "Ita; ego sum Ulīxēs. 25 Nōlī autem appellāre mē nōmine meō."

Pēnelopē, quae haec verba nōn audīverat, dīxit, "Crās procī mē conjugem novum dēligere cōgent. Crās arcum Ulīxis in ātrium portārī jubēbō. Ille quī arcum tendere potuerit mē in mātrimōnium dūcet." 30

20

RESCUE OF PENELOPE

Postrīdiē eīdem procī ad magnum ātrium properāvērunt. Quisque quidem crēdidit Pēnelopam sē conjugem dēlēctūram esse. Ulīxēs quoque, eandem vestem mendīcī gerēns, aderat.

Tum procī dīxērunt, "Multōs annōs, Tēlemache, patrem tuum expectās; propter amōrem patris honōrem tibi rēctē 5 dedimus, mātremque tuam invītam nūbere nōn coēgimus. Jam autem scīmus prō certō Ulīxem numquam reventūrum esse."

Interim Pēnelopē arcum Ulīxis et sagittās, arma gravia, in magnum ātrium portāvit. 10

Tum procīs dīxit, "Audīte mē, procī nōbilēs. Nūntiāvistis ūnum ē numerō vestrō conjugem meum futūrum esse. Hic est īdem arcus, hae eaedem sagittae quae Ulīxēs ōlim portābat. Ille quī hunc arcum tetenderit mē in mātrimōnium dūcet."

Quamquam omnēs procī temptāvērunt, nēmō arcum tendere poterat. 15

Subitō mendīcus dīxit, "Dā mihi arcum!"

Sine difficultāte arcum tetendit. Deinde magnā vōce clāmāvit, "Multa mīlia passuum nāvigāvī; jam ego Ulīxēs ipse adsum!" 20

Hīs verbīs audītīs, Tēlemachus arma cēpit et patrī auxilium dedit; eōdem tempore servī fīdī et cīvēs, quī sēcrētō arcessītī erant, in ātrium intrāvērunt ācriterque pugnāre incēpērunt. Pēnelopē fidēlis, omnibus procīs interfectīs, conjugī magnō gaudiō salūtem dedit. 25

21

REVELATION TO ULYSSES

Ulīxēs paucōs annōs in Ithacā cum uxōre fīliōque mānsit. Ōlim per somnia verba sacerdōtis iterum audīvit.

"Necesse erit tē relinquere uxōrem et fīlium, domum et amīcōs, et in longinquam terram iter facere. Quamquam ad Ithacam tūtus reveniēs, tamen per annōs longōs in illā terrā 5 longinquā habitābis.

"Cum in hanc terram perveniēs, relinque in lītore nāvem tuam; portā in umerō tuō rēmum longum; prōcēde in interiōrem partem terrae. Hīc virōs inveniēs quī nūllam scientiam maris habent, quī neque nāvēs neque nautās vīdērunt. 10

"Longō rēmō vīsō, incolae cōnfūsī rogābunt, 'Quae est rēs nova quam in umerō habēs? Estne arātrum? Estne hasta? Estne clāva nova?'

"Hīs verbīs audītīs, rēmum in terram fīgēs, et in illō locō templum aedificābis. Templō aedificātō, incolae tibi dīcent, 15 'Manē nōbīscum; dī ad nōs tē dūxērunt; signum in caelō vīdimus; verba ōrāculī audīvimus.'

"Diū in illā terrā manēbis et incolās multās artēs docēbis, sed eīs fābulās marium nāviumque nōn nārrābis. Nōn semper autem in hāc terrā longinquā habitābis. Multōs post annōs 20 dī tē, jam senem, in Ithacam iterum vocābunt.

"Fīliō Tēlemachō et līberīs Tēlemachī vīsīs, dī tibi mortem quiētam in marī dabunt. Post mortem ad īnsulās beātās portāberis, ubi pācem aeternam habēbis."

I Change active verbs to passive and make other changes necessary to construct a sensible sentence. Translate.

1 Dea Athēna vestēs et faciem ejus mūtāverat.
2 Magnā cum difficultāte Eumaeus canēs lapidibus reppulit.
3 Ulīxēs casam Eumaeī petit.

I I Change passive verbs to active and make other changes necessary to construct a sensible sentence. Translate.

1 Decem annōs ā deīs in multīs terrīs errāre coāctus erat.
2 Decem annōs bellum circum mūrōs ā Trōjānīs gerēbātur.
3 Ab amīcīs in casam ductus est ubi eī vīnum datum est.

I I I Change each direct quotation into indirect statement, and each indirect statement into a direct quotation.

1 Ulīxēs dīxit, "Nūllam pecūniam habeō."
2 Eumaeus dīxit, "Tēlemachus Ithacam relīquit."
3 Dīximus Ulīxem reventūrum esse.
4 Ulīxēs nārrāvit, "Decem annōs circum mūrōs Trōjae pugnāvī."
5 Eumaeus dīxit Ulīxem ab uxōre expectārī.
6 Servus nūntiat, "Urbs vestra tempestāte vāstāta est."

I V Change each statement to a command.

1 Impetum facitis.
2 Ad mare īs.
3 Nōs ad imperātōrem dūcis.
4 Urbem expugnātis.
5 Clauditis fenestrās.
6 Dēlētis urbēs.

V Translate the words underlined, using an ablative absolute each time.

1 <u>With Ulysses as leader</u> the Greeks arrived home safely.
2 <u>After Troy had been captured</u>, many Greeks departed.
3 <u>When the cloak has been made</u>, one of the suitors will marry Penelope.

V I Give the best possible translation for each ablative absolute.

1 Sacrificiō factō, Graecī ventōs secundōs expectāvērunt.
2 Mente mūtātā, puella domī nōn mānsit.
3 Ūndecim labōribus perfectīs, Herculēs fortiter ultimum suscēpit.

VII Supply the correct participle for each blank.

1 Avēs _____ nōs semper dēlectant. (singing)
2 Puerī dē perīculō _____ dīligentius prōcessērunt. (warned)
3 Quī _____ vīvit, līber numquam erit. (fearing)
4 Omnēs cēnam ā mātre _____ laudant. (prepared)
5 Leō Androclem _____ nōn vulnerāvit. (recognizing)
6 Mīles _____ in castra revēnit. (wounded)

VIII Substitute a participle or participial phrase for the part of the sentence underlined, and make other necessary changes. Translate.

1 Castra in lītore posuērunt et statim nūntiōs ad rēgiam mīsērunt.
2 Mīles quī amīcitiam petēbat rēgīnae dōna pretiōsa dedit.
3 Advenam nōn expectāmus, quod ōmina incerta erant.
4 Rēx, quamquam ā deīs monitus erat, tamen mentem nōn mūtāvit.
5 Sī tempestās classem ad vada pellit, nāvēs maximō in perīculō sunt.

IX Use a form of **volō/nōlō** to replace each word or phrase underlined. Translate.

1 Agricolae avēs īngentēs ex agrīs expellere temptābant.
2 Advenās prope portās dux dēprehendere nōn cupit.
3 Ad arcem in colle sēcrētō appropinquāre nōn temptābō.
4 Signum proeliī tubīs dare cōnstituerāmus.

X Change from indirect statement to direct quotation, making all necessary changes. Translate.

1 Mīlitēs nūntiant, sacrificiō datō, deōs ventōs secundōs missūrōs esse.
2 Māter puellae dīxit rēgem suam fīliam sacrificāre numquam voluisse.

XI Change from direct quotation to indirect statement, making all necessary changes. Translate.

1 Pater servō fīdō dīcit, "Fīlia mea servārī nōn potest."
2 Puella prōmīsit, "Brevī tempore exercitūs Graecī ex portū nāvigābunt."
3 Servus scrībet, "Dominus meus tōtam noctem doluit."

XII Change active verbs to passive and vice versa. Make other necessary changes. Translate.

1 Nūntius māne ā mīlite ipsō excitābitur.
2 Mātrēs fīliōs monent.
3 Saxa ā puerīs jaciēbantur.
4 Cīvēs ducem sapientem dēligunt.
5 Pīrātī captīvōs diū tenēbant.

XIII Choose the most appropriate meaning of the verb in each expression, and translate the whole phrase.

1 negōtia gerere	(a) carry
2 galeam gerere	(b) wage
3 bellum gerere	(c) behave
4 sē gerere	(d) wear
5 gerere scūtum	(e) conduct

XIV In each pair of phrases, the same verb has two different meanings. Bring out this difference in translating each expression.

1 nautās accipere
  dōna accipere
2 grātiās agere
  equōs agere
3 sagittam āmittere
  calceum āmittere
4 pecūniam recipere
  sē recipere
5 in mātrimōnium dūcere
  aquam dūcere
6 memoriā tenēre
  hastam tenēre

XV Choose the correct verb form to complete each sentence.

1 Virum hanc epistulam scrīptam/scrībere/scrībentem vīdimus.
2 Incolae arma nova gerēns/gerentem/gerentēs in vincula conjiciuntur.
3 Fīlia Agamemnonis ad āram prōcēdite/prōcēdit/prōcēdere.
4 Omnia tēcta urbis nostrae dēlērī/dēlēns/dēlēre nunc sentīs.
5 Mīlitibus revenientēs/revenientem/revenientibus praemia victōriae prōmissa sunt.

XVI Supply a suitable pronoun or adjective for each sentence.

1 _____ scelera dux ferōx in animō habet?
2 Frūmentum nōn erat bonum _____ nāvēs portāverant.
3 Ōmina adversa erunt avēs _____ circum umerōs ejus volābunt.
4 _____ dē causā incolae vīcī ā rēge auxilia postulāvērunt.
5 Hic puer est Pūblius _____ avunculus in Galliam iit.

USEFUL   LATIN   (An index of miscellaneous material in this book)

Latin Lives Today	12	Derivatives of **alta, antīqua, magna**
LLT/Sing It in Latin	15	Derivatives of **longa, lāta/**"America"
LLT/What's in a Name?	23	Derivatives of **prīma/** Geographical names
Latin Lives Today	25	Words related to **cōpia**
Latin Lives Today	28	Words related to **initiō, nōminant, via,** etc.
Latin Lives Today	38	Derivatives of **alba, maritima, pulchra, arida**
Latin Lives Today	42	Derivatives of **beāta, fābula, schola,** etc.
Latin Lives Today	45	Derivatives of **flamma, nauta, amīca, benigna**
Latin Lives Today	50	Derivatives of **portō, lūna, unda, stella,** etc.
A Roman Banquét	60	Menu (three courses)
Say It in Latin	61	Remarks suitable for table conversation
Latin Lives Today	68	Derivatives of **maneō, sedeō, stō,** etc.
Motto	71	**Labōrāre est ōrāre** (Benedictine Monks)
Latin Lives Today	80	English words related to **sōla**
Latin Lives Today	85	Derivatives of **gladius, focus, ager, deus,** etc.
Latin Lives Today	91	Derivatives of **caelum, verbum**
Useful Latin	100	Medical Latin used in prescriptions
The Planets	101	Their mythological names (with one exception)
Latin Lives Today	104	Derivatives of **pecūnia, rīpa, annus,** etc.
Latin Lives Today	111	Derivatives of **Vulcānus/Volcānus**
Useful Latin	120	Latin verbs borrowed as English nouns
Trade Names	122	Products with names of Latin origin
Useful Latin Expressions	133	Four idiomatic Latin phrases
Some Interesting Perfects	172	**Vēnī, vīdī, vīcī!** (Caesar), etc.
Say It in Latin	182	Latin expressions for classroom conversation
Useful Latin Phrases	187	Fifteen Latin phrases used in modern writing
Latin Lives Today	195	Names of months and their Latin origins
Useful Latin	201	Common abbreviations of Latin words
Useful Latin	211	Phrases, proverbs, and sayings often quoted
Motto	216	**In hōc signō vincēs** (Emperor Constantine)
Salute to the Flag	225	**Fidēs Obligāta** (Pledge of Allegiance)
Latin Lives Today	227	Derivatives of **spēlunca, fūmus, lateō, currō,** etc.
Useful Latin	271	Mottoes and idioms containing comparative adjectives
Motto	279	**Citius, Altius, Fortius** (Olympic Games)
Changing Times	280	Examples of illogical changes in meanings of words
Latin Lives Today	340	Derivatives of **dēserō, īnstruō, intrōdūcō, trahō**
The Beatitudes in Latin	355	Matthew V:3-12 (See English New Testament)
Mottoes	357	Four favorite Latin sayings
Say It in Latin	384	Three expressions pertaining to the stage

394

THE ROMAN CALENDAR had three points in each month from which the days were counted backward in giving dates.

Kalendae (the Kalends) were the first of each month.

Īdūs (the Ides) were the thirteenth or the fifteenth.

Nōnae (the Nones) were nine days before the Ides. (We would say eight days, whereas the Romans counted both the first and the last days of a series.)

In March, May, July, and October the Ides were the fifteenth; in all other months, the thirteenth. Thus, the Nones of March, May, July, and October were the seventh; of all other months, the fifth.

The day before each date-point was given as **prīdiē**.

December 31 = **pr. Kal. Jān. (prīdiē Kalendās Jānuāriās)**

March 6 = **pr. Nōn. Mār. (prīdiē Nōnās Mārtiās)**

April 12 = **pr. Īd.   Apr. (prīdiē Īdūs Aprīlēs)**

In other dates a Roman numeral shows the number of days before each date-point. Why does the Roman numeral II never appear in a date? (Remember the Roman method of counting both ends of a series.)

Latin words used to designate the months are adjectives. In the form given here they modify **mēnsis** (often omitted); e.g., **(mēnsis) Aprīlis; (mēnsis) Jūnius.**

Jānuārius	**Aprīlis**	**Jūlius** [1]	**Octōber**
Februārius	**Māius**	**Augustus** [1]	**November**
Mārtius	**Jūnius**	**September**	**December**

These adjectives may also modify a date-point.

K. Apr. or **Kal. Apr. (Kalendae Aprīlēs)** = April 1

pr. Kal. Apr. (prīdiē Kalendās Aprīlēs) = March 31

a. d. III Kal. Apr. (ante diem tertium Kalendās Aprīlēs) = ?

Īd. Mār. (Īdibus Mārtiīs) = on March 15 (on the Ides of March)

pr. Īd. Mār. (prīdiē Īdūs Mārtiās) = ?

a. d. VIII Kal. Jān. = December 25; **a. d. IV Nōn. Jūl.** = ?

Say in Latin: March 1, 5, 6, 7; January 1, 10, 13.

---

[1]Earlier names were **Quīntīlis** for **Jūlius** and **Sextīlis** for **Augustus.**

LATIN FOR FUN

"I'm in a hurry to get home so I'll go with Ulysses."

Through History with J. Wesley Smith

"Maybe this'll teach you to watch how you change traffic lanes on the Appian Way."

Through History with J. Wesley Smith

"I said, it's stuffy in here."

"Don't take chances—call the humane society people."

"X, IX, VIII, VII, VI, V, IV, III . . ."

PRONUNCIATION OF LATIN is determined by the sounds of the letters (vowels, diphthongs, consonants) and by the number and length of syllables in a word.

SOUNDS OF VOWELS AND DIPHTHONGS

Long Vowels	Short Vowels	Diphthongs
ā (father)	a (aha)	ae (like)
ē (they)	e (met)	au (round)
ī (meet)	i (pin)	eu (ĕ+oo)
ō (lone)	o (obey)	oe (boil)
ū (cool)	u (full)	ui (ruin)

CONSONANTS are in general the same as in English. Note, however, these sounds of letters and groups of letters.

g is hard (good)	c = k (cook)	bs = ps (cups)
s is soft (say)	i = y (yes)	bt = pt (kept)
ngu (language)	qu = kw (quick)	ch = k (look)
p (spin)	x = ks (extra)	ph = p (put)
t (stop)	v = w (wet)	th = t (ten)

SYLLABLES A Latin word has as many syllables as it contains vowels or diphthongs. A syllable is long if it contains a long vowel or a diphthong or if it ends in a consonant; otherwise it is short: **mo ne ō, au di ē tis, vi a, pic tū rae.**

WORD DIVISION If there are not more than two consonants between vowels, one goes with the vowel that follows: **la cū na, por tō, al tus, ve ni ō.**

If there are more than two consonants, the division is usually made after the first consonant: **ob scū rus, tem plum, mōn strum, pul chra.** Exception: **temp tō**

Compound words are separated into their elements: **ex it, ab est, in e ō, post e ā.**

When x occurs between two vowels, it goes with the first: **max i mum, dīx it, dūx i mus.**

ACCENT falls on the first syllable of a two-syllable word. In a longer word the accent falls on the next to last syllable if it is long. If that syllable is short, the one immediately preceding it is stressed: **al'tus, an ti'qua, a gri'co la.**

GENERAL VOCABULARY

This word list is a combined Latin-English and English-Latin vocabulary, including proper names and their definitions. Starred words have been taught through their likeness to other Latin words (e.g., **absum**) or to English words (e.g., **accūsō**). Double-starred words are identical in Latin and English (e.g., **color**). Words marked with symbol (°) appear only in special vocabularies or in optional readings. Entries marked thus are not among the 848 words of this list that are considered basic. A number at the end of an entry refers to the page where the Latin word is given in a lesson vocabulary, paradigm, or grammatical explanation, or where a pertinent treatment of derivation or word formation occurs.

A

ā, ab (with abl.), from, away from 26; by 303

able (be), **possum, posse, potuī**

about, **dē** (with abl.)

*__absum, -esse, āfuī, āfutūrus,__ be absent 177

°**accendō, -ere, -cendī, -cēnsum,** light, set fire to

*__accipiō, -ere, -cēpī, -ceptum,__ take, receive 147

*__accūsō, -āre, -āvī, -ātum,__ accuse, blame 64

ācer, ācris, ācre, sharp, fierce 263

acerbus, -a, -um, harsh, biting 368

acervus, -ī, M., heap, pile 287

*__Achāia, -ae,__ F., Achae'a, Roman province of Greece

**__Achillēs, -is,__ M., Achil'les, Greek hero in the Trojan War

ācriter (adv.), fiercely 241

across, **trāns** (with acc.)

*__acūtus, -a, -um,__ sharp, pointed 348

ad (with acc.), to, toward, 26; near, at 65

addūcō, -ere, -dūxī, -ductum, lead, bring to; influence 277

adhūc (adv.), till now 315

**__Admētus, -ī,__ M., Adme'tus, ruler in Thes'saly

*__adōrnātus, -a, -um,__ decorated 109

*__adōrnō, -āre, -āvī, -ātum,__ adorn 64

*__adōrō, -āre, -āvī, -ātum,__ worship 64

adsum, -esse, -fuī, -futūrus, be present 177

advena, -ae, M./F., stranger 353

Advena (see 167), foreigner

*__adventus, -ūs,__ M., arrival, advent

*__adversus, -a, -um,__ unfavorable 8, 92

**__Aeacus, -ī,__ M., Ae'acus, legendary king, grandfather of Achil'les

*__aedifīcium, -ī,__ N., building 142

aedificō, -āre, -āvī, -ātum, build, construct 109

aeger, -gra, -grum, sick, ill 147

*__Aegyptus, -ī,__ F., E'gypt

**__Aenēās, -ae,__ M., Aene'as, Trojan leader, hero of Aene'id

**__Aeolia, -ae,__ F., Aeo'lia, small island off the coast of Sic'ily

**__Aeolus, -ī,__ M., Ae'olus, ruler of the Aeo'lian Islands and of the winds

**__Aesculāpius, -ī,__ M., Aescula'pius, god of medicine

aestāte, in summer 55

aetās, -ātis, F., age 315

*aeternus, -a, -um, everlasting

**Aetna, -ae, F., Et′na (or Aet′na), volcano in Sic′ily

*afflīciō, -ere, -fēcī, -fectum, influence, afflict, affect 373

**Āfrica, -ae, F., Af′rica

afterwards, **posteā** (adv.)

**Agamemnōn, -onis, M., Ag′amem′non, Greek leader in Tro′jan War

ager, agrī, M., field 83

*agitō, -āre, -āvī, -ātum, drive, disturb, agitate 64; hunt (animals) 327

agmen, -inis, N., marching army, marching column 277

agō, -ere, ēgī, āctum, drive, act, do 189; **grātiās agere,** give thanks 185; **vītam agere,** live 241; (with adv.) treat 299

agricola, -ae, M., farmer 43

*agricultūra, -ae, F., agriculture 8

āla, -ae, F., wing 135

ālātus, -a, -um, winged 185

*Albānus, -a, -um, Al′ban

*Albis, -is, M., the Elbe (river)

albus, -a, -um, white 35

Alcestis, -is, F., Alces′tis, wife of Adme′tus; **Alcestī (dat.)

aliquandō (adv.), at some time 139

aliter (adv.), otherwise 142

alius, -a, -ud, other, another 139; **aliī . . . aliī,** some . . . others 339

*Alpēs, -ium, F., the Alps

also, **quoque** (adv.)

altar, **āra, -ae,** F.

alter, -a, -um, other, the other 251; **alter . . . alter,** one . . . the other

altus, -a, -um, high, tall, deep 10

always **semper** (adv.)

**Amāta, -ae, F., Ama′ta, queen of La′tium

*ambulō, -āre, -āvī, -ātum, walk 49

*amīcitia, -ae, F., friendship 197

*amīcus, -ī, M., friend 83

*amīcus, -a, -um, friendly 43

amita, -ae, F., aunt 35

āmittō, -ere, -mīsī, -missum, lose, let go 174

amō, -āre, -āvī, -ātum, love 49

amoenus, -a, -um, pleasant 189

*amor, -ōris, M., love 327

**Anchīsēs, -ae, M., Anchi′ses, father of Aene′as

ancient times (in), **antīquitus** (adv.)

°ancilla, -ae, F., maid

*ancora, -ae, F., anchor 344

**Ancus, -ī, M., An′cus (Mar′cius), fourth king of Rome

and, **et** (conj.); **-que; and so, itaque**

**Androclēs, -is, M., An′drocles, name of a Roman slave

**Andromeda, -ae, F., Androm′eda, an E′thio′pian princess

*angelus, -ī, M., angel 92

angustus, -a, -um, narrow 35

anicula, -ae, F., little old woman 303

**animal, -ālis (-ium), N., animal 8, 238

animus, -ī, M., mind; **in animō habēre,** intend, have in mind 131

*annus, -ī, M., year 103

*ante (with acc.), in front of, before 161

*antīquitus (adv.), in ancient times 43

*antīquus, -a, -um, old 10

*ānxius, -a, -um, anxious, uneasy

°aper, aprī, M., wild boar

aperiō, -īre, -uī, apertum, open 135

apertus, -a, -um, open 89

*apis, -is (-ium), F., bee 353

**Apollō, Apollinis, M., Apol'lo, god
of the sun

*appāreō, -ēre, -uī, -itum, appear 113

appellō, -āre, -āvī, -ātum, name 115

**Appius Claudius, Appiī Claudiī,
M., Ap'pius Clau'dius, Roman patriot

appropinquō, -āre, -āvī, -ātum,
approach 215

apud (with acc.), at, with 139

aqua, -ae, F., water 13

*Aqua, -ae, F., aqueduct, conduit;
Aq'ua Ap'pia, aqueduct constructed by Ap'pius Clau'dius

*aquaeductus, -ūs, M., aqueduct

*aquila, -ae, F., eagle 287

āra, -ae, F., altar 39

**Arabia, -ae, F., Ara'bia

**Arachnē, -ēs, F., Arach'ne, a girl
skilled in weaving

°arātrum, -ī, N., plough

*arbor, -oris, F., tree 242, 277

arca, -ae, F., box, chest 155

**Arcadia, -ae, F., Arca'dia, a district
in Greece

°arcessō, -ere, -īvī, -itum, summon

°arcus, -ūs, M., bow, arch

*ārdeō, -ēre, ārsī, glow, burn 142

are (they), **sunt**

**arēna, -ae, F., sand; arena 8

**Argō, -ūs, F., the Ar'go, Ja'son's ship

*Argonautae, -ārum, M., the Ar'go-
nauts, the crew of Ja'son's ship

**Argus, -ī, M., Ar'gus, builder of
Ja'son's ship

*Ariadna, -ae, F., Ariad'ne, a Cre'tan
princess

*āridus, -a, -um, dry, arid 8, 92

ariēs, -etis, M., ram 299

*arma, -ōrum, N. pl., weapons 98

*armātus, -a, -um, armed 221

arō, -āre, -āvī, -ātum, plow 311

around, **circum** (with acc.)

arrive, **perveniō (IV)**

*ars, artis (-ium), F., art, skill

arx, arcis, (-ium), F., citadel, fortress
234, 339

**Ascanius, -ī, M., Asca'nius, son of
Aene'as

*ascendō, -ere, -scendī, -scēnsum,
climb, ascend 64

ask, **rogō (I);** ask for, **ōrō (I)**

at (conj.), but; yet 315

at, **ad** (with acc.); **apud** (with acc.)

āter, -tra, -trum, black 161

**Athēna, -ae, F., Athe'na, goddess of
wisdom and of war

*Athēnae, -ārum, F. pl., Ath'ens

*Athēniēnsis, -e, Athe'nian, of Athens

**Atlās, -antis, M., At'las, giant who
held the heavens on his shoulders

atque (conj.), and, and also 89

**ātrium, -ī, N., hall, main room 109

attack, **oppugnō (I); impetus, -ūs,** M.

attonitus, -a, -um, stunned 303

*audācia, -ae, F., boldness 197

*audācter (adv.), boldly 303

*audāx, gen., **-ācis,** daring, bold

audeō, -ēre (irreg. perf.), dare 335

*audiō, -īre, -īvī, -ītum, hear, listen 89

*augeō, -ēre, auxī, auctum, increase,
grow 233

**Aulis, -idis, F., Au'lis, a Greek port

aunt, **amita, -ae,** F.; **mātertera,**
-ae, F. (See p. 246.)

aureus, -a, -um, golden, of gold 95

aurum, -ī, N., gold 155

aut (conj.), or; **aut . . . aut,** either . . .
or 118

autem (adv.), however, but; moreover
69

401

*auxilium, -ī, N., help, aid 131; pl., auxiliary troops, reinforcements 263
*avidē (adv.), eagerly, avidly 185
*avis, -is (-ium), F., bird 287
avunculus, -ī, M., uncle 221

B

*Babylōnicus, -a, -um, Babylo'nian
bāca, -ae, F., berry, small fruit 115
bad, **malus, -a, -um**
*barbarus, -a, -um, barbarian 217
be, **sum, esse, fuī, futūrus**
be able, **possum, posse, potuī**
beast, **bēstia, -ae,** F.
beātus, -a, -um, happy 39
bellum, -ī, N., war 103; **bellum gerere,** wage war 237
bene (adv.), well 109
beneficium, -ī, N., good deed 193
*benignē (adv.), kindly 189
*benignitās, -ātis, F., kindness 351
*benignus, -a, -um, kind 43
best, **optimus, -a, -um**
*bēstia, -ae, F., wild beast 33
*bibō, -ere, bibī, bibitum, drink 155
bonus, -a, -um, good 21
*bōs, bovis, M., ox; F., cow 333
boy, **puer, puerī,** M.
bracchium, -ī, N., arm 95
*brevis, -e, short 263
*breviter (adv.), briefly 278
bridge, **pōns, pontis (-ium),** M.
**Briganta, -ae, F., Brigan'ta, a name
bright, **clārus, -a, -um**
*Britan'nia, -ae, F., Brit'ain
*Britan'nus, -ī, M., Brit'on
build, **aedificō (I)**
building, **aedificium, -ī,** N.
but (conj.), **sed; autem** (never first)
by (pers. agent), **ā/ab** (with abl.)

C

cadō, -ere, cecidī, cāsūrus, fall (down) 174
**cādūceus, -ī, M., wand, staff 98
caecus, -a, -um, blind 221
caedēs, -is (-ium), F., slaughter 368
caelum, -ī, N., sky, heaven 89
**Caesar Augustus, Caesaris Augustī, M., title of Roman emperor
*calamitās, -ātis, F., disaster 351
calceus, -ī, M., shoe 303
**Calchās, -antis, M., Cal'chas, soothsayer to the Greeks before Troy
calidus, -a, -um, warm, hot 118
call, **nōminō (I); vocō (I)**
**Callistō, -ūs, F., Callis'to, Arca'dian princess changed to a bear
**Camillus, -ī, M., Camil'lus, Roman leader in the capture of Ve'ii
*Campī Ēlysiī, M. pl., Ely'sian Fields, place where heroes and virtuous people lived after death
*campus, -ī, M., field 177
can, **possum, posse, potuī**
*canis, -is, M./F., dog 242
*cantō, -āre, -āvī, -ātum, sing, play (an instrument) 293
capiō, -ere, cēpī, captum, take, seize 131
*Capitōlium, -ī, N., the Cap'itol, temple of Ju'piter in Rome; the Cap'itoline (one of Rome's seven hills)
*captīvus, -ī, M., prisoner, captive 92
capture, **capiō (III); dēprehendō (III)**
**Capua, -ae, F., Cap'ua, city in Italy
*caput, -itis, N., head 237
carry, **portō (I); gerō (III)**
*Carthāgō, -inis, F., Car'thage, a city in North Africa

cārus, -a, -um, dear, beloved 51

casa, -ae, F., cottage, small house 13

*****Cassiopēa, -ae,** F., Cas'siope'ia, queen of E'thio'pia

*****castellum, -ī,** N., castle, fortress 92

castra, -ōrum, N. pl., camp 221; **castra pōnere,** set up camp 255

*****cāsus, -ūs,** M., happening, fall 92

°**catēna, -ae,** F., chain

cauda, -ae, F., tail 305

*****causa, -ae,** F., cause 8

cavalry, **equitēs, -um,** M. pl.

caveō, -ēre, cāvī, cautum, beware (of) 303

*****caverna, -ae,** F., cave, cavern 8

cecidī (See **cadō.**)

*****celeritās, -ātis,** F., swiftness 305

*****celeriter** (adv.), quickly, fast 69

*****cēlō, -āre, -āvī, -ātum,** conceal 49

*****Celticus, -a, -um,** Cel'tic

cēna, -ae, F., dinner, meal 155

*****Centaurus, -ī,** M., Cen'taur, legendary creature, part man, part horse

*****centum** (indecl.), a hundred 92

*****centūriō, -ōnis,** M., centurion 253

cēpit, he (she, it) seized, took 118

******Cerberus, -ī,** M., Cer'berus, three-headed dog of the lower world

******Cerēs, -eris,** F., Ce'res, goddess of agriculture

certāmen, -inis, N., contest 311

*****certē** (adv.), surely, certainly 193

*****certus, -a, -um,** sure, certain

°**cerva, -ae,** F., doe

cervus, -ī, M., stag, deer 255

cēterī, -ae, -a, other, remaining; (as noun), the others 197

change, **mūtō (I)**

******Charōn, -ontis,** M., Cha'ron, ferryman in the lower world

******Chīrōn, -ōnis,** M., Chi'ron, a Centaur

*****chorda, -ae,** F., string 8

cibus, -ī, M., food 155

******cicātrīx, -īcis,** F., scar, cicatrix

******Circē, -ēs,** F., Cir'ce, an enchantress

*****circum** (with acc.), around 39

*****circumspectō, -āre, -āvī, -ātum,** look around 197

*****cisterna, -ae,** F., cistern, reservoir 8

citadel, **arx, arcis (-ium),** F.

citizen, **cīvis, -is (-ium),** M./F.

city, **urbs, urbis (-ium),** F.

*****cīvis, -is (-ium),** M./F., citizen 242, 249

clāmō, -āre, -āvī, -ātum, shout 51

******clāmor, -ōris,** M., loud cry, shout 8

clārus, -a, -um, bright, clear 49

*****classis, -is (-ium),** F., fleet; class 351

*****claudō, -ere, clausī, clausum,** shut, close 289

clāva, -ae, F., club, stick 118

clear, **clārus, -a, -um**

cloak, **palla, -ae,** F.

club, **clāva, -ae,** F.

******Clytemnestra, -ae,** F., Cly'tem nes'-tra, wife of Ag'amem'non

cognōscō, -ere, cognōvī, cognitum, come to know, recognize 147

cōgō, -ere, coēgī, coāctum, compel, force 249

******Colchis, -idis,** F., Col'chis, country on the eastern shore of the Black Sea

colligō, -ere, -lēgī, -lēctum, bring together, collect 147

collis, -is (-ium), M., hill, height 365

*****colloquium, -ī,** N., conversation 197

colō, -ere, -uī, cultum, cultivate 265

*****colōnia, -ae,** F., estate; colony 30

******color, -ōris,** M., color 8

columba, -ae, F., dove 161

coma, -ae, F., hair 95

come, veniō (IV)

comes, -itis, M./F., companion 277

*committō, -ere, -mīsī, -missum, commit, entrust; **proelium committere,** begin battle 233

concerning, dē (with abl.)

*concilium, -ī, N., council 103

*concurrō, -ere, -currī, -cursum, run together, dash together 305

*condiciō, -ōnis, F., condition 293

*condūcō, -ere, -dūxī, -ductum, escort, lead, conduct 123

*cōnficiō, -ere, -fēcī, -fectum, accomplish, finish; consume; weaken 315

*cōnfirmō, -āre, -āvī, -ātum, strengthen, assure, confirm 356

*cōnflīgō, -ere, -flixī, -flictum, strike together, bring together 305

*cōnfūsus, -a, -um, bewildered

°conjiciō, -ere, -jēcī, -jectum, throw

*conjungō, -ere, -jūnxī, -jūnctum, join together 368

*conjūnx, -jugis, M./F., husband, wife; spouse 289

conquer, vincō (III)

cōnscendō, -ere, -scendī, -scēnsum, embark, go aboard ship 315

*cōnsilium, -ī, N., plan; **cōnsilium capere,** form a plan 118

*cōnspectus, -ūs, M., sight, view 368

cōnspiciō, -ere, -spexī, -spectum, catch sight of, look at 161

cōnstituō, -ere, -stituī, -stitūtum, decide 185

*cōnstruō, -ere, -strūxī, -strūctum, build, construct 251

**cōnsul, cōnsulis, M., consul 8

*cōnsūmō, -ere, -sūmpsī, -sūmptum, consume, destroy; spend 64

*contāctus, -ūs, M., touch, contact

*contendō, -ere, -tendī, -tentum, hurry; insist, contend 303

*contrā (with acc.), against 348

*contrōversia, -ae, F., dispute 30

*conveniō, -īre, -vēnī, -ventum, come together, convene 123

*convocō, -āre, -āvī, -ātum, summon, call together 109

*cōpia, -ae, F., supply, abundance 24; pl., troops, forces 233

cornū, -ūs, N., horn; wing of an army, flank 368

*corōna, -ae, F., crown 95

*corpus, -oris, N., body 237

cotīdiē (adv.), daily 289

cottage, casa, -ae, F.

*crās (adv.), tomorrow 215

**creātor, -ōris, M., maker 8, 241

*crēdō, -ere, -didī, -ditum, trust in, believe 329

*creō, -āre, -āvī, -ātum, create 64

*Crēta, -ae, F., Crete, an island

crista, -ae, F., crest of a bird 177

*crūdēlis, -e, cruel 287

*crūdēlitās, -ātis, F., cruelty

*crūdēliter (adv.), cruelly 299

cucurrī (See **currō.)**

°culpō, -āre, -āvī, -ātum, blame

cum (prep. with abl.), with 35; (conj.), when 49

**Cūmae, -ārum, F. pl., Cu'mae, city on the coast of Campa'nia

*Cupīdō, -inis, M., Cu'pid, god of love

cupidus, -a, -um, desirous (of), eager (for) 249

cupiō, -ere, -īvī, -ītum, desire, wish (for) 131

cūr (adv.), why 49

cūra, -ae, F., care, anxiety 109

*cūriōsus, -a, -um, curious 92, 280

*cūrō, -āre, -āvī, -ātum, care for, care, take care of; cure 118

*currō, -ere, cucurrī, cursum, run, hasten 223

°currus, -ūs, M., chariot, car

*custōdiō, -īre, -īvī, -ītum, guard, watch 142

*custōs, -ōdis, M., guard, watchman 251

D

**Daedalus, -ī, M., Daed'alus, character of Greek legend

**Daniēl, -is; Daniēlī (dat.), M., Dan'iel, biblical character

*Dānuvius, -ī, M., the Dan'ube (river)

**Daphnē, -ēs, F., Daph'ne, woodland nymph

dark, obscūrus, -a, -um

dat, (he, she) gives 39

daughter, filia, -ae, F. (dat./abl. pl. end in -ābus)

day (by), interdiū (adv.)

daytime (in the), interdiū (adv.)

dē (with abl.), about, concerning 35; down from, away from 76

dea, -ae, F., goddess 43

dēbeō, -ēre, -uī, -itum, ought (to); owe 131

*dēcēdō, -ere, -cessī, -cessum, depart; ē vītā dēcēdere, die 293

*decem, ten 233

decemvirī, -ōrum, M. pl., magistrates who drew up the XII tables 249

*dēclārō, -āre, -āvī, -ātum, reveal, declare 64

*dēclīnō, -āre, -āvī, -ātum, turn aside, deviate; shun 374

dedī (See dō.)

deep, altus, -a, -um

defend, dēfendō (III)

*dēfendō, -ere, -fendī, -fēnsum, protect, defend 64

deinde (adv.), next, then 98

°dēlectō, -āre, -āvī, -ātum, please, delight

dēleō, -ēre, dēlēvī, dēlētum, destroy, erase, blot out 174

dēligō, -ere, -lēgī, -lēctum, pick, choose 142

**Dēlos, -ī, F., De'los, an island in the Aege'an Sea

*dēmēns, gen., -entis, insane, out of one's mind 373

dēnique (adv.), finally, at last 69

*dēns, dentis (-ium), M., tooth 235, 311

*dēnsus, -a, -um, thick, dense 69

depart, dēcēdō (III)

dēpellō, -ere, -pulī, -pulsum, drive from or away 217

dēpōnō, -ere, -posuī, -positum, lay down; put aside; dislodge 249

*dēportō, -āre, -āvī, -ātum, carry away, remove 251

dēprehendō, -ere, -hendī, -hēnsum, seize, catch 185

*dēscendō, -ere, -scendī, -scēnsum, go down, descend 64

*dēserō, -ere, -uī, -sertum, abandon, desert 339

*dēsertus, -a, -um, deserted

dēsiderō, -āre, -āvī, -ātum, wish, desire 73

*dēsignātus, -a, -um, pointed out, designated, elect 371

dēsiliō, -īre, -uī, -sultum, leap down 251

*dēsistō, -ere, -stitī, -stitum, stop, cease; desist from 293 *dēspērō, -āre, -āvī, -ātum, despair (of) 315

destroy, vāstō (I), dēleō (II)

**Deucaliōn, -ōnis, M., Deuca'lion, character in Greek legend

deus, -ī, M., god (pl. dī or deī) 83

*dexter, -tra, -trum, right; ā dextrā, on the right 263

*dextra, -ae, F., right hand; right (as opposed to left) 368

**Diāna, -ae, F., Dian'a, goddess of the moon and of hunting

dīcō, -ere, dīxī, dictum, say 43; salūtem dicere, greet 255

**Dīdō, -ōnis, F., Di'do, queen of Car'thage

diēs, diēī, M. or F., day 371

*difficilis, -e, difficult 274

*difficultās, -ātis, F., difficulty 253

*dīligēns, gen., -entis, careful

*dīligenter (adv.), carefully 142

*dīmittō, -ere, -mīsī, -missum, send away, dismiss 185

discēdō, -ere, -cessī, -cessum, go away, depart 157

*discipulus, -ī, M., pupil, student 138

discō, -ere, didicī, learn 139

**Discordia, -ae, F., Discor'dia, the goddess of discord and quarrels

*dispōnō, -ere, -posuī, -positum, arrange, distribute, dispose 287

*disputō, -āre, -āvī, -ātum, discuss, argue, dispute 64

*dissimilis, -e, dissimilar, unlike 274

diū (adv.), long (of time only) 157

diūtius (adv.), longer

*dīvidō, -ere, -vīsī, -vīsum, divide, separate 64

*dīvīnus, -a, -um, divine, godly 92

dīvitiae, -ārum, F. pl., riches 327

°dīxit, (he, she) said

dō, dare, dedī, datum, give 59

doceō, -ēre, -uī, doctum, teach 139

*doleō, -ēre, -uī, -itūrus, grieve, suffer 152

*dolor, -ōris, M., grief, sorrow 241

dolus, -ī, M., fraud, deceit, trick 333

*domicilium, -ī, N., place of residence, domicile 92

*dominus, -ī, M., master, lord 215

°domī, at home; domum, (to) home

*dōnum, -ī, N., gift, offering 89

door, jānua, -ae, F.

*dormiō, -īre, -īvī, -ītum, sleep 157

dracō, -ōnis, M., dragon 299

*duae, duās (nom., acc.), F., two

*dubium, -ī, N., doubt 221

*dubius, -a, -um, doubtful 263

dūcō, -ere, dūxī, ductum, lead, bring, carry 21

dum (with pres. tense), while 135

*duo, duae, duo, two 284

duodecim, twelve 433

*dūrus, -a, -um, hard, difficult 217

dux, ducis, M., leader 233

E

ē, ex (with abl.), from, out of 73

earth, terra, -ae, F.

ecce, see! behold! 161

**Ēchō, -ūs, F., Ech'o, a wood nymph

*edō, -ere, ēdī, ēsum, eat 155

*efficiō, -ere, -fēcī, -fectum, make, produce, effect 287

*ego, I (pers. pron.) 54, note; 218

ēgregius, -a, -um, excellent, distinguished 139

*elephantus, -ī, M., elephant 92

*ēmittō, -ere, -mīsī, -missum, send out, give forth, emit 64

enemy (personal), **inimicus, -i,** M.,
inimica, -ae, F.; (public), **hostis,
-is,** M.; the enemy, **hostēs, -ium**
enim (conj.), for 311
*__ēnumerō, -āre, -āvī, -ātum,__ count,
enumerate 64
eō, ire, ii (īvī), itum, go 336
**__Epimētheus, -ī,__ M., Ep'ime'theus, hus-
band of Pando'ra
**__Ēpīrus, -ī,__ F., Epi'rus, a district of
ancient Greece
*__epistula, -ae,__ F., letter 263
*__eques, -itis,__ M., horseman; pl. cavalry
237
equus, -ī, M., horse 115
*__ērēctus, -a, -um,__ upright, erect 92
*__errō, -āre, -āvī, -ātum,__ wander,
stray, err 69
est, is 10
et (conj.), and 10; **et . . . et,** both . . .
and 39
etiam (adv.), also, even 135
**__Etrūria, -ae,__ F., Etru'ria, a district in
Italy, now Tus'cany
*__Etrūscus, -a, -um,__ Etrus'can
**__Eumaeus, -ī,__ M., Eumae'us, swineherd
of Ulys'ses
*__Eurōpa, -ae,__ F., Eu'rope
**__Euryalus, -ī,__ M., Eury'alus, young
Tro'jan warrior
**__Eurydicē, -ēs; Eurydicēn__ (acc.), F.,
Euryd'ice, wife of Or'pheus
*__ēvādō, -ere, -vāsī, -vāsum,__ go
away, escape, evade 305
**__Evander, -drī,__ M., Evan'der, founder
of an early Italian city
*__ēveniō, -īre, -vēnī, -ventum,__ come
forth; happen 311
*__ēvocō, -āre, -āvī, -ātum,__ call forth,
evoke 98

*__excitō, -āre, -āvī, -ātum,__ awaken,
stir up, arouse 157
*__exeō, -īre, -iī (-īvī), -itum,__ go out
337
exercitus, -ūs, M., army 369
*__exilium, -ī,__ N., banishment, exile 92
*__expectō, -āre, -āvī, -ātum,__ wait for
69
*__expellō, -ere, -pulī, -pulsum,__ drive
out, expel 335
*__expīrō, -āre, -āvī, -ātum,__ breathe
out, expire 311
*__explōrātor, -ōris,__ M., scout 255
*__explōrō, -āre, -āvī, -ātum,__ explore,
investigate 64
expugnō, -āre, -āvī, -ātum, take by
storm, overcome, capture 373
exquīrō, -ere, -quīsīvī, -quīsītum,
seek out, search for 345
*__extinguō, -ere, -tīnxī, -tīnctum,__ put
out, extinguish 353
*__extrā__ (with acc.), beyond, outside 223

F

*__fābula, -ae,__ F., story, fable 39
*__faciem__ (acc. sing.), **faciēs** (nom. sing.
and nom., acc. pl.) F., face(s)
*__facile__ (adv.), easily 193
*__facilis, -e,__ easy 263
faciō, -ere, fēcī, factum, do, make
147; **iter facere,** travel, march
*__factum, -ī,__ N., deed, act, event 311
faithful, **fidus, -a, -um; fidēlis, -e**
*__fāma, -ae,__ F., fame 28
*__familia, -ae,__ F., family 30
far away, **longinquus, -a, -um**
farmer, **agricola, -ae,** M.
*__Fāta, -ōrum,__ N. pl., Fates, the three
goddesses of human destiny
fear, **timeō (II)**

407

fēlix, gen., **-īcis,** happy, successful, fortunate 263

*fēmina, -ae, F., woman 69

fenestra, -ae, F., window 55

°fer! ferte! carry! bring! 160, 161

*ferōx, gen., **-ōcis,** wild, ferocious 265

ferus, -a, -um, wild, fierce 171

fessus, -a, -um, weary, tired 299

few, **paucī, -ae, -a**

°fibula, -ae, F., pin, brooch

*fidēlis, -e, faithful, loyal

*fidus, -a, -um, faithful 209

field, **campus, -ī,** M.; **ager, agrī,** M.

fight, **pugnō (I)**

°figō, -ere, fīxī, fixum, fasten

*figūra, -ae, F., shape, figure 33

*filia, -ae, F., daughter 51

*filius, -ī, M., son 131

°filum, -ī, N., thread

*finiō, -īre, -īvī, -ītum, finish 327

*finis, -is (-ium), M. or F., limit, end; M. pl., boundaries, territory 241

finitimus, -a, -um, neighboring; (as noun) M. pl., neighbors 233

fireplace, **focus, -ī,** M.

*firmiter (adv.), firmly 237

*firmus, -a, -um, firm, strong 8, 92

first (at first), **primō** (adv.)

first, **primus, -a, -um**

flame, **flamma, -ae,** F.

*flamma, -ae, F., flame 43

*flammeus, -a, -um, flaming 118

flāvus, -a, -um, yellow 251

flūmen, -inis, N., river 251

*fluō, -ere, flūxī, flūxum, flow 135

fluvius, -ī, M., stream, river 83

fly, **volō (I)**

focus, -ī, M., hearth, fireplace 83

fodiō, -ere, fōdī, fossum, dig 345

*foedus, -eris, N., treaty, league 371

*folium, -ī, N., leaf 95

*fōns, fontis (-ium), M., spring, well, fountain 251, 287

forest, **silva, -ae,** F.

*fōrma, -ae, F., shape, beauty 8

formīca, -ae, F., ant 174

fōrmōsus, -a, -um, handsome 197

fortasse (adv.), perhaps 189

forte (adv.), by chance 193

*fortis, -e, strong, brave 265

*fortitūdō, -inis, F., bravery 253

*fortūna, -ae, F., fortune 8

forum, -ī, N., forum, market place 8; **Forum, Roman Forum

fountain, **fōns, fontis (-ium),** M.

*frangō, -ere, frēgī, frāctum, break 371

*frāter, -tris, M., brother 242, 246

free, **liberō (I)**

friend, **amīcus, -ī,** M.; **amica, -ae,** F.

*frīgidus, -a, -um, cold, frigid 8, 92

from (away from), **ā** or **ab** (with abl.)

from (down from), **dē** (with abl.)

from (out from), **ē/ex** (with abl.)

frūmentum, -ī, N., grain 131

*frūstrā (adv.), in vain 274

*fugiō, -ere, fūgī, fugitūrus, flee, escape 171

*fugitīvus, -ī, M., fugitive 92

°fulmen, -inis, N., lightning; thunderbolt

*fūmus, -ī, M., smoke 223

**furor, -ōris, M., rage, fury, furor 8

*futūrus, -a, -um, future 8, 92

G

**Galba, -ae, M., Gal'ba, a name

galea, -ae, F., helmet 109

*Gallia, -ae, F., Gaul (the country)

*Gallus, -a, -um, Gaulish, of Gaul

*Gallus, -ī, M., a Gaul

gaudium, -ī, N., joy · 98

geminus, -a, -um, twin 161

*gemma, -ae, F., gem, jewel 49

gēns, gentis (-ium), F., nation, tribe, clan 344

*genus, -eris, N., kind, sort 255

*Germānia, -ae, F., Ger'many

gerō, -ere, gessī, gestum, wear; carry, conduct, do 135; **bellum gerere,** wage war 237

**Gideōn, -ōnis, M., Gid'eon, hero of Is'rael who defeated the Mid'ianites

gift, **dōnum, -ī,** N.

girl, **puella, -ae,** F.

give, **dō, dare, dedī, datum**

gladius, -ī, M., sword 83

*glōria, -ae, F., glory 30

god, **deus, -ī,** M.

goddess, **dea, -ae,** F. (dat./abl. pl. end in **-ābus**)

good, **bonus, -a, -um**

*Gorgō, -onis, F., Gor'gon, a monstrous woman with snakes for hair

gracilis, -e, slender, thin 274

*Graecia, -ae, F., Greece

*Graecus, -a, -um, Greek (also as noun)

grāmen, -inis, N., grass 368

grātiās agere, give thanks 185

grātus, -a, -um, pleasing 76

*gravis, -e, heavy, serious, hard 287

*graviter (adv.), gravely

grieve, **doleō (II)**

gustō, -āre, -āvī, -ātum, taste 189

H

habeō, -ēre, -uī, -itum, have, hold 10

*habitō, -āre, -āvī, -ātum, live in, dwell, inhabit 39

**Haeduī, -ōrum, M. pl., Haed'ui, a Gallic tribe

happy, **laetus, -a, -um**

*Harpyiae, -ārum, F., Har'pies, mythical monsters, half bird, half woman

hasta, -ae, F., spear, javelin 83

he (himself), **ipse**

head, **caput, capitis,** N.

hear, **audiō (IV)**

heaven, **caelum, -ī,** N.

**Hector, -oris, M., Hec'tor, Tro'jan prince, slain by Achil'les

*Helena, -ae, F., Hel'en, queen of Spar'ta, abducted by Par'is

**Helenus, -ī, M., Hel'enus, Tro'jan prince and soothsayer

**Hellē, -ēs, F., Hel'le, sister of Phrix'us

help, **juvō (I)**

*Helvētiī, -ōrum, M. pl., the Helve'tians, a Gallic tribe

her (possessive), when reflexive, **suus, -a, -um;** when not reflexive, **ejus**

*herba, -ae, F., herb, grass, plant 39

**Herculāneum, -ī, N., Her'cula'neum, Italian city near Mt. Vesu'vius

Herculēs, -is, M., Her'cules, hero of Greek mythology; **Herculī (dat.)

heu, alas! oh! 263

heus, hello! hi there! 197

Hibernia, -ae, F., Ire'land

hic, haec, hoc, this; pl., these 194

hīc (adv.), here 161

hieme, in winter 55

high, **altus, -a, -um**

his (possessive), when reflexive, **suus, -a, -um;** when not reflexive, **ejus**

Hispānia, -ae, F., Spain

hodiē (adv.), today 73

home, **domus, -ūs (-ī),** F.; at home, **domī;** (to) home, **domum**

*Homērus, -ī, M., Ho'mer, author of
the Od'yssey and the Il'iad

homō, -inis, M., man, human 251

**honor, -ōris, M., honor 8, 234

hōra, -ae, F., hour 109

**Horātius, -ī, M., Hora'tius, heroic
defender of the Tiber bridge

horse, equus, -ī, M.

*hortus, -ī, M., garden 155

*hostis, -is (-ium), M., enemy; pl., the
enemy 242, 251

house, vīlla, -ae, F.; tēctum, -ī, N.

hūc (adv.), here, to this place 109

*humilis, -e, low; humble 274

**humus, -ī, F., ground, soil 344

hurry, properō (I)

I

ibi (adv.), there, in that place 147

Īcarius, -a, -um, Icarian

**Īcarus, -ī, M., Ic'arus, son of
Daed'alus

ictus, -ūs, M., thrust, blow 374

**Īda, -ae, F., I'da, mountain near Troy

īdem, eadem, idem, the same 200

idōneus, -a, -um, fit, suitable 345

igitur (adv.), therefore 113

°ignāvus, -a, -um, cowardly

*ignis, -is (-ium), M., fire 311

ignōtus, -a, -um, unknown 348

ill, aeger, -gra, -grum

ille, illa, illud, that; pl., those 194

*immortālis, -e, immortal 296

imperātor, -ōris, M., commander,
leader; emperor 255

imperātum, -ī, N., command 368

imperium, -ī, N., government, authority; empire 249

**impetus, -ūs, M., attack 368

impiger, -gra, -grum, industrious 55

*implōrō, -āre, -āvī, -ātum, beseech,
beg, implore 356

in, in (with abl.)

*in (with abl.), in, on 13; (with acc.),
into, to, against, toward, upon 24

*incendō, -ere, -cendī, -cēnsum, set
fire to, burn; enrage 353

*incertus, -a, -um, uncertain 356

incipiō, -ere, -cēpī, -ceptum, begin
197

*incognitus, -a, -um, unknown

incola, -ae, M. or F., inhabitant 39

incolumis, -e, safe, unharmed 303

*incrēdibilis, -e, incredible 166

*infāns, infantis, M. or F., child, infant

infantry, peditēs, -um, M. pl.

infēlīx, gen., -īcis, unhappy 269

*inflō, -āre, -āvī, -ātum, blow (into),
inflate 353

in front of, prō (with abl.)

*ingenium, -ī, N., ability, talent, genius

ingēns, gen., ingentis, huge 311

inimīcus, -a, -um, unfriendly; (as a
noun) M./F., enemy 109

°initiō, in the beginning

*initium, -ī, N., beginning 103

*injūria, -ae, F., harm, injury 30

*injūstus, -a, -um, unfair, unjust 92

inquit, (he, she) says, said 139

*insānus, -a, -um, insane 92

*insigne, -is (-ium), N., mark, badge;
pl., insignia 365

*instrūmentum, -ī, N., tool 92

instruō, -ere, -strūxī, -strūctum,
build up, construct, equip 339

*insula, -ae, F., island 33

*intellegō, -ere, -lēxī, -lēctum, under-
stand, perceive, know

*intelligentia, -ae, F., intelligence 30

inter (with acc.), between, among 33

interdiū (adv.), in the day time 65

interdum (adv.), sometimes 24

intereā (adv.), meanwhile 315

interficiō, -ere, -fēcī, -fectum, kill 139; **sē interficere,** commit suicide

**interim (adv.), meanwhile 131

interior, gen., **-ōris, interior

*intervāllum, -ī, N., distance 92

into, **in** (with acc.)

intrā (with acc.), within, inside 339

*intrō, -āre, -āvī, -ātum, enter

*intrōdūcō, -ere, -dūxī, -ductum, lead into, introduce 339

*invādō, -ere, -vāsī, -vāsum, enter, invade 174

*inveniō, -īre, -vēnī, -ventum, come upon, find 177

invidia, -ae, F., envy, hatred 305

*invidiōsus, -a, -um, envious 73

invītus, -a, -um, unwilling 98

**Īphigenīa, -ae, F., Iph'igeni'a, daughter of Ag'amem'non

ipse, ipsa, ipsum, self; himself, herself, etc. 198

*īra, -ae, F., wrath, anger, ire 335

*īrātus, -a, -um, angry, irate 51

**Īris, Īridis, F., I'ris, messenger of Ju'no; goddess of the rainbow

is, **est**

is, ea, id, that, this 185

island, **īnsula, -ae,** F.

*Īsraēlītae, -ārum, M., Is'raelites'

ita (adv.), yes; thus, in this way 49

*Ītalia, -ae, F., It'aly

itaque (conj.), and so, therefore 24

°item (adv.), also, likewise

*iter, itineris, N., journey, trip 277

iterum (adv.), again 55

**Ithaca, -ae, F., Ith'aca, Greek island

itself, **ipse, -a, -um;** (if reflexive), **suī**

J

jaceō, -ēre, -uī, lie, recline 237

jaciō, -ere, jēcī, jactum, throw, hurl, fling 200

jactō, -āre, -āvī, -ātum, hurl 109

jam (adv.), now, already 157; **jam prīdem,** for a long time now 303

**Jāniculum, -ī, N., Janic'ulum, a hill on the west bank of the Tiber

jānua, -ae, F., door, entrance 55

*Jānuārius, -a, -um, belonging to Ja'nus, of Ja'nus

**Jānus, -ī, M., Ja'nus, god of doors and beginnings

**Jāsōn, -onis, M., Ja'son, Greek hero

jewel, **gemma, -ae,** F.

°Jovī, Jovis (dat., gen.), see **Juppiter.**

jubeō, -ēre, jussī, jussum, order, command 293

*jūdex, -icis, M., judge 327

*jūdicium, -ī, N., judgment 269

*jungō, -ere, jūnxī, jūnctum, yoke, join 311

**Jūnō, -ōnis, F., Ju'no, queen of gods

*Juppiter, Jovis, M., Ju'piter, king of gods

°jūre jūrandō (abl. sing.), by an oath

°jūrō, -āre, -āvī, -ātum, take oath, swear

°jussū, by order (of)

°jussum, -ī, N., order, command

just, **jūstus, -a, -um**

*jūstitia, -ae, F., justice 30

*jūstus, -a, -um, just, fair 8, 92

**Jūturna, -ae, F., Jutur'na, a nymph, sister of Tur'nus

*juvenis, -is, M., young man, youth 242, 263

juvō, -āre, jūvī, jūtum, help, aid 83

K

kill, **necō (I), interficiō/occidō (III)**

kind, **benignus, -a, -um**

king, **rēx, rēgis,** M.

L

**labor, -ōris, M., work, labor, effort

*labōrō, -āre, -āvī, -ātum, work 55;
bene labōrāre, work hard 109

lacrima, -ae, F., tear 282

lacrimō, -āre, -āvī, -ātum, weep,
cry 197

*lacūna, -ae, F., pond, pool 51

*lacus, -ūs, M., lake

laetus, -a, -um, happy 55

**Lāocoōn, -ontis, M., Laoc'oön, Tro'-
jan priest

*lapis, lapidis, M., stone 335

large, **magnus, -a, -um**

largest, **maximus, -a, -um**

last (at), **dēnique, tandem** (advs.)

lātē (adv.), widely 278

*lateō, -ēre, -uī, hide, be hidden 215

*Latīnus, -a, -um, Latin

**Latīnus, -ī, M., Lati'nus, king of
La'tium

**Latium, -ī, N., La'tium, a district of
Italy (surrounding Rome)

**Lātōna, -ae, F., Lato'na, mother of
Apol'lo and Dian'a

lātus, -a, -um, wide, broad 13

*laudō, -āre, -āvī, -ātum, praise 73

*laureus, -a, -um, laurel, of laurel 95

*laurus, -ī, F., laurel tree 95

**Lāvīnia, -ae, F., Lavin'ia, Latin princess, bride of Aene'as

*lavō, -āre, lāvī, lautum, wash, bathe,
lave 64

law, **lēx, lēgis,** F.

lead, **dūcō (III)**

leader, **dux, ducis,** M.

lēgātus, -ī, M., ambassador, envoy;
staff officer 233

°**lēge, -em, -ēs, -is,** see **lēx**

*legiō, -ōnis, F., legion, division of the
Roman army (4000-6000 men) 253, 255

legō, -ere, lēgī, lēctum, collect,
gather together; read 249

lentē (adv.), slowly 69

*leō, -ōnis, M., lion 252, 255

levis, -e, light (not heavy)

*lēx, lēgis, F., law 234, 249

libenter (adv.), gladly, willingly 147

*liber, -brī, M., book 269

*liber, libera, liberum, free 76

**liberātor, -ōris, M., rescuer

liberī, -ōrum, M. pl., children 189

ligneus, -a, -um, wooden 118

lignum, -ī, N., wood 251

°**ligō, -āre, -āvī, -ātum,** tie, bind

lingua, -ae, F., tongue, language 33

little, **parvus, -a, -um**

lītus, -oris, N., shore, beach 344

live (dwell), **habitō (I);** (be alive),
vīvō (III); vītam agere

**locus, -ī, M., place; (pl. usually N.,
loca) 138

long (adj.), **longus, -a, -um;** (adv.)
diū (of time)

*longaevus, -a, -um, old, aged

*longē (adv.), far (away) 217

longinquus, -a, -um, distant 49

*longus, -a, -um, long 10

**lōtus, -ī, F., lotus, a fruit-bearing tree

love, **amō (I); amor, -ōris,** M.

lūceō, -ēre, lūxī, shine 135

lucerna, -ae, F., lantern, lamp 89

**Lūcia, -ae, F., Lu'cia

**Lūcius, -ī, M., Lu'cius or Luke

*lūdō, -ere, lūsī, lūsum, play 299

°lūdus, -ī, M., game, sport

*lūmen, -inis, N., light 315

*lūna, -ae, F., moon 49

lutum, -ī, N., mud, dirt 251

*lūx, lūcis, F., light 277

*lyra, -ae, F., lyre 8

M

**Macedonia, -ae, F., Mac'edo'nia,
a country between Thes'saly and
Thrace

maestus, -a, -um, sad 131

*maga, -ae, F., sorceress 177

*magicus, -a, -um, magic 8, 92

magister, -trī, M., master, school-
master, teacher 138

*magistrātus, -ūs, M., magistrate

**Magna (-ae) Graecia (-ae), F.,
Mag'na Grae'cia, collective name
of Greek colonies in southern Italy

magnopere (adv.), greatly 215

magnus, -a, -um, large, great 10

make, faciō (III)

*male (adv.), badly, unsuccessfully 265

maleficium, -ī, N., evil deed 193

mālum, -ī, N., apple 327

malus, -a, -um, bad, evil, wicked 156,
157; (as a noun) N., evil 157

man, vir, virī, M.; homō, -inis, M.

māne (adv.), early, in the morning 209

maneō, -ēre, mānsī, mānsūrus,
stay, remain 65

**Mānlius, -ī, M., Man'lius, Roman hero

*manus, -ūs, F., hand; band 369

many, multī, -ae, -a; very many, a
great many, plūrimī, -ae, -a

**Mārcus, -ī, M., Marcus or Mark

mare, maris (-ium), N., sea 299;
terrā marīque, on land and sea

*maritimus, -a, -um, of the sea; (with
ōra) seacoast 35

marry (of bridegroom), in mātrimōnium dūcō (III); (of bride), nūbō
(III)

**Mārs, Mārtis, M., Mars, god of war

master, magister, -trī, M.; dominus,
-ī, M.

*māter, mātris, F., mother 161, 234, 242

*mātrimōnium, -ī, N., matrimony, mar-
riage 92; in mātrimōnium dūcere,
marry (said of bridegroom) 177

maximē (adv., superlative of magnopere), very greatly, most 278

*maximus, -a, -um (superlative of
magnus), greatest, very great

*mē (acc., abl.), me 218

**Mēdēa, -ae, F., Mede'a, princess of
Col'chis, an enchantress

*medicīna, -ae, F., medicine 8

*medicus, -a, -um, medical; (as noun)
M., doctor, physician 147

*Mediterrāneus, -a, -um, Med'iterra'-
nean; Mare Mediterrāneum, N.,
the Med'iterra'nean Sea

*medius, -a, -um, mid; middle of 142

**Medūsa, -ae, F., Medu'sa, a Gor'gon

*Melita, -ae, F., Mal'ta, an island in the
Med'iterra'nean

*memoria, -ae, F., memory 30; me-
moriā tenēre, remember

*mendicus, -ī, M., beggar 335

**Menelāus, -ī, M., Men'ela'us, brother
of Ag'amem'non, husband of Helen

*mēns, mentis (-ium), F., mind 348

mēnsis, -is, M., month 282

mercātor, -ōris, M., trader 333

*Mercurius, -ī, M., Mer'cury, messen-
ger of the gods

*merīdiēs, -ēī, M., noon

messenger, **nūntius, -ī,** M.; **nūntia,
-ae,** F.

meus, -a, -um, my, mine 35

****Mīdās, Mīdae,** M., Mi'das, king who
was granted the golden touch

***Midianītae, -ārum,** M., the Mid'ia-
nites, an Arab tribe

***migrō, -āre, -āvī, -ātum,** migrate,
move, change 64

mihi (dat.), me, to me 218

***miles, -itis,** M., soldier 237

mille (indecl.), thousand 287; **milia,
-ium,** N. pl., thousands 287; **mille
passūs,** a mile; **milia passuum,**
miles 293

****Minerva, -ae,** Miner'va, goddess of
wisdom

***minimē** (adv.), no; not at all 49

***minimus, -a, -um** (superlative of
parvus), smallest, very small 156

***Minōtaurus, -ī,** M., Min'otaur, mythi-
cal monster with the head of a bull
and the body of a man

mīrus, -a, -um, wonderful, strange,
extraordinary 33

****Misēnum, -ī,** N., Mise'num, a pro-
montory and town in Italy

***miser, -a, -um,** unhappy, poor 55

miserable, **miser, -a, -um**

misericordia, -ae, F., pity 315

mittō, -ere, mīsī, missum, send 131

***modus, -ī,** M., way, manner 92, 287

moenia, -ium, N. pl., walls (of a city),
fortifications 368

moneō, -ēre, -uī, -itum, warn, ad-
monish, advise 55

***mōns, montis (-ium),** M., mountain
235, 251

mōnstrō, -āre, -āvī, -ātum, show,
point out 39

***mōnstrum, -ī,** N., monster 92

moon, **lūna, -ae,** F.

mora, -ae, F., delay 115

morbus, -ī, M., disease, sickness 98

***mors, mortis (-ium),** F., death 287

***mortālis, -e,** mortal; (as noun) M. pl.,
mortals 296

***mortuus, -a, -um,** dead 103 (also as
noun)

mountain, **mōns, montis (-ium),** M.

***moveō, -ēre, mōvī, mōtum,** move
64; **castra movēre,** break camp

mox (adv.), soon 35

***multitūdō, -inis,** F., multitude 250, 253

multum (adv.), much, deeply 174

multus, -a, -um, much; pl., many 28

mūniō, -īre, -īvī, -ītum, fortify, build;
(with **viam**), build a road 241

***mūrus, -ī,** M., wall 217

***mūsica, -ae,** F., music 8

mūtō, -āre, -āvī, -ātum, change 95

my, **meus, -a, -um**

N

nam (conj.), for 237

****Narcissus, -ī,** M., Narcis'sus, a handsome youth of mythology

***nārrō, -āre, -āvī, -ātum,** tell 39

natō, -āre, -āvī, -ātum, swim, float
251

***nātūra, -ae,** F., nature 8

nauta, -ae, M., sailor 43

nāvicula, -ae, F., small boat 103

***nāvigō, -āre, -āvī, -ātum,** sail,
navigate 64

***nāvis, -is (-ium),** F., ship, boat;
nāvis longa, warship 233

-ne, attached to word to indicate
question 33

nē . . . quidem (adv.), not even 348

near, **prope** (with acc.); **propinquus, -a, -um** (with dat.)

*__necesse__ (indecl. adj.), necessary 311

necō, -āre, -āvī, -ātum, kill 43

*__neglegō, -ere, -lēxī, -lēctum,__ disregard, neglect 282

*__negōtium, -ī,__ N., business 221

neighboring, **finitimus, -a, -um**

nēmō, -inī (dat.), **-inem** (acc.), M./F. sing., no one, nobody 333

*__Neptūnus, -ī,__ M., Nep'tune, god of the sea

neque (conj.), nor, and not 113; **neque ... neque,** neither ... nor

°**nesciō, -īre, -īvī, -ītum,** not know

new, **novus, -a, -um**

night, **nox, noctis (-ium),** F.

night (at), **noctū** (adv.)

nihil, N. (indecl.), nothing 197

*__Nīlus, -ī,__ M., the Nile (river)

**__Nīsus, -ī,__ M., Ni'sus, a friend of Asca'nius

*__nōbilis, -e,__ high-born, noble 356

nōbīs (dat., abl.), (to) us 218

noctū (adv.), at night, by night 65

nōlī, nōlīte, do not ... 159, 366

nōlō, nōlle, nōluī, not want, be unwilling 365

no longer, **nōn jam** (adv.)

*__nōmen, -inis,__ N., name 289

nōminō, -āre, -āvī, -ātum, name, call 26

*__nōn__ (adv.), not 10; **nōn jam,** no longer 51; **nōn sōlum ... sed etiam,** not only ... but also 147

nōndum (adv.), not yet 249

nōnne, introduces questions, implying answer "yes" 50

nōs (nom., acc. pl.), we, us 54, note; 218

noster, -tra, -trum, our 39

not, **nōn**

nōtus, -a, -um, famous, noted 33

novem, nine 269

novus, -a, -um, new, strange 13

nox, noctis (-ium), F., night 339

°**nūbēs, nūbis (-ium),** F., cloud

°**nūbō, -ere, nūpsī, nūptum,** marry, be married (said of bride)

*__nūdus, -a, -um,__ uncovered, nude 92

nūllus, -a, -um, no, none 65; (as noun supplies genitive and ablative of **nēmō**), no one

__Numa, -ae,__ M., or **Numa Pompilius, -ī, M., Nu'ma Pompil'ius, second king of Rome

*__numerus, -ī,__ M., number 171

numquam (adv.), never 233

nunc (adv.), now 35

nūntia, -ae, F., messenger 135

*__nūntiō, -āre, -āvī, -ātum,__ report 277

nūntius, -ī, M., messenger; news 135

nusquam (adv.), nowhere 303

°**nūtrix, -īcis,** F., nurse

*__nympha, -ae,__ F., nymph 76

O

Ō, ō, O! Oh!

ob (with acc.), because of 299

*__obscūrus, -a, -um,__ dark, dim 33

*__obtineō, -ēre, -uī, -tentum,__ possess, occupy, obtain 191, 233

occidō, -ere, -cidī, -cāsum, fall, fall down; **sōl occidit,** the sun set 315

occīdō, -ere, -cīdī, -cīsum, cut down, kill 174, 191

*__occupō, -āre, -āvī, -ātum,__ seize, occupy 103

*__occurrō, -ere, -currī, -cursum,__ run against, run to meet 64, 263

*Ōceanus, -ī, M., the Ocean 92

*oculus, -ī, M., eye 177

**odium, -ī, N., hatred 374

often, saepe (adv.)

*oleum, -ī, N., oil 115

ōlim (adv.), once, some day 49

*olīva, -ae, F., olive 8

**Olympus, -ī, M., Olym′pus, mountain
in Thes′saly, the home of the gods

**ōmen, -inis, N., omen, sign 8, 335

omnis, -e, all, every, whole 263

on, in (with abl.)

one, ūnus, -a, -um (See p. 284.)

open, apertus, -a, -um

oppidum, -ī, N., town 115

*opprimō, -ere, -pressī, -pressum,
press down, oppress 311

oppugnō, -āre, -āvī, -ātum, attack,
besiege 123, 263

*optimus, -a, -um (superlative of
bonus), best, very good 115

ōra, -ae, F., coast, shore 28

*ōrāculum, -ī, N., oracle 243

*orbis, -is (-ium), M., circle, ring 327;
orbis terrārum, the world

**Orcus, -ī, M., Or′cus, lower world,
abode of the dead

**Orestēs, -is, M., Ores′tes, son of
Ag′amem′non

**Ōriōn, -ōnis, M., Ori′on, a hunter,
transformed into a constellation

ōrō, -āre, -āvī, -ātum, ask for, beg
for, pray (to) 51

**Orpheus, -ī, M., Or′pheus, mythical
singer

ostendō, -ere, -tendī, -tentum, show,
display 333

ought, dēbeō (II)

overcome, superō (I), vincō (III)

ovis, -is (-ium), F., sheep 287

P

°pāce, pācem, pācis, see pāx

Padus, -ī, M., the Po (river)

paene (adv.), almost 351

*paenīnsula, -ae, F., peninsula 33

palace, rēgia, -ae, F.

*palla, -ae, F., long robe, mantle;
curtain, tapestry 135

**Pallās, -antis, M., Pal′las, son of
Evan′der

**Pandōra, -ae, F., Pando′ra, mythical
character, wife of Ep′ime′theus

**Paris, -idis, M., Par′is, Tro′jan prince

parō, -āre, -āvī, -ātum, prepare,
furnish 147

*pars, partis (-ium), F., part, portion;
direction, side 233

part, pars, partis (-ium), F.

parvus, -a, -um, small, little 10

passus, -ūs, M., step, pace; mīlia
passuum, miles 293

pāstor, -ōris, M., shepherd

*pater, -tris, M., father 161, 242

*patria, -ae, F., native country 138

paucī, -ae, -a, few 147

paulātim (adv.), little by little 233

paulisper (adv.), a little while 315

pāx, pācis, F., peace 233

pecūnia, -ae, F., money 103

°pede, see pēs

*pedes, -itis, M., foot soldier; pl.,
infantry 237

**Peliās, -ae, M., Pe′lias, uncle of
Ja′son

°pellis, -is (-ium), F., hide, skin

*pellō, -ere, pepulī, pulsum, beat,
rout; drive 351

**Pēnelopē, -ēs (Pēnelopa, -ae) F.,
Penel′ope, wife of Ulys′ses

*penna, -ae, F., feather 177

pepuli (See pellō.)

per (with acc.), through 21

*pereō, -īre, -iī (-īvī), -itūrus, perish, die 209

perficiō, -ere, -fēcī, -fectum, finish, accomplish 249

*perfidus, -a, -um, faithless 255

periculōsus, -a, -um, dangerous 39

periculum, -ī, N., danger 98

peritus, -a, -um, skilled, expert 109

permōtus, -a, -um, disturbed 251

*perpetuus, -a, -um, continuous

**Perseus, -ī, M., Per'seus, legendary Greek hero

*perterreō, -ēre, -terruī, -territum, frighten 123

*perterritus, -a, -um, terrified 303

*pertineō, -ēre, -uī, extend, pertain (to) 191

perveniō, -īre, -vēnī, -ventum, arrive at, reach 303

*pēs, pedis, M., foot, paw 293

*pessimus, -a, -um (superlative of malus), worst, very bad 156

*pestilentia, -ae, F., pestilence 30

petō, -ere, -īvī, -ītum, pursue, seek, ask (for), look for 185

**Phaëthōn, -ontis, M., Pha'ëthon, son of Apol'lo

°phōca, -ae, F., seal, sea lion

**Phoebus, -ī, M., Phoe'bus Apol'lo, god of the sun

*Phoenicēs, -um, M., Phoeni'cians, ancient navigators and merchants

**Phoenicia, -ae, F., Phoeni'cia, a small strip of the coast of Syr'ia

**Phrixus, -ī, M., Phrix'us, brother of Hel'le

*pictūra, -ae, F., picture 13

**Picus, -ī, M., Pi'cus, legendary king, changed into a woodpecker (picus)

piger, -gra, -grum, lazy 55

*pīrāta, -ae, M., pirate 43

*pius, -a, -um, dutiful, reverent 200

place, locus, -ī, M. (pl. loca, N.); pōnō (III)

*placidus, -a, -um, calm, placid 299

pleasing, grātus, -a, -um

*Plēiades, -adum, F., the Ple'iades, the Seven Stars

**Plēionē, -ēs, F., Pleio'ne, wife of At'las, mother of the Ple'iades

plēnus, -a, -um, full 287

*Plīnius, -ī, M., Plin'y, the Elder, author of a Natural History; the Younger, nephew of the Elder, also a writer

plumbeus, -a, -um, made of lead 95

plūrimus, -a, -um (superlative of multus), most, very large; pl., a great many, very many 156

plūs, gen., plūris; pl., plūrēs, plūra, more; several 278

**Plūtō, -ōnis, M., Plu'to, king of the lower world

poena, -ae, F., penalty 197

*poēta, -ae, M., poet 8

**Polydōrus, -ī, M., Pol'ydo'rus, son of Pri'am

**Pompēiī, -ōrum, M. pl., Pompe'ii, a town in Italy destroyed by an eruption of Vesu'vius, A.D. 79

pōmum, -ī, N., fruit 189

pond, lacūna, -ae, F.

pōnō, -ere, posuī, positum, place, put 73; castra pōnere, set up camp 255

*pōns, pontis (-ium), M., bridge 235, 251

*populus, -ī, M., people 98

417

*porta, -ae, F., gate, door 135
*portō, -āre, -āvī, -ātum, carry 49
*portus, -ūs, M., harbor 92
possum, posse, potuī, be able (to), can 76
post (with acc.), after, behind 103
posteā (adv.), afterwards, later 26
*posterus, -a, -um, the next 371
postquam, after 189
postrīdiē (adv.), the next day 174
postulō, -āre, -āvī, -ātum, demand, ask for 76
posuit, (he, she) placed, put
*potēns, gen., -entis, powerful 263
*potentia, -ae, F., power, might 177
potestās, -ātis, F., power, control, authority 249
*praecipiō, -ere, -cēpī, -ceptum, teach, instruct 311
*praedīcō, -ere, -dīxī, -dictum, advise, foretell, predict 356
*praemium, -ī, N., reward, prize 155
*praesēns, gen., -entis, present, at hand 345
praeter (with acc.), except 118
praetereā (adv.), besides 237
praise, laudō (I)
prepare, parō (I)
*pretiōsus, -a, -um, costly, precious, expensive 237
pretium, -ī, N., price 269
*Priamus, -ī, M., Pri'am, king of Troy
prīdem (adv.), long ago; jam prīdem, for a long time now 303
*primō (adv.), (at) first 21
*primum (adv.), (at) first 161
*primus, -a, -um, first 21
*princeps, prīncipis, M., leader, chief (also adj.) first, chief 329
priusquam (conj.), before 305

prō (with abl.), in front of, before 69; for, for the sake of, in behalf of 131
*probō, -āre, -āvī, -ātum, approve; prove 249
*prōcēdō, -ere, -cessī, -cessum, proceed, go on 123, 171
proceed, prōcēdō (III)
procul (adv.), far, far away 35
°procus, -ī, M., suitor
proelium, -ī, N., battle 233
*prohibeō, -ēre, -uī, -itum, restrain, hinder, prohibit 335
**Promētheus, -ī, M., Prome'theus, one of the Ti'tans; he stole fire from heaven and brought it to earth
*prōmittō, -ere, -mīsī, -missum, promise 327
prope (with acc.), near 21
properō, -āre, -āvī, -ātum, hasten, hurry 89
propinquus, -a, -um, near 43
propter (with acc.), because of 113
prōra, -ae, F., bow of a ship 305
**Prōserpina, -ae, F., Proser'pina, daughter of Ce'res
*prōtegō, -ere, -tēxī, -tēctum, protect; cover 311
**Prōteus, -ī, M., Pro'teus, prophet and god of the sea, able to change himself into different shapes
*prōvincia, -ae, F., province 26
*prōvocātiō, -ōnis, F., challenge 371
*prōvocō, -āre, -āvī, -ātum, challenge, provoke 123, 193
*proximus, -a, -um, nearest, next 223
**Psȳchē, -ēs, Psȳchae (dat.); Psȳchēn (acc.), F., Psy'che, girl beloved by Cu'pid
**Pūblius, -ī, M., Pub'lius, a name
puella, -ae, F., girl 65

418

puer, puerī, M., boy 95

pugnō, -āre, -āvī, -ātum, fight 103

pulcher, -chra, -chrum, beautiful 35

pulsō, -āre, -āvī, -ātum, beat, knock (on) 374

*pūniō, -īre, -īvī, -ītum, punish 131

punish, pūniō (IV)

pupil, discipulus, -ī, M.

*purpureus, -a, -um, purple

*putō, -āre, -āvī, -ātum, think 329

**Pyrrha, -ae, F., Pyr'rha, wife of Deuca'lion; they were the legendary sole survivors of a great flood

**Pyrrhus, -ī, M., Pyr'rhus, king of Epi'rus, enemy of the Romans

Q

°quae, see quī, quae, quod

quaerō, -ere, -sīvī, -sītum, seek, search for 221

quam (adv.), how 241; (with comparative), than 265

quam ob rem, therefore, for this reason 299; why, for which reason

quamquam (conj.), although 147

°quās, see quī, quae, quod

°quasi (adv.), as if, as though

-que (attached to a word), and 83

queen, rēgīna, -ae, F.

°quercus, -ūs, F., oak

quī, quae, quod (interrogative adj.), which, what 223

quī, quae, quod (relative pronoun), who, which, that 209

°quid, see quis, quid

quidem (adv.), indeed, even 189

*quiētus, -a, -um, quiet, still 35

quīnque, five 233

quis, quid (interrog. pron.), who, what 221; sī quid, if anything

°quisque, quidque, (indef. pron.), each one, every one, each, every

°quō (adv.), where (to)

quod (conj.), because 51

quoque (adv.), also 24

°quotannīs (adv.), annually, every year

R

radius, -ī, M., ray 98

*rādīx, -īcis, F., root 345

rāmus, -ī, M., branch, bough 95

*rapidus, -a, -um, swift, rapid 8

*recēdō, -ere, -cessī, -cessum, withdraw, recede 123, 342, 373

*recipiō, -ere, -cēpī, -ceptum, take, get, or bring back 189; sē recipere, withdraw, retreat 237

recognize, recognōscō (III)

*recognōscō, -ere, -nōvī, -nitum, recognize 123, 335

rēctē (adv.), in a straight line; rightly 287

rēctus, -a, -um, straight 305

recūsō, -āre, -āvī, -ātum, refuse 95

reddō, -ere, reddidī, redditum, give back, return (with dir. obj.) 197

redeō, -īre, -iī, -itūrus, go back, return 337

*redūcō, -ere, -dūxī, -ductum, lead back 189

°rēgem, -ēs, -is, see rēx

*rēgia, -ae, F., palace 83

*rēgīna, -ae, F., queen 76

*regiō, -ōnis, F., region 253

*rēgius, -a, -um, of a king, regal 371

*rēgnō, -āre, -āvī, -ātum, be king, rule, reign 249

*rēgnum, -ī, N., kingdom, rule 103

regō, -ere, rēxī, rēctum, direct, rule, govern 135

419

*relinquō, -ere, -līquī, -lictum, leave, abandon 189

reliquus, -a, -um, remaining, rest of 265

remain, maneō (II)

*removeō, -ēre, -mōvī, -mōtum, remove 123

rēmus, -ī, M., oar 157

*repellō, -ere, reppulī, repulsum, drive back, drive away, repel 64

*reportō, -āre, -āvī, -ātum, carry back, bring back 64, 123

rēs, reī, F., thing; affair, fact, matter 371; rē vērā, in truth 299

*resistō, -ere, -stitī, stand still, resist (usually with dative) 305

respiciō, -ere, -spexī, -spectum, look back 293

*respondeō, -ēre, -spondī, -spōnsum, answer, reply 64

°retexō, -ere, -uī, -textum, unweave, unravel, ravel

*retineō, -ēre, -uī, -tentum, hold or keep back, retain 191, 315

*reveniō, -īre, -vēnī, -ventum, come back 123

*revocō, -āre, -āvī, -ātum, call again, call back; revoke 123

rēx, rēgis, M., king 73, 75, 235

*Rhēnus, -ī, M., the Rhine (river)

*Rhodanus, -ī, M., the Rhône (river)

*rīdeō, -ēre, rīsī, rīsum, laugh 269

rīpa, -ae, F., bank (of a river) 103

river, flūmen, -inis, N.

road, via, -ae, F.

rogō, -āre, -āvī, -ātum, ask 115

*Rōma, -ae, F., Rome

*Rōmānus, -a, -um, Roman (also as a noun)

*rosa, -ae, F., rose 8

rōstrum, -ī, N., beak 177

rule, regō (III)

**Rutulī, -ōrum, M., Rut'uli, ancient people inhabiting La'tium

S

*Sabīnī, -ōrum, M., the Sa'bines, people of ancient Italy

*saccus, -ī, M., bag, sack 157

*sacer, -cra, -crum, holy, sacred 142

sacerdōs, -dōtis, M. or F., priest or priestess 335

sacred, sacer, -cra, -crum

*sacrificium, -ī, N., sacrifice 92

*sacrificō, -āre, -āvī, -ātum, sacrifice, offer a sacrifice 64

saepe (adv.), often 51

saevus, -a, -um, fierce 287

safe, safely, tūtus, -a, -um

sagitta, -ae, F., arrow 65

**Sagittārius, -ī, M., archer; the constellation Sag'itta'rius

sail, nāvigō (I)

sailor, nauta, -ae, M.

*salūs, -ūtis, F., health, safety; greeting 250; salūtem dīcere, greet 34, note 1; 255; salūtem dare, greet

*salūtō, -āre, -āvī, -ātum, greet 64

same, idem, eadem, idem

sanguis, -inis, M., blood 345

*sānus, -a, -um, healthy, sane 8, 92

sapiēns, gen., -ientis, wise 289

sapientia, -ae, F., wisdom 83

satis (adj. and adv.), enough 233

saxum, -ī, N., rock 98

say, dīcō (III)

°scelus, -eris, N., crime, evil deed

*scēptrum, -ī, N., staff, scepter 92

*schola, -ae, F., school 39

school, schola, -ae, F.

*scientia, -ae, F., knowledge 30, 147

*sciō, -īre, -īvī, -ītum, know 333

*scrībō, -ere, scrīpsī, scrīptum, write 71

scūtum, -ī, N., shield 109

sē (acc., abl. sing./pl. of suī) 215

sea, of the sea, maritimus, -a, -um

seashore, ōra (-ae) maritima (-ae), F.

*sēcrētō (adv.), secretly, stealthily 118

*sēcrētus, -a, -um, secret; (also as a noun), sēcrētum, -ī, N. 92

**Secunda, -ae, F., Secun'da, a name

*secundus, -a, -um, second 152; favorable 189

sed (conj.), but 13

sedeō, -ēre, sēdī, sessum, sit 65

see, videō (II)

seize, occupō (I), capiō (III)

**Seleucus, -ī, M., Seleu'cus, a name

-self, -selves (himself, herself, etc.) when reflexive, suī, sibi, sē; when not reflexive, ipse, -a, -um

sella, -ae, F., seat, chair, stool 371

*sēmen, -inis, N., seed 287

sēmita, -ae, F., path 69

semper (adv.), always 55

**senātor, -ōris, M., senator 8, 241

*senātus, -ūs, M., senate 92

send, mittō (III)

°senex, gen., senis, old, aged; (as a noun) old man, old woman

*sentiō, -īre, sēnsī, sēnsum, perceive, feel, realize, sense 305

*sēparō, -āre, -āvī, -ātum, divide, separate 64

septem, seven 284

septimus, -a, -um, seventh 269

*sepulchrum, -ī, N., grave 92

*Sēquana, -ae, M., the Seq'uana (river), now the Seine

serō, -ere, sēvī, satum, sow 311

*serpēns, -entis, M. or F., snake 293

**Servius, -ī, M., Ser'vius, a name

servō, -āre, -āvī, -ātum, save, keep 73

servus, -ī, M., slave, servant 131

sex, six 269

**Sextus, -ī, M., Sex'tus, a name

ship, nāvis, -is (-ium), F.

shore, ōra, -ae, F.

shout, shouting, clāmor, -ōris, M.

sī (conj.), if 142

sibi (dat. sing./pl. of suī) 215

*Sibylla, -ae, F., a Sib'yl, prophetess and priestess of Apol'lo

*Sibyllīnus, -a, -um, Sibylline, of the Sibyl

sīc (adv.), thus, so

°siccō, -āre, -āvī,-ātum, dry

*Sicilia, -ae, F., Sic'ily

*significō, -āre, -āvī, -ātum, mean, signify 289

*signum, -ī, N., sign, mark, signal 92

*silēns, gen., -entis, silent 371

*silentium, -ī, N., silence 92, 371

*sileō, -ēre, -uī, be silent, keep still

silva, -ae, F., forest, woods 33

**Silvānus, -ī, M., Silva'nus, Latin god of forests and country

**Silvia, -ae, F., Sil'via or Syl'via

*similis, -e, similar, alike, like 274

simul atque (conj.), as soon as 345

sine (with abl.), without 103

sing, cantō (I)

*sinister, -tra, -trum, left 263; ā sinistrā, on the left 263

**Sinōn, -ōnis, M., Si'non, a Greek spy

Sinus (-ūs) Arabicus (-ī), M., the Arabian Gulf (the Red Sea)

slave, servus, -ī, M.

small, **parvus, -a, -um**

smallest, **minimus, -a, -um**

socius, -ī, M., companion, ally 157

*****sōl, sōlis,** M., sun 282

soldier, **miles, -itis,** M.

*****solea, -ae,** F., sole, sandal 8

solium, -ī, N., throne 303

******Solōn, -ōnis,** M., So'lon, a famous Athenian legislator

*****sōlus, -a, -um,** alone, only 69

sometimes **interdum** (adv.)

somnium, -ī, N., dream 174; **per somnia,** in a dream

somnus, -ī, M., sleep 157; **sē somnō dare,** sleep, go to sleep

son, **filius, -ī,** M.

sonus, -ī, M., sound 152

soon (adv.), **mox; jam** (with future)

soror, -ōris, F., sister 242, 299

******Sparta, -ae,** F., Spar'ta, ancient capital of Laco'nia, Greece

*****spatium, -ī,** N., space 92, 305

spear, **hasta, -ae,** F.

*****spectāculum, -ī,** N., sight, show 243

*****spectō, -āre, -āvī, -ātum,** watch, see, look (at) 55

speculum, -ī, N., mirror 185

spēlunca, -ae, F., cave, cavern 209

spēs, spei, F., hope 371; **Spēs,** the goddess of hope

*****spīna, -ae,** F., thorn 215

*****splendidus, -a, -um,** shining 8, 92

spring, **fōns, fontis (-ium),** M.

spūmōsus, -a, -um, foamy 303

star, **stella, -ae,** F.

statim (adv.), at once, immediately 76

*****statua, -ae,** F., statue 8

stay, **maneō (II)**

*****stella, -ae,** F., star 49

stō, stāre, stetī, stātūrus, stand 65

stream, **fluvius, -ī,** M.

strong, **validus, -a, -um**

*****studium, -ī,** N., eagerness, enthusiasm; loyalty, study 92

*****stupefaciō, -ere, -fēcī, -factum,** make senseless, stun 373

*****stupidus, -a, -um,** dull, stupid 8, 92

*****Stygius, -a, -um,** of the Styx

******Styx, Stygis,** F., Styx, chief river in the lower world

sub (with acc. or abl.), under 21, 24

subitō (adv.), suddenly 51

*****subdūcō, -ere, -dūxī, -ductum,** haul up, draw up 315

(Pōns) Sublicius, wooden pile bridge across the Ti'ber, built by An'cus

*****subterrāneus, -a, -um,** underground

suī (gen. of refl. pron.), of himself, of herself, of itself, of themselves 215

suitor, **procus, -ī,** M.

sum, esse, fuī, futūrus, be 36

summus, -a, -um, highest, greatest, utmost; highest part of, top of 249

*****sūmō, -ere, sūmpsī, sūmptum,** take, lay hold of 287

sunt, (they) are 21

*****super** (prep. with acc./abl.), above, over 353; (adv.), above, besides

*****superbē** (adv.), proudly 274

superbus, -a, -um, proud 73

superō, -āre, -āvī, -ātum, overcome, defeat, surpass 139

suprā (adv.; prep. with acc.), above, over 287

*****surgō, -ere, surrēxī, surrēctum,** rise, get up, stand up 345

°**suscipiō, -ere, -cēpī, -ceptum,** take up, receive, undertake

*****suspiciō, -ōnis,** F., suspicion 253

suus, -a, -um, his/her/its/their 189

**Symplēgadēs, -um, F. pl., the Sympleg'ades, legendary Clashing Rocks at the entrance to the Black Sea

T

*tabernāculum, -ī, N., tent 255

*tabula, -ae, F., table, tablet 30

*tacitus, -a, -um, silent, tacit 92, 197

taeda, -ae, F., torch 118

take, **capiō (III)**

take back, **recipiō (III)**

take possession of, **occupō (I)**

tam (adv.), so, so much 76

tamen (adv.), still, nevertheless 174

Tamesis, -is, M., the Thames (river)

tandem (adv.), at last, at length 249

tantum (adv.), only, merely 185

tantus, -a, -um, so great 265

*Tarentīnī, -ōrum, M., Tar'entines

**Tarentum, -ī, N., Taren'tum, city in southern Italy

**Tarpēia, -ae, F., Tarpe'ia, daughter of Spu'rius Tarpe'ius, the commander of the citadel at Rome

*Tarquinius Superbus, -ī -ī, M., Tar'quin the Proud, last king of Rome

Tartarus, -ī, M., **Tartara, -ōrum, N., Tar'tarus, the lower world

**Tatius, -ī, M., Ta'tius, a Sa'bine king

Taurī, -ōrum, M., Taurians, ancient inhabitants of Black Sea region

taurus, -ī, M., bull 311

tē (acc., abl. of **tū**), you (sing.) 218

teach, **doceō (II)**

teacher, **magister, -trī,** M.

tēctum, -ī, N., roof, house 174

tēla, -ae, F., web, texture 193

**Tēlemachus, -ī, M., Telem'achus, son of Ulys'ses and Penel'ope

tēlum, -ī, N., weapon, spear 373

temerē (adv.), rashly, boldly 193

*tempestās, -ātis, F., storm, weather

temple, **templum, -ī,** N.

*templum, -ī, N., temple 92

*temptō, -āre, -āvī, -ātum, try, attempt 69

*tempus, -oris, N., time 237

°tendō, -ere, tetendī, tentum, stretch, extend

teneō, -ēre, -uī, hold, keep 189

*tepidus, -a, -um, lukewarm, tepid 8

tergum, -ī, N., back 200

terra, -ae, land, country, earth 21; **terrā marīque,** on land and sea

*terreō, -ēre, -uī, -itum, frighten 193

*territus, -a, -um, frightened 69

**terror, -ōris, M., fear, fright 348

tertius, -a, -um, third 269

texō, -ere, -uī, textum, weave 193

that, **ille, illa, illud; is, ea, id**

their (when reflexive), **suus, -a, -um;** (when not reflexive), **eōrum, eārum**

themselves (reflexive), gen., **suī**

these, **hī, hae, haec; eī, eae, ea**

**Thēseus, -ī, M., The'seus, slayer of the Min'otaur

*Thessalia, -ae, F., Thes'saly, a district of Greece

**Thetis, -idis, F., The'tis, mother of Achil'les

this, **hic, haec, hoc; is, ea, id**

those, **illī, illae, illa; eī, eae, ea**

*Thrācia, -ae, F., Thrace, a district in Greece

through, **per** (with acc.)

*Tiberis, -is, M., the Ti'ber (river)

tibi (dat.), (to) you (sing.) 218

timeō, -ēre, -uī, fear, be afraid 43

*timidus, -a, -um, fearful, timid 8

time, **tempus, temporis,** N.

°**timor, -ōris,** M., fear

*****Titānus, -ī,** M., Ti'tan, one of the giants of Greek mythology

******Titus, -ī,** M., Ti'tus

to, **ad, in** (preps. with acc.)

*****tolerō, -āre, -āvī, -ātum,** endure, bear, tolerate 368

*****tōtus, -a, -um,** whole, entire 287

town, **oppidum, -ī,** N.

trahō, -ere, trāxī, tractum, draw, drag, pull 339

*****trāns** (with acc.), across 98

*****trānseō, -īre, -iī (-īvī), -itum,** go across, cross over 251

*****trānsfigō, -ere, -fixī, -fixum,** pierce through, transfix 374

*****trānsportō, -āre, -portāvī, -portātum,** convey, carry across 123

tree, **arbor, -oris,** F.

*****tremō, -ere, -uī,** tremble, quake 251

trēs, tria, three 284

*****tridēns, -entis,** M., three-pronged spear, trident

*****Trōja, -ae,** F., Troy, city in Asia Minor

*****Trōjānus, -a, -um,** Tro'jan (also as noun)

try, **temptō (I)**

tū, you (nom. sing.) 54, note; 218

*****tuba, -ae,** F., trumpet 353

******Tullia, -ae,** F., Tul'lia, a name

tum (adv.), then 95

tumulus, -ī, M., mound of earth 344

******Turnus, -ī,** M., Tur'nus, king of the Rut'uli, killed by Aene'as

tūtus, -a, -um, safe, safely 142

tuus, -a, -um, your, yours (addressed to one person) 39

twin, twin-born, **geminus, -a, -um**

*****tyrannus, -ī,** M., tyrant 249

******Tyrrhus, -ī,** M., Tyr'rhus, a shepherd

U

ubi (adv.), where 49; (conj.), when 118

*****Ulixēs, Ulixis,** M., Ulys'ses, king of Ith'aca, hero of Ho'mer's Od'yssey

*****ultimus, -a, -um,** last 269

umbra, -ae, F., shade; ghost 103

umerus, -ī, M., shoulder 374

unda, -ae, F., wave 49

undique (adv.), from all sides, everywhere 277

*****unguentum, -ī,** N., ointment 311

ūnus, -a, -um, one 284

*****urbs, urbis (-ium),** F., city 233

*****urna, -ae,** F., jar, pitcher, urn 8

ursa, -ae, F., bear 69

usque ad (with acc.), till 315

°**ut** (adv. and conj.), as

utrimque (adv.), from both sides 305

uxor, -ōris, F., wife 157, 188, 242

V

vadum, -ī, N., shoal, shallow 348

valeō, -ēre, -uī, -itūrus, be well, be strong 60; **valē,** farewell, goodby 35

*****validus, -a, -um,** strong; well 8, 109

vāstō, -āre, -āvī, -ātum, lay waste, destroy 43

*****vehementer** (adv.), violently 277

*****vehiculum, -ī,** N., vehicle 243

******Vēiī, -ōrum,** M., Ve'ii, an old town in Etru'ria, once a rival of Rome

vellus, -eris, N., fleece 287

vēlum, -ī, N., sail, veil 157

°**vēnātor, -ōris,** M., hunter

*****venēnum, -ī,** N., poison 311

veniō, -īre, vēnī, ventum, come 131

*****ventus, -ī,** M., wind 157

******Venus, -eris,** F., Ve'nus, Roman goddess of love and beauty; the planet

*verbum, -ī, N., word 89
*vērō (adv.), in truth, indeed 233
*vērum, -ī, N., truth 215
*vērus, -a, -um, true 193
*vesperī, in the evening 155
**Vesta, -ae, F., Ves'ta, Roman goddess
  of the hearth
  vester, -tra, -trum, your, yours (ad-
    dressed to more than one person)
    218, note
*vēstigium, -ī, N., footprint, trace 282
  vestis, -is (-ium), F., clothing 333
**Vesuvius, -ī, M., Vesu'vius, volcano
  near Her'cula'neum and Pompe'ii
*vexō, -āre, -āvī, -ātum, shake; vex,
  annoy 265
  via, -ae, F., way, road, street 13
*Via (-ae) Appia (-ae), F., Ap'pian
  Way, famous Roman road
*vīcinus, -ī, M., neighbor; vīcinus, -a,
  -um, neighboring 147
**victor, -ōris, M., victor, conqueror
*victōria, -ae, F., victory 30
  vīcus, -ī, M., village 83
  videō, -ēre, vīdī, vīsum, see 35
  vigilō, -āre, -āvī, -ātum, stand
    watch, be on guard; be awake, be
    vigilant 103, 265
  vīgintī, twenty 265
**villa, -ae, F., farmhouse, villa 10
  village, vīcus, -ī, M.
*vinciō, -īre, vīnxī, vīnctum, bind
  vincō, -ere, vīcī, victum, conquer,
    overcome 131
°vinculum, -ī, N., chain, bond
*vīnum, -ī, N., wine
  vir, virī, M., man 113
*virgō, -inis, F., unmarried woman 252,
  368; (Virgō) Vestālis, Ves'tal Virgin
*virtūs, -tūtis, F., courage, virtue 250

*vīta, -ae, F., life 131
  vītō, -āre, -āvī, -ātum, avoid 98
*vīvō, -ere, vīxī, victum, live 293
  vīvus, -a, -um, alive, living 161
  vōbīs (dat., abl. pl.), (to) you 218
  vocō, -āre, -āvī, -ātum, call 35
  volō, velle, voluī, wish, want, will 365
  volō, -āre, -āvī, fly 55
*voluntās, -ātis, F., will, wish 329
  vōs (nom., acc. pl.) you 54, note; 218
*vōx, vōcis, F., voice 263; magnā
  vōce, in a loud voice 209; parvā
  vōce, in a low voice 221
*Vulcānus, -ī, M., Vul'can, god of fire
  vulnerō, -āre, -āvī, -ātum, wound 95

W

walk, ambulō (I)
wander, errō (I)
want, cupiō (III), dēsīderō (I), volō
  (velle); not want, nōlō (nōlle)
warn, moneō (II)
water, aqua, -ae, F.
wave, unda, -ae, F.
which (rel. pron.), quī, quae, quod;
  (interrog. pron.), quis, quid; (interrog. adj.), quī, quae, quod
why, cūr
wild, ferus, -a, -um
window, fenestra, -ae, F.
wish, dēsīderō (I), cupiō (III), volō
  (velle); voluntās, -ātis, F.
with, cum (with abl.); apud (with acc.)
work, labōrō (I); labor, -ōris, M.
worship, adōrō (I)
worst, pessimus, -a, -um
wound, vulnerō (I)

Z

**Zephyrus, -ī, M., Zeph'yrus, west wind

425

SUMMARY OF GRAMMAR

NOUNS AND ADJECTIVES

Declensions I and II

nouns

	Singular	Singular	Singular	Singular	Singular	Singular
Nom.	casa (F.)	sonus (M.)	puer (M.)	ager (M.)	vir (M.)	dōnum (N.)
Gen.	casae	sonī	puerī	agrī	virī	dōnī
Dat.	casae	sonō	puerō	agrō	virō	dōnō
Acc.	casam	sonum	puerum	agrum	virum	dōnum
Abl.	casā	sonō	puerō	agrō	virō	dōnō
	Plural	Plural	Plural	Plural	Plural	Plural
Nom.	casae	sonī	puerī	agrī	virī	dōna
Gen.	casārum	sonōrum	puerōrum	agrōrum	virōrum	dōnōrum
Dat.	casīs	sonīs	puerīs	agrīs	virīs	dōnīs
Acc.	casās	sonōs	puerōs	agrōs	virōs	dōna
Abl.	casīs	sonīs	puerīs	agrīs	virīs	dōnīs

adjectives

	Singular M.	Singular F.	Singular N.	Plural M.	Plural F.	Plural N.
Nom.	bonus	bona	bonum	bonī	bonae	bona
Gen.	bonī	bonae	bonī	bonōrum	bonārum	bonōrum
Dat.	bonō	bonae	bonō	bonīs	bonīs	bonīs
Acc.	bonum	bonam	bonum	bonōs	bonās	bona
Abl.	bonō	bonā	bonō	bonīs	bonīs	bonīs
Nom.	liber	libera	liberum	liberī	liberae	libera
Gen.	liberī	liberae	liberī	liberōrum	liberārum	liberōrum
Dat.	liberō	liberae	liberō	liberīs	liberīs	liberīs
Acc.	liberum	liberam	liberum	liberōs	liberās	libera
Abl.	liberō	liberā	liberō	liberīs	liberīs	liberīs
Nom.	sacer	sacra	sacrum	sacrī	sacrae	sacra
Gen.	sacrī	sacrae	sacrī	sacrōrum	sacrārum	sacrōrum
Dat.	sacrō	sacrae	sacrō	sacrīs	sacrīs	sacrīs
Acc.	sacrum	sacram	sacrum	sacrōs	sacrās	sacra
Abl.	sacrō	sacrā	sacrō	sacrīs	sacrīs	sacrīs

426

Declension III

masculine/feminine nouns

	Singular	Singular	Singular	Singular	Singular	Singular
Nom.	lēx (F.)	mīles (M.)	frāter (M.)	collis (M.)	nūbēs (F.)	nox (F.)
Gen.	lēgis	mīlitis	frātris	collis	nūbis	noctis
Dat.	lēgī	mīlitī	frātrī	collī	nūbī	noctī
Acc.	lēgem	mīlitem	frātrem	collem	nūbem	noctem
Abl.	lēge	mīlite	frātre	colle	nūbe	nocte
	Plural	Plural	Plural	Plural	Plural	Plural
Nom.	lēgēs	mīlitēs	frātrēs	collēs	nūbēs	noctēs
Gen.	lēgum	mīlitum	frātrum	collium	nūbium	noctium
Dat.	lēgibus	mīlitibus	frātribus	collibus	nūbibus	noctibus
Acc.	lēgēs	mīlitēs	frātrēs	collēs	nūbēs	noctēs
Abl.	lēgibus	mīlitibus	frātribus	collibus	nūbibus	noctibus

neuter nouns

	Singular	Singular	Singular	Singular	Singular	Singular
Nom.	ōmen	caput	opus	iter	mare	animal
Gen.	ōminis	capitis	operis	itineris	maris	animālis
Dat.	ōminī	capitī	operī	itinerī	marī	animālī
Acc.	ōmen	caput	opus	iter	mare	animal
Abl.	ōmine	capite	opere	itinere	marī	animālī
	Plural	Plural	Plural	Plural	Plural	Plural
Nom.	ōmina	capita	opera	itinera	maria	animālia
Gen.	ōminum	capitum	operum	itinerum	marium	animālium
Dat.	ōminibus	capitibus	operibus	itineribus	maribus	animālibus
Acc.	ōmina	capita	opera	itinera	maria	animālia
Abl.	ōminibus	capitibus	operibus	itineribus	maribus	animālibus

Declension IV

m./f. nouns   ### neuter nouns

Declension V

m./f. nouns

	Singular	Plural	Singular	Plural	Singular	Plural
Nom.	exercitus (M.)	exercitūs	cornū	cornua	rēs (F.)	rēs
Gen.	exercitūs	exercituum	cornūs	cornuum	reī	rērum
Dat.	exercituī	exercitibus	cornū	cornibus	reī	rēbus
Acc.	exercitum	exercitūs	cornū	cornua	rem	rēs
Abl.	exercitū	exercitibus	cornū	cornibus	rē	rēbus

427

Declension III (continued)

adjectives

3-ending

	Singular (M.)	Singuiar (F.)	Singular (N.)
Nom.	ācer	ācris	ācre
Gen.	ācris	ācris	ācris
Dat.	ācrī	ācrī	ācrī
Acc.	ācrem	ācrem	ācre
Abl.	ācrī	ācrī	ācrī

	Plural (M./F.)	Plural (N.)
Nom.	ācrēs	ācria
Gen.	ācrium	ācrium
Dat.	ācribus	ācribus
Acc.	ācrēs	ācria
Abl.	ācribus	ācribus

2-ending

	Singular (M/F.)	Singular (N.)
Nom.	facilis	facile
Gen.	facilis	facilis
Dat.	facilī	facilī
Acc.	facilem	facile
Abl.	facilī	facilī

	Plural (M./F.)	Plural (N.)
Nom.	facilēs	facilia
Gen.	facilium	facilium
Dat.	facilibus	facilibus
Acc.	facilēs	facilia
Abl.	facilibus	facilibus

1-ending

	Singular (M./F.)	Singular (N.)
Nom.	fēlix	fēlix
Gen.	fēlicis	fēlicis
Dat.	fēlicī	fēlicī
Acc.	fēlicem	fēlix
Abl.	fēlicī	fēlicī

	Plural (M./F.)	Plural (N.)
Nom.	fēlicēs	fēlicia
Gen.	fēlicium	fēlicium
Dat.	fēlicibus	fēlicibus
Acc.	fēlicēs	fēlicia
Abl.	fēlicibus	fēlicibus

Present Participle

	Singular (M./F.)	Singular (N.)
Nom.	portāns	portāns
Gen.	portantis	portantis
Dat.	portantī	portantī
Acc.	portantem	portāns
Abl.	portante/tī	portante/tī

	Plural (M./F.)	Plural (N.)
Nom.	portantēs	portantia
Gen.	portantium	portantium
Dat.	portantibus	portantibus
Acc.	portantēs	portantia
Abl.	portantibus	portantibus

IRREGULAR ADJECTIVES[1]

	Singular (M.)	Singular (F.)	Singular (N.)	Singular (M.)	Singular (F.)	Singular (N.)
Nom.	sōlus	sōla	sōlum	alter	altera	alterum
Gen.	sōlius	sōlius	sōlius	alterīus	alterīus	alterius
Dat.	sōlī	sōlī	sōlī	alterī	alterī	alterī
Acc.	sōlum	sōlam	sōlum	alterum	alteram	alterum
Abl.	sōlō	sōlā	sōlō	alterō	alterā	alterō

[1]alius, sōlus, ūllus, ūnus, tōtus, nūllus; alter, neuter, uter

428

COMPARISON

Regular Adjectives/Adverbs

	positive		superlative	
Adjectives	Adverbs		Adjectives	Adverbs
lātus, -a, -um	lātē		lātissimus, -a, -um	lātissimē
fortis, forte	fortiter		fortissimus, -a, -um	fortissimē
ācer, ācris, ācre	ācriter		ācerrimus, -a, -um	ācerrimē
facilis, facile	facile		facillimus, -a, -um	facillimē
fēlix, gen., -icis	fēliciter		fēlicissimus, -a, -um	fēlicissimē

Irregular Adjectives/Adverbs

	positive		superlative	
Adjectives	Adverbs		Adjectives	Adverbs
bonus, -a, -um	bene		optimus, -a, -um	optimē
malus, -a, -um	male		pessimus, -a, -um	pessimē
magnus, -a, -um	magnopere		maximus, -a, -um	maximē
parvus, -a, -um	parum		minimus, -a, -um	minimē
multus, -a, -um	multum		plūrimus, -a, -um	plūrimē

Comparatives of Adjectives/Adverbs

regular			irregular		
Adjectives (M./F.)	Adjectives (N.)	Adverbs	Adjectives (M./F.)	Adjectives (N.)	Adverbs
lātior	lātius	lātius	melior	melius	melius
fortior	fortius	fortius	pejor	pejus	pejus
ācrior	ācrius	ācrius	major	majus	magis
facilior	facilius	facilius	minor	minus	minus
fēlicior	fēlicius	fēlicius	—	[1]plūs	plūs

Declension of Comparative Adjectives

	Singular (M./F.)	Singular (N.)	Plural (M./F.)	Plural (N.)
Nom.	lātior	lātius	lātiōrēs	lātiōra
Gen.	lātiōris	lātiōris	lātiōrum	lātiōrum
Dat.	lātiōrī	lātiōrī	lātiōribus	lātiōribus
Acc.	lātiōrem	lātius	lātiōrēs	lātiōra
Abl.	lātiōre	lātiōre	lātiōribus	lātiōribus

[1]Used in singular as noun only.

PRONOUNS

First Person

	personal	reflexive
	Singular	**Singular**
Nom.	**ego**	—
Gen.	**meī**	**meī**
Dat.	**mihi**	**mihi**
Acc.	**mē**	**mē**
Abl.	**mē**	**mē**
	Plural	**Plural**
Nom.	**nōs**	—
Gen.	**nostrī**	**nostrī**
Dat.	**nōbīs**	**nōbīs**
Acc.	**nōs**	**nōs**
Abl.	**nōbīs**	**nōbīs**

Second Person

	personal	reflexive
	Singular	**Singular**
Nom.	**tū**	—
Gen.	**tuī**	**tuī**
Dat.	**tibi**	**tibi**
Acc.	**tē**	**tē**
Abl.	**tē**	**tē**
	Plural	**Plural**
Nom.	**vōs**	—
Gen.	**vestrī**	**vestrī**
Dat.	**vōbīs**	**vōbīs**
Acc.	**vōs**	**vōs**
Abl.	**vōbīs**	**vōbīs**

Third Person

not reflexive

(Forms of a demonstrative—usually **is, ea, id**—are used as third-person pronouns)

Third Person

reflexive

	Nom.	Gen.	Dat.	Acc.	Abl.
Sing.		**suī**	**sibi**	**sē**	**sē**
Plur.		**suī**	**sibi**	**sē**	**sē**

POSSESSIVE MODIFIERS

Referring to Singular Antecedent

1st person   **meus, -a, -um**
2nd person   **tuus, -a, -um** (of one person)
3rd person   **suus, -a, -um** (reflexive)
             ejus (not reflexive) gen. sing. of **is, ea, id**

For declension, see **bonus**, p. 426

Referring to Plural Antecedent

1st person   **noster, -tra, -trum**
2nd person   **vester, -tra, -trum** (of more than one)
3rd person   **suus, -a, -um** (reflexive)
             eōrum, eārum, eōrum (not reflexive) gen. pl. of **is, ea, id**

For declension, see **sacer, bonus,** p. 426

DEMONSTRATIVES

	Singular (M.)	Singular (F.)	Singular (N.)	Plural (M.)	Plural (F.)	Plural (N.)
Nom.	is	ea	id	eī	eae	ea
Gen.	ejus	ejus	ejus	eōrum	eārum	eōrum
Dat.	eī	eī	eī	eīs	eīs	eīs
Acc.	eum	eam	id	eōs	eās	ea
Abl.	eō	eā	eō	eīs	eīs	eīs

	Singular (M.)	Singular (F.)	Singular (N.)	Plural (M.)	Plural (F.)	Plural (N.)
Nom.	hic	haec	hoc	hī	hae	haec
Gen.	hujus	hujus	hujus	hōrum	hārum	hōrum
Dat.	huic	huic	huic	hīs	hīs	hīs
Acc.	hunc	hanc	hoc	hōs	hās	haec
Abl.	hōc	hāc	hōc	hīs	hīs	hīs

	Singular (M.)	Singular (F.)	Singular (N.)	Plural (M.)	Plural (F.)	Plural (N.)
Nom.	ille	illa	illud	illī	illae	illa
Gen.	illīus	illīus	illīus	illōrum	illārum	illōrum
Dat.	illī	illī	illī	illīs	illīs	illīs
Acc.	illum	illam	illud	illōs	illās	illa
Abl.	illō	illā	illō	illīs	illīs	illīs

IDENTIFYING PRONOUN

	Singular (M.)	Singular (F.)	Singular (N.)	Plural (M.)	Plural (F.)	Plural (N.)
Nom.	īdem	eadem	idem	eīdem	eaedem	eadem
Gen.	ejusdem	ejusdem	ejusdem	eōrundem	eārundem	eōrundem
Dat.	eīdem	eīdem	eīdem	eisdem	eisdem	eisdem
Acc.	eundem	eandem	idem	eōsdem	eāsdem	eadem
Abl.	eōdem	eādem	eōdem	eīsdem	eīsdem	eīsdem

INTENSIVE PRONOUN

	Singular (M.)	Singular (F.)	Singular (N.)	Plural (M.)	Plural (F.)	Plural (N.)
Nom.	ipse	ipsa	ipsum	ipsī	ipsae	ipsa
Gen.	ipsīus	ipsīus	ipsīus	ipsōrum	ipsārum	ipsōrum
Dat.	ipsī	ipsī	ipsī	ipsīs	ipsīs	ipsīs
Acc.	ipsum	ipsam	ipsum	ipsōs	ipsās	ipsa
Abl.	ipsō	ipsā	ipsō	ipsīs	ipsīs	ipsīs

RELATIVE PRONOUNS

	Singular (M.)	Singular (F.)	Singular (N.)	Plural (M.)	Plural (F.)	Plural (N.)
Nom.	quī	quae	quod	quī	quae	quae
Gen.	cujus	cujus	cujus	quōrum	quārum	quōrum
Dat.	cui	cui	cui	quibus	quibus	quibus
Acc.	quem	quam	quod	quōs	quās	quae
Abl.	quō	quā	quō	quibus	quibus	quibus

INTERROGATIVE PRONOUNS

	Singular (M.)	Singular (F.)	Singular (N.)	Plural (M.)	Plural (F.)	Plural (N.)
Nom.	quis	quis	quid	quī	quae	quae
Gen.	cujus	cujus	cujus	quōrum	quārum	quōrum
Dat.	cui	cui	cui	quibus	quibus	quibus
Acc.	quem	quem	quid	quōs	quās	quae
Abl.	quō	quō	quō	quibus	quibus	quibus

INTERROGATIVE ADJECTIVES

	Singular (M.)	Singular (F.)	Singular (N.)	Plural (M.)	Plural (F.)	Plural (N.)
Nom.	quī/quis	quī/quis	quid	quī	quae	quae
Gen.	cujus	cujus	cujus	quōrum	quārum	quōrum
Dat.	cui	cui	cui	quibus	quibus	quibus
Acc.	quem	quam	quid	quōs	quās	quae
Abl.	quō	quā	quō	quibus	quibus	quibus

DECLINABLE NUMBERS

	M.	F.	N.	M.	F.	N.
Nom.	ūnus	ūna	ūnum	duo	duae	duo
Gen.	ūnīus	ūnīus	ūnīus	duōrum	duārum	duōrum
Dat.	ūnī	ūnī	ūnī	duōbus	duābus	duōbus
Acc.	ūnum	ūnam	ūnum	duōs	duās	duo
Abl.	ūnō	ūnā	ūnō	duōbus	duābus	duōbus

	M.	F.	N.			N. Pl.
Nom.	trēs	trēs	tria	**mille** (Sing.) is an in-		milia
Gen.	trium	trium	trium	declinable adjective;		milium
Dat.	tribus	tribus	tribus	**milia** (Pl.) is a neuter		milibus
Acc.	trēs	trēs	tria	noun.		milia
Abl.	tribus	tribus	tribus			milibus

ROMAN NUMERALS

[1]ūnus, -a, -um	I	[2]prīmus	[1]sex	VI	[2]sextus
duo, duae, duo	II	secundus	septem	VII	septimus
trēs, trēs, tria	III	tertius	octō	VIII	octāvus
quattuor	IV	quārtus	novem	IX	nōnus
quīnque	V	quīntus	decem	X	decimus
		[1]ūndecim	XI		[2]ūndecimus
		duodecim	XII		duodecimus
		tredecim	XIII		tertius decimus
		quattuordecim	XIV		quārtus decimus
		quīndecim	XV		quīntus decimus
		sēdecim	XVI		sextus decimus
		septendecim	XVII		septimus decimus
		duodēvīgintī	XVIII		duodēvīcēsimus
		ūndēvīgintī	XIX		ūndēvīcēsimus
		vīgintī	XX		vīcēsimus
vīgintī ūnus, -a, -um/ūnus et vīgintī	XXI				vīcēsimus prīmus
		duodētrīgintā	XXVIII		duodētrīcēsimus
		ūndētrīgintā	XXIX		ūndētrīcēsimus
		trīgintā	XXX		trīcēsimus
		quadrāgintā	XL		quadrāgēsimus
		quīnquāgintā	L		quīnquāgēsimus
		sexāgintā	LX		sexāgēsimus
		septuāgintā	LXX		septuāgēsimus
		octōgintā	LXXX		octōgēsimus
		nōnāgintā	XC		nōnāgēsimus
		centum	C		centēsimus
		centum (et) ūnus	CI		centēsimus (et) prīmus
		ducentī, -ae, -a	CC		ducentēsimus
		trecentī, -ae, -a	CCC		trecentēsimus
		quadringentī	CCCC		quadringentēsimus
		quīngentī	D		quīngentēsimus
		sescentī	DC		sescentēsimus
		septingentī	DCC		septingentēsimus
		octingentī	DCCC		octingentēsimus
		nōngentī	DCCCC		nōngentēsimus
		mīlle	M		mīllēsimus

[1]Cardinal numerals. (For declension of **ūnus, duo, trēs, mīlia,** see p. 432.)

[2]Ordinal numerals· **primus, secundus,** etc. (For declension, see **bonus,** p. 426.)

VERBS

Conjugations I, II, III, III-iō, IV

principal parts

I	portō	portāre	portāvī	portātum
II	moneō	monēre	monuī	monitum
III	dūcō	dūcere	dūxī	ductum
III-iō	capiō	capere	cēpī	captum
IV	audiō	audīre	audīvī	audītum

indicative active (present system)

Present

Singular	Singular	Singular	Singular	Singular
portō	moneō	dūcō	capiō	audiō
portās	monēs	dūcis	capis	audīs
portat	monet	dūcit	capit	audit
Plural	Plural	Plural	Plural	Plural
portāmus	monēmus	dūcimus	capimus	audīmus
portātis	monētis	dūcitis	capitis	audītis
portant	monent	dūcunt	capiunt	audiunt

Imperfect

Singular	Singular	Singular	Singular	Singular
portābam	monēbam	dūcēbam	capiēbam	audiēbam
portābās	monēbās	dūcēbās	capiēbās	audiēbās
portābat	monēbat	dūcēbat	capiēbat	audiēbat
Plural	Plural	Plural	Plural	Plural
portābāmus	monēbāmus	dūcēbāmus	capiēbāmus	audiēbāmus
portābātis	monēbātis	dūcēbātis	capiēbātis	audiēbātis
portābant	monēbant	dūcēbant	capiēbant	audiēbant

Future

Singular	Singular	Singular	Singular	Singular
portābō	monēbō	dūcam	capiam	audiam
portābis	monēbis	dūcēs	capiēs	audiēs
portābit	monēbit	dūcet	capiet	audiet
Plural	Plural	Plural	Plural	Plural
portābimus	monēbimus	dūcēmus	capiēmus	audiēmus
portābitis	monēbitis	dūcētis	capiētis	audiētis
portābunt	monēbunt	dūcent	capient	audient

imperatives

Singular	Plural
portā	portāte
monē	monēte
*dūc	dūcite
cape	capite
audī	audīte

*Other irregular imperatives: **dīc, fac, fer** (sing.); **ferte** (pl.)

indicative passive (present system)

Present

Singular	Singular	Singular	Singular	Singular
portor	moneor	dūcor	capior	audior
portāris/-re	monēris/-re	dūceris/-re	caperis/-re	audīris/-re
portātur	monētur	dūcitur	capitur	audītur
Plural	Plural	Plural	Plural	Plural
portāmur	monēmur	dūcimur	capimur	audīmur
portāminī	monēminī	dūciminī	capiminī	audīminī
portantur	monentur	dūcuntur	capiuntur	audiuntur

Imperfect

Singular	Singular	Singular	Singular	Singular
portābar	monēbar	dūcēbar	capiēbar	audiēbar
portābāris/-re	monēbāris/-re	dūcēbāris/-re	capiēbāris/-re	audiēbāris/-re
portābātur	monēbātur	dūcēbātur	capiēbātur	audiēbātur
Plural	Plural	Plural	Plural	Plural
portābāmur	monēbāmur	dūcēbāmur	capiēbāmur	audiēbāmur
portābāminī	monēbāminī	dūcēbāminī	capiēbāminī	audiēbāminī
portābantur	monēbantur	dūcēbantur	capiēbantur	audiēbantur

Future

Singular	Singular	Singular	Singular	Singular
portābor	monēbor	dūcar	capiar	audiar
portāberis/-re	monēberis/-re	dūcēris/-re	capiēris/-re	audiēris/-re
portābitur	monēbitur	dūcētur	capiētur	audiētur
Plural	Plural	Plural	Plural	Plural
portābimur	monēbimur	dūcēmur	capiēmur	audiēmur
portābiminī	monēbiminī	dūcēminī	capiēminī	audiēminī
portābuntur	monēbuntur	dūcentur	capientur	audientur

Conjugations I, II, III, III-iō, IV

infinitives (active)

Present	Perfect	Future
portāre	portāvisse	portātūrum esse
monēre	monuisse	monitūrum esse
dūcere	dūxisse	ductūrum esse
capere	cēpisse	captūrum esse
audīre	audīvisse	audītūrum esse

participles (active)

Present (See p. 428)	Future
portāns	portātūrus, -a, -um
monēns	monitūrus, -a, -um
ducēns	ductūrus, -a, -um
capiēns	captūrus, -a, -um
audiēns	audītūrus, -a, -um

indicative active (perfect system)

Perfect

Singular	Singular	Singular	Singular	Singular
portāvī	monuī	dūxī	cēpī	audīvī
portāvistī	monuistī	dūxistī	cēpistī	audīvistī
portāvit	monuit	dūxit	cēpit	audīvit

Plural	Plural	Plural	Plural	Plural
portāvimus	monuimus	dūximus	cēpimus	audīvimus
portāvistis	monuistis	dūxistis	cēpistis	audīvistis
portāvērunt	monuērunt	dūxērunt	cēpērunt	audīvērunt

Past Perfect

Singular	Singular	Singular	Singular	Singular
portāveram	monueram	dūxeram	cēperam	audīveram
portāverās	monuerās	dūxerās	cēperās	audīverās
portāverat	monuerat	dūxerat	cēperat	audīverat

Plural	Plural	Plural	Plural	Plural
portāverāmus	monuerāmus	dūxerāmus	cēperāmus	audīverāmus
portāverātis	monuerātis	dūxerātis	cēperātis	audīverātis
portāverant	monuerant	dūxerant	cēperant	audīverant

Future Perfect

Singular	Singular	Singular	Singular	Singular
portāverō	monuerō	dūxerō	cēperō	audīverō
portāveris	monueris	dūxeris	cēperis	audīveris
portāverit	monuerit	dūxerit	cēperit	audīverit

Plural	Plural	Plural	Plural	Plural
portāverimus	monuerimus	dūxerimus	cēperimus	audīverimus
portāveritis	monueritis	dūxeritis	cēperitis	audīveritis
portāverint	monuerint	dūxerint	cēperint	audīverint

436

Conjugations I, II, III, III-iō, IV

infinitives (passive)   participles (passive)

Present	Perfect	Future	Perfect	Future
portārī	portātum esse	portātum īrī	portātus, -a, -um	portandus, -a, -um
monērī	monitum esse	monitum īrī	monitus, -a, -um	monendus, -a, -um
dūcī	ductum esse	ductum īrī	ductus, -a, -um	dūcendus, -a, -um
capī	captum esse	captum īrī	captus, -a, -um	capiendus, -a, -um
audīrī	audītum esse	audītum īrī	audītus, -a, -um	audiendus, -a, -um

indicative passive (perfect system)

Perfect

Singular	Singular	Singuiar	Singular	Singular
portātus sum	monitus sum	ductus sum	captus sum	audītus sum
portātus es	monitus es	ductus es	captus es	audītus es
portātus est	monitus est	ductus est	captus est	audītus est

Plural	Plural	Plural	Plural	Plural
portātī sumus	monitī sumus	ductī sumus	captī sumus	audītī sumus
portātī estis	monitī estis	ductī estis	captī estis	audītī estis
portātī sunt	monitī sunt	ductī sunt	captī sunt	audītī sunt

Past Perfect

Singular	Singular	Singular	Singular	Singular
portātus eram	monitus eram	ductus eram	captus eram	audītus eram
portātus erās	monitus erās	ductus erās	captus erās	audītus erās
portātus erat	monitus erat	ductus erat	captus erat	audītus erat

Plural	Plural	Plural	Plural	Plural
portātī erāmus	monitī erāmus	ductī erāmus	captī erāmus	audītī erāmus
portātī erātis	monitī erātis	ductī erātis	captī erātis	audītī erātis
portātī erant	monitī erant	ductī erant	captī erant	audītī erant

Future Perfect

Singular	Singular	Singular	Singular	Singular
portātus erō	monitus erō	ductus erō	captus erō	audītus erō
portātus eris	monitus eris	ductus eris	captus eris	audītus eris
portātus erit	monitus erit	ductus erit	captus erit	audītus erit

Plural	Plural	Plural	Plural	Plural
portātī erimus	monitī erimus	ductī erimus	captī erimus	audītī erimus
portātī eritis	monitī eritis	ductī eritis	captī eritis	audītī eritis
portātī erunt	monitī erunt	ductī erunt	captī erunt	audītī erunt

Irregular Verbs

principal parts

sum	esse	fuī	futūrus
possum	posse	potuī	——
eō	īre	[1]iī	itum
volō	velle	voluī	——
nōlō	nōlle	nōluī	——

indicative (present system)

Present

Singular	Singular	Singular	Singular	Singular
sum	possum	eō	volō	nōlō
es	potes	īs	vīs	nōn vīs
est	potest	it	vult	nōn vult
Plural	Plural	Plural	Plural	Plural
sumus	possumus	īmus	volumus	nōlumus
estis	potestis	ītis	vultis	nōn vultis
sunt	possunt	eunt	volunt	nōlunt

Imperfect

Singular	Singular	Singular	Singular	Singular
eram	poteram	ībam	volēbam	nōlēbam
erās	poterās	ībās	volēbās	nōlēbās
erat	poterat	ībat	volēbat	nōlēbat
Plural	Plural	Plural	Plural	Plural
erāmus	poterāmus	ībāmus	volēbāmus	nōlēbāmus
erātis	poterātis	ībātis	volēbātis	nōlēbātis
erant	poterant	ībant	volēbant	nōlēbant

Future

Singular	Singular	Singular	Singular	Singular
erō	poterō	ībō	volam	nōlam
eris	poteris	ībis	volēs	nōlēs
erit	poterit	ībit	volet	nōlet
Plural	Plural	Plural	Plural	Plural
erimus	poterimus	ībimus	volēmus	nōlēmus
eritis	poteritis	ībitis	volētis	nōlētis
erunt	poterunt	ībunt	volent	nōlent

[1]Also **īvī,** with alternate perfect stem **īv-**

infinitives			participles			imperatives	
Present	Perfect	Future	Present		Future	Singular	Plural
esse	**fuisse**	**futūrum esse**	——	**futūrus, -a, -um**		**es**	**este**
posse	**potuisse**	——					
īre	**isse/iisse**	**itūrum esse**	**iēns**	**itūrus, -a, -um**		**ī**	**īte**
velle	**voluisse**	——	**volēns**			——	——
nōlle	**nōluisse**	——	**nōlēns**			**nōli**	**nōlite**

indicative (perfect system)

Perfect

Singular	Singular	Singular	Singular	Singular
fuī	**potuī**	[1]**iī**	**voluī**	**nōluī**
fuistī	**potuistī**	**īstī/iistī**	**voluistī**	**nōluistī**
fuit	**potuit**	**iit**	**voluit**	**nōluit**
Plural	Plural	Plural	Plural	Plural
fuimus	**potuimus**	**iimus**	**voluimus**	**nōluimus**
fuistis	**potuistis**	**īstis/iistis**	**voluistis**	**nōluistis**
fuērunt	**potuērunt**	**iērunt**	**voluērunt**	**nōluērunt**

Past Perfect

Singular	Singular	Singular	Singular	Singular
fueram	**potueram**	[1]**ieram**	**volueram**	**nōlueram**
fuerās	**potuerās**	**ierās**	**voluerās**	**nōluerās**
fuerat	**potuerat**	**ierat**	**voluerāt**	**nōluerat**
Plural	Plural	Plural	Plural	Plural
fuerāmus	**potuerāmus**	**ierāmus**	**voluerāmus**	**nōluerāmus**
fuerātis	**potuerātis**	**ierātis**	**voluerātis**	**nōluerātis**
fuerant	**potuerant**	**ierant**	**voluerant**	**nōluerant**

Future Perfect

Singular	Singular	Singular	Singular	Singular
fuerō	**potuerō**	[1]**ierō**	**voluerō**	**nōluerō**
fueris	**potueris**	**ieris**	**volueris**	**nōlueris**
fuerit	**potuerit**	**ierit**	**voluerit**	**nōluerit**
Plural	Plural	Plural	Plural	Plural
fuerimus	**potuerimus**	**ierimus**	**voluerimus**	**nōluerimus**
fueritis	**potueritis**	**ieritis**	**volueritis**	**nōlueritis**
fuerint	**potuerint**	**ierint**	**voluerint**	**nōluerint**

[1]With stem **iv-** these forms are **ivī**, etc., **iveram**, etc., **iverō**, etc.

NOUNS (CASE USES)

Nominative
1. Subject **Virī in agrīs labōrant.**
2. Predicate noun **Puer fīlius agricolae est.**

Vocative **Vidē, amīce, ursam. Venīte, puellae, nōbīscum.**

Genitive **Casae agricolārum sunt parvae.**

Dative
1. Indirect object **Puerō dōnum dabimus.**
2. With adjectives meaning near, dear, kind, pleasing, friendly, unfriendly, similar, and dissimilar **Dea fēminīs cāra est.**
3. With verbs such as **resistō** and **crēdō** **Vir pīrātae resistit.**

Accusative
1. Direct object **Magister discipulōs laudat.**
2. Extent (of time) **Multōs annōs bellum gerēbant.**
   Extent (of space) **Pauca mīlia passuum ambulāvimus.**
3. With prepositions **ad, ante, apud, circum, contrā, extrā, inter, intrā, ob, per, post, praeter, prope, propter, super, suprā, trāns;** and also with **in** and **sub** (motion implied)
4. Subject of infinitive in indirect statement **Amīcōs manēre dīxit.**

Ablative
A. (With prepositions **ā/ab, cum, dē, ē/ex, in, prō, sine, sub**) in phrases answering these questions:
1. By whom? (agent with passive verb) **Ab amītā vocātur.**
2. In what manner? **Rēx cum sapientiā regit.**
3. With whom? (accompanied by whom?) **Cum sociīs fugit.**
4. Where? (in, on, under, in front of?) **Prō ārā stābam.**
5. From what place? (away, out, down from) **Ab Āfricā nāvigāvit. Columba ē fenestrā volāvit. Dē monte dēscendunt.**
B. (Without preposition) in phrases answering these questions:
1. When? (at, in, or within what time?) **Eō diē eam vīdī.**
2. How? (with, by, or by what means?) **Signum tubā dabō.**
C. Ablative absolute (two nouns, noun and pronoun, noun and adjective and/or participle) **Caesare duce/Tē duce/Duce praesente mīlitēs laetī erant.**

Any Case
Appositive (same case as word it explains) **Līberī, fīliī rēgis, adsunt.**

PRONOUNS

1 Demonstrative **Hic (vir) est altus.**
2 Interrogative **Cui praemium dās?**
3 Personal **Videō eum.**
4 Reflexive **Ego mē in cavernā cēlāvī.**
5 Relative **Templum quod vīdī erat pulcherrimum.**

   Case uses of pronouns in general are the same as for nouns, depending on use in the pronoun's own clause.

   A pronoun agrees in gender and number with the noun for which it
stands. **Eae (puellae) ursam timent.**

ADJECTIVES

Agreement

   The gender, number, and case of an adjective depend on the word
modified. **Agricolae territī ab agrīs fūgērunt.**

   A participle used as an adjective modifies a noun or pronoun with
which it agrees in gender, number, and case. **Fēminae dolentēs
auxilium deōs ōrant. In casā ā nautīs aedificātā habitō.**

VERBS

Present System: Present, Imperfect, Future Tenses
Perfect System: Perfect, Past Perfect, Future Perfect Tenses

Active Voice (Subject acts.) **Vir puerum juvat.**
Passive Voice (Subject is acted upon.) **Puer ā virō juvātur.**

Indicative Mood (States fact or asks question.) **Sēmita est lāta. Estne
sēmita lāta?**
Imperative Mood (Expresses command.) **Nārrāte nōbīs fābulās!**
Subjunctive Mood (Indicates a wish, hope, possibility, or mild command.)
Līberī veniant. Hīc maneāmus.

Infinitive (sometimes referred to as a mood)

1 Complementary (Completes such verbs as **possum, volō, nōlō,
dēbeō.**) **Poterātisne verba ōrāculī audīre?**
2 With imperatives of **nōlō** (**nōlī, nōlīte**) to form the negative imperative **Nōlī īre. Nōlīte, līberī, in viam currere.**
3 Verb in indirect statement **Nautās īnsulam custōdīre sentīmus.**

Participle (sometimes referred to as a mood)

As verb may denote action and have direct object. **Advenae, oppidum dēsertum invenientēs, omnia aedificia dēlēvērunt.**

INDEX OF GRAMMAR

ablative absolute, 345, 348, 440
  of accompaniment, 353, 440
  of agent, 303, 353, 354, 440
  of manner, 353, 440
  of means, 103, 354, 440
  of place, 14, 22, 25, 353, 440
  of time, 283, 354, 440
  "versatile" (review), 353, 354
  with prepositions, 14, 22, 25, 353, 440
  without preposition, 103, 354, 440
accent 15, 398
accusative of direct object, 12, 22, 440
  of extent of space, 294, 440
  of extent of time, 294, 440
  in indirect statement, 330, 440
  with prepositions, 22, 25, 440
active voice 299, 441
adjectives agreement of, 95, 96, 441
  comparative degree of, 266, 267
  comparison of, 266, 270, 274, 275
  declensions I-II, 91, 101, 426; III, 263, 264, 428
  demonstrative, 186, 431
  interrogative, 224, 432
  irregular, 156, 270, 428, 429
  as nouns, 102
  position of, 27, 28, 95
  possessive, 190, 430
  predicate, 12, 330
  reflexive, 189, 430
  superlative degree of, 152, 153, 156, 266, 267, 270
  with dative, 44, 440
adverbs 74, 278, 429
agreement adjective with noun, 95, 96
  participle in passive verb forms, 315
  verb and subject, 37

answers to questions 50
apposition 26, 440
cases 12, 14, 21, 22, 29, 33, 40, 53, 67, 440
case endings of nouns 101, 234, 239, 369, 371, 426, 427
  declension I, 12, 14, 21, 22, 23, 29, 33, 40, 44, 52, 53, 101, 426
  declension II, 83, 84, 90, 101, 239, 426
  declension III, 233-235, 238, 239, 427
  declension IV, 369, 427
  declension V, 371, 427
clauses 69, 210
commands 66, 158, 159, 366, 441
comparison of adjectives, 266, 267, 270, 274, 275, 429
  of adverbs, 278, 429
compound verbs 123, 337
conjugations 58, 131, 434-439
  I-II, 58, 99, 110, 139, 300, 312, 313, 315, 316, 434-437
  III-IV, 131, 133, 135, 139, 158, 171, 300, 312, 313, 315, 316, 434-437
conjunctions 70, 74
consonants 10, 14, 398, 445
dative of indirect object, 39, 440
  position of, 40
  with adjectives, 44, 440
declension of adjectives, 91, 101, 263, 264, 426, 428
  of comparative adjectives, 266, 267, 270, 274, 275, 429
  of nouns, 52, 83, 84, 90, 101, 233, 234, 369, 371, 426, 427
  of participles, 290, 428
  of superlative adjectives, 153, 156, 266, 270, 271, 274, 275, 429

demonstratives 185, 186, 193, 194, 431, 441

diphthongs 14, 398, 446

direct object 12, 440

enclitics -cum, 210, 219; -ne, 50

eō and compounds 336, 337, 438, 439

extent of space/time, 294, 440

future perfect tense 312, 313, 315, 316, 336, 436, 437, 439

future tense sum/possum, 36, 77, 438

    conjugations I-II, 99, 300, 434

    conjugations III-IV, 135, 136, 300, 434

    eō and compounds, 336, 337, 438

    volō/nōlō, 366, 438

gender explained, 90

    declensions I-II, 44, 52, 83, 90

    declension III, 234, 238, 242, 250, 252

    declensions IV-V, 369, 371

genitive 33, 242, 440

hic, ille, is 185, 193, 194, 431

īdem 200, 431

imperative mood 66, 441

    conjugations I-II, 66, 435

    conjugations III-IV, 158, 435

    irregular formations, 161, 336, 435

    irregular verbs, 159, 336, 366, 439

imperfect tense 59, 139, 140, 300, 336, 434, 435, 438

    distinguished from perfect, 143

in with ablative, 14; with accusative, 25

indicative mood 66, 441

indirect discourse see indirect quotation and indirect statement

indirect object 39, 440

indirect quotation 330

indirect statement 330, 334, 441

infinitives present active, 58, 133, 327, 331, 436; passive, 327, 437

    perfect active, 333, 436; passive, 334, 437

infinitives (cont.)

    future active, 329, 340, 436

    complementary, 77, 366, 441

    of eō and compounds, 336, 337, 439

    of sum/possum, 439

    of volō/nōlō, 439

    tense of, in indirect statement, 331, 334

intensive ipse, 198, 431

interrogative adjective 224, 432

interrogative pronoun 221, 222, 432, 441

ipse 198, 431

is 185, 431

mīlle/mīlia 287, 432

mood imperative, 66, 441

    indicative, 66, 441

    infinitive, 58, 441

    participle, 290, 291, 305, 306, 315, 339, 340, 441

    subjunctive, 380, 381, 441

-ne sign of a question, 50

negative commands 159, 366

"neuter law" 90, 237

nōli/nōlīte in negative commands 159, 366, 441

nōlō 365, 366, 438, 439

    with complementary infinitive, 366

nominative 12, 21, 440

nōnne sign of a question, 50

nouns declensions of, 52, 83, 84, 90, 233, 234, 237, 369, 371, 426, 427

    gender of, 44, 90, 234, 237

number of nouns, 21, 22

    of verbs, 36

numbers (one to ten) 284; 432, 433

nunc/jam 158

object direct, 12, 440; indirect, 39, 440

order of words 11, 27, 28, 33, 40, 44, 67, 95

participles agreement of, 290, 315, 334, 339, 340, 441

present, 290, 428, 436

perfect, 305, 306, 437; used in passive voice, 315, 316, 334, 437

future active, 339, 436; used in infinitive, 340, 436

translation of, 291, 306, 339

used in infinitives, 334, 340, 436, 437

passive voice 299, 300, 315, 316, 334, 441

past perfect tense 312, 313, 315, 316, 336, 337, 436, 437, 439

perfect stem 113, 118-119

perfect system of verbs 315, 316, 441

perfect tense active, 110, 171, 174, 177, 336, 337; passive, 315, 316

contrasted with imperfect, 143

translation of, 110-111, 172, 316

person endings of verbs 36, 99, 110, 135, 299

persons of verbs 36-37, 110, 299

personal pronouns 218, 430, 441

phrases 14, 25

possession 33, 242

possessive adjectives 190, 430

possessive pronouns 190, 430

possum conjugation of, 76, 77, 438, 439

translation of, 77

with complementary infinitive, 77

predicate adjective, 12, 330

noun, 12, 300, 330, 440

in indirect statement, 330

with passive voice, 300

prefixes 123, 337

prepositions with ablative, 14, 22, 25, 74, 353, 440

with accusative, 22, 25, 74, 440

present stem 58, 99, 139

present system of verbs 148, 300, 441

present tense sum/possum, 36, 77, 438

conjugations I-II, 58, 300, 434

conjugations III-IV, 131, 133, 171, 300, 434

eō and compounds, 336, 337, 438

volō/nōlō, 366, 438

principal parts of verbs 113, 306, 336

pronouns demonstrative, 186, 193, 194, 431, 441

interrogative, 219, 221, 222, 432, 441

personal, 218, 219, 430, 441

reflexive, 215, 219, 430, 441

relative, 209, 210, 219, 432, 441

pronunciation 10, 15, 398

questions -ne, nōnne, 50

ubi and cūr, 49

quī and quis, 221, 224

quotations direct, 330

indirect, 330

reflexive adjectives 189, 430

reflexive pronouns 215, 219, 430, 441

relative pronouns 209, 210, 432, 441

sounds summary of, 10, 398

statement indirect, 330, 331, 334

stems of verbs present, 58, 99, 139

perfect, 113, 118-119

participial, 315, 316, 334

sub 25

subject 12, 440; omitted, 37

in indirect statement, 330

subjunctive mood 380, 381, 441

substantive use of adjectives 102

suffixes 243, 253, 280, 296

sum conjugation of, 36, 438, 439

compounds of, 76, 77, 438, 439

position of, 11

with predicate, 12

superlative of adjectives, 152, 156, 267, 429; of adverbs, 278, 429

syllabication 14, 398

tense explained, 36

   present, 36, 58, 131-132

   imperfect, 36, 59, 139, 140

   future, 36, 99, 135, 136

   perfect, 110, 171, 174-175, 315, 316, 336, 337

   past perfect, 312, 313, 315, 316, 336, 337

   future perfect, 312, 313, 315, 316, 336, 337

tenses table of, 36, 77, 148, 177, 313, 316, 336, 366, 434-439

verbs agreement of, 37

   endings of, 23, 29, 36, 99, 110, 299, 381

   person and number of, 36

verbs (cont.)

   position of, 11

   principal parts, 113, 306, 434, 438

   stems of, 58, 113, 118-119

   without expressed subject, 37

vocative 67, 84, 440

voice active, 299, 441

   passive, 299, 300, 315, 316, 441

volō 365, 366, 438, 439

   with complementary infinitive, 366

vowels 10, 14, 398, 446

word division 14, 398

word mastery 8, 30, 64, 71, 92, 123, 166, 191, 241, 243, 246, 253, 280, 296, 342, 360

GRAMMATICAL TERMS

adjective word that describes or qualifies a noun or pronoun

adverb word that describes or qualifies a verb, adjective, another adverb, or an entire clause

antecedent word, phrase, or clause to which a pronoun refers

apposition relationship of an appositive to the noun it explains

appositive noun set beside another noun to define its meaning

base form of a noun without any ending, found by dropping genitive singular ending

case means of relating a noun or pronoun to other parts of a sentence, as in Latin by endings

clause group of words containing a subject and predicate

comparison changes in the form of an adjective or adverb to show greater degree of quality or characteristic than the simple word

complementary infinitive infinitive that completes the meaning of the verb with which it is used

conjugation arrangement of verb forms in regular order

conjunction word that joins words, phrases, or clauses

consonant sound produced by complete or partial blockage of the breath stream; also letter representing such a sound: **b, c, d, f, g, h, j, k, l, m, n, p, q, r, s, t, v, x, z**

declension arrangement of cases and numbers of a noun, adjective, or pronoun in regular order

445

derivative word that has its source in another word

diphthong sound produced by pronouncing two vowels together in one syllable: **ae, au, oe, eu, ui**

expletive filler serving as formal subject to anticipate the real subject

gender grouping of nouns into classes: masculine, feminine, neuter

interjection exclamatory word or phrase without grammatical connection

noun name of a person, place, or thing

number the form of a noun, pronoun, or verb which shows it to be singular or plural

participle verbal adjective that can not only modify a noun or pronoun, but also retain verb force in expressing simple tense and possibly in taking an object

parts of speech classification of words by use: nouns, adjectives, pronouns, verbs, adverbs, prepositions, conjunctions, interjections

person classification for pronouns and verbs to distinguish between the speaker (first person), the one spoken to (second person), and person or thing spoken about (third person)

phrase word group serving as a unit, without subject or predicate

predicate verb and words used with it to make a statement about the subject

predicate adjective, predicate noun adjective or noun which follows forms of esse and similar linking verbs and applies to the subject

preposition word that relates a noun or pronoun to some other idea in the sentence

principal parts key forms of a verb from which all other forms can easily be derived

pronoun substitute for a noun to refer to the noun without naming it

reflexive pronoun or adjective that refers specifically to the subject of the clause or sentence

sentence word or group of words expressing a complete thought

stem common element in related verb forms, to which verb endings are added; in Latin there are present, perfect, and participial stems

stress increased force given to certain syllables in speaking; accent

subject person, thing, or idea about which the verb makes a statement or asks a question

syllable part of a word uttered in a single breath impulse; a Latin word has as many syllables as it has vowels or diphthongs

tense form of a verb that indicates the time of an action or condition

verb word expressing action, occurrence, existence, or state of being

vocative case used in addressing a person

voice form of the verb indicating the relation of an action to the subject as the doer or the receiver

vowel speech sound allowing relatively free passage of air through mouth and nose; also the letter representing such a sound; specifically, the letters **a, e, i, o, u,** and **y**

ACKNOWLEDGMENTS

The courtesy of persons and institutions which permits reproduction of the pictures on the pages listed is gratefully acknowledged. Accademia Nazionale dei Lincei, Rome, and De Antonis 199; Fratelli Alinari 75, 363; Fratelli Alinari and Art Reference Bureau 16 left, 17 center left, 87 top left and center, 124 bottom left and center, 183, 385; D. Anderson and Art Reference Bureau 126 second row left, 272 left, 273 bottom; Peter D. Arnott, University of Iowa 258 top right; Art Color Slides, Inc. 19 top right, 134, 306; Ollie Atkins, The Saturday Evening Post 248; Ehemals Staatliche Museen Berlin, Museum Dahlem, Gemäldegalerie 99, 208, 283, 309 bottom right; Bernisches Historisches Museum 72; Better Homes and Gardens magazine 13; Major F.A.C. Boothby 165 second row right; Brera Museum, Milan 93; Trustees of the British Museum 86 top left and center, 125 third row right, 145 upper left margin, 165 bottom right, 181 top left, 258 left margin (2), 272 center, 273 top left, 297, 308 top left, 310; Brogi and Art Reference Bureau 126 top right, 151; Brunner & Co., Como 259 center right; Bureau of Public Roads, Department of Commerce 213 second row; Caisse Nationale des Monuments Historiques 144 right; Chicago Natural History Museum 20 margin, 228 top left; Collections of the Corning Museum of Glass 325; Drawing by Richard Decker, copr. ©1958, The New Yorker Magazine, Inc. 397 bottom; William Egli 11, 17 top right, 126 bottom right, 220, 261; Enit 2; Elfi Finne 24; Fitzwilliam Museum, Cambridge, England 52; The Fogg Art Museum, Harvard University, Grenville L. Winthrop Collection 289; French Government Tourist Office 259 top left; Robert Emmett Ginna and Horizon, A Magazine of the Arts 314; Harrow School Museum 145 third row; The Hermitage, Leningrad 207; C. M. Hutchinson 32, 78, 206, 232; Kelsey Museum of Archaeology, University of Michigan 145 second row center; Kunsthistorisches Museum of Vienna 364; Edward Laning, detail of sketch for the ceiling in the New York Public Library 117; Trustees of the London Museum 40, 165 third row; The Louvre and Photographie Giraudon 63, 102, 107, 247, 323, 350; Mauritshuis, The Hague 66; The Metropolitan Museum of Art, Rogers Fund 1918, 18 top left, Edith Perry Chapman Fund 1952, 124 right, Rogers Fund 1921, 169, Purchase 1900, 181 top right, Gift of Henry G. Marquand 1897, 214, Rogers Fund 1916, 229 top right; Musée du Bardo, Tunis 245 top; Musée National Suisse, Zurich 273 center left; Museo Arqueológico, Barcelona 272 top right; Museo Capitolino, Fot. S.P.Q.R., X Rip.180 bottom; Museum für Kunsthandwerk, Frankfurt am Main and Horizon, A Magazine of the Arts 285; Museum of Fine Arts, Boston 19 third row center, 57 top right; Museum of São Paulo, Brazil 293; Museum, Sousse, Tunisia by Louis Foucher 47; The Trustees of The National Gallery, London 328, 386; The National Geographic Society 165 bottom left; Betty Neal 273 center right, 309 center; The Oriental Institute of The University of Chicago 205 top left and center; Palazzo Doria, Rome and De Antonis 377; Parke, Davis & Co. 146; Oliver Wendell Holmes Library, Phillips Academy, Andover, Mass. 362; Rheinisches Landesmuseum, Trier, Germany 145 top, and second row right, 165 top; Römisch-Germanisches Zentral-Museum, Mainz 20 second row center (2); Royal Ontario Museum of Archaeology 125 top left, 145 lower left margin, 229 third row right, bottom; Scala, Florence 97, 137, 158, 192, 196, 240, 252, 270, 332; Burr Shafer, reprinted courtesy of the Saturday Review, the copyright owner 396 (2), 397 top and center; Soprinten-denza delle Antichità della Calabria 281; Soprintendenza Monumenti e Scavi in Libia, Archivio Fotografico della Libia Occidentale 308 bottom right; Spanish National Tourist Office 212 top left, 213 bottom left and right, 258 bottom right; Staatliche Kunstsammlungen, Ministerium f. Volksbildung, Dresden 56 top; Städtisches Museum, Wiesbaden 153; The Tate Gallery 319; The University Museum, University of Pennsylvania 155; Archivio Fotografico Gallerie e Musei Vaticani 129, 277, 352, 357, 370; Archivio Fotografico Gallerie e Musei Vaticani and D. Anderson 55; Villa Giulia and A.F.I. Naples 238; The Walters Gallery, Baltimore 19 third row left, 20 center left, 82, 87 top right, 125 second row, third row right.

Special thanks are due to Raymond V. Schoder, S.J. for a large number of transparencies reproduced on the pages listed. Some of these required also the generous permission of those in charge of institutions whose collections include objects photographed. 9, 16 top right, 17 top left, center right, bottom left and right, 18 bottom left, 19 second row left, third row right, 20 top right, center right, bottom left and right, 22, 27, 31, 41, 42, 48, 57 center left and bottom, 70, 81, 86 top right, 87 second row left and right, and bottom, 126 top left, bottom left, 127, 141, 164 right, 165 second row left, 170, 173, 180 top, 181 bottom, 188, 204 top, 205 center and bottom, 212 top right and bottom, 213 first and third row, 218, 224, 228 top right and bottom, 229 third row left, 231, 244 top right and bottom, 245 center left and bottom, 259 top and bottom, 262, 266, 273 top right, 275, 308 top right, 309 top, and bottom left, 367.

Raymond V. Schoder, S.J. and Biblioteca Vaticana 19 top left; Trustees of the British Museum 164 left; Glyptotek und Museum Antiker Kleinkunst, Munich 57 top; Kunsthistorisches Museum of Vienna 204 bottom; The Metropolitan Museum of Art 126 second row center; Musée Archéologique, Timgad 345; Musée du Bardo, Tunis 308 bottom left, 343; Musée National Suisse, Zurich 125 center left, bottom left; Musei Capitolini 184; Museo Provinciale Campano, Capua 145 bottom; Museo Provinciale, Paestum 114; Museum, Sousse, Tunisia by Louis Foucher 229 top left; The Trustees of The National Gallery, London 338; Rijksmuseum G.M. Kam, Nijmegen 20 top left, 56 bottom center; Services des Antiquités de l'Algérie 36; Soprintendenza alle Antichità della Campania 18 right, 56 center left, 57 center right (2), 88, 108, 112, 125 top right, 132, 144 center, 229 second row, 244 left, 258 bottom left, 298, 302; Soprintendenza alle Antichità dell'Etruria 205 top right, 380; Soprintendenza alle Antichità del Piemonte 56 bottom right; Soprintendenza alle Antichità di Roma 19 bottom, 56 bottom left, 272 bottom right.